CRIMES
OF WAR

Crimes of War: What the Public Should Know.
©Crimes of War Project, 1999 and 2007

Concept: Gilles Peress, Anna Cataldi, and Roy Gutman
Editors: Roy Gutman, David Rieff, and Anthony Dworkin
Editor of Photography/Research: Sheryl A. Mendez
Legal Editor, First Edition: Kenneth Anderson
Legal Editor, Second Edition: Michael N. Schmitt
Consultant, Military Law: General A.P.V. Rogers
General Counsel: Ron Goldfarb
Project Manager, First Edition: Peggy Lampl
Creative Direction/Design: Jeff Streeper
Design, First Edition: Brooke Hellewell
Design Assistance: Amy Stevens and Ed Pirnik

Printed in Singapore.
First Edition 1999
Second Edition (revised) 2007

The text of this book is composed in Officina Sans
with the display set in Officina Sans.
Composition and Production by Modern IDENTITY
Manufacturing by Tien Wan Press.

Library of Congress Cataloging-in-Publication Data

Crimes of War : What the Public Should Know / Roy Gutman,
David Rieff, and Anthony Dworkin, editors. — Rev. and
expanded ed. p. cm.
ISBN-13: 978-0-393-32846-2 (pbk.)
ISBN-10: 0-393-32846-5 (pbk.)
1. War crimes. I. Gutman, Roy. II. Rieff, David. III.
Dworkin, Anthony Ross.
K5301.C75 2007
341.6'9--dc22
2006036978

For information contact:
W.W. Norton & Company, Inc.
500 Fifth Avenue
New York, New York 10110
www.wwnorton.com

W.W. Norton & Company Ltd.,
Castle House
75-76 Wells Street
London W1T 3QT

1 2 3 4 5 6 7 8 9 0

CRIMES OF WAR

WHAT THE PUBLIC SHOULD KNOW
REVISED AND UPDATED EDITION

Edited by Roy Gutman, David Rieff, and Anthony Dworkin
Photography Edited by Sheryl A. Mendez

W. W. NORTON & COMPANY   NEW YORK · LONDON

TABLE OF CONTENTS

PREFACE TO THE SECOND EDITION

By Roy Gutman, David Rieff and Anthony Dworkin

When the first edition of this book appeared in 1999, on the eve of the fiftieth anniversary of the Geneva Conventions, it seemed as if the greatest challenge to international humanitarian law—the code of conduct for belligerents in war first drafted in the mid-nineteenth century and reformulated after World War II and the Holocaust—no longer came from States with functioning legal systems but rather from rogue actors. Whether guerrilla bands or repressive States, they were prepared to employ any method from terror to torture, from mass rape to ethnic cleansing, from crimes against humanity to genocide itself, to suppress rebellions or advance particular ethnic, tribal, or clan interests. After the massacre of Bosnians at Srebrenica and of Rwandan innocents at the Nyarubuye Catholic Mission, it was easy to believe, as we put it at the time, that "the locus of conflict [had] shifted to the poor world, where governments and insurgent groups routinely have disregarded the legal regime" of international humanitarian law.

Few of us thought the day had actually come when the leading powers would carry out their commitment in Article One of the four 1949 Geneva Conventions, not only to respect the rules but also ensure respect for them in all circumstances. The authors and editors knew from bitter personal experience how alternately cynical and passive our own governments could be. While it was laudable that the major powers had created special tribunals for the former Yugoslavia and for Rwanda, the action was in fact a substitute for military interventions that might have halted the crimes as they were being committed. The slaughter in Chechnya proceeded with scarcely a word from Washington or the governments of the European Union. Increasingly it seemed as if systematic crimes against civilian populations, the illegal conduct of belligerents up to and including genocide—the gravest crime of all under humanitarian law—were in danger of becoming the norm rather than the exception in conflict zones from the Caucasus to the Sudan.

And yet, in the post-Cold War, pre-9/11 world, there was reason to think that heightened public consciousness of international humanitarian norms might pressure governments to go beyond lip service and act on the basis of these norms. News coverage had helped force governments to protest the greatest abuses and shame the perpetrators into halting them, so the media saw news value in identifying crimes in real time. In setting up ad hoc tribunals, the international community declared the excesses to be unacceptable and devised a transparent process that could establish a historic record of what had actually happened. Many, particularly human rights advocates, saw a glimmer of hope that the establishment of new judicial institutions would prefigure a different, less cynical, attitude toward war crimes and crimes against humanity and a new determination to translate the laws of war into actual practice, both during conflicts and in their aftermath. Reality of course fell short of these hopes. The tribunals never had their own police powers, and major countries, starting with the United States, allowed impunity to take hold in the former Yugoslavia by refusing to risk a soldier's life to capture an indicted war criminal. On the heels of the two ad hoc tribunals for the former Yugoslavia and Rwanda, the United Nations established a permanent International Criminal Court, and, although the United States kept its distance, the ICC's legitimacy was not in question in Europe and most other parts of the world. From its inception the ICC had at least some practical impact—notably in helping prompt the withdrawal of five African states from the Democratic Republic of Congo in 2002 just before their leaders would have been subject to indictment for the crimes that were committed there.

To those who signed on to its provisions, the ICC was an emblem of the decline of maximalist interpretations of State sovereignty, and of the heightened consciousness of international humanitarian law, as much as it was an effective short-term legal instrument. Thus, the legitimacy of international legal regimes that imposed limits on what States could do while prosecuting armed conflicts seemed to have grown stronger by the end of the millennium. In a world of mass migration, the free movement of capital, and communications that recognized no national boundaries, the idea that States could do more or less anything they wanted within their own borders—which had been the bedrock assumption of international relations theory and practice since the Peace of Westphalia in the 17th century—no longer made the sense it once had. After all, in such a world why shouldn't an international court, or, in extreme cases, the courts of another country have the right to bring war criminals to justice? Was this not in keeping with the spirit of the millennium, the spirit of what then-United Nations Secretary General Kofi Annan had dubbed "the rights of the person"?

Of course it remains true that the law was being applied selectively, with one set of rules for the formerly colonized and another for the former colonizer. Nonetheless, a two-tiered system of international justice still seemed to most of us like a vast improvement over no international system of justice at all. In other words, while the limitations of the new international legal regime were obvious, the progress it represented for humanity as a whole seemed undeniable. And who was to say that it might not lead over the long term to greater justice and equity? Such radical transformations as that envisioned by the expansion of international justice cannot be properly evaluated using criteria of short-term results.

Viewed from the vantage point of 2007, five years into the so-called "Global War on Terror," the hope placed in international justice may seem terribly naïve. Our own error was not in putting excessive faith in international institutions, but in assuming that the commitment to international humanitarian law on the part of well-off Western countries was permanent—in short, that if the world had not yet turned the moral corner, these countries either had or could be pressurized into doing so. And a grievous error it was.

The new U.S. administration, which came to office in 2001 by a decision of the U.S. Supreme Court following the closest election in history, viewed the International Criminal Court as already an intolerable infringement of the sovereignty of a democratic State. One of President George W. Bush's very first actions was to withdraw the signature of adherence to the new court that his predecessor, Bill Clinton, had given in his last days as President. That was a harbinger of a radical shift in attitude that followed the attacks of September 11, 2001. On its own, and without consulting Congress or the Courts, the new administration decided unilaterally to reinterpret the 1949 Geneva Conventions, a document to which the United States is a State Party and which was ratified by the U.S. Senate, and dispense with many of the most fundamental commitments.

The attacks of September 11, and the subsequent wars launched by the United States and Great Britain in Afghanistan and Iraq, proved how tenuous those commitments were, especially on the part of the United States. The assault directed by Osama bin Laden against principally civilian targets, from airliners to the World Trade Center, could have been denounced as a monumental crime against humanity under international humanitarian law. But rather than rally the world—every society, every ethnic group, every religion—behind the universal norms and the Conventions to which every State is a party, President George W. Bush chose a unilateral course, emphasizing American military power and the drive for revenge. Far from drawing upon the moral power of a body of law incorporating the lessons of history and of the worst excesses of humankind in war, the Bush Administration argued that international humanitarian law was not binding on Washington in this war. The terrorists, administration lawyers insisted, were "unlawful combatants" and as such were exempt from the protections afforded by the Geneva Conventions. They could be held in secret, locked up indefinitely without trial or even a procedure for determining if they were combatants or noncombatants, and, though the Bush Administration insisted otherwise, they could be tortured. In short, the United States government in effect released itself from the obligation to obey the norms of the laws of war to which the world had believed that it had irrevocably committed itself.

In a very short time, the United States went from being the guarantor of the regime of humanitarian law to becoming a major violator of it. The jihadis committed crimes against humanity by targeting and killing innocent civilians wholesale; the American government violated the law by systematically denying its protections to detainees—refusing even after two adverse Supreme Court rulings to set up a transparent system that would differentiate between war criminals, combatants, and civilians often captured far from the battlefield. The selection of the U.S. Naval Base at Guantanamo Bay, Cuba, as the site of the biggest of the new prisons gave the administration what it claimed was a legal basis for avoiding any code to cover those detained—whether the Geneva Conventions, the Uniform Code of Military Justice, the civil and criminal codes of the United States, or even the laws of Cuba. In March 2003, the Bush administration launched its invasion of Iraq and publicly acknowledged the applicability of the Geneva Conventions and other international codes. But the precedent of abusive interrogation techniques and no legal protection had been established, and when insurgents began assaulting the U.S. forces in Iraq, the American military imported techniques from the "black hole" of Guantanamo into Abu Ghraib prison. The ensuing scandal proved enormously costly to America's military presence in Iraq and to its prestige around the world. The international news media arrived late to this story, another sign that increased consciousness of humanitarian law had been a fleeting phenomenon of the late 1990s.

Whether the suspension of humanitarian law will prove to be an anomalous development that will be rectified when a new administration takes office, or whether instead it represents a permanent transformation of the context in which international humanitarian law is applied, is unknowable at the time of this writing. The Congressional decisions authorizing military tribunals, curtailing habeas corpus, and winking at torture are not encouraging. On the other hand, perhaps a shred of comfort can be taken from the fact that much of the criticism of post-9/11 U.S. policies on these questions has been couched in terms of international humanitarian law.

Clearly if the United States and the other well-off Western countries give themselves a blanket exception to the laws of war as they go about prosecuting the war against radical Islamism, then they will at best remain a set of norms taught in law schools. If the United States has no deep commitment to these legal norms, there is no reason to expect that the countries of the poor world will take up the slack.

Despite the Bush administration's assault on international humanitarian law, and its avoidance of accountability under law for those it has detained, our conviction remains the same as in 1999: this form of law is imperfect but it is not obsolete. The better the principles are understood by the general public, the more likely that governments might be shamed into observing them and pressing for their global implementation. If on the other hand, great powers join the rogue States in diluting and actively subverting these legal norms, or carving out exceptions to them, then our future is a world in which wholesale violations of the laws of war will be the norm. In other words, we shall see the triumph of the old barbarism, not the faint glimmers of humanity slowly growing less cruel.

Whether a book like this can affect the debate at a time when people are afraid and governments seem prepared to do everything in their power to legitimize and even foment this great fear is an open question. But that does not make it less imperative to try. The choice is stark: law or lawlessness. It is against this backdrop that we offer this revised new edition of *Crimes of War*.

PREFACE TO THE FIRST EDITION

By Roy Gutman and David Rieff

In the early 1990s, while Western leaders were still congratulating themselves over the end of communism and the fall of the Soviet empire, the security structure that helped bring about those events began to come apart. The American-led North Atlantic Alliance that had for four decades effectively counterbalanced the Russian domination of eastern Europe proved incapable of dealing with a single Yugoslav despot, Slobodan Milosevic. The alliance that had confronted the prospect of nuclear apocalypse could not develop a coherent response to a small conventional conflict in southeastern Europe.

War had returned to the European continent. First in Croatia and then in Bosnia, it was being fought seemingly without respect for the rules of warfare that had been drafted in the wake of World War II and the Holocaust. These codes of conduct in war were a lesser-known element in the architecture of international security put into place after 1945. They were an effort to prevent a repetition of the worst of the abuses of World War II: the concentration camps, the mass deportations, the terror bombing. They enabled postwar governments in Europe and North America to at least assure their publics that the lessons had been learned and standards set.

It is no exaggeration to say that these codes were intended to establish even in war a firebreak between civilization and barbarism. The Nuremberg Tribunal of 1945 set down the principle that there were such things as crimes against humanity, systematic crimes against civilians that can occur inside a country but that might be tried anywhere else. The Genocide Convention of 1948 gave legal meaning and force to the worst crime in the lexicon. The 1949 Geneva Conventions codified and advanced the rules governing wars between States, differentiating legal conduct from illegal and criminal acts in war. Together with the two Additional Protocols of 1977, the Geneva Conventions are the central summation of the agreed rules governing the conduct of war. Scholars and humanitarian organizations, hoping to emphasize the protections under law for noncombatants, call this field international humanitarian law. Militaries prefer to speak of the laws of war, and include in that definition the issues connected with the causes of war. In well-off Western countries, the canons of international humanitarian law took hold—once the sometimes savage colonial wars had ended. Contrast, say, the American military's conduct in Vietnam, where many of the standards of international humanitarian law were violated, with its attempt to adhere scrupulously to these norms in the Gulf War. Unfortunately, the locus of conflict shifted to the poor world, where governments and insurgent groups routinely have disregarded the legal regime. And in the immediate post-Cold War era, no major Western power felt it had any stake in Third World conflicts unless oil was involved.

Small wonder, then, that less than two years after the fall of the Berlin Wall, the structure of international humanitarian law seemed on the brink of collapse. It took a war in Europe—Croatia in 1991—to stir public interest. The war in Bosnia-Herzegovina (1992), the Rwandan genocide (1994), and Chechnya (1995) amplified the alarm bell, though it should have been sounded a good deal earlier.

Bosnia was the trigger. In the heart of "civilized" Europe, Serbian forces had set up concentration camps, deported non-Serbs in cattle cars, destroyed towns and villages, organized the systematic rape of Croat and Muslim women, and targeted civilians in the name of ethnic cleansing. The great Western alliance watched passively, and were it not for the glare of media attention as had occurred more than two decades earlier in Vietnam, and the public outcry in western Europe and North America, the savagery might have had no bounds.

In response to the public outcry, major powers sent in food and medicine and UN forces to monitor the distribution of aid, but more as an excuse to deflect public opinion than a policy response that squarely addressed the cause of a man-made disaster. Belatedly, and well after the worst crimes had occurred, major powers set up the first war crimes tribunals since Nuremberg, first for Bosnia and then in Rwanda. They did so, at least in part, in response to pressure from human rights, relief, religious, and other non-governmental organizations and from the news media.

This, in itself, was a singular departure. Non-governmental organizations and committed individuals can rightly claim credit for the conception, drafting, and adoption in 1948 of the UN Universal Declaration on Human Rights and the Genocide Convention, but the public historically have been bit players in curbing crimes of war. The implementation of international standards had always been up to governments, the militaries, and the Geneva-based International Committee of the Red Cross, which for over a century has helped in the drafting, oversight, and implementation of the Geneva Conventions.

No one yet knows whether the rise to prominence of non-governmental organizations will help shift the responsibility toward a world order based on collaboration between governments, intergovernmental organizations like the United Nations, and private groups. Perhaps, on the other hand, the talk of entering an era of international law and ending the old hard edged conception of State sovereignty is overstated. Whatever structures of world politics emerge in the next century, the editors and writers of this book—lawyers, journalists, and scholars—contend that the laws of war belong to everyone. They are among the great achievements of civilization, and in this era of uncertainty and disorder more relevant than ever.

For the time being, accountability is not the rule, but the exception, in conflict. And realistically, international humanitarian law will not take hold without the support of governments. But as public interest grows in international humanitarian law, and this once esoteric field begins to generate news, a sense of change is in the air. Whether the story concerns the sentencing for genocide of a Rwandan mayor—the first such sentence handed down since Nuremberg—the effort to send war crimes investigators to

Kosovo, a Spanish prosecutor's attempt to put the former Chilean dictator Augusto Pinochet on trial for crimes against his people, or the U.S. government decision to award a bounty of up to $5 million for the capture of indicted Bosnian war criminals, the pattern represents a radical shift.

The question now is whether the new paradigm will prove enduring, and whether the rule of law set out in international treaties can truly be made to apply to conflict. There is ample reason for skepticism. What is certain is that it will not happen without public awareness and public engagement. And without a command of the most basic facts about the laws of war, there can be neither.

The need is pressing. Wars today increasingly are fought not between armies where officers are bound by notions of honor but by fighters, many of them children, who are not soldiers in any conventional sense of the word. The goal of these conflicts is often ethnic cleansing—the forcible expulsion of the civilian population of one's enemy—not the victory of one army over another.

The principal victims of this kind of war—slaughter is often the better term for it—are civilians. As horrible as the death toll was in World War I, the millions who died were, by and large, killed on the battlefield—soldiers killed by soldiers, not civilians killed by lawless or random or planned savagery. The rough proportion of military to civilian casualties was ninety to ten. In World War II, the proportions were roughly even. Today for every ten military casualties there are on the order of ninety civilian deaths. The reality of our era, as demonstrated in Angola, Somalia, Bosnia, Rwanda, and Chechnya, is that torture is rampant, murdering civilians commonplace, and driving the survivors from their homes often the main goal of a particular military offensive.

This book is published on the eve of the fiftieth anniversary—in August 1999—of the Geneva Conventions, with the aim of encouraging public knowledge of the principles of conduct in war. It consists of three types of articles. The heart of the law, and of this book, are the grave breaches, or serious war crimes, delineated in the four Geneva Conventions of 1949 and the First Additional Protocol of 1977. The editors sought to find a clear example of each breach, irrespective of countries or adversaries, and then asked working reporters who had been at the scene to provide a graphic case study of what they had seen. These articles are labeled *crime*. Leading scholars in the United States and abroad contributed shorter articles on technical topics, most labeled *the law*. There are also essay-length articles by journalists or scholars on major themes, labeled *key terms*. To provide a broader overview of contemporary conflict, the editors asked reporters and one historian to take a fresh and critical look at recent conflicts and examine them in the light of the crimes of war. These *case studies* offer insights into the dynamics of crimes in nine wars and can be read as a book within a book. Complementing the case studies are three experts' overviews of the applicable law: "Categories of War Crimes" by Steven Ratner, "Crimes against Humanity" by Cherif Bassiouni, and "Genocide" by Diane Orentlicher. Every article was vetted by our legal editor, Kenneth Anderson, his colleagues at American University's Washington College of Law, and by leading military law experts in the United States and Britain.

The A-to-Z format, the use of bold-face type to indicate cross-references, and the graphic design are intended to make the book easy to use, and the photographs to provide visual bookmarks, while documenting the reality behind the words. The texts recount some of the most compelling reportage of contemporary journalism. Sydney Schanberg's case study of

Cambodia, Roger Cohen's article on ethnic cleansing in Bosnia, Gwynne Roberts's account of the gassing of Kurdish civilians in Halabja and the aftermath, Frank Smyth's tale of arrest in Iraq, Ed Vulliamy's account on concentration camps, and Corinne Dufka's account of child soldiers in Liberia are a few of the articles that provide the raison d'être for this book.

Crimes of War was conceived as a handbook for reporters. But just as war is too important to be left to the generals, war coverage is too important to be left uncritically to the news media. The general public, too, should know the moral and legal benchmarks contained in the law. One reason for a commonality of interest is that coverage of contemporary conflicts increasingly is available to the public without a filter or a framework or context. A second is that every close observer has a restricted field of vision.

Journalists who cover wars and humanitarian emergencies of the post-Cold War world know far better than their audiences or their critics how much they are operating in uncharted territory. Understanding what is going on in the midst of all the havoc, confusion, and disinformation is anything but simple. And almost nothing in their training prepares reporters to be able to make the necessary distinctions between legal, illegal, and criminal acts. Is it a war crime under international law or a horrible, destructive, but legal act of war when one sees a hospital being shelled in Sarajevo, a humanitarian aid convoy blocked at a checkpoint on the Dagestan-Chechen border, or combat in which no prisoners are taken in Sri Lanka? Is it a legitimate sanction on the part of a State when the homes of alleged terrorists are reduced to rubble, as happens regularly in Israel, or is it a war crime? When combatants insert themselves amongst the civilian population, as was the case in Vietnam and more recently in Rwanda, does this violate the international conventions?

The best single indicator of a major war crime often is a massive displacement of civilians. But people may be fleeing for their lives from the scene of crime or the immediate threat of crimes, as in South Sudan at many points during the civil war there; or because their leaders ordered them out, but are intending to return militarily to destroy the other side, as the Serbs fleeing Croatian Slavonia did in 1991. They may be fleeing at the insistence of their political leaders, who intend to depict them as the victims of crime, as in the case of the Tajiks who fled into Afghanistan in 1993; or because they and their leaders have committed massive crimes and fear justice or retribution, as in the case of the Rwandan Hutus who fled into eastern Zaire in 1994 in the wake of the genocide. Determinations as these are hard to make in the best of circumstances, but all the more so under deadline pressure.

Sometimes the laws of war are frustratingly counterintuitive. International humanitarian law, as the contents of this book exemplify, does not address the causes or origins of a particular war, or which side was right and which side was wrong, only the method by which it is fought. So it is entirely possible, for example, for an aggressor to stage a war of conquest in accordance with the Geneva Conventions or for a defender to commit war crimes in a legitimate war of self-defense. But the fact that the law cannot answer every question, or shield us from every moral dilemma that war occasions, does not mean it has no answers or provides no bulwark against barbarism and crime.

In any case, understanding, while always difficult, is never more so than in war when the lure of easy explanations may be hard to resist. The British journalist Lindsey Hilsum maintains that when a journalist reports that the situation on the ground is one of anarchy, or resorts to such reductive clichés as describing a particular conflict as the product of ancient ethnic or tribal hatreds, the chances are that he or she has not fully understood what was going on.

Obviously, journalists have a primary role, but they are not the only people focused on the brutality of contemporary conflict. Groups such as Human Rights Watch, Amnesty International, and the German Society for Threatened Peoples increasingly have turned their focus to violations of humanitarian law; but they cannot take on the entire responsibility of uncovering crimes of war. Watch groups have exceptional expertise and devoted staffers, but they also have finite resources and may arrive late at the scene, have limited access, and are sometimes slow to produce their reports. And like many private groups, dependent on external fund-raising, each has its separate mandate and agenda.

Relief and aid workers in the field have become the eyes and ears of the world in conflict zones. Usually, they are the first on the scene and the last to leave. But their mandate and their training usually does not encompass trying to stop or even report on war crimes, and they are at risk of expulsion, with all that this entails for the endangered populations they are trying to serve, if they publicly cross that line. Yet knowledge of what is legal, illegal, and criminal in warfare will permit them or any other observers to alert those who do have the mandate and the means to inform the world or to act.

For the general public, *Crimes of War* should make it possible to become better informed consumers of the news by laying out the benchmarks for monitoring the watchdogs and governments. Just what steps governments should take to counter wholesale violations of the codes of war is not the subject of this book. Sometimes merely turning the spotlight on gross violations of humanitarian law can affect behavior in a small theater of war; other times, as in the Balkans, only military intervention or the threat of it can do any good. Our hope is that if the principles of law are widely understood, and if the news media and other observers present the relevant facts to the public, informed debate will provide the answers.

Joseph Pulitzer put it most succinctly when he wrote, "There is not a crime which does not live in secrecy. Get these things out in the open, describe them, attack them, ridicule them in the press, and sooner or later, public opinion will sweep them away." That, at least, is the hope of those who have contributed to this book.

Auschwitz, Poland, 1979.

FOREWORD

By Richard Goldstone

Reporters and other observers at the frontline of conflict often voice frustration that their reports and efforts hardly dent the public consciousness and do little to change an intolerable situation; but the fact is that accurate, timely, and thoughtful coverage of war crimes can have an impact far beyond any immediate calculation.

A dramatic illustration of the impact of that kind of reporting was the establishment of the United Nations International Criminal Tribunal for the former Yugoslavia. Visual and written reports from journalists of the plight of the victims of ethnic cleansing in Bosnia jolted the Security Council into taking the unprecedented step of creating an international court as its own sub-organ. Never before had it even been contemplated or suggested that it should use its peacekeeping powers to that end. That ethnic cleansing was happening in Europe and that the Cold War had come to an end were crucial to the endeavor. There can be no doubt, however, that it was media exposure that triggered the decision.

More recently, gruesome photographs of the torture and abuse of prisoners detained by the United States military in the Abu Ghraib prison in Iraq horrified the American people, and the shock waves reverberated around the world. The photographs and media comment on them have resulted in the trial and conviction of some of the perpetrators responsible for those war crimes. As of this writing, the debate still continues as to whether responsibility should be followed further up the chain of command. The outcome of that debate, I suggest, will depend in part on the attention given to the issue by the media.

Another recent example of the consequences of media publicity of war crimes comes from the province of Darfur in Sudan. The Security Council and a number of Western and African governments have devoted much attention to many credible reports of ethnic cleansing taking place there. The State Department in Washington D.C. has determined that genocide is being perpetrated in Darfur. Similar, if not more egregious, war crimes are being committed elsewhere in Africa. Millions of deaths have been the result of civil war in the Democratic Republic of Congo. Those crimes have received little media attention and, in consequence, meager attention from international organizations, whether the United Nations or the African Union. There can be no doubt that in this field media attention directly affects political consequences.

The successes of the United Nations ad hoc tribunals for the former Yugoslavia and Rwanda led to the diplomatic conference in Rome in 1998 when 120 nations adopted a new treaty for a permanent international criminal court. It came into force with effect from the beginning of July 2002 after the requisite 60 nations ratified the treaty. That number has since grown to over 100 nations. Hybrid international criminal tribunals have been established in Sierra Leone and East Timor. These developments signal the end of impunity for war criminals. It is certainly no exaggeration to ascribe these positive developments to the efforts of the media. It has been the most important medium for the dissemination of the work of international criminal courts.

Prior to the establishment of the Yugoslavia Tribunal, little attention was given to international humanitarian law (the Law of War) outside military colleges in some democratic nations. It was taught in few, if any, law schools. That has changed. Hardly a day passes without reference to war crimes and humanitarian law in the media. The subject is now widely taught in many law schools around the world.

In consequence of these developments, journalism has gained a new dimension. Compared to judicial bodies, journalists have very different mandates, modes of operating, routes to access information, and thresholds of proof. These functions of courts and journalists should not be confused. It is important that reporters stay reporters—that is, uncover the facts and write the stories (and the stories behind the stories) for the general public. Humanitarian law pragmatically accepts the reality of war, as must we all. If carefully applied, knowledge of that law will assist the public in grasping a critical but often hidden dynamic in conflict.

The first edition of this book, and the Crimes of War Project, has made a signal contribution to the improvement of the quality of war reporting and to the resulting enhancement of public awareness of the subject. Developments in humanitarian law have required journalists to become knowledgeable on the topic and to keep updating that knowledge.

In the foreword to the first edition, I raised the question as to whether the role of reporters should extend to taking part in tribunal prosecutions. I pointed out that not infrequently journalists come across evidence of war crimes—as eyewitnesses, in discovering a mass grave, or through being privy to statements made by commanders in the heat of action. Like aid workers and Red Cross or Red Crescent delegates, if reporters become identified as would-be witnesses, their safety and future access to fields of battle will be compromised. I suggested that the law takes too little account of that reality.

A qualified privilege for journalists has been the subject of debate in a number of legal jurisdictions. It came before the Yugoslavia Tribunal in 2002 during the trial of Radoslav Brdjanin. Jonathan Randal, a war correspondent of the *Washington Post*, refused to testify in the trial. He sought to have his subpoena set aside. He was unsuccessful before a trial chamber and took the matter on appeal. The Appeals Chamber ruled in his favor. The judges recognized a public interest in the work of war correspondents and society's interest in protecting the integrity of their newsgathering process. They held that compelling war correspondents to testify in a war crimes tribunal could adversely affect their ability to carry out their work. Firstly, witnesses might speak less freely to them and they might be refused access to war zones; and secondly, they might become the targets rather than the observers of those committing violations of humanitarian law.

The Appeals Chamber held that a balance has to be struck between the interests of justice in having all relevant evidence placed before the tribunal and the benefits to society of having the newsgathering function performed without unnecessary constraints. The outcome is a two-pronged test that must be satisfied:

"First, the petitioning party [the party seeking to obtain the war correspondent's testimony] must demonstrate that the evidence sought is of direct and important value in determining a core issue in the case. Second, it must demonstrate that the evidence sought cannot reasonably be obtained elsewhere."

In the 2000 case of Blagoje Simic, a trial chamber granted absolute immunity to a former employee of the International Committee of the Red Cross in order to protect the impartiality of that body. These developments constitute an important recognition of the essential and courageous work performed in times of war by war correspondents and humanitarian workers.

Humanitarian law and international human rights law have never been more developed; yet so many innocent civilians continue to be the victims of war crimes. This state of affairs will not improve absent a mechanism to enforce those laws and the norms they embody. The international community is coming to realize this—hence the two ad hoc tribunals, the International Criminal Court, and the hybrid tribunals. However, a reason for pessimism is the contradictory policy of the United States—on the one hand, support for the United Nations ad hoc and hybrid tribunals, yet, on the other, the negative and harmful attitude directed toward the permanent court. Strong media support for international criminal justice can play a crucial role in achieving a reversal of that approach.

If new enforcement mechanisms are to succeed they will need the continued vigilance of the media and greater public awareness. To that end this unique publication is an invaluable resource.

Near the Rwandan border, Zaire, 1994.

International Humanitarian Law: An Overview

By Lawrence Weschler

Justice may be many things at the Yugoslavia War Crimes Tribunal in The Hague, but one thing it decidedly is not is swift. At times the pace of the proceedings in the court's main hearing chamber—a gleaming, light-filled, technologically almost-futuristic cubicle encapsulated behind a wall of bulletproof glass—can seem positively Dickensian. The proceedings tend to lurch forward and then become bogged down in a thicket of minute-seeming legalistic distinctions, and there are mornings when even the most attentive mind can wander.

One such morning several years back, near the outset of the whole exercise, I found my own attention wandering into a book of history I'd brought along just in case—though of Holland, as it happened, not of Yugoslavia. I was reading about the earliest stages of human habitation of the Netherlands in the lowland marshes and swampfields north of the Rhine River delta, terrain much of whose elevation is pitched so low that it was regularly subject to catastrophic flooding. It was not all that surprising, therefore, to learn that through many centuries this muddy floodplain went largely uninhabited and that it wasn't until around the year 800 that the first tentative forays at serious colonization were undertaken as tiny communities pitched precarious clusters of hovels atop artificially piled mounds, known as terps.

With the passing generations, some of these terps were in turn joined together by painstakingly raised landbridges, which served both as connecting paths and as protective dikes. Any given triangle, say, of such dikes, joining together three outlying terps, incidentally proved capable of shielding the terrain it enclosed from outside flooding, but that only led to a new problem: what to do with all the rain and groundwater trapped and festering within the enclosure. Initial attempts at draining these patches of pestilential marshland, the so-called polders, have been documented as early as 1150, but the real breakthrough came with the introduction of windmills in the fifteenth and especially the sixteenth centuries. Eventually "gangs" of dozens of coordinated windmills were being deployed, each in turn raising the stagnant marshwaters a few inches up and over the dikes and into a surrounding network of irrigation and navigation canals. Polder after polder was thus reclaimed—hundreds, thousands, and presently hundreds of thousands of acres of uncommonly fertile land in a process that continues to this day.

Half-listening to the drone of the ongoing trial, I suddenly realized how in a sense the judges and prosecutors and investigators there in The Hague had set themselves a remarkably similar sort of reclamatory challenge. The tribunal's founding president and chief judge, the Italian Antonio Cassese; its founding prosecutor, the South African Richard Goldstone; and his successors, the Canadian Louise Arbour and the Swiss Carla del Ponte, have all repeatedly cast their work in terms of an attempt to stem the historic cycle of floodtides of ethnic bloodletting that recurrently afflict places like the former Yugoslavia, or Rwanda, the other principal locus of the tribunal's mandate. In both places, these jurists have repeatedly insisted, the propensity for ethnic mayhem is far from endemic or inevitable. "For the great majority of their histories," as Justice Goldstone insisted early on, "the Croats and Serbs and Muslims, and the Tutsis and the Hutus, have lived in relative peace with one another, and they were all doing so relatively nicely until just recently. Such interethnic violence usually gets stoked by specific individuals intent on immediate political or material advantage, who then call forth the legacies of earlier and previously unaddressed grievances... It is they, not the group as a whole, who need to be held to account, through a fair and meticulously detailed presentation of the evidence, precisely so that the next time around no one will be able to claim that all Serbs did this, or all Croats or all Hutus—so that people will be able to see how it is specific individuals in their communities who are continually endeavoring to manipulate them in that fashion. I really believe that is the only way the cycle can be broken."

In this context, it occurred to me that each of these individual prosecutions was like a single mound, a terp cast out upon the moral swampland of the war's aftermath—and the entire tribunal enterprise a system of interconnected dikes and sluices and pumps and windmills and canals designed to reclaim for each of the regions the possibility of a fertile regeneration.

But the tribunals weren't merely attempting to reclaim such a possibility for Yugoslavia and Rwanda alone. Sitting there in the spectator's gallery at the tribunal, I recalled that old jurists' saw to the effect that if international law exists at the vanishing point of law, the law of war exists, even more emphatically, at the vanishing point of international law; and it occurred to me how there, on the infinite marshy borderland, these jurists and lawyers and investigators, and the diplomats who'd carved out the immediate occasion for their labors, and the human rights monitors and (yes) journalists who'd painstakingly (and often at great risk) gathered up the initial shards and planks required for their effort, were all engaged—fact by fact, testimony by testimony, case by case—in the latest instance of a decades-long, at times maddeningly halting, vexed, and compromised effort to expand the territory of law itself.

I say "decades-long," but in fact people have been working this border terrain for centuries and indeed millennia. The marshland into which the current pioneers have been inserting their tentative new foundations is hardly virgin territory, and they have continually been coming upon the water-logged ruins of earlier efforts, bulwarks that seemed to hold for a time but then crumpled and are now having to be reconceived. We moderns pride ourselves on our various treaties, conventions, proclamations, and protocols—as though we were the first ever to have conceived of such a daft and brilliant scheme (the placing, after all, of humane constraints upon the very practice of war!)—but centuries ago there were already entire systems in place (the product, in part, of carefully elaborated disputations by thinkers ranging from Augustine through Aquinas). Consider, for example, the remarkable sway of chivalry in medieval Europe (or, alternatively, of the various samurai codes in Tokugawa Japan): the way everything from the requirements for proper warning through behavior on the battlefield, treatment of noncombatants, the protection of prisoners, and the victor's responsibilities following his opponent's surrender were all meticulously stipulated, stipulations which in turn were often rigorously observed for fear of loss of knightly honor (a disgrace more scathing, in some instances, than defeat itself). Of course, such codes had their limits. For one thing, in the case of chivalry, they tended to rely on fairly stylized face-to-face relations between combatants (as much a product of the imperatives of ransom as those of mercy) and hence failed to survive the introduction of munitions and artillery into the battlefield. Beyond that, they were tied to notions of Christian nobility and therefore tended to get jettisoned when the war-making involved non-Christian opponents, as in the unspeakably gruesome Crusades. And when Christendom itself began breaking up, with the onset of the Protestant Reformation, Christians took to treating each other as heathen heretics. The wars of religion that ravaged sixteenth- and seventeenth-century Europe were among the most harrowing and anarchic of all time, and much of the early theorizing behind what was to become the modern law of war (from Grotius through Montaigne and Rousseau) arose in the appalled shadow of such seemingly limitless mayhem.

The most recent campaign to plot and posit an international humanitarian legal order (a law, that is, of war, governing the interactions between combatant forces and between those forces and noncombatants during times of military conflict—as opposed to the doctrine of human rights more generally conceived, which is understood to apply to all people at all times) is generally thought to have gotten launched in the mid-nineteenth century, in part as a response to the exponential increase in the potential for mayhem occasioned by the convergence of mass conscription and technological progress. During the Crimean War of 1854, for example, eighty thousand members of the three hundred thousand in the Franco-British expeditionary force perished under conditions of horrendous disorder and distress. Five years later, in June 1859, when a huge Austrian army clashed with a Franco-Italian force in the Battle of Solferino, close to forty thousand died within just a few days—with the majority, perhaps, expiring due to untreated wounds. A young Swiss businessman named Jean-Henri Dunant, happening upon the scene, was so "seized with horror and pity" that he dedicated the rest of his life to addressing the appalling situation. He established the International Committee of the Red Cross in 1863 and then convened an international conference that culminated in the Geneva Convention of 1864 "for the amelioration of the conditions of the wounded in armies in the field." During those same years, in America, with the Civil War raging, though with a specific eye toward the requirements of the peace that would need to follow, President Abraham Lincoln authorized a New York professor, Francis Lieber, to prepare a draft of the rules of military engagement, especially as regards the treatment of prisoners of war; the Lieber Code, which Lincoln thereupon promulgated as binding on all Union forces, was to have a profound effect on subsequent such codifications.

International humanitarian law, as it was to develop over the next century, was determinedly agnostic on the question of the legality of war itself. Phrased differently, it assumed war as a given and strove to channel its excesses. For a long while, the principal tracks upon which this process occurred were associated with two cities—The Hague, where conferences in 1899 and 1907 tended to focus on the conduct of war (permissible weapons and the like); and Geneva, where further conventions, under the auspices of the League of Nations in 1925 and the International Committee of the Red Cross in 1929, 1949, and 1977, built on the work of the original 1864 convention. These conferences often tended to address the toxic legacy of the immediately prior war. The 1925 Geneva Protocol, for example, prohibited the use of poisonous gases and biological weapons. The four Geneva Conventions of 1949 dealt, respectively, with the wounded and sick on land; the wound-

ed, sick, and shipwrecked at sea; prisoners of war; and perhaps most significantly, the fate of civilian noncombatants. A 1954 convention in The
Hague addressed the protection of cultural monuments. And two 1977 protocols to the 1949 Geneva Conventions, the fruit of a marathon three-year
drafting session, among other things partially extended the terms of those
earlier conventions on international conflicts to wars of national liberation
and civil wars. The Nuremberg Tribunals of Nazi leaders (and to a lesser
extent the Tokyo Trials of Japanese officials) staked out new territory with
the development and promulgation of the notion of "crimes against humanity," territory further consolidated in 1948 with the United Nations
Convention on the Prevention and Punishment of the Crime of Genocide.

The past century and a half, in short, has seen a remarkable project of
constructive expansion out there on the infinite borderland. Indeed, the
interconnecting bulwarks and dikes and bastions of international humanitarian law constitute one of the true wonders of our age—the astonishing and
heartening achievement of generations of legal and diplomatic artisans.
Their masterful monument has proven, at best, of only middling effective-
ness. The porous ramparts sag and leak, and seem subject to random
collapse. Although the various conventions and codes project a magisterial
all-inclusiveness, what they've most pointedly lacked, at least until recently,
has been any effective means of enforcing their magisterial norms, and
specifically of holding individuals criminally accountable, both to their victims and to the entire world community, for their violation. True, such
individual prosecutions formed the core of the Nuremberg and Tokyo trials,
but those prosecutions were arguably instances of victor's justice and in any
case there weren't any other such trials for almost fifty years thereafter.
There have been internal national human rights prosecutions following the
collapse of dictatorships—Greece, Argentina, Ethiopia—and there have been
cases where governments as such, though not individuals, have been ruled
in violation of various human rights norms: Turkey, Honduras, Uruguay.

But the vast armature of international humanitarian law has stood
largely mute, palsied in part by the fear of most national governing elites—
and in particular the successive leaderships of the five permanent Security
Council members most in a position to invoke those norms—that the glare
of such attention might one day be turned on their own actions. (In the
United States this tenor of concern often took the form of the anxious
assertion that "by that logic Henry Kissinger could have been held liable
for the Christmas bombing of Hanoi"—as well he might have been.)

Against this backdrop, the sudden lurch forward with the establishment
of the two ad hoc criminal tribunals on Yugoslavia and Rwanda during the
mid-1990s came as virtually a fluke (notwithstanding the years and years of
prior lobbying by committed human rights lawyers and activists for State
accountability and an end to individual impunity), their establishment
arguably having primarily grown out of the panicky overreaction of the
Security Council's permanent five, shamed at the spectacle of their own gap-
ing failure to take any more consequent action to stop the carnage itself as
it was happening. (At least this way they could be seen to be doing something.) No sooner had the tribunals been constituted than several of the
permanent five, perhaps realizing the implications of their mistake, seemed
to think better of the entire project. They filibustered the appointment of
the permanent prosecutor for over a year and then imposed all sorts of procedural and budgetary constraints on the efficient operation of the
Yugoslavia tribunal. In particular, for a long while, the international peacekeeping forces on the ground were ordered to bend over backward to avoid
even encountering, let alone arresting, the indicted war criminals plainly in

their midst. And yet, somehow, the tribunals persisted, against enormous odds.

Perhaps most significantly, ad hoc though they were, they seemed to be steadily expanding the terrain of the possible along the borderland of international humanitarian legal practice. And meanwhile, to everyone's astonishment, the rudiments of a permanent International Criminal Court seemed to be taking shape, most notably in the summer of 1998 in Rome, where an international diplomatic conference eventually brokered a treaty calling for an establishment of a modest, admittedly compromised, though still surprisingly robust version of just such a tribunal. The United States, initially one of the fiercest rhetorical advocates of a permanent court, seemed to become spooked all over again by perceived threats to its own sovereignty and at least initially demurred, lurching from confounded paralysis to a last-minute signing-on to the treaty under President Clinton, a signature that was then almost immediately repudiated under the new president, George W. Bush, whose administration redoubled its efforts to sabotage the fledgling court's development. Notwithstanding America's opposition, the new court gradually (indeed at times maddeningly haltingly) began to launch investigations (in the Democratic Republic of the Congo, northern Uganda, and Darfur) and to issue a first tentative stream of indictments. Meanwhile, other nationally based, though internationally supported, tribunals (for example in Sierra Leone, Cambodia, and East Timor) began to gather strength, and (somewhat more problematically, perhaps) the deposed and presently captured Saddam Hussein came to trial for his depredations in Baghdad. And in South America, as renewed democratic regimes began at last to step out from under the shadow of the military dictatorships that had preceded them, one after another they began to revisit the blanket amnesties those militaries, in taking their leave, had forced upon them, reopening old cases and even bringing some of the worst offenders to justice after all.

Suddenly, improbably, unlike anything anyone had seen in almost fifty years, there were all kinds of concrete activity taking place out there along the infinite borderland.

It is against that backdrop that a consortium of international journalists—many of them longtime frontline war correspondents—came up with the idea for the guide you hold in your hands. Although they'd witnessed and reported on many war crimes, as technically defined, over the years, they'd done so without any particular expectation that the perpetrators would ever be brought to justice. No, stronger than that: they'd done so in the near-certainty that the perpetrators, as usual, would get off scot-free, and that the regime of impunity would persist inviolate.

Suddenly, however, that sorry state of affairs seems to be changing. Suddenly, it's going to matter whether, say, there was or wasn't a machine gun emplacement nestled in the rafters of that hospital, or a cannon in its courtyard. It's going to matter whether armed troops were accompanying the column of refugees fleeing that collapsing enclave, or whether the defenders had raised a white flag and were attempting to surrender when they were shot. By virtue of their profession, war correspondents may well find themselves among the first outside witnesses on the scene at war crimes. As such, they're going to need to be informed witnesses, and the rest of us are going to have to become a far better informed and engaged public.

Hence this book, now entering its second edition, vastly updated to take in the advances and setbacks of the last seven years. The turn away from the received standards of international humanitarian law evident in the United States' armed confrontation with al-Qaeda, discussed elsewhere in this new edition, now stands in counterpoint to the gradual reclamatory project of international justice. It does not negate it.

NOTE: Terms in bold face are cross references to other articles.

A

Act of War

By David Turns

Until 1945, an act of war in the traditional, historical sense was understood to mean any act by a State that would effectively terminate the normal international law of peacetime and activate the international law of war. The decision was invariably that of the target State and was generally preceded by a statement warning that certain acts would be considered acts of war and would trigger hostilities. Belligerent and neutral States also used the term. Belligerents would interpret as acts of war any action that seemed to assist the enemy; neutrals, any infringement of their neutrality.

In 1945, the United Nations Charter banned the first use of force, putting an end to declarations of war. Article 2(4) of the Charter states: "All members shall refrain in their international relations from the threat or use of force against the territorial integrity or political independence of any State." The last formal declaration of war was made by the U.S.S.R. against Japan in 1945. An example of modern State practice is provided by the United Kingdom, which during the Suez War (1956) and the Falkland Islands War (1982) strenuously denied that it was at war with, respectively, Egypt and Argentina. Britain applied the law of international armed conflict in its military operations, nevertheless.

The term "act of **aggression**" has to all intents and purposes subsumed the legal term "act of war" and made it irrelevant, although "act of war" is still used rhetorically by States that feel threatened. The People's Republic of China stated in 1997 that any attempt by the Republic of China (Taiwan) to declare independence would be regarded as an act of war; and in August 1998, the U.S. Secretary of State, Madeleine Albright, said that Osama bin Laden, the reputed mastermind of truck-bomb attacks on two U.S. embassies in Africa, had "declared war on the United States and struck first." In the domestic law of many States, "act of war" is also used in some contexts, such as insurance and reparations claims, to refer to any use of force in any armed conflict.

Following the terrorist attacks on the World Trade Center and the Pentagon on 11 September 2001, U.S. President George W. Bush declared that America had been attacked and that the terrorists' actions constituted "acts of war" (they were also implicitly recognized by the UN Security Council as giving rise to a right of self-defense, albeit against a non-State group rather than a State). This was followed by the U.S. Congress passing a Resolution to give war powers to the President for the prosecution of the "war." Even so, use of the term "acts of war" to describe the terrorist attacks of 9/11 is, in legal terms, fairly meaningless—acts of war are committed by sovereign States—and it should be viewed, again, as primarily rhetorical in nature. (See **terrorism**.)

EXTRA

RACE RESULTS | **Los Angeles Times** | **NIGHT Pictorial**

LIBERTY UNDER THE LAW — EQUAL RIGHTS — TRUE INDUSTRIAL FREEDOM

LXI | Three Parts — 38 Pages | *** | MONDAY MORNING, DECEMBER 8, 1941. | Page A | DAILY, FIVE CEN

IT'S WAR!

Hostilities Declared by Japanese
350 Reported Killed in Hawaii Raid

U.S. Battleships Hit; Die in Honolulu

NEW YORK, Dec. 7. (A.P.)—Three hundred and y men were killed by a direct bomb hit on Hickam ld an N.B.C. observer reported tonight from Hono-u.

In addition to these casualties from an air raid by anes which the observer identified as Japanese, he d three United States ships, including the battleship lahoma, were attacked in Pearl Harbor.

Several of the attacking planes, which came from e south, were shot down, he said.

HONOLULU, Dec. 7. (A.P.)—Japanese bombs killed east seven persons and injured many others, three ously, in a surprise morning aerial attack on Honolulu y.

Army officials announced that two Japanese planes had shot down in the Honolulu area.

he dead included three Caucasians, two Japanese and -year-old Portuguese girl.

everal fires were started in the city area, but all were ediately controlled.

vernor Joseph B. Poindexter proclaimed M-Day emergency se measures immediately in effect. He appointed Eduard Doty arge of the Major Disaster Council.

M-Day proclamation establishes civilian-military control of and roads, and permits the Governor to issue food ration lations.

st reports said that 10 or more persons were injured when en-planes sprayed bullets on the streets of Wahiawa, a town of 3000 population, about 20 miles northwest of Honolulu.

s report indicated the aerial attack was aimed at points on the island shu other than Honolulu and the heavily fortified Pearl Harbor naval

e attack ended at around 9:25 a.m., (11:55 a.m. P.S.T.) lasting for ap-

Turn to Page B, Column F

LATE WAR BULLETINS

SHANGHAI, Dec. 8 (Monday.) (A.P.)—The Japanese have sunk the British gunboat Petrel as it lay off the International Settlement waterfront.

HONOLULU, Dec. 7. (U.P.) — Parachute troops were sighted off Pearl Harbor today.

TOKYO, Dec. 8 (Monday.) (A.P.)—An emergency session of the Japanese Cabinet was held at Premier Tojo's official residence at 7 a.m. today (2 p.m. Sunday, P.S.T.)

NEW YORK, Dec. 7. (U.P.)—The U.S.S. Oklahoma, a battleship, was set afire in today's air attack on Pearl Harbor, an N.B.C. broadcast from Honolulu said.

WASHINGTON, Dec. 7. (A.P.)—The Navy Department announced tonight that a censorship had been placed on all outgoing cablegrams and radio messages from the United States and its outlying possessions.

LONDON, Dec. 7. (AP)—The House of Commons was summoned tonight for a session tomorrow.

The House of Lords also was called.

An announcement from Prime Minister

Turn to Page B, Column 3

Air Guards, Attention!

To chief observers: All observation posts:
A.W.S. (Aircraft Warning Service) You are directed to activate your observation posts immediately and to see t h a t the post is fully manned at all times.

By order Brig. Gen. William O. Ryan, Commander, Ft. Interceptor Command.

Air Bombs Rained on Pacific Bases

WASHINGTON, Dec. 7. (A.P.)—The White House announced early tonight that the Navy had advised th President that Japan has attacked the island of Guam

WASHINGTON, Dec. 7.—Japan declared upon the United States today. An electrified nation mediately united for a terrific struggle ahead. Presid Roosevelt was expected to ask Congress for a declara of war tomorrow.

During the day, Japanese planes bombed Manila, Honol Pearl Harbor, and Hickam Field, Hawaii, without warning. broadcast from Honolulu, some 350 soldiers were reported dea Hickam Field, with numerous casualties at the other points of tack. (The attack on Manila was announced by the White Hou The Associated Press correspondent there reported at 1:25 p (P.S.T.) that Manila was quiet.) President Roosevelt said he ho the report of the bombing of the Philippine capital "at least is roneous."

Then, the Tokyo government announced that Japan had tered a state of war with the United States and Great Britain of 6 a.m., tomorrow (1 p.m. P.S.T. Sunday.)

But President Roosevelt hardly waited for the Japanese de ration. As soon as he heard of the bombing he ordered the A and Navy to carry out previously prepared and highly secret p for the defense of the country.

Army airmen engaged Japanese fighting planes over Honol In the city below them, the White House said, a heavy loss of had been inflicted, together with extensive damage to property

At the same time, the Chief Executive called his Cabinet int traordinary session for 8:30 p.m., and invited Congressional l ers to join the group a half-hour later.

Prior to this meeting, Mr. Roosevelt began the draft of a special me to Congress and if the general sentiment in official Washington quarters any indication, Japan's declaration of war would be met in like terms by Commander-in-Chief.

From a high Congressional source, it was learned that the President mentioned the possibility of a joint session of Congress tomorrow. This urally led to speculation that the Chief Executive would address it and person, as did Woodrow Wilson in 1917, that it declare war.

Turn to Page B, Colu

Japan attacked Pearl Harbor on December 7, 1941, and one day later the United States formally declared war.

29

A

Afghanistan

By Patricia Gossman

Conflict has raged in Afghanistan since April 1978. It has been marked by brutality on a massive scale. Although the major fighting ended with the defeat of the Taliban in 2001, conflict continues especially in the south and east of the country, and many of those responsible for war crimes in earlier phases of the war continue to wield power. During every phase of the fighting, Afghan and foreign armed factions committed crimes against humanity and serious war crimes. These included large-scale massacres, disappearances and summary executions of tens of thousands of Afghans, indiscriminate bombing and rocketing that killed hundreds of thousands of civilians, torture, mass rape and other atrocities. There has never been any serious effort, international or domestic, to account for these crimes.

Afghanistan's quarter-century of war began on April 27, 1978, when the People's Democratic Party of Afghanistan (PDPA), a small, Marxist-Leninist party, launched a coup, overthrowing and killing then-President Mohammed Daoud Khan and most of his family. The PDPA then embarked on an ambitious and ruthless campaign to transform Afghanistan into a modern socialist state. Mass arrests and executions began shortly after the coup. Among the thousands of victims were individuals (or entire families) that the new regime considered as potential opponents: leaders of social, political, or religious groups, professionals of every kind and other members of the educated class.

Lacking popular support to carry out its political agenda, the PDPA found itself in a situation spiraling out of control. The repression sparked uprisings throughout the country and mutinies within the Afghan army that threatened to destabilize the regime. The disintegration of the army marked a turning point for Soviet policy and led to the decision to invade on December 25, 1979, ostensibly in response to a request for military support from the exiled deputy prime minister Babrak Kamal, who was then installed as a puppet leader.

Civilian takes cover from artillery bombardment by Taliban seeking to seize Kabul, 1995.

A

The Soviet occupation brought about a shift in tactics in the war as the resistance forces began to coalesce around a number of factions largely organized along ethnic lines. They did not control the cities, but moved mainly in the rural areas where they enjoyed popular support. Most of the factions maintained headquarters or political representatives in Pakistan or Iran, where they also established conduits for vast amounts of military assistance that began to flow principally from the U.S. through Pakistan. Aware that the mass arrests and executions carried out earlier by the PDPA had only fueled the resistance and nearly destroyed the Army, the Soviets employed more systematic means of intelligence gathering. The secret police, the KhAD, was modeled on the Soviet KGB. It engaged in widespread summary executions, detentions and torture of suspected mujahidin (resistance) supporters. Torture survivors from this period whom I have interviewed regularly identified Soviet personnel supervising the torture.

Mujahidin began to organize even before the December 1979 Russian invasion. Badakhshan, 1979.

In the countryside, Soviet forces bombed routinely and indiscriminately; the aim was both to demoralize the civilian population supporting the resistance and to destroy its means of providing food and shelter to the mujahidin. Thus, irrigation systems, cropland and other rural resources were bombed as well as villages. The bombing killed countless civilians and devastated the countryside. From the early 1980s on, most refugees arriving in Pakistan reported they had fled because of the bombing. In all, some five million Afghans fled the country. In addition to the bombing, Soviet and Afghan forces carried out reprisals against civilians, executing any they believed to support the resistance. Soviet forces also sowed mines throughout the country; many remain a threat to Afghans living in rural areas today.

Desertions from the Afghan army had so decimated the military that Soviet forces and advisors were deployed in great numbers; Soviet personnel made decisions for the state, and for the PDPA officials who nominally governed it. Thus, some responsibility for war crimes committed during this period may rest with those Soviet officers as well as with senior Afghan officials. The members of the politburos of the two countries' ruling parties could also be held accountable for the decisions and policies during this period. No one knows how many Afghans died in the ten years following the revolution, but the number may be as high as one million.

In February 1986 the Soviet Union, under President Gorbachev, reached a decision to withdraw its forces by the end of 1988. The head of KhAD, Najibullah, was "elected" general secretary of the PDPA and subsequently became president of the Revolutionary Council. The Geneva Accords, outlining the provisions of the Soviet withdrawal, were signed on April 14, 1988, by Afghanistan, Pakistan, the U.S. and the USSR. Military and economic aid from the U.S. and USSR continued to their respective clients.

A fighter loyal to Ahmad Shah Massoud, with support from a tank belonging to General Rashid Dostum, fights off the Pakistan-backed Hekmatyar faction in the battle for Kabul, 1992.

Without the Soviet army, the Najibullah government increasingly relied for its defense on regional militias, paying for their loyalty with Soviet-provided cash and weapons. Although some were regular army divisions, the militias operated outside ordinary chain of command within the military, and were largely autonomous within their areas of control. Militia forces were responsible for waylaying and robbing travelers, including returning refugees, extorting money from traders, kidnapping, looting property, forcibly taking land, and planting mines without mapping or marking them.

A number of mujahidin groups also committed war crimes during this period. Many of those based in Pakistan who had the support of Pakistani military and intelligence agencies operated with impunity and had considerable control over the Afghan refugee population. One of the most powerful of these was Hizb-i Islami, headed by Gulbuddin Hekmatyar. These mujahidin carried out assassinations and maintained secret detention facilities in Pakistan; persons detained there included Afghan refugees who opposed the mujahidin leaders, or who worked for foreign NGOs, especially those employing women.

The demise of the Soviet Union meant the end of Soviet aid, and of the Najibullah regime. When the Najibullah government collapsed in April 1992, Kabul was engulfed in civil war as the multiple factions that had participated in the struggle against the PDPA regime and the Soviet occupation, along with the militias, fought for control of territory. Despite efforts by the UN and some of the neighboring countries to mediate, there was no agreement on a power-sharing settlement. The factional fighting fell largely along ethnic lines, and groups frequently targeted civilians from rival ethnic groups.

In many cases, the atrocities were carried out on the orders or with the direct knowledge of senior commanders and party leaders. However, senior commanders secured the loyalty of their subordinates at a cost, and operated with the knowledge that any effort to weaken the power of the commanders under them might lead them to switch sides, taking their troops with them. While this fact does not absolve the leaders of responsibility for the actions of their forces, it is critical in understanding command and control within the armed factions.

On April 26, 1992, most of the party leaders in Pakistan announced that they had reached agreement on an interim government that would hold power until a council could be convened and elections subsequently held. As defense minister of the new government, Ahmad Shah Massoud attempted to gain control first of Kabul itself—an objective that eluded him for three years. His principal foe was Hizb-i Islami, whose rocket attacks killed thousands of civilians between 1992 and 1995. Every major armed faction in Kabul had an arsenal of heavy weaponry that they used in battles that raged in the streets of Kabul during this period. Rape, as well as other targeted attacks on civilians, was ethnically based. In many cases, it was used as a means of ethnic cleansing. In one of the most notorious incidents of the civil war, hundreds of ethnic Shia Hazaras were raped and killed in a February 1993 massacre. Survivors I have spoken to identified commanders responsible for the killings and rape who continue to operate with impunity in Kabul. The leader of one of the factions responsible, Abdul Rasul Sayyaf, was elected to parliament in September 2005.

The Taliban emerged out of the chaos of the post-1992 period. In this group's first successful military operation, the Taliban disarmed and executed a notoriously predatory commander in Kandahar. The Taliban moved on to take on other commanders and very quickly attracted the support of Pakistan, who needed a client it thought would protect Pakistan's interests. By 1995 the Taliban took control of Herat, and in 1996, Kabul. The Taliban's actions with respect to women have been well documented, as they imposed harsh restrictions on girls' schools and employment for women

The Taliban were highly centralized, with regional governors in all strategic provinces reporting directly to the group's leader, Mullah Omar. The influence of non-Afghans over Mullah Omar increased after Osama bin Laden returned to Afghanistan in 1996 and in 1997 moved to Kandahar.

In May 1997 the largest single massacre of the war took place. Mainly Uzbek troops under General Malik Pahlawan captured over 3,000 Taliban soldiers at Mazar-i-Sharif and executed them. Some were taken to a desert location and shot; others were thrown down wells. One of the few survivors described to me how he crawled from under the bodies until he reached a village where the residents were willing to shelter him. Gen. Malik continues to live in Kabul.

The major war crimes of the Taliban were committed between 1997 and 2001 as they moved outside their ethnic Pashtun heartland. In areas where they encountered resistance, Taliban forces responded by massacring civilians and other noncombatants, and burning down villages. In August 1998, they massacred at least 2,000 people, mainly Hazara civilians, in Mazar-i-Sharif, exacting what they said was revenge for the massacre of their own troops the previous year. In July 1999, the Taliban launched a major offensive across the plain north of Kabul known as Shamali (meaning "North"), summarily executing civilians, and burning down villages, fields and orchards. The devastation was incalculable. In both of these operations, the Taliban had considerable support from Pakistan.

When the United States intervened in Afghanistan in late 2001, its forces sought allies on the ground among the commanders of the so-called "Northern Alliance" opposed to the Taliban. The U.S.'s overriding objective in Afghanistan was to defeat al-Qaeda and remove the Taliban from power with

In the voting booth at a mosque in Kabul during the October 2004 Presidential election.

minimal U.S. casualties. The fact that many of these new allies had records that included not only grave breaches of international humanitarian law, but in some cases criminal ties to narcotics trafficking and other illicit activities, apparently posed no obstacle. The U.S. provided arms, cash and other support to commanders whom it believed could keep the Taliban and al-Qaeda at bay. But the U.S. failed to achieve that objective. Athough a new central government was established under President Hamid Karzai in 2002, the Taliban remain a lethal force, with support flowing across the border from the "tribal areas" of Pakistan. Meanwhile a number of the commanders the U.S. has backed have strengthened their positions against rivals, and have continued to engage in abuse and criminal activities.

In mid-November, 2001, Northern Alliance forces surrounded the last Taliban stronghold in Kunduz. When the Taliban forces and the Pakistani and Arab fighters with them surrendered, thousands were taken into custody and transported to prison facilities under the control of General Dostum at Shiberghan and Qala-i-Jangi, near Mazar-i-Sharif. At least two hundred detainees (and, according to some sources, many more) reportedly died en route in the overcrowded container trucks used to transport them and were buried in mass graves in the desert area of Dasht-i-Leili near Shiberghan. Gen. Dostum later acknowledged that some two hundred prisoners had suffocated due to inadvertent overcrowding. A full investigation of the incident has never taken place.

Not all Afghan commanders and leaders involved in the long years of conflict engaged in war crimes; many should enjoy the right to participate in politics. However, too many with criminal records have secured places in political office or security agencies. By allying itself—for the sake of political expediency—with local commanders with long records of past crimes, the U.S. has jeopardized prospects for establishing stable and accountable institutions in Afghanistan, and has helped reinforce a pattern of impunity that undermines the legitimacy of the political process.

U.S. forces have also committed grave abuses. These have included crude and brutal methods of **torture** that have sometimes led to death, the use of secret **detention** facilities that facilitate torture; and unacknowledged detentions that are tantamount to **disappearances**, in violation of prohibitions on prolonged arbitrary detention in customary international humanitarian law and human rights law. During Cherif Bassiouni's tenure as UN Independent Expert on Human Rights in Afghanistan, the U.S. blocked his efforts to inspect U.S. detention facilities. Bassiouni had particularly condemned the United States' use of "firebases" to hold detainees—facilities not accessible to the ICRC. Under U.S. pressure, in 2005 the UN Human Rights Commission did not renew Bassiouni's mandate.

In January 2005, the Afghan Independent Human Rights Commission published the results of a national survey which showed overwhelming support for measures to keep war criminals out of power and to begin a truth process to account for past crimes. Before the September 2005 parliamentary elections, an electoral complaint commission received hundreds of submissions from Afghans charging candidates with war crimes and human rights violations. The fact that many candidates known to have illegal militias were not removed from the ballot was seen as one factor in the low voter turnout. After months of delay, in December 2005, the cabinet of President Hamid Karzai's administration adopted an action plan on transitional justice that was based on the Human Rights Commission's recommendations. A year later, few of the recommended steps had taken place. While some Afghans see the need to find a way to address the past, others, as well as some senior U.S. officials, argue that rocking the boat will lead to greater instability. In fact, the failure to scrutinize the records of those vying for power has led to the entrenchment of persons who continue to terrorize civilians and otherwise undermine the political process.

(See **detention and interrogation; Guantanamo; terrorism**.)

Aggression

By Steven R. Ratner

Aggression in international law is defined as the use of force by one State against another, not justified by self-defense or other legally recognized exceptions. The illegality of aggression is perhaps the most fundamental norm of modern international law and its prevention the chief purpose of the United Nations. Even before the UN, the League of Nations made the prevention of aggression a core aim; and the post-World War II Allied tribunals regarded aggression as a crime under the rubric **crimes against peace**.

The most authoritative definition comes from the UN General Assembly. (The UN Charter never defines the term, instead banning the threat or use of force.) In 1974, it completed a twenty-year project to define aggression. Member States claimed that a definition would help the UN—principally the Security Council, charged by the Charter with addressing aggression—in responding more consistently and promptly. While it reflects a broad international consensus, it is not a treaty, though it may represent **customary international law**.

The definition begins by stating that "[t]he first use of armed force by a State in contravention of the Charter" constitutes prima facie evidence of aggression. The definition is somewhat limiting, and perhaps circular, in that the first use of force by a State would not be aggression if undertaken in a way consistent with the Charter. Thus, for example, the deployment of U.S. forces to Somalia in 1992, while the first use of force, would not be aggression because it was authorized by the Security Council under Chapter VII of the Charter. A number of States have accepted that a State's first use of force to extricate its citizens from another State when they are in imminent danger, and the other State is not able to protect them, is not aggression (e.g., Israel's 1976 Entebbe raid) and may be a form of self-defense. Some scholars and human rights activists have advocated a broader right of non-UN-approved intervention to prevent large-scale human rights abuses.

Moreover, most States seem willing to accept, albeit tacitly, a limited right of a State to a first use of armed force—so-called anticipatory self-defense—where it is facing a certain, imminent, and catastrophic attack, such as was faced by Israel on the eve of the June 1967 war. However, the assertion by the United States government in its 2002 National Security Strategy of a broader right of preemptive self-defense to deal with "rogue States and terrorists" possessing weapons of mass destruction elicited significant criticism internationally. Foreign governments and others also condemned the war in Iraq in 2003 in part because they rejected U.S claims that the action was authorized by prior Security Council resolutions (the U.S. did not make a legal argument that the war was taken as a matter of self-defense) and concluded that it was thus aggression under the Charter.

The General Assembly's definition also offers an illustrative list of acts of aggression: invasion, attack, or occupation of whatever duration; bombardment; blockade; attack on another State's armed forces; unauthorized use of military forces stationed in a foreign State; allowing territory to be used for aggression; and sending armed bands or similar groups to carry out aggression or substantial involvement therein.

Acts of aggression such as these trigger the two key lawful uses of force mentioned in the Charter: (a) individual or collective self-defense; and (b) force approved by the UN itself. Thus, the Iraqi invasion of Kuwait triggered the right of Kuwait and its allies to engage in self-defense, as well as the right of the UN to approve the use of force against Iraq under Chapter VII.

Despite its prohibition in international law, aggression remains a feature of international life. Although the classic attack on another State is not as rampant as before World War II, more subtle forms of armed intervention persist, and the responses of the international community remain plagued by timidity and inconsistency.

(See **humanitarian intervention**; **just and unjust war**.)

Israel's first use of force in the Six-Day War would not be classified as aggression but as anticipatory self-defense to avert a certain and catastrophic attack. Port Suez, June 1967.

Apartheid

By Steven R. Ratner

Nelson Mandela described apartheid as "the color line that all too often determines who is rich and who is poor... who lives in luxury and who lives in squalor... who shall get food, clothing, and health care... and who will live and who will die."

Apartheid was the system of racial discrimination and separation that governed South Africa from 1948 until its abolition in the early 1990s. Building on years of discrimination against blacks, the National Party adopted apartheid as a model for separate development of races, though it served only to preserve white superiority. It classified persons as either white, Bantu (black), colored (mixed race), or Asian. Its manifestations included ineligibility from voting, separate living areas and schools, internal travel passes for blacks, and white control of the legal system.

As part of its decades-long efforts to eliminate the practice, the UN adopted in 1973 the International Convention on the Suppression and Punishment of the Crime of Apartheid, which 101 States have ratified. It characterizes apartheid as a crime for which individuals can be held accountable. The convention defines apartheid as a series of "inhuman acts committed for the purpose of establishing and maintaining domination by one racial group of persons over any other racial group of persons and systematically oppressing them." It also declares apartheid a crime against humanity.

The Geneva Conventions commit States to a policy of nondiscrimination in treating the sick and wounded, the shipwrecked and stranded, captured combatants and civilians under an occupation regime or caught up in conflict. Apartheid has also been labeled a war crime in international conflicts under Additional Protocol I to the Geneva Conventions. Protocol I lists as grave breaches apartheid "and other inhuman and degrading practices involving outrages upon personal dignity, based on racial discrimination." The inclusion of apartheid as a grave breach stemmed from the international campaign to isolate South Africa and was opposed by several Western powers as not sufficiently connected to armed conflict.

The most recent attempt to criminalize apartheid was in the Rome Statute of the International Criminal Court (ICC), which lists apartheid as a crime against humanity, defining it generically as inhumane acts "committed in the context of an institutionalized regime of systematic oppression and domination by one racial group over any other racial group or groups... with the intention of maintaining that regime."

Despite the Apartheid Convention's (and now the ICC's) geographically unconfined definition, states and non-governmental organizations (NGOs) have only rarely referred to systems outside South Africa as apartheid. Groups such as the Kurds, the Tamils, the South Sudanese, or other indigenous peoples do suffer systematic discrimination that might well meet the definition of apartheid, even if those practices lack all the legal trappings of the South African model. But the term has not been invoked by victims or their advocates, no doubt because it is still associated with South Africa. Thus, the likelihood that individuals will be prosecuted domestically or internationally in the near future for apartheid remains small.

A

Arab-Israeli Wars

By Benny Morris

On November 2, 1948, an Israel Defense Forces (IDF) patrol visited the campsite of a small Bedouin subtribe, Arab al Mawasa, just west of the Sea of Galilee in northern Israel. The area, along with the rest of upper central Galilee, had been conquered by the IDF three to four days before in an armored offensive code-named Operation Hiram.

The patrol, in search of arms, scoured the area. On nearby "Hill 213" the troops found the decapitated remains of two Israeli soldiers who had been missing since a skirmish one month before. According to the 103rd Battalion's patrol report, "The men [then] torched the Arabs' homes [tents?]. The men returned to base with 19 Arab males. At the base the males were sorted out and those who had taken part in enemy operations against our army were identified and then taken under Haim [Hayun]'s command to a designated place and there 14 of them were liquidated. The rest are being transferred to a prisoner of war camp."[1]

Few such documents have surfaced in Israel's archives during the past fifty years, partly because soldiers and officers who committed atrocities rarely left written descriptions behind, partly because those that do exist are mostly deposited in the IDF Archive, where internal censors make sure that documents explicitly pertaining to massacres or expulsions never see the light of day. But occasionally slips occur.

We now know, on the basis of United Nations, American, and British documents and a handful that surfaced in Israel's civilian archives (the Israel State Archive, party political archives, private papers collections, etc.) during the 1980s and 1990s, of more than a dozen massacres of Arabs by Jewish troops in the course of the first Arab-Israeli war of 1948. These range in size from the shooting of a handful or several dozen civilians arbitrarily selected and lined up against a village wall after its conquest (as occurred, for example, in Majd al Kurum, Bi'na and Dir al Assad, Ilaboun, Jish, Saliha, Safsaf, and Sasa during Hiram) to the slaughter of some 250 civilians and detainees during a firefight in the town of Lydda, southeast of Tel Aviv, on the afternoon of July 12, 1948.

Over the years, the release of new documents and newspaper interviews with witnesses and participants has uncovered Israeli massacres of Arab civilians and prisoners of war in the subsequent wars of 1956, 1967, 1973, and 1982. The revelations came as a shock to much of the Israeli public, which was nurtured on a belief in its own moral superiority and on a doctrine of "purity of arms." Jewish troops, it was believed, in the mainstream Jewish underground, the Haganah, before 1948, and in the IDF since then, had been trained not to sully their arms by committing atrocities. When an atrocity nonetheless came to light, it was always dismissed as a rare exception, a unique occurrence.

The truth is otherwise—and not surprisingly. Underlying the series of Arab-Israeli wars has been a deep hatred by each side of the other and deep existential fears, both among Israeli Jews and Palestinian Arabs. Moreover, the wars have been at least partly fought in areas crowded with civilians (the whole of Palestine in 1948, the Gaza Strip in 1956 and 1967, the West

Bank and Golan Heights in 1967, and southern Lebanon and Beirut in 1982). Almost inevitably, civilians were hurt and killed, sometimes deliberately, more often unintentionally.

The bloodiest and most atrocity-ridden of these wars was, without doubt, the 1948 war of independence, which began, from November 1947 to May 1948, as a civil/guerrilla war between Palestine's thoroughly intermixed Arab and Jewish communities, but ended, from May 1948 to January 1949, as a conventional war between the invading Arab States' armies and the newborn State of Israel. The fact that the Arabs had launched the war—the Palestinian Arabs in November–December 1947 and the Arab States in May 1948—and that the war was protracted and extremely costly for the Jews (who lost six thousand dead, or 1 percent of a total population of 650,000) only exacerbated anger toward the Arabs and heightened the propensity to commit atrocities. The willingness to commit atrocities on each side was also fed by reports—sometimes accurate, sometimes fantastic—of atrocities committed by the other

Prime Minister David Ben-Gurion reads Israel's proclamation of independence, Jerusalem, 1948.

side; retaliation was a frequent motive for Arabs and Israelis alike.

Two out of the three massacres committed by Arabs against Jews during the 1948 war were triggered by Jewish atrocities against Arabs. On December 30, 1947, Irgun Zvai Leumi (National Military Organization, or IZL) terrorists threw a bomb at an Arab bus stop at the entrance to the Haifa Oil Refinery outside Haifa. Half a dozen Arabs were killed, and more were injured. The Arab workers inside the refinery immediately retaliated by turning on their Jewish coworkers with knives, crowbars, and sticks, killing thirty-nine of them. (In turn, the Haganah responded on the night of December 31 by raiding the nearby Arab village of Balad ash Sheikh, where many of the workers lived, blowing up several dozen houses and killing about sixty Arabs.)

Similarly, the Arab irregulars' attack on the convoy of doctors, nurses, students, and Haganah militiamen making its way through East Jerusalem to Mount Scopus (the Mount Scopus Convoy) on April 13 was also a retaliation for the assault by Jewish (IZL-Lehi-Haganah) troops on the Arab village of Deir Yassin, just west of Jerusalem, on April 9, 1948, in which about one hundred villagers were killed during the fighting or just afterward.

The third and largest Arab atrocity of the war, the massacre by irregulars of dozens of surrendering Haganah troops, including some twenty women, at Kfar Etzion in the Etzion Bloc of settlements just north of Hebron, on May 13, was unprovoked by any immediate Jewish attack or atrocity.

But overall, the Jewish forces—Haganah, IZL, Lehi (Lohamei Herut Yisrael, or Freedom Fighters of Israel, or "Stern Gang," as the British authorities called them), and IDF—committed far more atrocities in 1948 than did Arab forces, if only because they were in a far better position to do so.

The Haganah, and subsequently the IDF, overran large Arab-populated areas—some four hundred villages and towns—whereas Arab forces conquered or overran fewer than a dozen Jewish settlements in the course of the war. To this must be added the fact that the civil war in Palestine, which ended in mid-May 1948, raged in a country nominally ruled by a British administration. Neither Jews nor Arabs could legally hold prisoners and, for months, neither had facilities to hold large numbers, so prisoners either were not taken or were shot.

Massacres apart, 1948 was characterized by a great deal of random killing by Jewish troops of Arab civilians. Patrols and ambushes would randomly kill civilians scavenging for food or trying to cross the front lines for other reasons.

From the available evidence, it would appear that not one Jewish soldier or officer was ever punished in connection with these atrocities. Similarly, so far as the evidence allows, no Arab irregular or regular soldier was ever tried or punished for murdering Israelis.

The atrocities did not stop at killings; many Arab villagers and townspeople were expelled from their homes by conquering Jewish units. The largest of these expulsions took place in the towns of Lydda and Ramle on July 12 and 13, when upward of fifty thousand people were dispatched onto roads eastward. In retrospect, it is clear that what occurred in 1948 in Palestine was a variety of **ethnic cleansing** of Arab areas by Jews. It is impossible to say how many of the 700,000 or so Palestinians who became refugees in 1948 were physically expelled, as distinct from simply fleeing a combat zone. What is certain is that almost all were barred by the Israeli government decision of June 1948 and, consequently, by IDF fire, from returning to their homes or areas. Similarly, almost all of the four hundred or so Arab villages overrun and depopulated by Israel were in the course of 1948 or immediately thereafter razed to the ground, partly in order to prevent the refugees from returning. No Jewish soldier or commander was ever tried or punished for expelling an Arab community or destroying an Arab village (though as far as the evidence allows, neither was any Jewish soldier or official ever tried or punished for not expelling Arabs or for not destroying an Arab village or urban neighborhood).

In the course of the war Arab soldiers or irregulars expelled a handful of Jewish communities. Indeed, Arabs expelled Jewish communities from every site they overran, but there were less than a dozen such sites. These included the Jewish Quarter of the Old City of Jerusalem, most of whose buildings were subsequently razed; the Etzion Bloc of settlements—Kfar Etzion, Massu'ot Yitzhak, Revadim, and Ein Tzurim (again, the buildings were razed to the ground by their looters-conquerors); and Kfar Darom, in the Gaza Strip. (All these sites were resettled by Jews after Israel conquered the West Bank and Gaza Strip in the 1967 war. On the other hand, the hundreds of sites from which Arabs were driven out in 1948, and the buildings razed, remained uninhabited or were resettled with Jews.)

Following 1948, IDF discipline and ethics gradually improved. There-after, in each subsequent war, and in the interregnum between wars, there were progressively fewer atrocities, a point Gen. Rafael Eitan, the IDF chief of general staff, went out of his way to make when assailed for his troops'

A Palestinian woman blocked from returning to her home by the armistice line established after the 1948 Arab-Israeli war. Burj village, West Bank, 1948; a Palestinian woman asking why her family has been massacred, Sabra, Beirut, Lebanon, 1982.

behavior during the 1982 invasion of Lebanon.

In October–November 1956, the IDF overran the Gaza Strip, where it remained in control until March 1957. During the battle for this heavily pop-ulated zone and during the first weeks of occupation, the IDF killed some five hundred civilians, either in actual combat or in a subsequent series of massacres. Elsewhere during the Sinai-Suez War, IDF troops reportedly killed fleeing, and often unarmed, Egyptian troops by the hundreds and, occasion-ally, Egyptian prisoners of war. For example, at the end of October 1956, the IDF Paratroop Brigade killed some three dozen POWs near the Mitle Pass. Revelation of this affair in 1995 prompted Egyptian protests to Jerusalem and a demand for an investigation (whose results were never made public).

During the 1967 Six-Day and October 1973 wars, there were cases of IDF troops killing fleeing, and often unarmed, Arab troops and murdering POWs. Again, the victorious Israelis had greater opportunity to commit atrocities than their Arab foes, but there is evidence also that Arab troops, when given the chance, killed off surrendering Israelis and POWs. Such incidents occurred in the 1973 war's first days, when the Syrians overran part of the Golan Heights and the Egyptians overran the IDF's Bar-Lev Line along the east bank of the Suez Canal. Arab civilians and security forces also killed downed Israeli pilots on both fronts.

On the other hand, in the aftermath of these two wars there were almost no reports of atrocities by IDF troops vis-à-vis Arab civilians. Indeed, both the 1967 war (when the IDF overran crowded cities in the West Bank and Gaza Strip) and the 1973 war (when the IDF conquered the populated west bank of the Suez Canal) were marked by almost no civilian casualties.

However, in the immediate wake of the June 1967 war, the IDF destroyed more than half a dozen Arab villages in the West Bank (Imwas, Yalu, Beit Nuba, Khirbet Beit Mirsim, Nabi Samwil, etc.) and expelled their inhabitants. The area of the first three villages was subsequently turned into a nature reserve, Park Canada, which remains to this day a favorite Israeli picnic spot.

Altogether, during and in the immediate aftermath of the 1967 war some 200,000 to 300,000 Palestinians left the West Bank and Gaza Strip for Jordan, many of them refugees for the second time, having moved to the West Bank in 1948 from areas that had become Israeli. In addition, fifty thousand to ninety thousand Syrian civilians (the exact number is disputed) fled their homes or were driven out of the Golan Heights during the IDF conquest. As in 1948, very few of these refugees, from the West Bank, Gaza, and the Golan, were allowed back by Israel, and most still live in camps in Jordan and Syria.

In 1982, as well, the IDF troops who overran southern Lebanon, including Beirut and much of the Beirut–Damascus road, committed few deliberate atrocities, despite the fact that the war was waged in a heavily populated area in which there were more than half a dozen Palestinian refugee camps that stiffly resisted the invaders. Nonetheless, thousands of Palestinian and Lebanese civilians were killed by Israeli airmen, guns, and tanks as the invading force slowly pushed northward, laying down before it a curtain of fire in order to soften resistance and keep down IDF casualties. The exact number of Arab civilians killed is a matter of dispute (Israeli officials spoke of "hundreds"; the Lebanese and Palestinians of "thousands," and even, in one report, of as many as eighteen thousand). What is not disputed is that whole streets and blocks of Lebanese cities—Tyre, Sidon, and Beirut—were destroyed and a number of refugee camps were largely demolished (Rashidiye near Tyre, Ein al Hilwe near Sidon, and others) during the fighting.

Israel's invasion of Lebanon, according to Israeli government spokesmen, was caused or provoked by Palestinian "terrorism" against Israeli targets from southern Lebanon. In fact, during the years between July 1981 and June 1982, when the invasion was launched, there had been practically no terrorist attacks from Lebanon against Israel. But between 1969 and 1981, southern Lebanon had served as a base for Palestine Liberation Organization (PLO) attacks against Israeli targets, the most famous of which was the Coast Road Raid of March 1978, when seaborne Palestinian terrorists from Lebanon commandeered an Israeli bus on the road between Tel Aviv and Haifa and killed more than thirty of its passengers.

In September 1982, the largest deliberate atrocity of the Lebanon War took place, the massacre of several hundred Palestinian refugees (again the exact number is disputed, though apparently some five hundred died) in the Sabra and Shatilla camps or neighborhoods of southern Beirut at the hands of Lebanese Christian militiamen of the Phalange Party. While these militiamen, who were Israel's allies, had been let or sent into the camps by the occupying Israeli troops, the Israelis had not intended or planned the massacre, though Israel's defense minister, Ariel Sharon, was subsequently removed from his post on the recommendation of a commission of inquiry. The Kahan Commission found him "negligent" and indirectly responsible for what had happened. The massacre, and the previous destruction of the refugee camps in the south, had meshed with Sharon's policy of pushing the refugee communities as far northward and away from Israel's border as possible, and with the Phalange desire to rid Lebanon altogether of its (largely Muslim) Palestinian population.

In the years since, reports of only two deliberate atrocities, in which a handful of Lebanese villagers and Palestinians died, have surfaced in the Israeli press, and it is doubtful whether many more actually occurred. But during the years 1982–1985, as Israel's security forces struggled unsuccessfully to suppress the Shiite resistance campaign against their occupation of southern Lebanon, Shiite militants were occasionally executed by Israeli

Israeli troops with Egyptian POWs during the Yom Kippur War, Sinai, 1973.

security men, thousands of suspects were detained without trial, **torture** was used systematically against suspects, and houses of resistance fighters were occasionally demolished.

The Arab-Israeli wars also gave rise, of course, to Israel's control of a foreign-populated territory (whether or not technically regarded as occupation of enemy territory in the West Bank and Gaza), resulting in resistance to that presence and Israeli efforts to suppress it.

From 1967 until 1995, Israel occupied and governed the Palestinian-populated West Bank and Gaza Strip, with the population increasing in number during this period from about 1 million to 2 million.

Periodically, groups of local inhabitants banded together to resist the occupation, occasionally using nonviolent political measures (strikes, school closures, demonstrations), at other times employing violence—which the Palestinians called "armed resistance" and the Israelis "**terrorism.**" These acts, both within the occupied territories and in Israel proper, as well as along Israel's borders with Jordan and Lebanon, often involved deliberate attacks on civilians, which would qualify as terrorism on any ordinary definition. For example, in the bouts of Palestinian Islamic fundamentalist terrorism during 1994–1996, suicide bombers destroyed Israeli buses in the centers of Tel Aviv and Jerusalem, killing dozens of Israeli civilians.

Israel responded to both forms of activism, violent and nonviolent, with a range of measures, many of which violated international law and human rights conventions. Over the decades, for example, Israel has expelled without trial from the territories hundreds of political activists, some of whom were suspected of links to "terrorism"; others were merely suspected of political "agitation" and "incitement."

Severe punishments were usually reserved for persons suspected of what Israeli authorities characterized as terrorism or abetting terrorism. In the course of 1967–1981, the Israeli authorities demolished or sealed some thirteen hundred homes, usually of suspected terrorists. Another seven

Israeli soldiers with Egyptian prisoners of war under Egyptian artillery fire during the Yom Kippur War, Sinai, 1973.

hundred or so homes were destroyed or sealed off during the Intifada, the semiviolent Palestinian uprising of 1987–1993. The homes in question generally also housed brothers and sisters, parents, and children of the suspects, rendering the measure a limited form of **collective punishment.** Usually, the families were not allowed to rebuild their homes. The homes were usually demolished before the suspect was brought to trial or convicted of any crime.

By far the most common antiresistance measure was arrest. During the thirty years of occupation more than fifty thousand Palestinians passed through the Israeli prison system, most of them during the Intifada years. Thousands more were detained on administrative orders, meaning that they were never tried or convicted by any court of law. The military authorities have the power to detain persons for six months without trial, renewable with a judge's permission. In 1999, Israel's jails held more than one hundred administrative detainees, a few of whom had spent years in prison without ever having stood trial.

But most of the prisoners—Israel's prisons in 1999 held about five thousand Palestinian prisoners—were tried by military courts. The courts freed very few suspects, and sentences have often been criticized as being unreasonably severe. A boy of fifteen could spend a year or two in jail for throwing a stone at a car. On the other hand, Israeli military and civilian courts have tended to be extremely lenient toward Israeli soldiers or civilians who killed Palestinians, often making do with suspended sentences or orders to do community service. Israel's General Security Service (and, less frequently, IDF and police units) has systematically employed various forms of **torture**, such as sleep deprivation, beatings, cold showers, and painful postures, against terrorist suspects over the years.[2]

In the course of the Intifada, IDF troops killed with regular and plastic-coated bullets about one thousand Palestinians, many of them minors. Most were killed during clashes between soldiers and stone-throwing rioters.

Palestinian youths in clash with Israeli soldiers. Ramallah, West Bank, 2000.

During the Intifada, dozens of suspected terrorists were killed by Israeli military and police undercover units who were often accused of acting like **death squads**. Israeli spokesmen countered that the peculiar conditions of operation of such units—small squads dressed as Arabs operating in the middle of Arab towns and without close support of regular troops—made haste with the trigger finger an imperative of survival. But over the six years of the Intifada, only a handful of such undercover troops were ever killed or injured by Arabs, raising questions as to whether they were typically in great peril during their operations.

Apart from specific action against suspected terrorists and their supporters, IDF troops frequently resorted to wholesale collective measures in order to suppress rebelliousness among the West Bank and Gaza populations. Often, twenty-four-hour or dusk-to-dawn curfews were imposed on whole cities or villages—preventing the inhabitants from going to work or otherwise living a normal life for days on end. Occasionally—such as during or after a nationally motivated strike—the authorities would close down schools, universities, or businesses. Sometimes the troops would cut off water, electricity, or telephone lines to specific localities as a form of punishment. Lastly, the security forces often arrested, and subjected to interrogation, family members of suspected terrorists in order to discover the suspects' whereabouts.

Israel's administration of the occupied territories has been a target of criticism, in part because Israel claims that it is not legally obliged to implement provisions of the Fourth Geneva Convention relating to the occupation of territory. Israel is a party to all four Geneva Conventions but did not sign the two Additional Protocols of 1977.

The Government says in actual practice it applies what it calls the "humanitarian provisions" of the Fourth Convention to the territories, without specifying which provisions are "humanitarian." The position has been assailed by Palestinians and the Arab States and is not accepted by Israel's principal ally, the United States, or any other major power.

One reason that Israel refused to apply the Fourth Geneva Convention as a matter of law, is that the Labor government in power in 1967 feared that by applying the convention, whose second article refers to "all cases of partial or total occupation of the territory of a High Contracting Party," it would effectively acknowledge Jordan as the previous sovereign. Israel viewed Jordan as a belligerent occupier that had unlawfully invaded and illegally annexed the West Bank.

In common practice, Israeli courts, guided by Supreme Court guidelines, operate in light of accepted international customary law and those international conventions adopted into internal Israeli law. Thus there is something of a dichotomy between Israel's official public position in international forums and legal practice vis-à-vis the territories.

In summation, the Arab-Israeli wars, like most wars, have resulted in atrocities, mostly committed by the winning side or the side in a position to commit such atrocities, both against soldiers and civilians. The number and frequency of the atrocities has diminished over the years, in part because the wars have been shorter (the 1948 war lasted a full year, the 1967 war a bare six days), in part because of greater discipline among the Israeli troops. On the other hand, the increased firepower in Israeli hands has meant that troops, when advancing through built-up areas, as in 1982, have tended to lay down curtains of fire that have resulted in large numbers of civilian casualties, something that did not occur in the previous wars, when the IDF had less firepower or was not engaged in built-up areas.

At the same time, the decades of Israeli occupation of the West Bank, Gaza Strip, and Golan Heights has resulted in the systematic deployment of a variety of measures that are contrary to international humanitarian law, including torture of suspected terrorists, house demolitions, administrative detention without **due process**, and **deportations**.

1. "C Company," 103rd Battalion report, signature illegible, November 2, 1948, IDF Archive 1096\49\\65.
2. B'Tselem, *The Interrogation of Palestinians during the Intifada*, 1991, Jerusalem; also B'Tselem, *Routine Torture: Interrogation Methods of the General Security Service*, Jerusalem, 1998.

The Second Intifada and After

By Orna Ben-Naftali and Aeyal Gross

The Second Intifada, also known as the al-Aqsa Intifada, broke out in September 2000 following a visit by Israel's then-opposition leader Ariel Sharon to Jerusalem's Temple Mount (or Haram al-Sharif). Since the site is sacred in both the Islamic and Jewish religions, and the question of sovereignty over it has been one of the thorniest issues in negotiations between Israel and the Palestinians, it is not surprising that Sharon's visit was considered a deliberate provocation.

The following day, Palestinian demonstrators gathered around the al-Aqsa mosque threw stones at Jewish worshippers at the Western Wall below, and Israeli security services responded by firing rubber-coated metal bullets and live ammunition at the crowd. Five Palestinians were killed. Palestinian

Al-Aqsa Martyrs' Brigades fighters moving weapons which they smuggled into Gaza via tunnels after the cease-fire, May 2005.

demonstrations throughout the territories and within Israel followed, and the vicious cycle of violence known as "the Second Intifada" began. By February 2005, when Palestinian leader Mahmoud Abbas agreed to a mutual truce with Prime Minister Sharon and persuaded the main Palestinian armed groups to declare a cease-fire, 3,307 Palestinians, including 654 children, and 972 Israelis, including 117 children, had been killed.

Sharon's visit was only the spark that set off the uprising, not its root cause. After seven years of the Oslo peace process, both Israelis and Palestinians had lost faith in its underlying premise that small steps on both sides could build trust between the two parties. Many Israelis felt that their withdrawal from Palestinian territory had not brought them greater security, while Palestinians saw an expansion of settlements and no genuine Israeli interest in creating a viable Palestinian state. The failure of the Camp David Summit in July 2000 entrenched these views. From an Israeli perspective, the

49

Palestinian refusal to accept what Israelis regarded as the most generous land offer they had ever made showed that the Palestinians were not negotiating in good faith and had never accepted Israel's right to exist securely. Many Israelis came to believe that the subsequent uprising was orchestrated by Palestinian leader Yasser Arafat to pressure Israel into concessions he could not achieve through negotiation.

Many Palestinians, for their part, felt that the Israeli proposals at Camp David ignored the basic requirement of justice that the State of Palestine should control all the land the Palestinians had occupied before 1967 and were designed to prevent the emergence of a truly viable Palestinian state. Palestinians complained that Israel's negotiating strategy aimed not at a fair settlement but at making the Palestinians appear responsible for the breakdown of talks. From their perspective, the Second Intifada was a spontaneous response to a series of setbacks and provocations.

Israel's heavy use of force against civilian demonstrators in the early

Palestinians protest Israel's construction of a wall of separation, Qalqilya, West Bank, 2003.

days of the uprising set the pattern for what was to follow. This period also gave the Intifada its emblematic images and hastened a mutual process of dehumanizing the enemy. At the end of September, a Palestinian man named Jamal al-Dura and his 12 year old son Mohammed were caught up in an armed clash between Israeli and Palestinian forces in Gaza; the son was killed and the father wounded by Israeli fire. The entire sequence of events was filmed by French television, and the pictures became for Palestinians a symbol of Israeli lack of concern for Palestinian lives. A couple of weeks later, two Israeli reserve soldiers lost their way and mistakenly ended up in Ramallah. A Palestinian mob gathered outside the police station where the soldiers had been taken, and were given access to them. The images of the body of one of the soldiers being thrown from the window of the police station with a Palestinian policeman waving bloody hands at the crowd became a symbol of Palestinian barbarism imprinted on the Israeli consciousness.

It was clear from the start that this Intifada, as distinct from the first one, was going to be fought with weapons not stones. The Israeli army's heavy-handed tactics—including the use of tanks, helicopters and live ammunition against demonstrators—blurred any distinction between combat and civilian zones. Unable to confront the Israeli military directly, Palestinian fighters increasingly struck back with attacks on civilian targets. Suicide bombing in public places in Israel was unleashed in the summer of 2001 and became the main expression and tactic of the Intifada, generating a deep sense of insecurity and anger among Israelis that translated into political support for ever tougher responses. Israel argued that the Palestinian security forces were involved in terrorist attacks, a charge that led to a further escalation of hostility and distrust.

A 2002 report by Human Rights Watch determined that the leaders of Hamas and Islamic Jihad openly espoused suicide bombing attacks against Israeli civilians, and appeared to be able to turn the bombings on and off at

will. While the report did not find evidence that Arafat and the Palestinian Authority planned or ordered suicide bombings or other attacks on Israeli civilians, it said there were important steps that Arafat and the PA could and should have taken to prevent or deter such attacks. After 2001 Palestinians also fired Qassam missiles at targets within Israel, mostly from the Gaza Strip. Qassam attacks became more significant after 2003, causing a number of deaths and injuries as well as damage to property.

Israel's measures taken to repress the Intifada included the destruction of Palestinian security facilities; an increasing use of targeted killing of suspected perpetrators of violence, including political leaders; the administrative detention of thousands of Palestinians, including minors, often for more than a year on the basis of secret evidence; and aerial bombardments. Following "Terrible March" of 2002, when 133 Israelis were killed in suicide bombings, including 30 guests at the Park Hotel in the resort town of Netanyah during Passover dinner, Israel broadened its operations to include ground invasions of refugee camps and the military re-occupation of some territories from which it had previously withdrawn. The fiercest fighting to place in the Jenin refugee camp, where 52 Palestinians were killed, according to the local hospital. The Israel Defense Forces (IDF) designated some areas of military action as "closed military zones", barring access to the outside world and denying access to NGOs and to a UN fact-finding mission. During the operations, the IDF used Palestinians as human **shields**, in clear violation of international humanitarian law. The fact that there was only one soldier convicted for this practice—and then sentenced only to 28 days imprisonment—attests to the impunity enjoyed by Israeli soldiers. The practice was later banned by the Israeli High Court of Justice.

Israeli military actions led to enormous hardship for Palestinian civilians. Thousands of houses were razed, many more damaged and tens of thousands of fruit trees were uprooted; commercial and public facilities were destroyed. Palestinians were subjected to daily curfews and road closures, and movement between Palestinian towns and villages was further curtailed by an intricate system of checkpoints. These measures had a devastating effect on the Palestinian economy, bringing two thirds of the population below the poverty line. Far from complying with the rule that all feasible measures should be taken to minimize harm to civilians, Israel's military policies suggested that the principle of distinction had been abandoned. Many Israeli actions appeared to violate the rule of **proportionality** and laws against **wanton destruction** and **collective punishment**.

The Palestinians sought to justify the Intifada as a legitimate struggle against an oppressive occupying power, based on their inherent right of self-determination. While the right of self-determination may involve a right of resistance to those who frustrate its realization, it does not follow that all means are thereby legitimate. The deliberate and widespread killing of **civilians**, either by suicide bombing or by the indiscriminate firing of Qassam rockets, was both a crime against humanity and a war crime. The use in hostilities of children under the age of 15, the use of ambulances to transfer weapons and combatants in violation of the prohibition on **perfidy**, and the defiling of the bodies of Israeli soldiers may all be considered crimes under the laws of war.

Some aspects of Israel's response to the Second Intifada remain particularly disputed, reflecting the unique complexity of the Israeli-Palestinian situation. This consists of a long-term occupation; a Palestinian Authority which is certainly not a State but is also not a non-governmental entity; the existence of Palestinian police as well as paramilitary forces; and the related blurring of the lines between occupation and self-government in the occupied territories. The eruption of the Intifada under these conditions created a situation that did not fit neatly into the boxes of international law.

Israel's policy of targeted killing of suspected militants has been the focus of enormous controversy. Israel defends targeted killings as a lawful use of force against enemy fighters during an armed conflict. But critics say that many targeted killings take place outside the context of hostilities, and therefore violate restrictions on the deliberate taking of life. Other critics say that even if an armed conflict is taking place, the victims of many Israeli strikes were not taking a direct part in hostilities, and therefore were not legitimate targets. The meaning that should be given to the concept of "taking a direct part in hostilities" in the circumstances of contemporary conflict is the subject of fierce disagreement.

The wall or separation barrier that Israel is constructing to prevent attacks against Israeli territory and settlements from Palestinian areas of the West Bank has provoked even greater argument. The barrier extends repeatedly into areas occupied by Israel in 1967, and in many places cuts

Palestinians off from other Palestinians or from their own land. The Israeli High Court of Justice ruled that the route of the barrier in specific places violated the principle of proportionality because the severe injury caused to the Palestinians was excessive in relation to the purported security benefit. But the court rejected the argument that it was inherently unlawful for the barrier to extend beyond the Green Line marking Israel's 1967 borders, and upheld other portions of the barrier as a proportionate response to the security threat Israel faced.

However the International Court of Justice, in an advisory opinion that Israel has said it will ignore, determined that the construction of the barrier in occupied territory was inherently illegal, as its route was designed to incorporate illegal settlements and effect the de facto annexation of the areas it enclosed. Notwithstanding Israel's official response to the Advisory Opinion, its shadow effect is considered as having prompted the Israeli Supreme Court to look into the barrier issue more carefully than it had before.

Realizing that the massive use of force by Israel had not crushed Palestinian resolve, and perhaps hoping ultimately to save what he could from the settlement enterprise in the West Bank, Israeli Prime Minister Sharon ordered an Israeli pullout from the Gaza Strip in the summer of 2005. Following Sharon's stroke, his successor Ehud Olmert announced plans for a progressive disengagement from many parts of the West Bank—suggesting that the separation barrier might in time become an effective unilateral boundary. In the meantime, Israel's continuing control over the Gaza Strip's borders, coastline and airspace, as well as its economy and trade, telecommunications, population registry and infrastructure mean that the occupation —now forty years old—may not yet have truly ended.

In the summer of 2006, Hezbollah launched a surprise attack on an Israeli army post at the Israeli-Lebanese border, killing eight soldiers and seizing two others. At the same time, Hezbollah launched a volley of shells against Israel. In response, Israel attacked targets in Lebanon. The conflict escalated to what became known in Israel as the Second Lebanese War, and ended only following Security Council Resolution 1701 which established a strengthened UN force to patrol Southern Lebanon alongside the Lebanese army. While Israel had, under *jus ad bellum*, the right to respond to the armed attack by Hezbollah, the customary law of self-defense requires that any response be proportionate to the threat, and many people questioned whether Israel's offensive met that requirement.

Regarding *jus in bello*, the conflict was characterized by the deaths of civilians on both sides of the border. Hezbollah's attacks, which were not directed at military targets, clearly violated the rules of distinction. Israel was also accused of failing to observe the rules of distinction and proportionality. At the same time Israel conducted extensive military actions in Gaza, following the firing of Qassam missiles from Gaza and the seizure of an Israeli soldier by Hamas. Hundreds of Palestinians died, and by the humanitarian crisis in Gaza became worse then ever.

Following these developments, the Israeli government dismissed the idea of unilateral disengagement from the West Bank as "not on its agenda." At the time of writing, no end to the occupation is in sight.
(See **occupation; terrorism**.)

Israel's Views of the Application of IHL to the West Bank and Gaza Strip

By Kenneth Anderson

Although the West Bank and Gaza are referred to by nearly all other States as "occupied territories," implying that all Israeli activities in them are governed by the Fourth Geneva Convention of 1949, Israel calls them "administered areas" and has a different view of its obligations and their legal status.

The Israeli government view, laid out in legal memoranda issued by its Ministry of Foreign Affairs, is that the territories did not belong to any sovereign State at the time Israel captured them during the 1967 war. That is, Egypt did not claim the Gaza Strip, and Jordan may have claimed the West Bank, but Israel and the great majority of States did not recognize that claim; and Palestinians did not assert sovereignty over the territory at that time. In addition, UN resolutions 242 and 338, which call upon Israel to withdraw from occupied territory, did not say that other States claimed sovereignty at the time. Israel further argues that any Palestinian claims to sovereignty over the territories based upon the UN General Assembly partition resolution of 1947 were rendered invalid because the Palestinians and allied Arab states rejected the resolution and took up arms against it.

Accordingly, in the Israeli view, the Fourth Convention is inapplicable on its face, since under the second paragraph of Article 2 common to all four Conventions of 1949, the Conventions apply only to "occupation of the territory of a High Contracting Party." Formal recognition of the applicability of the Convention, Israel argued, implied a recognition of the sovereignty of the former administration.

Nevertheless, the Israeli government in official statements has pledged compliance with what it views as the humanitarian and customary provisions of the Convention—but without stipulating which articles it has in mind. Israel claims it has gone further than required in its protection of the local population of the territories. For example, although the Convention accepts the legality of the death penalty, it is not applied even to horrific acts of terrorism. Similarly, the Convention does not require that any provision be made for movement of the local population to and from territories, whereas Israel, within limits, permits such travel and trade, even to countries in a legal state of war with Israel.

The United Nations Security Council, the International Committee of the Red Cross, States, and scholars have criticized Israel's legal position. Critics note that Article 1 of the Fourth Geneva Convention requires a High Contracting Party to "respect and ensure respect" for the Convention "in all circumstances." Moreover, Article 4 stipulates that "persons protected by the Convention are those who, at any given moment, and in any manner whatsoever, find themselves, in case of a conflict or occupation, in the hands of a Party to the conflict or occupying power of which they are not nationals." Thus, critics agree, Israel should apply the full Convention, and it is an exaggeration to claim that accepting the applicability of the Convention implies acknowledging prior sovereignty.

Armistice

By Howard S. Levie

An armistice is not a peace treaty. While its main objective is to bring about a cease-fire, a halt to hostilities, that halt may be indefinite or for a specified period of time only. An armistice agreement does not terminate the state of war between the belligerents. A state of war continues to exist with all of its implications for the belligerents and for the neutrals. (The Korean Armistice Agreement did not specify a time period—and thus was subject to termination by either party. North Korea in fact denounced it in 1997.)

In time past, brief, local cease-fire agreements frequently were used for the purpose of removing the dead and the wounded from the battlefield.

In recent decades the armistice agreement has gained in importance because in a majority of cases it has not been succeeded by a treaty of peace as was formerly the almost universal custom, but remains as the only agreement entered into by the hostile nations bringing hostilities to an end.

The U.S. Army's "The Law of Land Warfare," issued in 1956, defines armistice and the subjects that it should cover. "An armistice (or truce, as it is sometimes called) is the cessation of active hostilities for a period agreed upon by the belligerents. It is not a partial or temporary peace; it is only the suspension of military operations to the extent agreed upon by the parties."

Of course, the parties may also include such provisions as they may desire and agree upon; it is extremely rare that armistice agreements impose obligations to address violations of the laws of armed conflict.

Effective Date and Time: It is particularly important to allow time for the information to reach outposts that would otherwise unwittingly violate the armistice agreement by continuing hostilities after it had become effective. Even in an era of instant communications, not every soldier or group of soldiers will be equipped to receive the information immediately.

Duration: In former days it was customary (but not required) to specify the length of time that the armistice agreement was to remain in force. In modern times such a provision has frequently been omitted, probably on the assumption that a peace treaty will be forthcoming in the not-too-distant future. When an armistice agreement contains no specific period of duration it remains in effect until formally denounced by one side. While there is no law requiring it, certainly it should be expected that the denunciation will be announced as becoming effective only after a specified period of time or at a specified future time, and not by the arrival of an artillery bombardment!

Line of Demarcation and Neutral Zone: While there is no specific provision in any convention on the law of war providing for a demarcation line and a neutral zone (the latter sometimes referred to as "no-man's-land"), inclusion of these items will go far in preventing incidents that neither side really wants and which can inadvertently and unintentionally result in the resumption of hostilities.

Relations with Inhabitants: In almost every armistice one side will be occupying some of the territory of the other side. This means that there will be enemy civilians in part of the territory it controls. The U.S. Army's Land Warfare Manual states that if there is no provision on this subject in the armistice agreement these relations remain unchanged, each belligerent "continuing to exercise the same rights as before, including the right to prevent or control all intercourse between the inhabitants within his lines and persons within the enemy lines."

Prohibited Acts: Rarely do armistice agreements prohibit specific acts by the belligerents other than the basic act of hostilities; and rarely is any action taken by the other belligerent when the opposing force has taken an action that it believes to be prohibited. However, any violation of the armistice agreement, including any hostile act, would certainly fall within the definition of being a "prohibited act." Although not specifically set forth in the Korean Armistice Agreement, certainly the frequent violations of the demilitarized zone by the North Koreans, the construction of tunnels under that zone, and the landing of commandos in South Korea, with such missions as to assassinate the president of the Republic of Korea, are prohibited acts.

Prisoners of War: This was the most difficult problem that confronted the negotiators during the negotiation of the Korean Armistice Agreement, and its solution took well over a year. The United Nations Command insisted on "voluntary repatriation," which meant that the prisoner of war was free to return to the army in which he was serving when captured, or to go else-where if he preferred. This was primarily because while the North Koreans occupied most of South Korea early in the conflict, they conscripted into their army all South Koreans of military age who had been captured or had surrendered. These men had no desire to be "repatriated" to North Korea. "Voluntary repatriation" is now accepted international law and a provision to that effect will undoubtedly be found in future armistice agreements.

Consultative Machinery: Provisions of the Korean Armistice Agreement furnish a good example of the commissions set up by armistice agreements. There was a Neutral Nations Repatriation Commission to oversee the armistice with respect to prisoners of war; a Military Armistice Commission (with joint observer teams) to oversee the implementation of the armistice itself; and a Neutral Nations Supervisory Commission (with its own inspection teams) to ensure compliance with certain of the provisions of the armistice agreement.

Miscellaneous Political-Military Matters: There are times when the negotiators of an armistice agreement are authorized by their governments to discuss political matters. (At times, governments have used diplomats in armistice negotiations. The Korean Armistice Agreement, for example, was negotiated by military officers, while the Agreement for the Cessation of Hostilities in Vietnam was negotiated by diplomats.) Thus, while the United Nations Command Delegation insisted that it could discuss military matters and not political matters, Article 4 of the Korean Armistice Agreement contained a provision by which the military commanders recommended to the governments that within three months of signing the Parties convene a political conference to settle certain questions beyond the authority of the military commanders.

B

Belligerent Status

By Ewen Allison and Robert K. Goldman

Historically, rebel groups seeking to overthrow a recognized government or to secede from a State have sought "belligerent status"—a legal standing akin to that accorded a government and bringing the law of international armed conflict into play for both sides.

A rebel group gained "belligerent status" when all of the following had occurred: it controlled territory in the State against which it was rebelling; it declared independence, if its goal was secession; it had well-organized armed forces; it began hostilities against the government; and, importantly, the government recognized it as a belligerent.

In more recent times, however, governments have simply refused to grant recognition to groups rebelling against them. Governments are loath to admit that they have lost effective control of territory, and are reluctant to grant legal standing to rebel groups.

This refusal has serious legal and humanitarian consequences. Where insurgents did not have belligerent status, a government would not be bound to treat insurgents according to the law of international armed conflict, thus often paving the way for savage and inhumane incidents.

As a countermeasure, the international community has arranged for certain minimum standards of humanitarian law to be triggered by facts on the ground without waiting for governments to recognize belligerents or a state of belligerency. A confrontation is deemed to be an internal (or in technical terms, "non-international") armed conflict when the fighting is intense, organized, and protracted enough to go beyond temporary disturbances and tensions. Necessarily, an internal armed conflict is confined within a State's borders and generally does not involve foreign States as parties. As soon as the situation on the ground meets these criteria, parties are expected to conform to a distinct body of humanitarian law crystallized most notably in Common Article 3 of the Geneva Conventions of 1949. If the rebel group has effective control over some part of national territory, the provisions of Additional Protocol II may also apply. In either case, the legal standing of the parties is unchanged.

In effect, humanitarian law sidesteps entirely the sensitive issue of recognition.

(See **international vs. internal armed conflict**.)

Biological Experiments

By Sheldon H. Harris

The Nazis were not the only nation to build death camps in the period leading up to World War II. The Japanese, too, had their concentration camps. The object was not, as with the Germans, the extermination of a people, but instead was to use incarcerated common criminals and prisoners of war as guinea pigs in biological and, to a lesser extent, chemical warfare experiments.

Lt. Gen. Shiro Ishii, the architect of Japan's chemical and biological warfare program.

The rationale was simple. The fanatical, right-wing militarists who dominated Japanese society from the late 1920s to the end of World War II believed that in order to achieve their goal of Japanese domination of East Asia, they would have to rely upon exotic weapons of war such as pathogenic and chemical arms. That was horrible enough. But those who originated the program did not believe that these weapons could simply be developed in laboratories and let loose against enemies on the battlefield. They had to be tried out on human subjects.

And so a vast network of death factories was constructed that, by the time World War II had begun, stretched from the remote steppes of Inner Mongolia to Singapore, and from Bangkok to Manila. The center of this empire of death was Ping Fan, a suburb of the city of Harbin in north China, where the architect of Japan's chemical and biological warfare program, Lt. Gen. Shiro Ishii, had his headquarters.

Each factory employed at least two thousand people, including (apart from the ordinary soldiers used to guard the facilities) some twenty thousand physicians, microbiologists, veterinarians, zoologists, and plant biologists.

At a conservative estimate, their diabolical research project of testing prospective pathogens and biological weapons on the camps' inmates involved between twelve and fifteen thousand men, women, and children.

Tens of thousands of others were killed in field tests that consisted of distributing food tainted with deadly pathogens; lacing water wells, streams, and reservoirs with other pathogens; creating cholera epidemics by injecting cholera into the veins of unsuspecting peasants, who were told they were being inoculated against the disease; and spraying or dropping various biological weapons on villages, towns, and cities from the air.

With the exception of few lesser participants, who were brought before a show trial by the Soviet authorities, most of the architects of Japan's biological warfare programs were never prosecuted for their crimes. The rea-

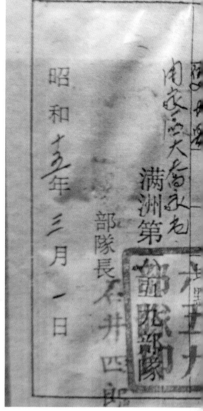

son for this was that after the U.S. occupation of Japan, American scientists eager to acquire the experimental data garnered from these biological experiments argued successfully that their Japanese colleagues had gained invaluable insights into how the human body reacted to certain pathogens—information that would greatly assist American biological weapons programs. The result was that the U.S. occupation authorities colluded in a cover-up of what had taken place.

The use of "bacteriological methods of warfare" has been banned under international law since the 1925 Geneva Protocol on chemical and biological weapons, which was a response to the horrors of poison gas as employed in World War I. In the so-called medical case at the Nuremberg War Crimes Trials two decades later, the defendants were charged with conducting medical and biological experiments on thousands of German and non-German subjects. The tribunal ruled that whatever right Germany had to experiment on German nationals who were prisoners, that right "may not be extended... to permit the practice upon nationals of other countries who... are subjected to experiments without their consent and under the most brutal and senseless conditions... To the extent that these experiments did not constitute war crimes, they constituted crimes against humanity."

These statutes alone should have made prosecutions of the architects of the Japanese biological warfare program almost mandatory. But they had everything to do with the Cold War and almost nothing to do with the state of international humanitarian law. That said, subsequent laws have only strengthened the prohibitions against the kinds of grave breaches of which

Lt. Gen. Ishii's unit occupied a 32-square-kilometer "no-man's-land" in Ping Fan, a suburb of Harbin, northern China, and every resident was required to carry an identity passbook.

the Japanese were guilty. Protocol I of the 1977 Additional Protocols to the Geneva Conventions explicitly forbids "medical and scientific experiments" even with the consent of the subject. And in the arms control field, the 1972 Biological Weapons Convention forbids "develop[ing]... microbial or biological agents or toxins [and] equipment" designed to use or deliver "such agents or toxins for hostile purposes or in an armed conflict."

But leaving aside prosecutions, the truth is hard enough to come by. Until the 1980s, the Japanese government denied the crimes committed by its doctors and scientists had even taken place. When the overwhelming weight of the evidence forced it to concede something had indeed occurred, the Japanese authorities insisted the program had been the work of renegade militarists. The government neither apologized nor offered compensation to those still alive who had been exposed to the germ warfare experiments, or to the families and heirs of those who had not survived them.

(See **biological weapons**; **chemical weapons**; **medical experiments on POWs**.)

B

Biological Weapons

By Terence Taylor

Potentially, biological weapons can cause many thousands of casualties with the use of a very small quantity of material. In terms of a threat to human life they are on a scale comparable to a nuclear weapon as a weapon of mass destruction, and some countries view them as the strategic equivalent.

Biological weapons (BW) can be developed from living organisms (for example, bacteria and viruses) or toxins (poisons) obtained from these organisms. Given the right technological expertise biological weapons are cheaper and easier to produce than nuclear weapons. Recent developments in biotechnology in civil industry, mainly in the pharmaceutical and veterinary medicine sectors, have made possible the easier production, storage, and weaponisation of some types of pathogenic organisms. Until the mid-1970s, while BW had some military value, the state of scientific and technological development was such that their effects were too unpredictable and the problems of their storage and handling too great; consequently, other weapons conferred greater advantages. The advances in civil industry, mainly in the past twenty years, have made possible the production of weapons that are more effective and have more predictable results. In particular, biotechnological capabilities have now advanced to the point that bacteria, viruses and toxins can be produced by synthetic means.

It is also easier to hide a BW program in civilian research and production facilities than either a nuclear or chemical one. The two biggest known post-World War II clandestine programs, in Russia (beginning in the days of the Soviet Union) and Iraq, used this technique. The hardest part of a BW program to conceal is the weapons end of the process, when the organism or toxin is put into a missile warhead, bomb, artillery round, or aerial spray tank. However, this activity can be done shortly prior to the intended use to achieve maximum surprise. Most at risk to these deadly weapons are unprotected civilian populations. For example, studies have shown that a missile delivering 30 kilograms of anthrax spores overhead an urban area could kill between 80,000 and 100,000 people if they had no special protection in an area of some 10 square kilometres. In comparison, a 12.5 kiloton (Hiroshima-size) nuclear weapon delivered over a similar area could kill between 23,000 and 80,000 people (but also cause severe structural damage). For a chemical agent to be delivered to achieve a similar casualty toll to the BW delivery described above, many more kilograms of agent would be required. For example, even three hundred kilograms of a highly lethal chemical agent, such as sarin nerve gas, delivered over a similar target could kill perhaps only 80 to 200 people and cover an area only a fraction of that covered by ten times less (in weight) of anthrax.

The Biological Weapons Convention (BWC), which entered into force in 1975, bans the research, development, production, stockpiling, or acquisition of biological and toxin weapons. The convention also bans delivery systems specifically designed for such weapons. While the BWC deals only with possession of these weapons, use in warfare was banned by the 1925 Geneva Protocol (which also similarly bans the use of **chemical weapons**);

although some States parties entered reservations asserting the right to use such weapons if an enemy State used them first, an absolute ban now exists as a matter of customary law. The 1925 Protocol was itself derived from an ancient customary law of war restricting the use of "poisonous" weapons or substances in armed conflict that had first been codified in the Hague Conventions of 1899 and 1907. To date 155 countries have ratified or acceded to the BWC.

The BWC contains no provision for monitoring or inspection, but there is a nonbinding "confidence-building" regime under which States may make declarations about their facilities that handle highly pathogenic organisms and give lists of publications which deal with them. Between 1993 and 2001 there was an attempt to negotiate a legally binding protocol for verification of compliance, including inspections, but consensus on a text was not achieved. The tension between the requirement for intrusive inspection measures and political, economic and other national security demands prevented a successful outcome.

While the United States and Britain had dismantled their BW programs well before the BWC came into force, it came to light by 1990 that the Soviet Union had been running an extensive illegal BW program. They took advantage of the more recent developments in biotechnology to carry their program forward to a much more advanced level. In April 1992, President Boris Yeltsin of Russia publicly admitted to the illegal BW program and announced a decree ending it. Convincing proof that the program has been fully dismantled has yet to be provided.

Iraq, although a signatory to the BWC, never ratified it and developed a comprehensive program using viruses, bacteria, and toxins. By the time of Operation Desert Storm in 1991, which resulted in the liberation of Kuwait, Iraq had missiles, aerial bombs, and artillery filled with biological agents and ready to use. They also had research and development programs on new agents and delivery means in progress. Neither the United States nor Britain knew the scale and scope of the program, but both took precautions, such as anthrax vaccination programs for the troops and prophylactics against nerve agent attacks. Britain also fielded a biological agent warning and detection system. Coalition bombing targeted chemical weapons plants but left the main BW sites untouched as the coalition was unaware of them.

Iraq only admitted to having a BW program in 1995 after more than four years of investigations by United Nations inspectors. However, Iraq still continued to hide important aspects of this weapons program for several years. After the coalition invasion of Iraq in March 2003, no evidence of a continuing program was discovered

Other smaller programs existed or still exist in other parts of the world. An example of one, now ended, was that in South Africa run by the apartheid regime until the early 1990s. This was a relatively small program aimed for assassination missions. However, it used advanced biotechnological techniques and it is possible that some of those who worked on the program have exported their skills elsewhere.

Biological weapons entered the realm of terrorism with the 2001 anthrax attack in the U.S. delivered through the mail system that affected people in several states. Five people died and 22 people were seriously ill. The perpetrator of this attack remains unknown. There is clear evidence that some terrorist groups, such as al-Qaeda and the Japanese Aum Shinrikyo, considered and experimented with biological weapons but there have been no other lethal terrorist attacks.

B

Blockade as Act of War

By Christopher Greenwood

Under the traditional concept of *blockade*, a belligerent was entitled to proclaim a blockade of all or part of the enemy's coast and to use warships to enforce that blockade. There was no legal obligation to comply with a blockade, but any merchant ship, whether belligerent or neutral, that was intercepted by the blockading State while attempting to run the blockade was liable to capture. Following the decision of a prize court, ship and cargo became the property of the blockading power. The traditional concept of the blockade was confined, therefore, to the law of naval warfare. *Blockade* today is a technical legal term that most people, including lawyers, use without much precision to describe a variety of conduct beyond maritime operations.

In order to be lawful, a naval blockade had to be formally declared and had to be effective, that is to say it had to be properly enforced by warships of the blockading State. At one time this meant stationing warships just off the coast of the State that was subject to blockade, but by the time of the two World Wars, blockades were often administered from a long distance. An effective blockade allowed a belligerent to cut off all maritime commerce between its enemy and the rest of the world. The purpose was not only to prevent goods from reaching the enemy (to a large extent that could be done without a blockade in any event) but also to prevent the enemy from exporting to the outside world and thereby sustaining its war economy. Blockades were used to great effect during the American Civil War and the two World Wars, but since 1945 there have been very few instances of anything that could properly be described as a blockade in this technical sense.

Today, however, the term *blockade* is frequently applied to maritime operations undertaken at the behest of the United Nations Security Council. The council has on several occasions authorized warships to intercept shipping suspected of violating economic **sanctions**. Following Iraq's invasion of Kuwait in 1990, for example, Resolution 661 imposed a ban on imports to, or exports from, Iraq and occupied Kuwait. Shortly afterward, Resolution 665 authorized states with naval forces in the region cooperating with the government of Kuwait to intercept shipping suspected of violating these sanctions. The result was in many ways very similar to that of a wartime blockade. Warships from several navies intercepted over ten thousand vessels between the summer of 1990 and the end of hostilities, and all maritime trade with Iraq and Kuwait was effectively cut off.

Nevertheless, operations of this kind differ from the traditional blockade in a number of ways. First, there is a legal duty resulting from the Security Council resolutions not to engage in sanctions breaking and any form of sanctions breaking is likely to lead to penalties. Second, the obligation to comply with the UN sanctions resolutions prevails over existing contracts and international agreements regarding shipping. Third, warships policing UN embargo operations of this kind are entitled to stop and search merchant shipping and to turn back ships suspected of sanctions breaking, but there are no provisions for the capture of ships or for prize court proceedings. For example, the owners of a Greek ship stopped by an American warship while trying to enter a Yugoslav port during the Yugoslav sanctions would probably be liable to penalties in the Greek courts but not in those of the United States. Finally, the imposition of a traditional blockade was generally regarded as an **act of war**, whereas enforcement of United Nations sanctions is a rather different act. Although sometimes there may be an armed conflict in place between the States whose warships are used to enforce sanctions and the target State (as was clearly the case in the **Gulf War** in 1991, and perhaps in the period leading up to it), that will not always be so. The enforcement of legal sanctions even by means of maritime embargoes is not necessarily an act of war.

In recent times, some commentators have also used the term *blockade* to describe land-based operations designed to cut off supplies to a particular town or area. These operations, which are more like the **sieges** of the past, are not really blockades at all. The large body of law relating to naval blockades is not applicable to them, there is no provision for the confiscation of property from those seeking to supply the besieged area, and the emphasis is on stopping supplies from getting in, rather than cutting off exports. There is also, as a result of Additional Protocol I to the Geneva Conventions, an obligation not to deprive the civilian population of the basic means of survival. The effect of this rule is far less clear-cut in naval operations, although a blockade that had as its sole purpose depriving the enemy population of food and other humanitarian supplies would be unlawful today.

(See **humanitarian aid, blocking of; starvation**.)

Bosnia

By Florence Hartmann

The conflict in Bosnia-Herzegovina, which began in April 1992 and ended in November 1995, has come to be seen as the model for wars of ethnic cleansing throughout the world. This was the most violent event Europe experienced since World War II, and the devastation of the small multiethnic state recalled the ruins of Germany after the Allied bombing. The methods of ethnic cleansing, used for conquest of territory, were a repudiation of the lessons of World War II as codified in the Geneva Conventions. Practically the only saving grace in Western policy making during the three-and-a-half-year war was the decision to launch an international war crimes tribunal to indict and try some of those responsible.

Everyone knows by now that the war was both the result of Yugoslavia's collapse and the event that ensured it could never be reconstituted. Long before the war began, Slobodan Milosevic in Serbia and, following his example, Franjo Tudjman in Croatia, had turned their backs on the Yugoslav ideal of an ethnically mixed federal State and set about carving out their own ethnically homogeneous States. With Milosevic's failure, in 1991, to take control of all of Yugoslavia, the die was cast for war.

Flatly rejecting proposals for a loosely based federation, refusing to adopt the democratic and Western market reforms that had swept the former Soviet bloc, and facing challenges in the streets from students, Milosevic opted for a military contest. He had effective control of the federal army and police, an aroused Serbian diaspora in the republics heading for independence, with ultranationalists at the fore, and the ability to manipulate all the key institutions in Serbia—the academics, the media, the Serbian Orthodox Church. Thus the wars over the succession to multinational Yugoslavia illustrated perfectly Clausewitz's idea that war is a continuation of politics by other means.

To strengthen his hold on his domestic power base, Milosevic made it

Civilians sprint to evade Serb snipers in "Sniper Alley." All too many were not fast enough. Sarajevo, 1992.

his mission to set Yugoslavia's ethnic and national groups against one another. In the end, he succeeded in chasing out of what remained of Yugoslavia all those national groups that refused to submit to the hegemony of the Serb people and of Milosevic's Socialist Party (the successor to the League of Communists).

The Serbian political project, first in Croatia, then in Bosnia-Herzegovina, envisaged the creation of ethnically homogeneous States, fashioned by seizing territory from other States. Ethnic cleansing meant using violence and deportations to remove any trace of the other ethnic communities who had previously cohabited with Serbs in the coveted territories. This "cleansing" was the goal of the war, not the unintended consequence. It was not the inability of the different ethnic groups to live together that brought on the conflict, but rather the political aim of separating them.

The violence unleashed grew directly out of the artificiality of the political agenda, which stood in total contradiction to the centuries-old

French UN peacekeepers explain ethnic divisions in central Bosnia, 1990.

multiethnic history of the Balkans. Simply put, the creation of ethnically homogeneous States in a region of historic mixing could not be achieved except through extreme violence. In Bosnia, cleansing clearly took the form of genocide, for it was aimed to eliminate enough of the population, starting with the annihilation of its elite, so it could no longer form a plurality. For the Serbs, war crimes served as a force multiplier—a means to achieve greater effect from other resources. They did not have enough military assets to achieve their ambitions otherwise.

Western governments, starting with the United States, chose not to intervene for three and a half years. In response to the atrocities reported by the media, relief organizations, and even their own diplomats, and to quell the public outcry over the haunting images of starved concentration camp inmates behind barbed wire, the UN Security Council passed resolutions its members then failed to implement and, in conjunction with the European Community, set up a diplomatic process which neither would back up by force. To evade their obligations under the 1948 Genocide Convention, which requires parties to prevent and punish genocide, Western leaders had frequent recourse to the term used by Serbian officials, ethnic cleansing, and then stated that all parties had committed the practice. They did not use the term genocide until the war had ended. The major powers recognized Bosnia-Herzegovina as a sovereign State, admitted it as a full member of the United Nations, and established diplomatic relations, meanwhile suspending the UN membership of the rump Yugoslavia and imposing sanctions on it for supporting the war. But they refused to identify the conflict as an international armed aggression and instead characterized it as a civil war and an ancient ethnic feud, a posture that permitted them to avoid their collective security obligations under the United Nations Charter. They also refused to document from their intelligence sources the links between the Serbian and Bosnian Serb armies—an integrated command structure, a single logistical infrastructure, and a common paymaster. A top American diplomat called the international failure to respond

Miljacka River, Sarajevo, spring 1992.

the worst crisis in European collective security since the 1930s.

    The evidence of concentration camps, systematic rape, massacres, torture, and mass deportation of civilians was undeniable, and in February 1993, largely at American behest, the Security Council set up an international war crimes tribunal in The Hague. But the major powers did not get around to naming a chief prosecutor until July 1994, and they gave no support to the Bosnian government when it brought a case for genocide against Serbia at the International Court of Justice in The Hague. Instead, Western governments repeatedly urged Bosnia to drop that case, which was finally decided in 2007. The Count ruled that Serbia was not responsible for genocide, but was guilty of failing to prevent and punish it.

    A key factor in incitement of ethnic hatreds, first in Serbia, and later in Croatia, was a media under the thumb of the country's political leaders. This psychological conditioning disguised the conflict in civil and ethnic terms by using the supreme alibi, namely that it would be impossible for the people of the former Yugoslavia to live together on the same territory. But it also awakened that barbarity which sleeps in all of us, and pushed the people to commit massive atrocities.

Historically, in conventional conflicts, defeating the enemy's army on the battlefield and seizing territory are usually each side's principal war aims. The killing and wounding of civilians, the destruction of property, and the creation of refugees or displaced people are often by-products of these aims. While much of this devastation is legal under international law, since the codes of war offer no complete guarantees for the safety of civilians caught in zones of combat, the essence of the laws of war is that suffering must be minimized. This makes it imperative that the civilian population should not be made the object of attack. Soldiers from proper armies who contravene these laws are subject to trial for war crimes. In Bosnia-Herzegovina, the killing of civilians was not a by-product of war, for the goal of ethnic cleansing was the annihilation of civilians.

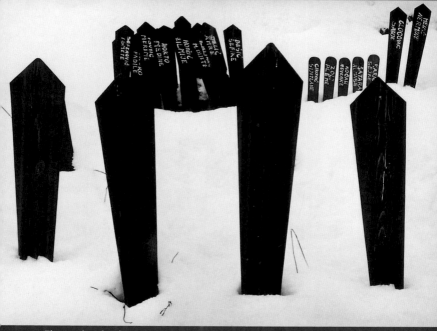

The tombs of unknown and known civilian children massacred by Serbs stand stark against the snow in the Lions Cemetery. Sarajevo, December 1995.

By the time Yugoslavia collapsed, the reputation of the Yugoslav Federal Army was irreparably stained, for under Milosevic's guidance the army coordinated and supported many of the militias who did the dirty work.

These were not the isolated, sporadic acts of militia factions running amok. To the contrary, the manner in which they were perpetrated, their ritualization, duration, and the pattern of commission across the territory under army control all testify that they were the product of a systematic policy, planned and coordinated at the highest political and military levels of the Yugoslav government.

To accomplish the war aim, there was probably no other way. In a multi-ethnic society like the former Yugoslavia before 1991, the annexation of territories while necessary could not be sufficient. Too many members of rival ethnic communities would have remained, and the more territories were conquered, the more difficult, paradoxically, it would become to occupy and administer them. Only ethnic cleansing, that is, the elimination of the other ethnic communities present in the coveted territories, could bring to fruition the war aims of the Serbs, and, later, of the Croats as well. Both Milosevic and Tudjman realized this from the start. The horrors and the goals of the war were one, or, more precisely, the success of the war depended on its horrors.

The war began on April 6, 1992, with the assault on key cities such as Bijeljina and Zvornik on the Bosnian-Serbian border by the Yugoslav Army and its allied paramilitary groups, followed by the siege of Sarajevo. Though planned over a long period, the order to activate the impressive military might secretly put in place around the Bosnian capital was held until the recognition of Bosnia-Herzegovina's independence by the Europeans and Americans.

From the very beginning of the conflict, terror was the method used to separate the communities. The violations of international humanitarian law that were committed during the war testify to the determination to reach this

goal. Bombardments of the civilian population, first of Sarajevo, then of besieged towns and villages; massacres during the capture of towns, followed by the forced evacuation of civilians to modify the ethnic structure of the particular area; illegal internment of the civilian population in concentration camps; torture; systematic rape; summary executions; appropriation and pillage of civilian property; systematic destruction of the cultural and religious heritage with the sole aim of eliminating any trace of non-Serbs in the conquered territories; using detainees as human shields on front lines and in minefields; and starvation of civilians who resisted—these were only some of the violations of international humanitarian law of which the Serbs were guilty.

Violence breeds violence. In 1993, emboldened by Milosevic's campaign of terror against the Muslims and the Western powers' consistent denial that genocide had taken place, the Croats entered the war against their former Muslim allies, using many of the same methods as the Serbs—terror, deportations, concentration camps, indiscriminate bombardments of civilians, massacres, the blocking of humanitarian aid, destruction of religious shrines, and appropriation of property.

They were encouraged by Slobodan Milosevic's support for a Greater Croatia (which would include western Herzegovina and a part of central Bosnia, where a majority of 800,000 Bosnian Croats lived). These grave breaches of the laws of armed conflict were always on a smaller scale than those of the Serbs.

Victims of a double aggression, the Muslims certainly committed violations of international humanitarian law. But the Sarajevo government never made ethnic cleansing their cardinal policy, as had their enemies. This does not excuse the acts of certain special units of the Bosnian Army, the summary executions of some Serbs in Sarajevo, and the establishment of several concentration camps in which sexual assaults, assassinations, and torture were reportedly regularly practiced.

In an exhaustive report to the United Nations, a special Commission of Experts, chaired by Cherif Bassiouni of DePaul University in Chicago, concluded that overall 90 percent of the crimes committed in Bosnia-Herzegovina were the responsibility of Serb extremists, 6 percent of Croat extremists, and 4 percent of Muslim extremists. These conform roughly to an assessment drafted by the American CIA.

Whatever the apportionment of blame, what is tragically clear is that the ethnic cleansers were all too successful in their work. Whether bringing the architects and perpetrators of these crimes to justice can reverse any of this remains to be seen.

(See **international vs. internal armed conflict; NATO and the Geneva Conventions; UN and the Geneva Conventions.**)

The Yugoslav War Crimes Tribunal

By Stéphanie Maupas

Since its creation by the UN Security Council in 1993, the International Criminal Tribunal for the former Yugoslavia (ICTY) has indicted 162 people, ranging from political and military leaders to low-level fighters. Unquestionably the most prominent of these was the former Serbian President Slobodan Milosevic. Described by the Tribunal's Chief Prosecutor as the key figure in the ten years of war that consumed the former Yugoslavia, Milosevic was voted out of office and then handed over to The Hague in June 2001 to face charges of genocide, crimes against humanity and war crimes. But the trial of the former strongman of Belgrade, which began in February 2002, was cut short. Milosevic was found dead in his prison cell on March 12, 2006, and thus remains legally innocent. As for his counterparts, the former Croatian President Franjo Tudjman and the Bosnian Alija Izetbegovic are both dead and beyond the reach of any possible indictment.

Over the course of ten years of proceedings, the Office of the Prosecutor has constructed a detailed but partial picture of the policy of ethnic cleansing that swept across the former Yugoslavia. One of the most significant moments was the admission of responsibility by the "Iron Lady" of the Bosnian Serbs, the former President of the Bosnian Serb Republic Biljana Plavsic. In December 2003 Plavsic pleaded guilty after having surrendered to the tribunal. She publicly acknowledged that there had been a plan of ethnic cleansing and charged Slobodan Milosevic with having been its principal architect. But her apparent change of heart remained tainted by nationalist political considerations. At the tribunal she admitted that she had given herself up to prevent the Serbian people from continuing to pay the price of the conflict.

Following in Plavsic's footsteps, several people involved in the Srebrenica massacre—which the tribunal ruled to be an act of genocide—admitted their responsibility. But despite these confessions, a large part of the Serbian population continued to reject the tribunal's legitimacy. In June 2005, a video recording of the execution of a group of young men by Serb paramilitaries was shown during the Milosevic trial. Rebroadcast in Serbia, this piece of evidence provoked much debate, but did not in the end really alter public perceptions about Serbia's role in the Balkan wars. The Tribunal also condemned the policy of ethnic cleansing in serveral trials of the directors or guards at the prison camps of Omarska, Keraterm and Trnopolje, where many thousands of non-Serbs were held in appalling conditions.

On the Croatian side, several military leaders were charged and convicted, but the problems the tribunal experienced in attempting to get hold of General

After the U.S.-led liberation of Kosovo in 1999, FBI forensic experts collect evidence of war crimes committed by Serb forces against Kosovar civilians for submission to the Hague Tribunal for the former Yugoslavia.

Ante Gotovina, who had recaptured the Krajina region of Croatia from the Serbs during "Operation Storm," and who is still regarded as a hero by many Croatians, suggested the country is not yet ready to confront its past. This impression was reinforced after Gotovina's arrest in December 2005, when it became clear that Zagreb would support his defense in court. Croatia refuses to give credence to the prosecutor's contention that it was guilty of the same policy for which it believes Belgrade to have been responsible: ethnic cleansing.

As for the Bosnian Muslim army, the prosecutor indicted its former chief of staff General Rasim Delic for murder, cruel treatment and rape by forces under his command, prompting protests in Sarajevo where he is seen as having inherited the mantle of Izetbegovic. Several officers in the Bosnian Muslim army have also been convicted, and their trials shed some preliminary light on the place of the *mujahidin* in the fledgling army. Finally, the first trial of members of the Kosovo Liberation Army (KLA) has also taken place, ending in two acquittals and one guilty verdict. At the beginning of March 2005, the Prime Minister of Kosovo and former member of the KLA Ramush Haradinaj was finally indicted by the tribunal's current Chief Prosecutor, Carla del Ponte, despite political pressure against the move.

Without its own police force, forced to rely on the cooperation of States, the tribunal has for ten years struggled to gain custody of and bring to trial the people who have been indicted. During the tribunal's early years NATO was reluctant to take any steps against indicted suspects who remained at large in Bosnian territory, though it has since arrested 29 people.

Incorporated in the Dayton peace agreement as one of the tools of reconciliation, the tribunal has brought more than 3600 witnesses to the stand. These "unrecognized heroes of international justice" have testified to "leave their mark in the history of humanity," a history "that must be written with several hands" as Carla del Ponte put it in opening the Milosevic trial. "This

People from the village of Zepce attempt to identify remains thought to be of their fellow villagers who disappeared during the war. Near Sarajevo, 2003.

tribunal will for its part only write one chapter—the most bloody and distressing, that of individual responsibility for those who commit grave breaches of international humanitarian law," she added.

But after September 11 the international community appeared suddenly to lose interest in the tribunal. Because of financial pressures, states imposed a fixed timetable on the court, which was firmly instructed to wrap up all of its cases by 2010. Courts in Bosnia, Croatia and Serbia were invited to take over the responsibility of trying those responsible for war crimes. The Prosecutor's Office in the Hague has transferred more than 900 cases to the Bosnian special court. For the Prosecutor, the mission of the tribunal remains only partly fulfilled, since the political and military leaders of the Bosnian Serbs have not stood trial. Accused of responsibility for the massacre of Srebrenica and the three-and-a-half year siege of Sarajevo, Radovan Karadzic and Ratko Mladic have escaped justice for over ten years.

Cambodia

By Sydney Schanberg

For three decades, without surcease, Cambodia was consumed by war, genocide, slave labor, forced marches, starvation, disease, and civil conflict. It is to Asia what the Holocaust was to Europe.

Roughly the size of Missouri, bordered by Thailand, Laos, and Vietnam, Cambodia had a population of perhaps 7 to 8 million in 1975 when the maniacal Khmer Rouge guerrillas swept into Phnom Penh and began the "purification" campaign that was the centerpiece of their extremist agrarian revolution. Four years later, the Khmer Rouge were pushed back into the jungle, leaving behind their legacy: 1.5 to 2 million Cambodians dead in what would become known to the world as "the Killing Fields." Twenty percent of the population was erased. In America that would be 50 to 60 million people.

Some scholars say that technically what happened in Cambodia cannot be called a genocide because for the most part, it was Khmers killing other Khmers, not someone trying to destroy a different "national, racial, ethnical or religious group"—which is how international law defines genocide.

To make such semantic or legalistic distinctions, however, is sometimes to forsake common sense—after all, the Khmer Rouge set out to erase an entire culture, a major foundation stone of which was Cambodia's religion, Theravada Buddhism. And this may help explain why, over the years, the law has proved so poor a guide to the reality of human slaughter. For, whether you call the mass killing in Cambodia a **genocide** or simply a **crime against humanity**, it was the same by either name. It was a visitation of evil.

One might thus reasonably pick Cambodia as a paradigm for the law's weakness in dealing with such crimes. International law after all depends for its legitimacy on the willingness of the world's nation-states to obey and enforce it. In Cambodia's case most nation-states expressed shock and horror —and did nothing. Even after the Vietnamese Army pushed the Khmer Rouge out of power in 1979, ended the genocide, were welcomed as liberators, and installed a pro-Hanoi government in Phnom Penh, Western nations saw to it that Cambodia's seat at the United Nations continued to be occupied for several years by those very same Khmer Rouge. Washington and its allies, while denouncing the Khmer Rouge crimes, were still slaves to Cold War ideology; they decided it was better to keep the Khmer Rouge in the UN seat than to have it go to a government in the orbit of Vietnam and its mentor, the Soviet Union. Realpolitik, not the law, was the governing force.

For the human record, let us examine exactly what the Khmer Rouge did to the Cambodian population. Their first act, within hours of military victory, was to kidnap it, herding everyone out of cities and towns into work camps deep in the countryside. All villages that touched on roads were similarly emptied. Cambodia, in fact, was transformed into one giant forced-labor camp under the fist of Angka, "the organization on high." That was the mild part.

The Khmer Rouge had actively sealed off the country. The world could not look in. The horror could begin. Led by Pol Pot, their Paris-educated, Maoist-influenced "Brother Number One," the new rulers proceeded to completely shatter the three underpinnings of Cambodian society—the family,

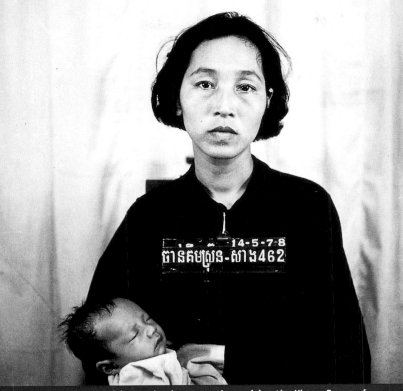

Their only epitaph: With macabre bureaucratic precision the Khmer Rouge photographed their victims before torturing and killing them. This picture is all that remains of a mother and child murdered in Tuol Sleng Prison sometime between 1975 and 1979. So were all of those on the following pages.

the Buddhist religion, and the village. In grueling migrations, people were marched to sites as far as possible from their home villages. Children were separated from parents and placed in youth groups, where they were indoctrinated to inform on their parents and other adults for any infractions of Angka's crushing rules. Marriage was forbidden except when arranged by Angka. The schools were shuttered, currency abolished, factories abandoned. Newspapers ceased to exist. Radio sets were taken away.

As for religion, Buddhist temples were razed or closed. Of the sixty thousand Buddhist monks only three thousand were found alive after the Khmer Rouge reign; the rest had either been massacred or succumbed to hard labor, disease, or torture. The Chams, a Muslim minority, were also targets for elimination.

Religion, however, was but a starting point. Simply put, the Khmer Rouge marked for potential extinction all Cambodians they deemed not "borisot" (pure)—meaning all those with an education, those raised in population centers, those "tainted" by anything foreign (including knowledge of a foreign language), even those who wore glasses. Anyone, that is, suspected of not being in step with their pathological agrarian master plan. All suspect Cambodians were labeled "new people" and kept apart from the "pure" populations. In some instances, the "new people" were given special identifying neckerchiefs—reminiscent of the yellow Star of David—so they could always be picked out of a crowd, as they often were when taken away for execution.

The Khmer Rouge had a pet slogan: "To spare you is no profit; to destroy you, no loss." With this incantation, at least 1.5 million Cambodians were erased.

I was in Phnom Penh when the Khmer Rouge marched in victorious on April 17, 1975, their faces cold, a deadness in their eyes. They ordered the city evacuated. Everyone was to head for the countryside to join the glorious revolution. They killed those who argued against leaving. Two million frightened people started walking out of the capital. The guerrilla soldiers even ordered the wounded out of the overflowing hospitals, where the casualties had been so heavy in the final few days of the war that the floors were slick with blood. There was no time for anything but emergency surgery. When the doctors ran out of surgical gloves, they simply dipped their hands in bowls of antiseptic and moved on to the next operating table. Somewhere between five thousand and ten thousand wounded were in the city's hospitals when the order to evacuate came. Most couldn't walk so their relatives wheeled them out of the buildings on their beds, with plasma and serum bags attached, and began pushing them along the boulevards out of the city toward the "revolution."

Foreigners were allowed to take refuge in the French embassy compound. I watched many Cambodian friends being herded out of Phnom Penh. Most of them I never saw again. All of us felt like betrayers, like people who were protected and didn't do enough to save our friends. We felt shame. We still do.

Two weeks later, the Khmer Rouge expelled us from the country, shipping us out on two truck convoys to the border with Thailand. With this act, Cambodia was sealed. The world could not look in. The killing could begin.

But the story of Cambodia's misery did not start with the Khmer Rouge. It began in March 1970, when a pro-Western junta headed by Gen. Lon Nol, with Washington's blessing, deposed Prince Norodom Sihanouk, who was out of the country. Sihanouk, a neutralist, had kept Cambodia out of the Vietnam War by making concessions to appease both sides. He allowed the Americans to secretly bomb Viet Cong sanctuaries inside Cambodia while he allowed the Vietnamese Communists to use Cambodia's port city, Kompong Som (also called Sihanoukville) to ship in supplies for those sanctuaries.

With Sihanouk gone, the Lon Nol group in effect declared war on Hanoi; and President Richard Nixon, pleased to have partisans—not neutralists—in Phnom Penh, ordered American troops to push into Cambodia from Vietnam for a six-week assault on the Communist sanctuaries. However, not having real confidence in Lon Nol, the president didn't inform him of the invasion on his sovereign territory until after it had begun and after Nixon had informed the American public on national television.

This was probably the moment that marked Cambodia's transformation into a pawn of the Cold War, with the Chinese backing the Khmer Rouge, the Soviets backing Hanoi, and the Americans backing the Lon Nol regime—all of them turning the entire country into a surrogate Cold War battlefield. The great irony in this turn of events is that the Khmer Rouge were no serious threat in 1970, being a motley collection of ineffectual guerrilla bands totaling at most three thousand to five thousand men, who could never have grown into the murderous force of seventy thousand to 100,000 that swept into Phnom Penh five years later without the American intervention and the subsequent expansion of Chinese and Russian aid to the Communist side. The enlarged war gave the Khmer Rouge status and recruitment power. It also gave them tutelage and advisory help from Hanoi's forces (at least for the first two years before deep rifts drove the two apart).

This five-year war was marked by barbarism by all sides. Cambodian warriors have a battlefield custom, going back centuries, of cutting the livers from the bodies of their vanquished foes, then cooking them in a stew and eating them. The belief is that this imparts strength and also provides talismanic protection against being killed by the enemy. In this and countless other ways, the international conventions that say respect must be shown to the fallen enemy were universally disregarded.

Early in the war, in a town south of Phnom Penh, Lon Nol troops had killed two Viet Cong and recovered their badly charred bodies, which they hung upside-down in the town square to swing gruesomely in the wind—thereby sending a message to all who might consider aiding the foe. Henry Kamm, my *New York Times* colleague, tried to tell the Lon Nol commander that treating the bodies in this manner violated the Geneva Conventions. The commander found this amusing. He left the bodies twisting.

With the Vietnamese Communist units moving deeper into Cambodia, the Lon Nol government began whipping up anti-Vietnamese fervor. This visited fear and worse upon the 200,000-strong ethnic Vietnamese community in the country who, though they were citizens of Cambodia and had lived there for generations, soon became the targets of a public frenzy. Massacres began occurring. Many of the Vietnamese lived along the rivers, earning their living as fishermen; their bodies were soon floating down the Mekong by the dozens. One government general, Sosthene Fernandez, a Cambodian of Filipino ancestry who later rose to become chief of the armed forces, began using ethnic Vietnamese civilians as protective shields for his advancing troops, marching them in front into the waiting guns of the Viet Cong. This, too, is against international law. Fernandez disagreed. "It is a new form of psychological warfare," he said.

Saigon raised bitter protests against these pogroms, and Cambodia's Vietnamese population was finally interned in protective custody in schools and other public buildings. Many were eventually moved under guard to South Vietnam as a temporary measure until emotions cooled.

As the war progressed, the country—at least the part held by the Lon Nol government—progressively shrank. The energized Khmer Rouge kept grabbing more and more territory until the area under government control, aside from the capital, was reduced to a handful of transport corridors and several province towns. The Phnom Penh airport and the Mekong River were its lone links to the outside world. To preserve these lines of supply, the Americans bombed Khmer Rouge and Viet Cong targets in the countryside on a daily basis. Since most of the raids were by giant, eight-engine B-52s, each carrying about twenty-five tons of bombs and thus laying down huge carpets of destruction, the bombing was anything but surgical, and frequently hit civilian villages. The result was thousands of refugees fleeing into Phnom Penh and the province towns. The capital swelled from a population of 600,000 at the start of the war to 2 million at its end in 1975. The American embassy in Phnom Penh—and Henry Kissinger's team in Washington—insisted that the refugees were fleeing only one thing: attacks by the brutal Khmer Rouge. But in fact they were fleeing both the Khmer Rouge and the American bombs. I visited refugee camps regularly and consistently heard both accounts.

Some peasants didn't flee at all; the Khmer Rouge used their anger about the bombing to recruit them as soldiers and porters.

The bombing raids illustrate what is pretty much an axiom in all wars: i.e., that so-called "conventional" weapons not forbidden by international law can produce the same horrific results as banned weapons.

In Cambodia, the B-52s carried napalm and dart cluster-bombs (since discontinued by the Pentagon). The raids were carried out by three of the mammoth planes in formation. Each plane can carry twenty-five to thirty tons of bombs, making the total load of a formation seventy-five to ninety tons. B-52s drop their bombs to form a grid, or "box," of destruction on the ground; the grid (an average one might be one kilometer wide and two kilometers long) can be altered to fit the size and shape of the troop concentration. Soldiers who manage to survive these massive explosions (which sometimes throw bodies and dirt as much as one hundred feet in the air) are often rendered unfit for further duty, having been put in permanent shock or made deaf or simply frightened to the bone of every sharp sound or movement. Such raids were what destroyed the retreating Iraqi troops on the road to Basra at the end of that war in 1991—the road that became known as the "Highway of Death."

In 1973, an accidental B-52 bombing of Neak Loeung, a government-held Mekong river town, killed and wounded some four hundred Cambodians, most of them civilians. The American embassy apologized and gave monetary gifts to victims' families on a sliding scale—a few hundred dollars for the loss of a limb, more for multiple limbs, and still more for a death. When civilians die in wars, the military calls it unintentional, even though everyone knows civilian deaths are inevitable, especially when the weapons spray their lethality over large spaces. The phrase used by the Pentagon for civilian deaths is "collateral damage"—just as napalm was called "soft ordnance"—the idea being to give war a softer, sanitized sound for the lay public.

Napalm, incidentally, was dropped by B-52s in the Vietnam and Cambodian wars, in the form of CBUs—Cluster Bomb Units. (Other planes dropped napalm in different containers and forms.) A CBU is a large bomb, say 750 pounds, that carries hundreds of smaller projectiles. A typical CBU is rigged to open, in the manner of a clamshell, a short distance above the ground, releasing its hail of explosive bomblets on the enemy troops beneath it. One variety was the CBU-3; its bomblets carried napalm, which set fire to the troops or robbed the air of oxygen, thus asphyxiating them. Another version carried special darts, which ripped through flesh or pinned the victims to trees or the ground. Sometimes it is hard for the layman to discern any great difference between these weapons and, for instance, the chemical arms banned by international law and custom. Both have a terror component. The napalm and darts have since been taken out of the American CBU inventory—because of their bad image—but conventional-bomblet CBUs are still used, as in the 1991 Gulf War with Iraq.

And what about plain old rockets? Should all of them be banned, since they are frequently used as instruments of terror against civilians? The Khmer Rouge sent rockets shrieking into Phnom Penh throughout that five-year war. These were not precisely aimed munitions by any definition. They were crudely produced Chinese projectiles with a fan-shaped tail that whistled as it cut through the air overhead; you knew when it began its downward plummet because the whistling suddenly stopped. These rockets were launched from the city's environs, set off from hand-fashioned wooden platforms; there was no aiming at specific military targets—the effort was simply to get them to land somewhere, anywhere, in the refugee-packed city. And land they did—on markets, in school rooms, in back-yards-spewing jagged metal and sliced limbs. The purpose was to demoralize the civilian population, and it worked.

An artillery piece can also be used as a weapon of terror against civilians. One afternoon in the summer of 1974, the Khmer Rouge trained a captured American-made 105 mm howitzer on Phnom Penh and fanned its muzzle across the city's southern edge. At first, as the shells fell in this half-moon arc, they exploded without result, but then the arc came to a colony of houses called Psar Deum Kor, and the death began. Fires started by the shells broke out and the houses were quickly in flames, whipped by high winds. Within a half hour, nearly two hundred people were dead and another two hundred wounded, virtually all civilians. The bodies were carted off on police pickup trucks. No military target was anywhere in the vicinity.

In the end—whether in Cambodia or any other killing field—there is nothing new either about the barbarity of people destroying people or, unfor-

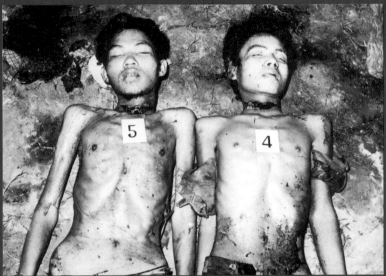

The Khmer Rouge killed more than 16,000 prisoners at their Tuol Sleng detention center between 1975 and 1979 and photgraphed the dead.

tunately, about its seeming inevitability in every age. One unchanging lesson is that war or genocide or crimes against humanity are states of violence that, where they exist, remove all breath from such notions as the law and civilized behavior.

Is it hopeless, then, to try to strengthen both the international law and its enforcement? No, never hopeless, not if you believe in the possibility of improvement, no matter how slight. Journalists are by blood and tradition committed to the belief, or at least to the tenet, of trying to keep bad things from getting any worse than they already are. Thus, this book.
(See **persecutions on political, racial, or religious grounds.**)

Carpet or Area Bombing

By Horst Fischer

C

Air attacks on a city that treat it as a single **military objective** instead of clearly distinguishing military objectives and attacking them individually are an example of area bombardment, often called carpet bombing. Many of the World War II attacks on cities targeted an area rather than individual military objectives. Legal arguments and military rationales were given for the strategic bombing campaign, among them to destroy the enemy's industry, to weaken the morale of the population, or simply to punish the adversary for its previous violations. The destruction of Rotterdam, Dresden, and Hiroshima are prominent examples. The Nuremberg Tribunal did not discuss area bombardment in any detail, and the practice, which flies in the face of all the civilian protections in the Fourth Geneva Convention of 1949, continued into the Cold War. The U.S. aerial campaigns against North Vietnam—in particular the so-called Christmas bombing of 1972 against Hanoi and Haiphong—are believed to have been illegal area bombardments.

An explicit ban on area bombardment was first codified in the 1977 Additional Protocol I, which applies to bombardments of cities, towns, villages, or other areas containing a concentration of civilians. An attack by bombardment by any method or means that treats as a single military objective a number of clearly separated and distinct military objectives is considered to be an **indiscriminate attack** and is prohibited. Launching such an attack in the knowledge that it will cause excessive loss of life, injury to civilians, or damage to civilian objects is considered a grave breach. Bombarding areas containing solely military targets is permitted. Important powers such as the United States, which are not party to Protocol I, accept this principle as binding **customary international law**.

Though the Protocol's wording makes it clear that attacks targeting cities as such are prohibited, declarations by States while negotiating the text suggest severe problems in applying it. States have made clear that "clearly separated" implies a significant distance between separate military objectives, but what is "significant" is highly subjective.

One obvious problem is the inaccuracy of aerial bombardment. This has been altered by newer precision-guided weapons; but these are available only to a few combatants, and then only in limited quantities. So long as the party to the conflict attempting to distinguish between targets employs weapons that can be used discriminately, it will be able to claim it has avoided crossing the line into violations of humanitarian law.

From recent conflicts it can be concluded that belligerents are aware of the restraints on area bombardment even if they are not bound by the rules of Protocol I. The major allied forces in the **Gulf War** claimed to have implemented the standards of Protocol I in attacking Iraqi military targets although not bound to do so.

The U.S. military command has acknowledged that the bombing of the Iraqi Basra area by American B-52 bombers in 1991 was an area bombardment. As the attacks had been directed solely against the combatants of the so-called Iraqi Republican Guard, the United States believed the attacks to have been lawful.

Bomb craters from B-52 strikes. Near Saigon, Vietnam, 1968.

Chechnya

By Barry Renfrew

C

Russia's disastrous war in Chechnya has witnessed butchery and savagery on a scale and intensity recalling World War II. During the 1990s massive formations of Russian tanks, artillery, and aircraft pounded Chechen cities and towns to charred ruins. Since then, Chechnya has endured years of guerrilla war and government security sweeps in which thousands of people have been killed or disappeared. The conflict has spilled into neighboring republics in southern Russia, destabilizing an already precarious region. Guerrillas have indiscriminately struck deep into the heart of Russia, killing hundreds of civilians, including children. Human rights and the laws of war appear meaningless to both sides.

The first phase of the war in Chechnya began in 1994. Both sides routinely committed atrocities during this conflict, though the far larger Russian military was guilty of more frequent excesses. Russian troops indiscriminately attacked towns and villages, killing and raping civilians, pillaging and burning homes. Chechen fighters executed prisoners and civilian opponents, attacked civilian targets in Russia and used civilians to shield their forces, and drove thousands of Russian civilians out of Chechnya in a systematic campaign.

There is no neat, simple answer as to why this war was so savage. It was a war inflamed by intense nationalism and ethnic hatred; a calamitously managed war that swiftly degenerated into a brutal campaign of suppression that only increased Chechen resistance; a war in which an ill-trained, disintegrating army, in truth little more than a mob, was pitted against a smaller, but highly motivated and skilled guerrilla force; a war in which a democratically elected government employed the ruthless methods and forces of Soviet totalitarianism against a civilian population. It was also a war between peoples and cultures that have waged merciless wars of conquest and extermination against each other for centuries with unrelenting medieval savagery.

Kill or be killed was the sole motivation of most soldiers in the disintegrating Russian Army, who were desperately fighting to stay alive rather than win a war. Win or die was the creed of Chechens inspired by fanatical patriotism and their Islamic belief in jihad, or holy war, against the traditional enemy. Many Russians saw Chechens as swarthy, treacherous savages and habitual criminals. The Chechens saw the Russians as ruthless conquerors and despoilers of their motherland.

Russia is a disparate patchwork of conquered ethnic and national groups, and every Russian government, whatever its ideology, has believed that the existence of Russia depends on preserving this empire at any cost. Many Russian

Russian special forces patrol the neighborhoods of Grozny, where almost every home was destroyed during the second invasion that began in 2000.

leaders and ordinary people were deeply aware that the dissolution of the Soviet Union had stripped away huge tracts of territory and much of their national pride, and feared that Russia was on the brink of disintegration. Putin's government viewed the idea of Chechen independence as a prelude to the unraveling of Russia and refused to consider any strategy but military victory.

The Chechens, an intensely nationalistic and martial people, were among the last to be conquered by czarist Russia in the nineteenth century. They never accepted Russian domination and Moscow's rule was correspondingly harsh. Soviet dictator Joseph Stalin deported virtually the entire Chechen nation, hundreds of thousands of men, women, and children, to Central Asia in the 1940s, where many perished in appalling conditions.

Chechnya declared independence after the Soviet Union collapsed in 1991. Most Chechens regard their right to independence as a fact of nature as indisputable as the mountains of their land. They see no need to justify their claim of independence through international law or history. A Chechen asked such a question would give you either a look of pity because you were clearly a fool or else a threatening retort that you must be an enemy.

International law has little to say on whether the Chechens have the right to secede or whether Russia was justified in using force to stop them. (Although international treaties often refer broadly to the self-determination of peoples, it is usually construed to refer to anti-colonial struggles of far-away peoples and not to parts of a nation.) But governments assert their

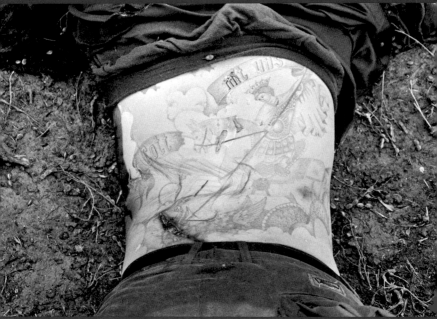

Mass grave of civilians, mostly ethnic Russians, killed in the bombing of Grozny shortly after the first Russian intervention. "Gott mit Uns" (God is with us) says tattoo in German. January 1995.

sovereign right to preserve their territorial integrity, by force if necessary—tacitly accepting the right of other States to do likewise.

Russian soldiers were bewildered when they were sent into Chechnya in December 1994. Women and children tried to block the Russian tanks, begging the troops to turn back. One Russian general halted his forces, saying it was not the role of the army to fight its own citizens.

That early uncertainty evaporated as Chechen forces inflicted heavy losses on the Russians. The ill-trained, poorly led Russian troops were mowed down by the hundreds in futile human-wave attacks against Chechen positions. What was supposed to be a swift police action turned into a gigantic disaster for the Russian military. Atrocities began almost at once, with Chechens literally tearing captured Russian airmen to bits while Russian forces indiscriminately bombed civilian settlements.

Grozny, the Chechen capital, was engulfed by a pitched battle. After infantry assaults failed, the Russian military set out to pulverize the city into submission. Russian aircraft bombarded Grozny while armored forces and artillery hammered the city from the ground.

The Russian assault fell mainly on Grozny's civilians, mostly ethnic Russians. The city's small Chechen population had fled to surrounding villages. Separatist forces operated from buildings filled with Russian civilians as shields.

Under international humanitarian law, the Russians were justified in seeking to capture the city because it was the rebels' main base and the location of legitimate military targets, regardless of the presence of civilians. The fact that Chechen forces had fortified large parts of the city also meant that apartment blocks and other civilian structures were legitimate targets if they were being put to military use. And many civilians perished not because of the Russians, but because Chechen forces were using them

Chechen woman shows portrait of missing relative, August 2002.

as human shields, and, at times, prevented them from leaving the city or being evacuated. A Russian strategy of capturing Grozny by destroying it as a whole target was illegitimate, however, under the rules of war because targeting must be discriminate and aimed at discrete individual objectives. Combatants may not lawfully treat all the targets in an area, such as an entire city, as a single, giant target.

Reporting from Grozny during the battle, I could see clearly that both sides would do anything to win. Talk of law or humanitarian concerns was meaningless to most Russian and Chechen commanders, especially those who indifferently sent their own troops to be slaughtered day after day in a war of attrition.

Chechen fighters, as well as using civilians as shields in battle, killed prisoners and civilian opponents, especially supporters of pro-Moscow Chechen political groups, frequently torturing and mutilating victims. Some captured Russian soldiers were tortured and executed, while others were treated well and released.

During this period, the West chose to see the war as an internal matter with no legal or practical basis for outside intervention. Although painfully aware that Russian forces were responsible for the deaths of thousands of civilians, the West believed it had to support Yeltsin as the best guarantor of moderate, pro-Western government in Moscow. Russian democracy was in its infancy, and powerful Communist and nationalist groups in Russia were calling for Yeltsin's removal and a return to the country's totalitarian past. Outside Russia there were scattered calls for sanctions, but Western reaction was confined to appeals for restraint and occasional rebukes.

By the summer of 1996 the war appeared to be winding down with Moscow claiming victory. In August, the separatists captured much of Grozny in a surprise attack. Moscow, seeing no hope for a military victory, pulled its forces out and tried to save face by saying a decision on Chechen independence would be made at a later date. The Chechens said they were independent.

Russian soldiers killed a mother of three in this room on January 25, 2000, according to her family. She was Russian and her husband Chechen.

After several years of low-level conflict, Russian forces forced their way back in to Chechnya in 2000 and restored direct rule after taking Grozny. Various attempts at finding a negotiated settlement failed and the Chechens fought on from the hills. Increasingly, the Russians have pursued a strategy of "Chechenization," putting local pro-Moscow forces in charge of security and claiming that the war is over. A series of referenda and elections has been staged in Chechnya under conditions that human rights groups reject as a climate of fear. By mid-2006, the dominant figure in Chechnya was the Russian-backed prime minister, Ramzan Kadyrov, son of the former president Akhmad Kadyrov who was assassinated in 2004. On the other side, the rebel forces have suffered the loss of some of their most influential leaders: Aslan Maskhadov, the main separatist leader, was killed in March 2005, and the military commander Shamil Basayev in July 2006.

There are few military engagements any more, but the bitterness and criminality of the conflict remain unchanged. During this second phase of the conflict, Russian forces and their Chechen allies have been accused of widespread abuses against civilians, including enforced disappearances, torture and indiscriminate killing. International and Russian human rights groups estimate that up to 5,000 civilians have been abducted by Russian or pro-Russian security forces. Many of the victims are never seen again, while survivors report being held incommunicado and tortured to try to force them to admit ties to the guerrillas. Kadyrov's security forces, the so-

called "kadyrovtsy," are now believed to carry out the majority of abductions. The International Helsinki Federation for Human Rights says that the *kadyrovtsy* operate a network of secret prisons and are responsible for up to 75% of the war crimes committed in Chechnya.

The Russian security forces in Chechnya remain poorly trained, demoralized, undisciplined and corrupt. There has been little accountability for abuses they have committed over the years: the handful of Russian officers and soldiers put on trial for crimes in Chechnya have mostly been acquitted or received modest sentences. In one of the few trials of Russian military personnel, two soldiers were acquitted of killing six civilians in 2005 after saying they were following the orders of their superiors: a defense that has been rejected since the Nuremberg Trials following the defeat of Nazi Germany.

At the same time Chechen attacks against civilian targets have been stepped up. Trying to take the war to the Russians, Chechen detachments have attacked several Russian cities, often using civilian hostages as human shields. In October 2002, Chechen fighters took over a Moscow theatre during the performance of a popular musical, leading to a rescue attempt in which over 100 hostages were killed by a gas released by Russian forces. Two years later, Chechens seized about 1,000 hostages at a school in the southern city of Beslan, a raid that left some 330 people dead, half of them children. Other attacks have been directed against hospitals, public concerts and residential areas.

Shamil Basayev, the Chechen military commander behind the school attack, who was later killed by Russian forces, said in a 2005 interview it was necessary to make every Russian feel the pain of the war. "Responsibility is with the whole of the Russian nation ... If the war doesn't come to each of them individually, it will never stop in Chechnya," he said.

There are persistent claims that some Chechen commanders have links to al-Qaeda and other international terrorist groups.

As Russia showed signs of swinging back to its authoritarian past under Vladamir Putin, who succeeded Yeltsin, the United States and other Western nations were more critical about growing evidence of human rights abuses in Chechnya. George Bush threatened in 2000 to cut off aid if Russia continued "killing women and children, leaving orphans and refugees" in Chechnya. The West's tone changed dramatically after the Sept. 11, 2001, attacks on New York City and Washington D.C. The United States, looking for allies in an international war on terrorism, was eager to accept help from Moscow, which portrayed the Chechen conflict as another front in the conflict against Islamic terrorism. The European Union, the U.S. State

Survivors wander the bullet-riddled corridors of Beslan's School No. 1 after Chechen separatists seized the school and hundreds of children. September 2004.

Department and others have occasionally urged Russia to curb human rights abuses in Chechnya, but there has been little action to back the censure and the issue has almost disappeared from international politics.

The Russian government has also managed to deflect domestic attention from Chechnya and there is little public discussion of the issue. Journalists, human rights groups and others are restricted and Chechnya remains a very dangerous place for outsiders and locals.

(See **wanton destruction**.)

Chemical Weapons

By Peter Pringle

In March 1984, an Iranian soldier attacking Iraq during the conflict between those two States came under fire from artillery shells that emitted a heavy smoke smelling of garlic. Within a few minutes, the soldier's eyes burned and his skin began to itch, redden, and blister. Five days later the skin on his neck, chest, and shoulders began to peel off. Shortly afterward, the soldier died.

A UN investigation of several such instances concluded that chemical weapons, including mustard gas and the nerve agent known as Tabun, had been used. By the end of the war, Iran claimed tens of thousands of chemical weapons casualties. There was no doubt that Iraq had broken the 1925 Geneva Protocol for the Prohibition of the Use of Asphyxiating, Poisonous, or other Gases, and of Bacteriological Methods of Warfare, nor that Iran had retaliated in kind, albeit briefly and less effectively.

Following the Iran-Iraq war, Saddam Hussein continued for some time to stockpile chemical and biological weapons, and there have been uncorroborated allegations of the use of such weapons by other States: the use of gas by South African-backed forces in Mozambique, by contestants in the conflict between Azerbaijan and Armenia, by Turks against Kurds, and in the Sudan civil war. More recently, there were also unverified claims by a Soviet-era defector that the Russians may have developed super-strains of germ weapons, and some of these may still exist in the Russian arsenal.

For the observer at the front line, accusations of the use of chemical and biological weapons are almost impossible to verify on the spot. Only after a prolonged investigation that involves examining the corpses of the victims, interviewing survivors, and searching for residues of the weapons ingredients and products of chemical reactions involving such ingredients, can the truth be known—and sometimes not even then.

Put together over the years, these reports of the use of banned weapons underscored the urgency of tightening international controls. The 1925 Geneva Protocol, eventually ratified by 133 States, effectively prohibited only the first use of chemical and biological weapons. Countries were not prevented from developing and stockpiling chemical weapons, and several parties to the Protocol reserved the right to use chemical weapons in retaliation if their enemy used them first. The ban did not apply against a country's own nationals, nor cover riot control gases, including CS gas. The 1972 Biological Weapons Convention renounced germ weapons totally, including their development and stockpiling. In 1993, the new Chemical Weapons Convention was opened for signature in Paris. It entered into force on April 29, 1997, and 180 States have ratified it, including the United States and Russia.

The essence of the fifty-thousand-word treaty is that each State party undertakes never, in any circumstances, to develop, produce, otherwise acquire, stockpile, or retain chemical weapons, or transfer them directly or indirectly to anyone; never to use chemical weapons or engage in any preparations for doing so; and never to assist, encourage, or induce, in any way, anyone to engage in any activity prohibited by the treaty.

By "chemical weapons" the treaty means munitions or other devices using toxic chemicals to cause death, temporary incapacitation, or permanent harm to humans or animals. The treaty does not prohibit the development of toxic chemicals for industrial, agricultural, research, medical, pharmaceutical, or other peaceful purposes, or purposes related to protection against chemical weapons, or law enforcement including domestic riot control. Riot control agents, such as CS gas, cannot be used as a method of warfare.

Each State undertakes to destroy, within ten years, its chemical stockpiles and production facilities that can produce more than one ton of chemical weapons per year.

In one respect the CWC has been a success: no weapons banned by the treaty have since been used, and chemical stockpiles and production facilities are being destroyed. However the changing nature of conflict and developments in weapons research have highlighted what some people see as dangerous loopholes in the treaty.

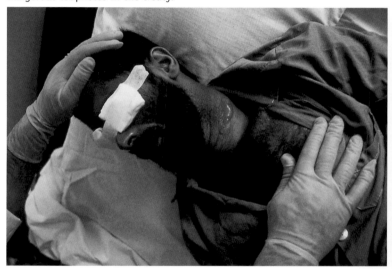

An Iranian victim of Iraqi chemical warfare is treated at a hospital in Tehran, 1986.

In October 2002, Russian special forces in Moscow used a knockout gas derived from the chemical fentanyl, a "calmative" agent, during the attempted rescue of several hundred theatergoers who had been taken hostage by Chechen fighters. More than 120 of the hostages died from the effect of the gas. As an incapacitant, fentanyl can be used only for purposes specifically recognized by the CWC, including law enforcement. The example of the Dubrovka theater siege shows how difficult it can be to distinguish between law enforcement and armed conflict, when armed groups mount attacks against civilians far from any recognizable military front line. This is particularly problematic as there has been extensive academic and military research in recent years into such so-called "nonlethal" gases.

The use of riot control gas is another gray area. In February 2003, U.S. Defense Secretary Donald Rumsfeld told Congress that he had formulated rules of engagement that would comply with the "straitjacket" of the CWC and still allow U.S. troops to use riot control agents in some circumstances, like when confronting enemy fighters hiding with civilians in a cave in Afghanistan. According to the U.S. view, the restriction on using riot control gas as a method of warfare only forbids its use in offensive military operations. By contrast, the United Kingdom has stated that riot control agents cannot be used "on any battlefield."

Child Soldiers

By Anna Cataldi and Jimmie Briggs

"I didn't think I would live," said Owo Peter, a thin, slightly built boy in his teens. "I can't return to my village because they would attack my family. If I am caught now, they will kill me with no explanation."

Peter, recovering from a serious gunshot wound at the World Vision Center in Gulu, Uganda, looked away as he recounted the story of how he'd been abducted and forced to fight by the Lord's Resistance Army rebel group. He said that he'd been snatched from his home in the village of Odek in northern Uganda by members of the LRA several years before, as he worked on the arts and crafts he sold by the side of the road. Somehow, the raggedy group of rebels—themselves children in their teens—knew that Peter had once served with the local home guard. As the guerrillas moved with him and other captives, the commanders singled him out for a beating with tree limbs. Ten grunts were chosen to lash his back, torso and legs. The guerrillas and their captives were headed to southern Sudan, where the rebel camp awaited.

Peter survived the journey despite his severe wounds, and remained at the rebel outpost for the next four years. His captors sent him, with very little training, into major battles. When Peter was shot in the arm during an incursion into Uganda, he saw his opportunity to escape. He was unable to say how many people he'd killed during his time as a child soldier.

One of the most alarming trends in armed conflict is the participation of children as active soldiers. Children as young as eight years of age are being forcibly recruited, coerced and induced to become combatants. Manipulated by adults, children have been drawn into violence that they are too young to resist and with consequences they cannot imagine.

Child soldiers are recruited in many different ways. Some are conscripted, others are press-ganged or kidnapped, and still others are forced to join armed groups to defend their families. Sometimes, children become soldiers simply in order to survive.

The employment of children in this way is anything but a recent phenomenon—for millennia, children have gone to war as drummer boys, messengers, porters, and servants—but the escalating number of children bearing arms in contemporary conflicts is terrifying. Non-governmental organizations estimate that there are now some 300,000 children serving as soldiers in over 30 conflicts around the world. Africa has the highest numbers of child soldiers, but they have also been used in Colombia, Sri Lanka, Nepal and many other places. Both boys and girls are affected. Human Rights Watch has said that in Uganda—as well as in Ethiopia and El Salvador—as many as a third of children pressed into service or recruited by armed groups are girls. Often they are forced to act as sex slaves in addition to their other tasks.

Many branches of international law forbid the recruitment of child soldiers. The two Additional Protocols of 1977, applying to international and internal conflicts respectively, impose on the parties to a conflict the obligation to do everything feasible to prevent children under fifteen from taking part in hostilities and to refrain from recruiting them into their armed forces. Using child soldiers below the age of fifteen is also generally agreed to be a violation of customary law. The 1998 Rome Statute of the International

Dean Chapman, Panos Pictures

Alvaro Ybarra Zavala, Agence VU

Marcus Bleasdale

Teun Voeten, *SIPA Press*

C

Marcus Bleasdale

Stephen Ferry, *Redux Pictures*

Criminal Court lists conscription or enlistment of children under the age of fifteen and using children to participate actively in hostilities as war crimes in international and non-international armed conflict.

Human rights law also addresses the issue of children in armed conflict. The 1989 Convention on the Rights of the Child (CRC), which has gained nearly universal acceptance, is the primary instrument. The convention defines a child as a person below the age of eighteen, but sets fifteen as a minimum age for going to war. Only two countries have not ratified it: Somalia and the United States. (In the United States, opposition is based in part on the Convention's prohibition on executing people for crimes committed between the ages of 16 and 18.) In January 2000, an Optional Protocol was passed to the CRC, requiring governments to take all feasible measures to prevent children below 18 from taking part in hostilities. The Protocol also forbids the forcible recruitment by governments of children below 18, and bans non-governmental forces from enlisting children below 18 in any circumstances.

In October 2005, the International Criminal Court announced that it had issued warrants for the arrest of five leaders of the Lord's Resistance Army, the first such step taken by the new court. The ICC prosecutor accused Joseph Kony, leader of the LRA, and four of his closest commanders of killing, raping and robbing civilians. The ICC chief prosecutor, Luis Moreno Ocampo, put a special emphasis on the LRA's systematic kidnapping of children, forcing them to fight and using girls as sex slaves.

(See **sexual violence: enslavement; slavery**.)

Preceding page, top left to right 1. A Karen soldier, Burma. 2. Maoist soldiers, Nepal. 3. Child soldiers in Liberia, 2003. 4. Young Russian conscripts, Chechnya. 5. Child soldier in Freetown, Sierra Leone. 6. Darfur, Sudan. 7. Gulu, northern Uganda, where children flee villages in late afternoon to avoid abduction and death. 8. A 15-year-old FARC guerrilla in Colombia.

In Liberia, Krahn militia men and boys spear a suspected NPFL member and beat him to death. Double Trouble is shown in flip-flops holding a stick.

Corinne Dufka, Reuters

Children as Killers

By Corinne Dufka

The Krahn militiamen, about two hundred of them, were advancing up Broad Street. Armed with AK-47s, machetes, fishing harpoons, and kitchen utensils, their objective was to take over the posh seaside neighborhood of Mamba Point from Charles Taylor's National Patriotic Front of Liberia (NPFL) militia. It was April 1996 and Monrovia, the Liberian capital, had plummeted into urban chaos, leaving hundreds dead and causing tens of thousands to flee the city in panic.

A commander heard a stirring within a building. "What's that?" the soldiers yelled excitedly. An unarmed man was pulled out from his hiding place on the second floor. We knew him as the caretaker, surely trying to stay out of harm's way. For the Krahn, he was the enemy.

Within minutes he was being chased like an animal by a group of ten soldiers. They ran him around in circles stabbing him with bayonets until, bleeding profusely, he was too tired to resist. The caretaker, a gentle but strapping man, did not last long. He was soon shot in the back with a pistol, and as he lay dying some of the soldiers took turns stabbing him in the back with a six-inch-long butcher knife.

Perhaps the last image he had before slipping into death was of Double Trouble, a nine-year-old boy soldier dressed in an oversize, faded, purple T-shirt and flip-flops, grabbing the knife and having his turn at plunging it in and out between the shoulders. He then grabbed an empty Coke bottle, which like a *tira de gracia* was broken over the dying man's head. Double Trouble stood up and looked around for the approval of his mates. Like he had just hit a home run. The score, 1–0. They slapped him on the back and cheered.

"Where's your mama?" I asked him after the battle. He had a soft, childish face that hardened between the eyes as he responded. "She dead." "And your daddy?" "He dead too. Everybody dead." "How old are you?" I asked. "Old enough to kill a man," he replied.

Double Trouble. One of thousands of child soldiers in Liberia. Most have experienced more loss and pain before the age of eight than the rest of us do in a lifetime. Many watched their parents killed in front of them, or worse, were forced to kill their loved ones as some sort of perverse initiation rite. But every child needs a family and soon the militia became theirs.

A few days later, a brief cease-fire between the two warring sides was agreed upon. The fighters relaxed. Boys will be boys, I thought, as I came upon a group of five NPFL child soldiers, the eldest not more than twelve, playing soccer on one of the most heavily contested corners of the urban war. I saw their rifles discarded on the street below a rain-soaked Liberian flag, and only then did it become clear that the white "ball" they maneuvered was a human skull. The decaying body lay some twenty meters away.

They kicked the "ball" over the debris of war—spent cartridges, old wallets, clothes dropped by fleeing civilians, and old photographs—and squealed with delight as it entered the goal posts marked by two rusting sardine cans. A glimpse of childhood and they were back behind the barricades the next morning. "Hey, white woman," a boy of about eleven with oversize tennis shoes, a looted hat with yellow flowers, and an AK-47 half his height yelled at me from behind a bullet-pocked wall. "No school today. Nope. Today we gunna kill da Krahn."

Civil Patrols

By Ewen Allison and Robert K. Goldman

In 1982, an army colonel ordered the Guatemalan village of Chichicastenango to form a "Civil Defense Patrol" to help put down an ongoing insurrection. The colonel made it clear that those who refused to sign a commitment to civil patrols would be seen as subversives and killed. The villagers signed.

Hundreds of thousands of Guatemalan civilians had to serve in civil patrols, essentially **paramilitary** groups formed from the civilian population as a means to control them and gain their assistance in the civil war. Already poor, patrollers were forced to purchase weapons and uniform shirts from the army. Members had to patrol continuously for up to twenty-four hours a week, and sometimes went on army-accompanied sweeps that lasted up to several weeks. Males of nearly all ages—even eight-year-olds—were compelled into service. Besides their combat duties, patrollers had to work as laborers for army soldiers. Those who refused to participate had to pay a fine, find a replacement, or face beatings and other severe punishments or even execution, all without trial. Recalcitrant villagers in Chichicastenango were put into a specially dug well fifteen meters deep.

Humanitarian law does not interfere with a government's right to suppress insurrections and implicitly allows a military draft. Human rights law takes a dim view of forcing people to serve in civil patrols. The Inter-American Commission on Human Rights has repeatedly declared that the institution of civil patrols in Guatemala was a restriction of liberty and a form of involuntary servitude, in violation of Articles 6, 7, and 22 of the American Convention on Human Rights.

Yet civil patrollers are not only victims, they are also victimizers. Patrollers in Guatemala beat, tortured, and even killed thousands of suspected subversives, even those who merely refused to serve in the patrols. Sometimes civil patrols were ordered to do these things by army or government officials, sometimes the patrols acted on their own initiative. In either case, patrollers violated not only the human rights of the victims but also the rules of internal armed conflict that call for humane treatment of non-combatants.

Governments are usually held responsible for violations of both humanitarian and human rights law perpetrated by patrollers. This is especially the case when the patrols are organized by government or army officials. Also, governments are held responsible under human rights law when they fail to suppress violations by privately organized armed groups.

(See **compelling military service**; **irregulars**.)

Civil War

By A. P. V. Rogers

C

Treaties on the laws of war were developed to deal with wars between States, not civil wars (or internal armed conflicts as they are now known). They only applied to the latter in the unlikely event that the **belligerent status** of the insurgents was recognized. It was not until after World War II that treaties started to include some provisions on internal armed conflicts to ensure some protection for the victims of those conflicts.

It is never easy to determine when a violent confrontation within a State goes beyond the realms of domestic criminal law and becomes an armed conflict to which international law applies. This is especially the case as the State will be reluctant to admit that it does not have the situation under control, yet dissidents will be quick to claim that theirs is a cause of international concern.

Assuming that threshold is crossed, the international legal rules governing internal armed conflicts are much less developed than those applying to armed conflicts between States. The rules are to be found in basic customary law principles and in Common Article 3 of the 1949 Geneva Conventions. Additionally, certain fundamental (known as "non-derogable") principles of human rights law provide protection for the victims of these conflicts. If dissident forces exercise sufficient control over part of the State's territory as to enable them to carry out sustained and concerted military operations and comply with their obligations under it, Protocol II of 1977 also applies.

The following are the most important rules that apply to all parties to internal armed conflicts:

1. All combat activity must be justified on military grounds; activity that is not militarily necessary is prohibited.

2. Attacks may be directed *only* against objects that make a contribution to the enemy's military effort and hence are of tactical or strategic importance. Incidental loss and damage must be minimized.

3. A distinction must always be made between combatants, who may take a direct part in hostilities and be attacked themselves, and noncombatants, who may not take a direct part in hostilities and may not be attacked or used as shields.

4. Noncombatants and their property must be spared as far as possible from the incidental effects of military operations. Stealing is an offense in war as in peace.

5. Prisoner of war status does not arise in internal armed conflict. Captured persons can be tried under the law of the State where the internal armed conflict is going on for any offenses they may have committed against that law. They have the protections listed in paragraph 6 and under human rights law. Sentences may only be carried out after a proper trial by a properly constituted court.

6. Persons who take no active part in hostilities (noncombatants, captured persons, the wounded, sick, and shipwrecked) are to be treated humanely and equally, irrespective of race, color, religion, sex, wealth, etc. That means there must be no murder, mutilation, cruel treatment, torture, rape, sexual assault, or other outrages on personal dignity, or humiliating or degrading treatment.

Ibo troops retreat during the Nigerian Civil War over the secession of Biafra, 1968.

7. Hostage taking is prohibited.

8. Starvation of noncombatants as a method of warfare is prohibited.

9. The wounded, sick, and shipwrecked must be collected and cared for.

10. Although it may be necessary to evacuate noncombatants from areas of danger, it is prohibited to move them for discriminatory reasons or to shield military targets from attack.

In internal armed conflicts to which Protocol II applies, the above rules are supplemented by more detailed provisions on the protection of the civilian population, especially children, the treatment of detainees, and the conduct of criminal prosecutions.

(See **international vs. internal armed conflict.**)

Civilian Immunity

By Heike Spieker

C

Civilians and civilian objects are protected under the laws of armed conflict by the principle of distinction. Under this principle, parties to an armed conflict must always distinguish between civilians and civilian objects on the one hand, and combatants and military targets on the other.

The meaning of the term was spelled out in Additional Protocol I of 1977. While a number of States have not ratified Protocol I, the obligation to uphold the principle of distinction is also valid as customary law.

The civilian population enjoys immunity insofar as it shall "enjoy general protection against dangers arising from military operations" and "shall not be the object of attack." The Protocol also prohibits actions whose primary purpose is to spread terror among the civilian population. Civilians retain their protected status "unless and for such time as they take a direct part in hostilities"—civilians who join in fighting forfeit their immunity from attack.

Additional Protocol I also prohibits so-called **indiscriminate attacks**, thereby obliging each party to an armed conflict under all circumstances to distinguish at all times between **combatants** and **military objectives**, and civilians or civilian objects. Examples of indiscriminate attack include **carpet bombing** or an attack which may be expected to cause **collateral damage** to civilian persons or objects "which would be excessive in relation to the concrete and direct military advantage anticipated."

Most experts in international law believe that the customary law principle of distinction as a rule applies in both international and non-international armed conflicts. This is supported by the International Committee of the Red Cross Study on Customary International Humanitarian Law. Yet the black letter law is much less explicit in non-international conflict. There is no explicit prohibition of indiscriminate attacks in Additional Protocol II addressing non-international armed conflicts specifically, and the Statute of the International Criminal Court does not criminalize indiscriminate attacks in non-international conflict.

Additional Protocol II does not explicitly distinguish between combatants and civilians and does not even mention the term "combatant." Non-State actors taking a direct part in non-international armed conflict are not granted any right to participate in hostilities and do not enjoy POW status in case of capture. However Protocol II does specify that civilians "shall enjoy general protection against the dangers arising from military operations... unless and for such time as they take a direct part in hostilities."

It explicitly prohibits making civilians as such the object of attack or undertaking acts or threats of violence the primary purpose of which is to spread terror among the civilian population.

Civilians, Illegal Targeting of

C

By Joel Greenberg

On July 25, 1993, Israel launched a massive retaliatory strike against Shiite Muslim guerrillas who had rocketed northern Israeli towns and killed seven Israeli soldiers in a month in the Israeli occupation zone in southern Lebanon.

Operation Accountability began with wide-ranging air strikes across Lebanon and ended six days later with an American-brokered cease-fire. Intensive Israeli air and artillery bombardments forced hundreds of thousands of civilians in southern Lebanon out of their towns and villages.

Israel's openly declared aim was to stop attacks by the Iranian-backed Hezbollah group through the massive displacement of Lebanese civilians. The plight of the refugees streaming north toward Beirut, it was hoped, would compel the Lebanese government and its patron, Syria, to rein in Hezbollah.

Yitzhak Rabin, the Israeli prime minister, put it this way: "The goal of the operation is to get the southern Lebanese population to move northward, hoping that this will tell the Lebanese government something about

the refugees who may get as far north as Beirut."

After issuing warnings, Israel proceeded to attack the hearts of villages, causing civilian casualties. Human Rights Watch said the Israeli Army also executed "what appear to have been calculated direct attacks on purely civilian targets."

The direct targeting of civilians is a breach of the laws of armed conflict. "The civilian population as such, as well as individual civilians, shall not be the object of attack. Acts or threats of violence the primary purpose of which is to spread terror among the civilian population are prohibited," states Additional Protocol I of 1977. Israel has not ratified Protocol I, but this provision, prohibiting direct attacks on civilians, is generally recognized as customary law, universally applicable regardless of ratification.

Nearly three years later, on April 11, 1996, Israel unleashed a similar offensive against Hezbollah, which led to another mass exodus of civilians in southern Lebanon. Operation Grapes of Wrath began with surgical air strikes and ended seventeen days later after an Israeli artillery barrage killed more than one hundred Lebanese refugees sheltering in a United Nations base.

As the bombardment by Israeli warplanes, gunships, and artillery

Was it deliberate? Three civilian passengers died in this minibus on a road near Tibnin, north of Bint Jbeil in southern Lebanon, July 2006. The family had decided to flee the village after hearing Israel's evacuation order, and were waving a large white flag outside the vehicle when they were hit by an Israeli air strike. Human Rights Watch concluded that the incident was at best a case of reckless disregard by Israel of its obligation to avoid targeting civilians. At worst, HRW said, it was a deliberate targeting of civilians.

spread northward, some 400,000 people fled their villages and towns, urged on by radio broadcasts and leaflets that warned them to leave or risk being hit. Amnesty International said that the language of the warnings was intended to threaten civilians, some of whom could not leave because they were too old or too sick to leave, or lacked transport, while others chose to remain to safeguard their property.

A warning broadcast on April 11 over the Voice of the South radio station of the Israeli-backed South Lebanon Army militia said: "If Hezbollah men happen to be near anybody's house, it will be hit." An April 13 message to residents of forty-five villages warned that "any presence in these villages will be regarded as subversive; that is, the subversive elements and whoever happens to be with them will be hit."

The warnings seemed to suggest that the civilians and civilian objects were being targeted as punishment for their association with Hezbollah, rather than being destroyed incident to a legitimate attack on Hezbollah. Whether this or the other possible interpretation—that Israeli authorities were simply cautioning they would hit Hezbollah targets and anyone in the way might well become regrettable civilian collateral damage—the warnings carried an echo of the American **free fire zone** doctrine in Vietnam.

Israeli public statements were more circumspect. When civilians stayed behind in Nabatiyeh al-Fowqa, and were killed in fighter-bomber rocket attacks, Prime Minister Shimon Peres declared: "We only hit at those buildings from which Katyushas were fired... But naturally Nabatiyeh was supposed to be vacant."

Brig. Gen. Giora Inbar, the commander of the Israeli army's liaison unit in southern Lebanon, indicated that the population displacement was not for military advantage but to send a political message: "The residents of southern Lebanon are under pressure... If they understand that the address for peace and quiet is the government of Lebanon, which will impose its authority on Hezbollah, then this pressure is worthwhile."

More bluntly, an Israeli colonel, identified only as "Z," told the Israeli newspaper *Ha'aretz* that if Lebanese leaders "cared about the 400,000 refugees from the south, they would have acted to stop the fighting, but it seems that until thousands of refugees don't leave [the city of] Sidon for Beirut, they won't care."

And the *Wall Street Journal* quoted an unnamed official as saying: "Even if you tie me up and whip me, I'm not going to admit on-the-record that our policy is to force out civilians to put pressure on the Lebanese government. But let's just say we hope Lebanon understands the message."

Displacement of civilians is permitted under the laws of war if it is for their own protection or required for imperative military reasons. In this instance, the International Committee of the Red Cross (ICRC) publicly criticized the attacks as "contrary to international humanitarian law." The ICRC said its rationale drew from the 1899 and 1907 Hague Conventions and Protocol I, Articles 51, 52, and 57, which prohibit: acts or threats of violence, the primary purpose of which is to spread terror among the civilian population; attacks which may be expected to cause incidental loss of civilian life, injury to civilians, damage to civilian objects or a combination thereof, which would be excessive in relation to the concrete and direct military advantage anticipated; and attacks by bombardment by any methods or means which treat as a single military objective a number of clearly separated and distinct military objectives located in a city, town, village or area containing a similar concentration of civilians or civilian objects.
(See **collateral damage**; **indiscriminate attack**.)

Collateral Damage

By Horst Fischer

C

Collateral or incidental damage occurs when attacks targeted at **military objectives** cause civilian casualties and damage to civilian objects. It often occurs if military objectives such as military equipment or soldiers are situated in cities or villages or close to civilians. Attacks that are expected to cause collateral damage are not prohibited *per se*, but the laws of armed conflict restrict **indiscriminate attacks**. Article 57 of the 1977 Additional Protocol I to the 1949 Geneva Conventions states that, in an international conflict, "constant care shall be taken to spare the civilian population, civilians, and civilian objects." In addition, under Article 51, **carpet bombing** is prohibited, as are attacks that employ methods and means of combat whose effects cannot be controlled. Finally, attacks are prohibited if the collateral damage expected from any attack is not proportional to the military advantage anticipated. Military commanders in deciding about attacks have to be aware of these rules and either refrain from launching an attack, suspend an attack if the principle of **proportionality** is likely to be violated, or replan an attack so that it complies with the laws of armed conflict.

In internal conflict, civilians have little legal protection from collateral or incidental damage. Additional Protocol II requires that, so long as they do not take part in hostilities, the civilian population and individual civilians "shall enjoy general protection against the dangers arising from military operations" and "shall not be the object of attack." Protocol II also prohibits acts or threats of violence whose primary purpose is "to spread terror among the civilian population."

Parties to recent major armed conflicts, such as the **Gulf War** and the wars in the former Yugoslavia, have used the term *collateral damage* as part of an effort to demonstrate that their attacks were lawful. The claim is either that no collateral damage was caused or that the damage was minimal or proportional. Neutral observers might reach different conclusions than the parties to these conflicts. The death of many civilians in Iraq during the Gulf War due to the the lack of electricity in hospitals, which was the result of the destruction of almost all Iraqi power plants by allied air attacks, has been asserted by Iraq as disproportionate collateral damage. On the other hand, NATO officials in spring and summer 1995 quite rightly claimed that NATO attacks on Bosnian Serb military targets in Bosnia-Herzegovina did not kill civilians in a disproportionate manner and that therefore collateral damage was proportional.

Thus, besides having legal implications, the term is often used to win political support for a specific method of warfare or to counter allegations of violations of humanitarian law. The observer is reminded that whatever the claims of governments or armed forces, attacks directly targeted at the civilian population are in violation of the basic principle of distinction and cannot be referred to as having caused collateral damage.

(See **civilian immunity**.)

Collective Punishment

By Daoud Kuttab

For fourteen years, George Qumsieh, a stonecutter, worked to build a three-story stone home in the West Bank town of Beit Sahour. In February 1981, he and his family—his wife, four daughters, and three sons—moved into their new home. Nine months later, Israeli soldiers arrived at the home to arrest their youngest son, Walid, aged fifteen. The army accused Walid of having thrown stones at an Israeli military vehicle four days earlier, as a result of which a side window was broken. No soldiers were reported to have been injured in the incident.

The following day, and before the Shin Bet (General Security Service) had completed its interrogation of Walid, more troops arrived at the Qumsieh home. Ariel Sharon, the newly appointed Likud defense minister, had promised an "iron fist" policy against Palestinians. Members of an Israeli engineering brigade placed explosives and blew up the Qumsiehs' stone house. Months later, Walid was sentenced to seven years in jail based on the confession of his friends.

Under the 1949 Geneva Conventions, which protects civilians in occupied territory, collective punishments are a war crime. Article 33 of the Fourth Convention states: "No protected person may be punished for an offense he or she has not personally committed," and "collective penalties and likewise all measures of intimidation or of terrorism are prohibited." Israel does not accept that the Fourth Geneva Convention applies to the West Bank *de jure*, but says it abides by the humanitarian provisions without specifying what the humanitarian provisions are.

By collective punishment, the drafters of the Geneva Conventions had in mind the reprisal killings of World Wars I and II. In the First World War, Germans executed Belgian villagers in mass retribution for resistance activity. In World War II, Nazis carried out a form of collective punishment to suppress resistance. Entire villages or towns or districts were held responsible for any resistance activity that took place there. The conventions, to counter this, reiterated the principle of individual responsibility. The International Committee of the Red Cross (ICRC) Commentary to the Conventions states that parties to a conflict often would resort to "intimidatory measures to terrorize the population" in hopes of preventing hostile acts, but such practices "strike at guilty and innocent alike. They are opposed to all principles based on humanity and justice."

The law of armed conflict applies similar protections to an internal conflict. Common Article 3 of the four Geneva Conventions of 1949 requires fair trials for all individuals before punishment; and Additional Protocol II of 1977 explicitly forbids collective punishment.

Israel's occupation of the West Bank differs from almost all other cases of occupation because it has continued for more than one generation. Demolition of Palestinian houses has been a regular event in the occupied territories. Most often, the army acts following a bombing directed against Israeli civilians. On July 30, 1997, two suicide bombers attacked a market in West Jerusalem, killing fifteen people, including the bombers themselves, and injuring 170. The army responded by punishing the families of those suspected of carrying out the bombing as well as the village they came from. Homes of the families of four residents were completely demolished, as were eight homes in East Jerusalem. For a month, Israeli soldiers barred almost everyone from entering or exiting the West Bank.

Officially, the army destroyed the houses because they were built illegally. However, an unnamed defense official stated that the demolitions were meant as a signal to the Palestinian authorities that they could not "resume normal life until they take certain measures to combat terrorism."

Other security measures by the Israeli Army are no less controversial but are more ambiguous under international law.

Take travel restrictions. Issa from Bethlehem and his fiancée, Farida, from Jerusalem decided to get married on September 13, 1997, in the Mar Elias Christian Church south of Jerusalem. Following the July explosion, the Israeli Army announced a tight closure of the territory under control of the Palestinian Authority. So a Palestinian from Bethlehem could not obtain permission to travel to Jerusalem; and had they decided to move the wedding to Bethlehem, Farida could not have gotten permission to enter the area under Palestinian Authority control. After three abortive attempts to cross Israeli checkpoints, the groom, dressed in his wedding finest, circumvented the restrictions, climbed walls, and walked hours on dirt roads to make the ceremony. Most of the guests stayed home.

Permanent checkpoints between Israel and the occupied West Bank were set up in March 1993, following a series of stabbings in Israel. Palestinians without valid permits were banned from entering Israel. Since then, Israel has repeatedly imposed a "total closure," preventing all Palestinians from reaching hospitals, schools, educational institutions, diplomatic missions, and places of worship in Jerusalem. Travel restrictions, while taken as punishment by those suffering under them, can be but are not necessarily a collective punishment; they may be a security measure in response to a security breach. Some advocates have argued that semipermanent restrictions border on collective punishment.

Cases of collective punishment sharply increased after the beginning of the second Palestinian intifada in October 2000, most notably travel restrictions. Following a suicide attack against Israeli civilians in March 2002, the Israeli army carried out military operations in Palestinian towns that caused widespread destruction of property, and restricted movement still further by banning travel between Palestinian cities and villages in addition to the existing restriction on travel between West Bank and Gaza. In 2004, the Israeli army conducted a far-reaching program of house demolitions in the Gaza town of Rafah following a number of ambushes against Israeli soldiers on a nearby road. According to the United Nations relief agency UNRWA, 180 homes were destroyed in a single week in May. Kofi Annan, then UN Secretary General, described the demolitions as a case of collective punishment.

Colombia

C

By Douglas Farah

Colombia is undergoing one of the world's most complex armed conflicts. For many years, unlike other guerrilla wars in Central and South America, the fighting in Colombia did not so much pit a government army against guerrilla forces as paramilitaries against guerrillas with the army providing tacit support. Recently, many of the paramilitaries have demobilized, but the war goes on and its legacy of violence and displacement continues to distort Colombian society.

Colombia has a long history of bloody political fighting, including the quasi civil war of the 1940s and 1950s known as La Violencia, which pitted armed militias of the Liberal and Conservative parties against each other and nearly destroyed the country. The violence never entirely ceased. It was remnants of the Liberal party militia that formed the first and most prominent guerrilla movement, the Revolutionary Armed Forces of Colombia (FARC), in the 1960s. And it was in response to the rekindled guerrilla threat, first from the FARC and then from the National Liberation Army (ELN), that the first paramilitary formations were set up as ancillary units to the Colombian army.

Colombia, then, has remained mired in a vicious circle of violence and retaliation for several decades. Much of it was cyclical and retaliatory in nature. Both the guerrillas and the paramilitaries regularly resorted to killing members of one another's families. And as they did so, the violence progressively grew more personal and unstoppable. But however bad the violence was in the past, the access of all sides to tens of millions of dollars of drug traffickers' money made the round of internecine fighting and political violence that began in the early 1980s more wide-reaching and less discriminating than ever before.

The money obtained from drug trafficking gave the guerrillas and the paramilitaries access to the international arms market while freeing them from previous constraints on how they used the new weapons they acquired. Their tactics changed as well, although this would probably have happened with or without the involvement of the narcotraffickers. Freed from dependence on States which once supported them as liberation movements (and which might have been expected to pressure them to refrain from certain types of operations), the principal guerrilla groups, the FARC and ELN, have increasingly resorted to kidnappings, assassinations of elected officials, and attacks on oil pipelines. The result has been further, massive displacement of the civilian population. For their part, the paramilitaries engaged in counterinsurgency have carried out massacres, enforced disappearances and torture. And though the number of crimes attributed to the paramilitaries has dropped since they agreed on a ceasefire in 2002, some paramilitary groups appear to be reforming as mafia-like organized crime syndicates, and continue to exercise control through violence and intimidation. A recent law designed to encourage the demobilization of fighters has been criticized for failing to promote accountability for past crimes, and the government has shown little will to stand up to paramilitary leaders.

Following the election of Alvaro Uribe as president in 2002, the

Colombian government stepped up its military campaign against the guerrillas. The guerrillas have been pushed back in some areas, but the army has faced repeated charges of killing civilians; on occasion they have allegedly dressed victims in guerrilla outfits so they could record them as having been killed during combat. The continued targeting of civilians by all sides has led to a major humanitarian crisis, one that continues to be largely unknown outside Colombia. It has been estimated that between two and three million people have become internally displaced from their homes because of the conflict.

The Colombian crisis would exist with or without the drug traffickers. But while they are not at the root of the war, or of the social and historical events that provoked it, they are at the root of the criminalization of the conflict, itself a malign development in contemporary Colombian history. The drug traffickers have shown themselves willing to work with and finance both sides. The situation is far from the ideological contest that marked the Colombian conflict thirty years ago. Guerrillas and paramilitaries alike have

A young girl passes the body of a man executed in Cucuta, Colombia, where a right-wing paramilitary group carried out a wave of killings, March 2005.

grown rich off the war, and the profits that the war has engendered make the prospect of peace that much more elusive.

In the wake of the narcotraffickers have come common criminals who are willing to work for any group willing to pay for their services, and, of course, are even less mindful of the laws of war than the guerrillas and paramilitaries themselves. Perhaps predictably, the violence of the conflict has spilled over into almost every corner of Colombian life. The country is among the most violent in the world. The annual homicide rate in Colombia reached 78 per 100,000 inhabitants a few years ago, and is currently about 44. In contrast, the homicide rate in the United States is about six per 100,000 inhabitants.

This mixture of war and crime—the fighting can be shown to wax and wane according to the amount of narcotics money being channeled to both sides—makes the Colombian conflict very difficult to understand. What is clear, however, is the readiness of all sides to commit grave violations of humanitarian law, although certain groups have tended to commit some violations more than others.

For example, while all sides rely on forced abductions, the FARC, and to a lesser extent the ELN, have come to use kidnapping and hostage taking of civilians both as a political weapon and as a means of obtaining funds. The FARC tends to target politicians and land owners—most notoriously the former presidential candidate Ingrid Betancourt who was seized in 2002—while the ELN has been more prone to kidnap foreigners, especially those whom they believe can be ransomed for large sums. But there are no hard and fast rules. And while kidnapping remains primarily the tool of the guerrillas, the tactic has also been used by right-wing paramilitary organizations.

Massacres and summary executions are another instance of a tactic which, while engaged in by all sides, has been more commonly used by one of the belligerents. It was the paramilitary squads, according to human rights

Colombian Army fighters mobilize in an abandoned building in rebel-held territory, Medio Atrato, Colombia, 2005.

reports, that were the main offenders. Fighters loyal to two former paramilitary leaders, the brothers Fidel and Carlos Castano (both now thought to be dead), were for many years seen as the most frequent users of the tactic. As has so often been the case in Colombia, the Castanos' war against the guerrillas was motivated in large part by family history. The brothers' father was kidnapped by the FARC in the 1970s and held for ransom. The family negotiated with the guerrillas and eventually paid a ransom, but the father was killed anyway, and his body dumped on family property. It is not surprising, in the Colombian context, that upon reaching manhood the Castano brothers founded paramilitary organizations that were responsible for some of the worst massacres Colombia has ever known.

In the case of the Castanos, political violence and crime soon became all but impossible to separate. Their forces were financed by the sale of cocaine, and, in late 1997, Carlos Castano was identified by the U.S. Drug

Enforcement Administration (DEA) as a major drug trafficker. In the field, the Castanos' fighters made a practice of going in the middle of the night to a civilian area with a list of suspected leftists, dragging those they could find from their homes, executing them, and dumping the bodies where they would be seen by as many people as possible. Apparently, it was in retaliation for these acts that the FARC kidnapped and then reportedly killed Fidel Castano in 1994. Carlos Castano is now believed to have been killed in 2004 at the orders of a third brother, Vicente Castano, to prevent his giving evidence to U.S. authorities about the family's drug-trafficking.

The practice of carrying out summary executions has been routinely compounded by the use of torture. Torture is used to extract information, but it is also employed as a punishment and as a deterrent to others. Such killings are only one element in the pattern of direct and indiscriminate attacks against the civilian population in which all sides have regularly engaged. The result of these attacks, which have been little reported even in

Civilians caught in the cross-fire between FARC and Colombian special forces, San Vincente, March, 2002.

the Colombian press, has been hundreds of thousands of internally displaced people both in areas controlled by the guerrillas and areas controlled by the paramilitaries. This toll of internally displaced may be the most catastrophic human effect of all of the Colombian conflict. Even less noted has been the environmental disaster the fighting has caused. Despite widespread international protests, the ELN has regularly blown up oil pipelines that run through virgin jungle, fouling waterways and killing wildlife.

Following the paramilitaries' declaration of a ceasefire in 2002, the government began negotiations over demobilization. At the center of the peace process has been the question of how far fighters who said they were ready to give up violence should be held to account for war crimes they had committed. The Justice and Peace Law, passed in 2005 after years of debate, allowed reduced sentences for war crimes charges without requiring full and truthful confessions, and did not oblige paramilitary leaders to use their often vast fortunes to compensate the relatives of victims. Altogether over 30,000 people have gone through the demobilization process, though many are thought to have been common criminals rather than paramilitaries. In the meantime, human rights organizations say that in many cases the paramilitary groups have kept their internal structures intact and evolved into drug-trafficking cartels that control local politics through intimidation and bribery. In May 2006, Colombia's Constitutional Court overturned parts of the demobilization law, saying that fighters should only benefit from its provisions if they confessed to their crimes and paid full compensation. These new obligations, if enforced by the government, may solve some of the problems of the demobilization process.

Although there has been a reduction in violence over the last couple of years, most independent observers believe that it is too soon to speak of a fundamental improvement in Colombia's prospects. Despite its riches and the talents of its people, Colombia remains a society totally permeated by vio-

Bullet hole from a stray bullet with a view of downtown Medellin. Colombia, 2002.

lence. In one sense, it is a very special case. But, at least to a degree, the drawn-out war in Colombia resembles some of the recent conflicts in Africa in which the decline of the State, and the triumph of a murderous criminality, has led to a fundamental undercutting of the very bases of humanitarian law.

Combatant Status

By A. P. V. Rogers

During an armed conflict, only "combatants" are permitted to "take a direct part in hostilities." Noncombatants who do so lose any protected status that they might have. That is likely to mean that they lose their protection from attack; they are not entitled to be treated as prisoners of war; and they are liable to be prosecuted either as war criminals or, where domestic law applies, as common criminals in respect of any attacks on people or property they have carried out. Some, but not all, authorities consider that unprivileged belligerency or unauthorised combatancy is a war crime in itself.

Combatants are all members of the armed forces of a party to the conflict except medical and religious personnel. Members of a **levée en masse** are also regarded as combatants. Combatants cannot be punished for their hostile acts and if captured can only be held as POWs until the end of hostilities.

The term "taking a direct part in hostilities" certainly includes attacking enemy combatants or military objectives and it may extend to some support activities but the precise meaning of the term remains controversial.

The armed forces consist of all organized armed forces, groups and units which: a. are under a command responsible for the conduct of its subordinates to a party to the conflict; b. are subject to an internal disciplinary system which enforces compliance with the law of armed conflict; and c. whose members, at least when deployed on military operations, wear uniform or combat gear that distinguishes them from the civilian population.

Medical and religious personnel, like civilians, are noncombatants. They may not take a direct part in hostilities and so long as they do not do so are legally protected from attack. Medical personnel may, however, use small arms in self-defence if unlawfully attacked. Religious personnel are not armed.

The composition of the armed forces is a matter for the State or faction concerned. Its components may be regular units, reservists, territorial defence units, citizens called up for part-time service or full-time soldiers as long as the conditions set out above are fulfilled. It is normal for members of the armed forces to have ranks, the more senior ranks having power to give orders to, and exercise discipline over, their subordinates.

Violation of the law of armed conflict does not mean loss of combatant status so long as those responsible are tried and punished. If members of an armed group consistently violate the law of armed conflict and are not punished, that is strong evidence that the group does not qualify as "armed forces", since it fails to meet the criterion of an internal disciplinary system, and that its members do not have combatant status.

In unusual circumstances where it is impossible to wear uniform or combat gear all the time, such as when operating in areas under adverse occupation, behind enemy lines or, in liberation conflicts, in areas controlled by government forces, combatants must, at the very least, carry their arms openly during military engagements or when visible to the enemy in military deployments preceding the launch of any attack.

C

When they surrender or are captured, combatants are entitled to be treated as prisoners of war, though this can mean their internment until the close of active hostilities. If there is any doubt about their status, this must be resolved by a properly constituted tribunal. Unauthorised combatants, or unprivileged belligerents, who surrender or are captured may also be interned if the security of the detaining State makes it absolutely necessary. Those of them who qualify as "protected persons" under the Geneva Civilian Convention are entitled to the protection of that convention. Others are entitled at the very least to the rights of humane treatment and of fair trial.

(See **Guantanamo; guerrillas; irregulars; mercenaries; prisoners of war; protected persons; soldiers, rights of.**)

Some 3,000 Taliban and al-Qaeda fighters captured in Kunduz are held in a prison controlled by General Abdul Rashid Dostum built to house 800. Shiberghan, Afghanistan. December 2001.

Command Responsibility

By Nomi Bar-Yaacov

C

In January 1988, barely one month into the Intifada uprising against Israeli occupation of the West Bank and Gaza Strip, Col. Yehuda Meir ordered troops under his command to round up twenty Palestinian men from Hawara and Beita, two Arab villages in the West Bank, bind them in handcuffs and blindfolds, and break their bones. The unit commander reporting to Meir passed on the order to his troops, but told them he did not require them to comply. Some soldiers refrained from doing so, but others carried out the order with such zeal that they broke their truncheons. The defense minister at the time, Yitzhak Rabin, publicly spoke of the need to "break the bones of Intifada rioters."

Although Meir was not present during the incident, he was the superior commanding officer in the area.

It took some months before military police, following a request by the International Committee of the Red Cross (ICRC), launched an investigation. The army chief of staff summoned Meir and offered him the choice: to appear before a disciplinary military court for a severe reprimand and discharge from the army, or to face a court-martial. Meir accepted the first option, under which he was to go to work for the State security service until he could begin retirement on his colonel's pension.

When word of the behind-the-scenes deal became public, the Association for Civil Rights in Israel petitioned the Israeli High Court of Justice, demanding that Meir be court-martialed.

The High Court ruled unanimously that Meir should be tried in a special military tribunal for torture, intentionally causing bodily harm, and grievous assault, which are grave breaches of the Geneva Conventions, and also for unbecoming conduct.

"These actions outrage every civilized person, and no lack of clarity can cover it up" Justice Moshe Bejski said. "Certainly, if the order is given by a senior officer, that officer must be aware that the morality of the Israeli Defense Forces forbids such behavior."

Following the High Court's decision, Meir went on trial before a special military tribunal in Tel Aviv in April 1991. He was found guilty, demoted to private's rank, and deprived of his colonel's pension.

Meir's case points to two critical issues of international humanitarian law (IHL). Can obedience to superior orders be a defense against allegations of war crimes? And how far up the chain of command does "command responsibility" reach?

The answer to the first question is that a claim of superior orders cannot serve as a defense against an allegation of grave breaches or other serious violations of IHL. It should be noted, however, that the illegality of the orders was blatant and undeniable in Meir's case. In other cases, the illegality may not be so apparent, and a war crimes prosecution may fail if the subordinate is not shown to have acted "willfully" in the sense of knowing or having reason to know that the order was illegal. In addition, although a claim of superior orders cannot serve as an affirmative defense, it may be part of a claim of duress—such as a threat to execute the subordinate for failure to carry out orders—that may be offered in mitigation.

The second issue is how far up the chain of command responsibility extends. Article 86 of Additional Protocol I to the 1949 Geneva Conventions states: "The fact that a breach of the Conventions or of this Protocol was committed by a subordinate does not absolve his superiors from penal or disciplinary responsibility, as the case may be, if they knew, or had information which would have enabled them to conclude in the circumstances at the time, that he was committing or was going to commit such a breach, and if they did not take all feasible measures within their power to prevent or repress the breach."

This rule applies to officers. Therefore command responsibility extends as high as any officer in the chain of command who knows or has reason to know that his subordinates are committing war crimes and fails to act to stop them. Although Israel has not ratified Additional Protocol I, it is clear from Israeli Supreme Court practice that its domestic law embraces these internationally recognized standards for superior orders and command responsibility. The United States, also not a party to the Protocol, similarly accepts this principle.

Under the 1998 statute of the new International Criminal Court, a military commander is liable for crimes that he "knew or should have known" about under circumstances at the time, and only for those crimes committed by forces under his "effective command and control." He is liable if he "failed to take all necessary and reasonable measures" to prevent and repress such crimes that subordinates "were committing or about to commit," or for failing to report such crimes to proper authorities.

Various cases have raised difficult questions, starting with the famous Yamashita case heard by an American military commission in the Philippines following World War II. This tribunal held the Japanese officer who had led the defense of the Philippines, General Tomoyuki Yamashita, to what many critics, including two dissenting U.S. Supreme Court opinions, thought to be an extraordinarily high standard of responsibility for the actions of his subordinates, under circumstances where he had lost almost all command, control, and communications over them. In practical terms, command responsibility is not taken to extend as far up the chain of command as might logically be implied, that is, to commanders in chief, and is generally confined to officers in some meaningful supervisory capacity.

The war crimes tribunals for former Yugoslavia and Rwanda have determined that the principle of command responsibility can apply to civilians and military officials outside a clear structure of command, if the accused had effective control over the people directly responsible for the crimes at the time they were committed, and knew or had reason to know about what was taking place.

Meir argued in his own defense that he was acting in accord with his understanding of orders given by his superiors. The tribunal rejected his argument. The judges concluded that political and high-ranking military officials had not given orders to break bones. Consequently, the State prosecutor's office decided not to pursue charges against Ehud Barak, the chief of staff at the time, Rabin, the minister of defense, or Maj. Gen. Yitzhak Mordechai, the commanding officer of the central zone.

Officers and soldiers who carried out Meir's orders in the Hawara and Beita affair were tried in special military courts. Their arguments that they were merely "obeying orders" were rejected and they served time in prison. (See **Arab-Israeli wars; willfulness**.)

Compelling Military Service

By Patrick J. Sloyan

C

It was the standard practice for American infantry in Vietnam, where boobytraps and minefields threatened unspeakable horrors. Lt. William Diehl still remembers the day as a platoon leader on a jungle patrol.

One of their prisoners, a suspected Viet Cong guerrilla, was brought to the front of the line of soldiers. A rope was placed around the prisoner's neck and the platoon point man prodded the prisoner to lead the way. They had not gone far when the human mine detector broke a tripwire and set off a buried

My Lai massacre victims: Approximately twenty villagers survived, only to be used as human mine detectors.

shell. This time, however, the tactic failed. The blast was so powerful that it killed the point man, ripping his heart from his chest. It also wounded Diehl. Some nights, Diehl can still see the point man's heart pulsating on the jungle trail. He was certain some Vietnamese children, their mothers and grandparents living nearby were responsible. "We always believed the mines were planted by the villagers," Diehl said.

Diehl's unit violated U.S. Army training and at least three of the laws of war. Prisoners, whether military POWs or enemy civilians, cannot be forced to serve in military operations, be involved in dangerous work, or be subjected to cruel or inhumane treatment. What Diehl observed in Vietnam was specifically banned by Article 52 of the Third Geneva Convention of 1949.

Using human mine detectors had become commonplace during the ten-year war. In the My Lai massacre on March 16, 1968, troops of the Americal Division destroyed an entire village and killed more than five hundred old men, women, children, and infants. Only about twenty were spared; "In case we hit the minefield," Lt. William Calley later told an Army court-martial.

The motive for making civilians walk through minefields was survival. Almost a third of the fifty-eight thousand American soldiers who died in Vietnam were killed by a boobytrap or a mine; 40 per cent of the 153,000 wounded fell to a similar weapon. But the Geneva Conventions of 1949, which cover international, and, as in the case of Vietnam, "internationalized" conflicts, leave no doubt it is a war crime to force a captured soldier or civilian to "walk the point."

"Compelling a prisoner of war to serve in the forces of the hostile power" is a grave breach, according to the Third Geneva Convention. Unless he volunteers, employing a POW on unhealthy or dangerous labor is banned. The Third Convention specifies that the "removal of mines or similar devices shall be considered as dangerous labor." POWs also cannot be forced to do dangerous work or work for which they are physically unsuited; they can only be forced to work in sectors that are not military in nature or purpose.

Under the Fourth Geneva Convention, civilians cannot be forced into military service but can be interned and compelled to work under the same conditions as nationals of the occupying power. Internees may volunteer to work for the "needs of the army of occupation" but not its "strategic or tactical requirements" such as digging trenches, or building fortifications and bases. Non-internees may not be compelled to work.

The U.S. Army was well aware of the practice of using enemy POWs and civilians to clear mines during the war and of its criminal nature. By the time of Calley's trial, the Infantry School at Fort Benning had produced a training film showing an army platoon in a Vietnamese village. The lieutenant tells his sergeant to take some of the villagers and run them through a suspected area. "You want me, Lieutenant, to take the villagers and run them through a minefield?" the sergeant asks. Pressed to repeat the order, the officer backs down.

During the 1991 **Gulf War**, the lesson was remembered. Norman Schwarzkopf, a lieutenant colonel in Calley's Americal Division in Vietnam, was in command. Confronted by desert belts of Iraqi landmines and aware that thousands of Iraqi prisoners would surrender rather than fight, Schwarzkopf ordered perhaps the most ambitious effort to prevent war crimes ever conducted on a battlefield. Every officer and enlisted soldier was lectured on the rules of land warfare and the proper treatment of prisoners. According to personnel in the International Committee of the Red Cross (ICRC) legal division, they were contacted almost daily by members of Schwarzkopf's staff on the finer points of the laws of war.
(See **forced labor**.)

Concentration Camps

By Ed Vulliamy

**The laws governing warfare and conflict make no reference to concentra-
tion camps. But for more than a century, concentration camps have been
a venue for wholesale war crimes and the symbol of the worst abuses
against civilians in wartime.**

It was a Spanish general, Valeriano Weyler, who established the first *recon-
centrados* or "concentration centers" in Cuba in his drive to suppress the
1895 rebellion. Britain introduced concentration camps on a massive scale
during the Boer War from 1899 to 1902. To deny the Boer guerrillas food and
intelligence, Gen. Lord Kitchener ordered the British Army to sweep the
Transvaal and Orange River territories of South Africa "clean." Civilians—
women, children, the elderly, and some men of fighting age—were herded
from their homes and concentrated in camps along railway lines, with a view
to their eventual removal from the territory. The Boers, to whom these camps
became a symbol of genocide, called them *laagers.*

The Nazis developed a vast network of *Konzentrationslager,* using them
at first to hold political prisoners, later slave labor, and finally to annihilate
European Jewry and to kill large numbers of Poles, Russians, and Gypsies. Of
the nearly 6 million Jews killed under Hitler's "Final Solution," 2 million died
in Auschwitz, the main extermination center.

No one in the post–World War II generation could have anticipated the
reappearance of such camps in Europe. On that August 1992 day when my
colleagues and I from the British television network ITN alighted from our
vans, it was hard to gauge who was more amazed to see whom. Before us,
there was a landscape of human misery that seemed to recall another time:
men, some of them skeletal, lined up behind a barbed wire fence, with
lantern jaws and xylophone ribcages visible beneath their putrefied skin.
They, in turn, saw a camera crew and a clutch of reporters advancing across
the withered summer grass.

This was Logor Trnopolje, a teeming mass of wretched humanity—
scared, sunburned, and driven out of house and home. Among them was the
figure of Fikret Alic, whose emaciated torso behind sharp knots of wire would
become the enduring symbol of Bosnia's war, of its cruelty and its echo of
the worst calamities of our century. Alic had come from yet another camp,
Kereterm, where he had broken down in tears, having been ordered to help
clear up some 150 corpses, the result of the previous night's massacre.

I ventured into Trnopolje, past families crammed against one another on
the floor of what had been a school, past stinking holes dug into the ground
for what were intended to be cesspits. "I can't tell you everything that goes
on," said one young inmate, Ibrahim Demirovic, "but they do whatever they
want." A gracious doctor, Idriz, had been put in charge of a "medical center"
where he gave us an undeveloped film—it showed his patients, beaten literally black and blue.

The day after the discovery of Trnopolje and Omarska, I shied from calling them concentration camps because of the inevitable association with the
bestial policies of the Third Reich. I reasoned that we must take extreme care
in relating genocides of our lifetime and the Holocaust, which was singular

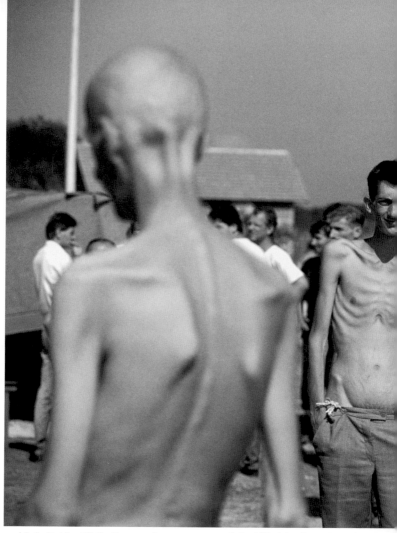

and inimitable. While thousands were purposefully killed in the gulag of Serbian camps, did that equate with the Nazis' industrial mass murder of Jews and others?

On reflection, *concentration camp* is exactly the right term for what we uncovered that day. For here civilian populations were literally *concentrated* —frog-marched in columns or bused to locations for illegal purposes of mal-treatment, torture, abuse, killing, and, crucially, enforced transfer, or **ethnic cleansing**. Indeed, the UN's independent Commission of Experts determined after a year long study that Trnopolje was a concentration camp, and Omarska and Keraterm "de facto death camps."

In general, the laws which would apply to concentration camps address the topic piecemeal, and the principal element is **unlawful con-finement**, a grave breach of the Fourth Geneva Convention. Confinement of civilians is not necessarily unlawful. "Foreign" civilians who pose a threat to a party to a conflict may be put in "places of internment" or given an "assigned residence." However, the threat they pose must be genuine, evi-denced by some clear action, not merely by their nationality. It is also lawful to remove civilians for their own security in an emergency, such as an impending battle, and set up temporary shelters for them. Even so, they

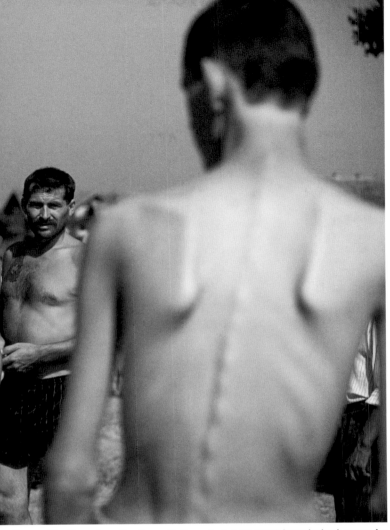

Images like these from the Trnopolje Camp in August 1992 brought back memories of the Nazi camps. But these were run by Serbs, for Bosnians.

must be returned home as soon as it is safe to do so and be well cared for in the meantime. Also, some civilians may be held or imprisoned as suspects or criminals, so long as they are given **due process**. In an internal conflict, noncombatants may be interned but are entitled to humane treatment and the judicial protections guaranteed by a regularly constituted court. None of these safeguards exist in concentration camps. Confinement under such conditions is thus unlawful. The arbitrary imprisonment of large numbers of civilians during conflicts—internal or international—can be a crime against humanity.

The themes of the "concentration" and "clearance" of civilians came to dominate the last phase of the Boer War, just as they dominated the entire Bosnian War, most notably in its early stages. As we know, the removal of Muslims and Croats from Serbian terrain was not a by-product of a war between armies, it was the *raw material*, the declared aim, of the Serbs.

The Boer War concentration camps aroused outrage and fury back in Britain, led by temperance crusader Emily Hobhouse. She described "deportations ... a burned-out population brought in by hundreds of convoys ...

semi-starvation in the camps . . . fever-stricken children lying on the bare earth . . . appalling mortality."

The camps provoked Lloyd George to thunder, "When is a war not a war? When it is carried on by methods of barbarism." Even the all-woman Fawcett Committee, which supported the British war but made intrepid inspections of the concentration camps, was struck by the conditions at Mafeking, where women were washing clothes in water fouled by excreta, or at Brandfort, where an epidemic killed 337 people in three weeks. These places were by no means Auschwitz or Belsen, but they *were* concentration camps.

The term concentration camp implies not so much a prison or assigned residence for POWs or even civilians, but a role in an overall process of "clearance." The fact that the Serbs sought to defend Trnopolje by describing it as a "transit camp" confirms the point: there is an entwinement between concentration camps and the forced movement or clearance of population.

In their description of Trnopolje in the trial verdict against Dusko Tadic, judges in The Hague noted that "there was no regular regime of interrogations or beating, as in other camps, but beatings and killings did occur." They referred to testimony about "dead people wrapped in paper and wired together, their tongues pulled out. . . and the slaughtered bodies of young girls and old men." The judges acknowledged that some inmates were allowed to forage for food in the village beyond the camp. But this "in effect amounted to imprisonment," since many were killed during these excursions, and survivors feared repeating them.

Moreover, "because this camp housed the largest number of women and girls, there were more rapes at this camp than any other. Girls between the ages of 16 and 19 were at the greatest risk . . . the youngest girl being 12 years of age." One girl serially raped by seven Serbian soldiers suffered "terrible pains . . . and hemorrhaging."

But what hallmarked Trnopolje was the fact that the camp was, as the judges said, "the culmination of the campaign of ethnic cleansing, since those Muslims and Croats who were not killed at the Omarska and Kereterm camps were, from Trnopolje, deported." This is one of the defining essences of concentration camps—that the detaining power wishes to be rid of their inmates, either by killing them, or else by enforced transit elsewhere.

In the case of Trnopolje, these transits—the concentration camp's purpose—were utterly terrifying. I went on one of them, in this instance of Muslims from the town of Sanski Most. Because they were **internal displacements**, from Serb-controlled northern Bosnia into government-held regions, they attracted little attention aside from the news media.

A year later, in September 1993, I found myself uncovering another concentration camp: Dretelj. This time the inmates were Muslims, their guards Bosnian-Croat. Most of the prisoners were locked away in the dank darkness of two underground hangars, dug into facing hillsides. The metal doors had been slid open for our visit, but many men preferred to stay inside, staring as though blind into the ether. "We're not really allowed out," said one. These men had been locked in here for up to seventy-two hours at a time, without food or water, drinking their own urine to survive. They all remembered the night in July 1993 when the Croat guards got drunk and began firing through the doors—between ten and twelve men died that night; the back wall of the hangar was pockmarked with bullets.

The plan was simple; the Bosnian Croat authorities explained them to the United Nations High Commission for Refugees (UNHCR) at a meeting in the coastal resort of Makarska during the week before our discovery of the camp. The proposal was to ship fifty thousand Muslim men to a transit camp at nearby Ljubuski, and thence to third countries. The Croatian Foreign Minister Mate Granic said his country would do all it could to help. Would the UNHCR? The aid workers were flabbergasted, caught in a heinous dilemma: to cooperate with the aim of Dretelj and three other concentration camps, or else to leave the men festering in conditions which had been hidden from the International Committee of the Red Cross for two months.

Any such fulfillment of the concentrations camps' goal is illegal **deportation** anyway. But in addition to its laws on confinement, the Fourth Geneva Convention of 1949 does regulate the transfer of internees—to take the Serbs' and Croats' own sanitized description of their concentration camps. This shall, says Article 127, "always be effected humanely," and as a general rule by rail or other means of transport. "If, as an exceptional measure, such removals have to be effected on foot, they may not take place unless the internees are in a fit state of health."

The convention continues: "When making decisions regarding the transfer of internees, the detaining power shall take their interests into account, and in particular shall not do anything to increase the difficulties of repatriating them or returning them to their own homes." At the time of writing, that provision, with regard to those "concentrated" at Trnopolje and Dretelj, remains infamously and horribly unfulfilled.

Congo, Democratic Republic of

By Gérard Prunier

The massive conflict lasting from 1996 to 2003 that drew in seven African countries and led to about three million deaths—the greatest number of fatalities in any war since World War Two—started as a direct consequence of the 1994 Rwandan genocide.

The Rwandan genocide, in which approximately 800,000 people were killed in a hundred days, took place between April and June 1994. Following the overthrow of the genocidal Hutu regime by Tutsi rebels, over a million and a half Hutu refugees fled Rwanda, with the majority going to Zaire (as it then was). Some left of their own free will but most were herded by the leaders of the *génocidaire*

government, which intended to use them as political hostages. The United Nations, having done nothing to stop the genocide, treated the massive refugee exodus simply as a humanitarian crisis, and provided the refugees with food and medical help. If this seemed an appropriate response, given the fact that most of the refugees were innocent civilians, it meant that the UN closed its eyes to the presence of 50,000 armed men from the former Forces Armées Rwandaises (FAR) and of perhaps as many armed militiamen from the notorious Interahamwe militia, a paramilitary force that had been at the forefront of the killing.

Thus over 100,000 armed men, guilty of the most heinous crimes, were allowed to settle a few miles away from the border of the country where they had committed a genocide. Like the rest of the refugees, they were fed by the international community, even as they trained to invade their country of origin. After two years of useless arguments with the United Nations, the new Rwandan government decided to take matters into its own hands and invaded Zaire in 1996.

After such a long wait, Rwanda had come to the conclusion that the UN was toothless and that Rwanda could do what it wanted in Central Africa. Paul Kagame, Rwanda's strongman, made a discreet deal with Washington: he—and a group of allied African countries that included Zimbabwe, Eritrea, Angola

Residents of Goma, eastern Congo, salute Laurent Kabila after his Rwandan-backed rebel army captures the town from the Mobutu government, May 1997.

and Uganda—would rid the Americans of the ageing and now useless Zairian leader, President Mobutu, at the same time as dismantling the Rwandan refugee camps. The ensuing "military campaign" was in fact a long walk through the enormous expanse of Zaire. The last stand of the Zairian tyranny was left to the troops of Jonas Savimbi, Mobutu's old Angolan guerilla ally, who fought a desperate pitched battle at Kikwit to try to stop the advance on the Zairian capital Kinshasa. The attempt was unsuccessful and long columns of victorious and exhausted boy-soldiers walked into the capital under the cautious cheers of a populace that did not know what to make of this extraordinary "campaign."

Meanwhile the Rwandans had taken advantage of their march across Zaire to track down and kill between 200,000 and 300,000 Hutu refugees. Some of those may have taken part in the genocide but the vast majority of the victims were women, old people and children—in other words, those who had no weapons and could not escape. Most of the real *génocidaires,* armed young men

Refugees flee after a rebel attack on Bule and Fataki, northeastern Congo, June 2003

in good health, managed to get away, some of them walking as far as Congo-Brazzaville or northern Angola.

The Rwandan government picked a forgotten Congolese radical, Laurent-Désiré Kabila, to be head of the new government. However it was the Rwandans who occupied all the key positions, civilian and military. For the next fourteen months, tiny Rwanda tried to run giant Zaire (which was now renamed the Democratic Republic of Congo to erase any memory of the Mobutu regime) as a kind of colony. As was predictable, this attempt failed.

"Africa's first world war": this is the name that many Africans gave to the massive conflict which re-ignited from the still-warm embers of the previous one on August 2, 1998. What happened was that all the participants in the first (or so-called "Mobutu") war fell out among themselves, taking sides with a kind of mindless automatism reminiscent of the deadly alliances which had set Europe on fire in August 1914 .

The war was initiated by President Kabila when, in July 1998, he suddenly decided to dispense with his overbearing Rwandan minders and sent them packing. Within a week the ousted Rwandans were back. They hijacked a number of civilian planes in the Eastern Congo and flew them to Kitona air base, near Kinshasa, hoping to take the capital by storm. Since Kabila's army was almost nonexistent, the Rwandan assault nearly succeeded. The only thing that stopped it was the decisive military intervention of the Angolan army, whose combat helicopters slaughtered the Rwandan troops as they approached Kinshasa.

The Angolan government came to Kabila's defense because it feared that if the Rwandans won they would strike an alliance with the Angolan rebel leader Jonas Savimbi, the head of the UNITA movement. Zimbabwe and Namibia quickly followed Angola's lead and sent troops to Kabila's assistance. Meanwhile, in alliance with Rwanda, Uganda and Burundi had occupied large chunks of the Eastern Congo. Once the Rwandan blitzkrieg had failed, the conflict turned into a bloody and slogging unsuccessful attempt at a remake of the "Mobutu war."

Bodies of Hema men executed by Lendu militia lie on the road north of Fataki, northeastern Congo. They were bound and impaled before being shot. June 2003.

Instead of the confused rabble which had made up Mobutu's army, the Rwandans were now facing professional troops who knew how to fight and who had reasonably good equipment. This time the fighting was fierce.

On the Northern front, the Mouvement de Libération du Congo (MLC), a Congolese rebel group sponsored and armed by Uganda, attempted to fight its way down the course of the Congo River to Kinshasa. The main fighting on this front was bloody but broadly complied with the rules of war. But massive violations of humanitarian law occurred in the rear of the fighting, where the MLC was trying to control diamond and gold mines. Mining towns were taken, lost and retaken in a wild melee and many civilians were killed. Rebel troops were repeatedly accused of cannibalism at the expense of their pygmy guides. Here cannibalism was not linked to traditional practices but was a deliberate modern form of terrorizing the population.

By far the worst crimes took place on the war's eastern front, which extended from the Province Orientale bordering on the Sudan, through North and South Kivu down to northeastern Katanga. In this region, the Ugandan and Rwandan armies supported various factions of the Rassemblement Congolais pour la Démocratie (RCD), a largely artificial organization made up of ambitious politicians, disaffected military men and child soldiers. Here the war reached its worst horrors. The Rwandan army, on the pretext of finding and destroying the former *génocidaires*, behaved in the most brutal fashion, slaughtering civilians and remorselessly stripping the country of all the mineral assets it could lay its hands on. This behavior triggered a violent reaction from local tribal militias called Mayi-Mayi who rose against the Rwandans and fought them. But given their undisciplined character and their use of child soldiers, these nationalist militias were often as cruel and destructive towards civilians as the Rwandans and their local allies. Villages were repeatedly looted by all sides, women were raped and adolescent boys forcibly inducted into the various armies. People fled the towns, hiding in the forest. Since malaria was rife and hospitals had run out of medicines, thousands died. In this most fertile country the fields were abandoned (cultivating them was too dangerous) and the refugees starved in the forests. Traders who still dared to venture on the potholed roads were attacked and the markets closed down.

Further north, the Ugandan Army had at first kept a modicum of respect for civilians, but it eventually became involved in a bloody agrarian conflict in the Ituri area of the Province Orientale. Ugandan officers sided with local warlords and condoned massive atrocities. During the years 1998 to 2001, at the height of the conflict, the whole eastern part of the Congo became an inferno of violence. In addition to the exactions of the Rwandan and Ugandan Armies, the RCD, and the Mayi-Mayi, the Interahamwe former *génocidaires* also committed atrocities in order to force the local peasants to give them support.

The war officially ended in April 2003 through a compromise peace sponsored by the South African government and all foreign military forces withdrew from the Democratic Republic of Congo. A coalition government was set up in Kinshasa, with the various rebel groups joining the government of Joseph Kabila (Laurent-Désiré Kabila had been murdered in January 2001 by one of his own bodyguards and his son had succeeded him). Nearly three million people had died, more than three-quarters through starvation and lack of medical care rather than the direct effects of combat. The country's infrastructure, already poor because of the neglect and corruption of the Mobutu years, had practically disappeared. There were no more roads, most schools were understaffed and in shambles, and the health system was almost nonexistent. The war had had another disastrous effect: thousands of women had been raped, many of them by men who were HIV positive. As a result AIDS spread rapidly throughout Eastern Congo. There was not the slightest foundation for a system of anti-retroviral drug distribution and even condoms were largely out of the reach of people who did not even have enough money to buy second-hand clothes (in this highly religious land attendance at Church services dropped drastically because people were ashamed to come into the house of God in dirty rags).

The peace agreement called for the creation of a national army but this proved difficult to achieve as the various armed groups were accustomed to obeying only their militia commanders and refused any centralized discipline. In Ituri, the Ugandans were reluctant to leave and continued their support of rival warlord militias, which colluded with them in looting the country through most of 2004. Ultimately a more aggressive approach by UN peacekeeping troops brought a modicum of order to this region in early 2005. However in North and South Kivu, armed groups of "demobilized" young men and children (often orphans) continued to brutalize the region, looting, killing and raping. In many ways, most of Congo remained hostage to the unending confusion of the East, where Rwanda kept its ties to armed groups in the hope of retaining influence and perhaps of one day making a military and economic comeback.

In Kinshasa, the transitional government remained divided between former rebels and former Kabila loyalists. Progress towards holding elections was slow, but after being postponed in 2005, legislative and presidential elections were held in June and July 2006 respectively. The elections were largely peaceful, except in Kinshasa where the rivalry between the incumbent Joseph Kabila and his closest rival, former MLC leader Jean-Pierre Bemba, exploded in an armed confrontation causing several casualties. In the second round of the presidential elections, held at the end of October

Goldmining in Wasta, northeastern Congo, is now under the control of fighting forces, which profit by exploiting Congo's mineral wealth. October 2004.

2006, Kabila secured a decisive victory and began a new five-year term as the country's elected leader. Early in 2007, the Congolese war became the subject of the likely first trial before the International Criminal Court, when a pre-trial chamber approved charges of forcibly recruiting child soldiers against the militia leader Thomas Lubanga.

For the Democratic Republic of Congo, the ghosts of the last war still seem uncomfortably alive, even though they are largely contained in the Eastern part of the country. It is to be hoped that a progressive normalization will follow the elections, and that the country's prodigious mineral riches and huge hydroelectric resources (Congo could supply power to the whole continent) will finally be harnessed for the economic development of what is potentially Africa's richest nation.

(See **courts and tribunals; refoulement; Rwanda**.)

Courts and Tribunals

C

By Charles Garraway

"Crimes against international law are committed by men, not by abstract entities, and only by punishing individuals who commit such crimes can the provisions of international law be enforced."

These words are taken from the judgment of the International Military Tribunal at Nuremberg. This was the first attempt in modern times to hold accountable in criminal proceedings before an international tribunal the per-petrators of crimes against international law. An earlier attempt at the end of World War I to establish a Tribunal to try the Kaiser for "a supreme offence against international morality and the sanctity of treaties" had collapsed when the Dutch authorities refused to hand him over for trial. War crimes tri-als were held before the Supreme Court in Leipzig but these were before domestic courts and were described by one commentator as a "judicial farce." The record of domestic courts in enforcing international law has not been impressive.

Following Nuremberg, and its sister Tribunal in Tokyo, the newly formed United Nations adopted the "Nuremberg Principles" establishing much of the jurisprudence but the Cold War prevented any further attempts to build on those foundations. Although consideration was given to the formation of an International Criminal Court to sit alongside the International Court of Justice, States were not prepared to give up their sovereign rights to that extent and the proposal was stalled.

It was only in the 1990s after the end of the Cold War that the project gained renewed support. This arose as a result of the atrocities committed during the breakup of the Yugoslav Republic and of the genocide in Rwanda. The United Nations Security Council established ad hoc Tribunals to try those responsible for genocide, crimes against humanity and war crimes. The Statutes of the Tribunals were based strongly on the Nuremberg precedent. In the case of Rwanda, the Statute broke new ground in granting international jurisdiction for the first time over war crimes committed in a non-interna-tional armed conflict.

These developments led on to renewed efforts to establish an International Criminal Court. After lengthy negotiations, a Statute was adopted in 1998 and the Court came into effect in 2002 after the Statute had received the necessary number of State ratifications. The Court is treaty based and only has jurisdiction where crimes listed in the Statute are com-mitted either by a national of a State Party or on the territory of a State Party. In addition, the Security Council can refer a situation to the Court under its binding powers, thus granting it jurisdiction. To date (2007), there have been three State referrals, Uganda, Democratic Republic of Congo and Central African Republic, and one referral by the Security Council, Darfur. The Prosecutor has opened investigations into all these except the Central African Republic where at the time of writing he is still carrying out a prelim-inary analysis.

The crimes listed in the Statute are genocide, crimes against humanity and war crimes with each crime closely defined both in the Statute itself and in a subsidiary document, "Elements of Crimes." The Court will also have jurisdiction in the future over aggression but subject to a definition being agreed and adopted by the States Parties. There are currently (2007) around 100 States Party to the Statute though there are some important absentees, including the United States, Russia and China. The United States originally signed the Statute but has since withdrawn its signature and has sought bilateral agreements with States to prevent its personnel being handed over to the ICC. It did not, however, oppose the Darfur referral in the Security Council but instead abstained on the vote.

The main difference between the International Criminal Court and the ad hoc Tribunals is in the nature of their jurisdiction. The ad hoc Tribunals were established by the United Nations Security Council under its binding powers and have compulsory jurisdiction with primacy over domestic State courts. The International Criminal Court on the other hand is designed to be "complementary" to domestic State Courts and will only be able to act where a State with jurisdiction is "unable" or "unwilling" to act itself. The onus is

TV set in a Kraljevo, Serbia, bar shows ex-President Slobodan Milosevic defending himself before the International Criminal Tribunal in The Hague, an important precursor for the International Criminal Court, 2002.

therefore placed on national courts to take responsibility. Already, many States Parties to the Statute have introduced national legislation, some for the first time, giving their domestic courts jurisdiction over the crimes listed in the Statute in order to ensure that they can take advantage of the "complementarity" provisions.

Whilst the International Criminal Court may provide a forum for some future conflicts, there remain many which fall outside its scope either because of timing (the International Criminal Court does not have retroactive jurisdiction) or because relevant States were not Parties to the International Criminal Court Statute. The trend in such cases has been towards placing greater responsibility on States themselves rather than establishing new international tribunals. The ad hoc Tribunals have been criticized for being too expensive, too remote (they are located outside the territories with which they deal) and too slow. Inevitably, they can only deal with a small number of major cases and some other forum will be required to deal with the vast majority of allegations. National authorities in both the former Yugoslavia and in Rwanda have had to wrestle with this problem and take action themselves, either by means of empowering local courts or by some form of extrajudicial process such as the tribal Gacaca proceedings adopted in Rwanda.

In Sierra Leone, by a treaty between the United Nations and the Government of Sierra Leone, a Special Court was established in 2002 to deal with the aftermath of the civil war in that country. This "hybrid" court has both international and Sierra Leonean judges and has jurisdiction not only over international crimes but also some crimes under national law as well.

In Cambodia, lengthy negotiations between the United Nations and the Cambodian authorities have led to the establishment of "Extraordinary Chambers," established under Cambodian law but with international support and assistance, to "prosecute those most responsible for crimes and serious violations of Cambodian and international law between 17 April 1975 and 6 January 1979" during the Pol Pot regime. However, this Court has been beset by financial and political difficulties and has not yet begun to function fully.

In East Timor Special Panels of Dili District Court were established and in Kosovo, UNMIK created the War and Ethnic Crimes Courts, all to deal with international crimes. Whilst these are national courts, they are staffed by both international and national personnel though operating primarily under domestic law provisions. The Timor Panels in particular have run into difficulties, due partly again to funding difficulties and partly due to the failure of the Panels to obtain jurisdiction over many of the indictees who are now located in Indonesia. The Kosovo Courts will be watched closely by the domestic courts in Croatia, Serbia and Montenegro and Bosnia-Herzegovina as the ad hoc Tribunal in The Hague winds down its work and begins to refer cases back to the national jurisdictions.

Similarly, in Iraq, a Special Tribunal was established during the occupation to try the leaders of the Saddam regime. The new Iraqi Government has now passed its own law, based on that passed by the Occupying Powers, creating "The Iraqi Higher Criminal Court." This Court has jurisdiction over genocide, crimes against humanity and war crimes as well as certain offences under Iraqi law principally involving the misuse of political power. The Court operates under a procedure that is a mixture of Iraqi and international law but is mainly staffed by Iraqi nationals. Originally the Court was required to appoint international advisers and observers to the various sections of the Court but that has, under the new law, become optional rather than obligatory. Initial indications are that international involvement has been limited, in part because the death sentence, suspended under the occupation, has now been restored. In the early trials, concern has been expressed about political interference both by the United States and by the Iraqi Government itself. Two presiding judges have been replaced during the proceedings. These concerns were particularly acute in respect of the appeals process culminating in the execution of Saddam Hussein and others.

Certainly States coming out of conflict and recovering from repressive regimes will face severe difficulties in coming to terms with the past. Each situation will be different and will require a slightly different solution. The move towards encouraging greater domestic involvement in judicial and other proceedings may assist in restoring the rule of law but international involvement will still be required to a greater or lesser extent to avoid allegations of vengeance or "victors' justice." However, the move towards individual accountability for international crimes is based firmly on the foundations laid long ago at Nuremberg where it was recognized that only by such accountability could international law be enforced.

Crimes against Humanity

By M. Cherif Bassiouni

The term *crimes against humanity* has come to mean anything atrocious committed on a large scale. This is not, however, the original meaning nor the technical one. The term originated in the 1907 Hague Convention preamble, which codified the customary law of armed conflict. This codification was based on existing State practices that derived from those values and principles deemed to constitute the "laws of humanity," as reflected throughout history in different cultures.

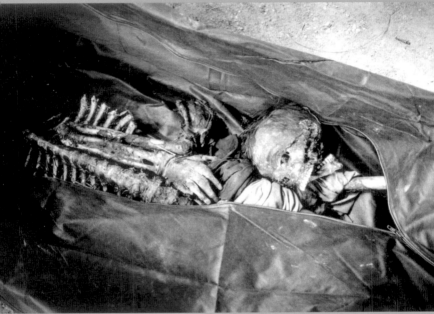

Human remains, wrists bound with cords, were buried in a mass grave at Khan Cala, a Russian Army base in Chechnya, and unearthed in February 2001.

After World War I, the Allies, in connection with the Treaty of Versailles, established in 1919 a commission to investigate war crimes that relied on the 1907 Hague Convention as the applicable law. In addition to war crimes committed by the Germans, the commission also found that Turkish officials committed "crimes against the laws of humanity" for killing Armenian nationals and residents during the period of the war. The United States and Japan strongly opposed the criminalization of such conduct on the grounds that crimes against the laws of humanity were violations of moral and not positive law.

In 1945, the United States and other Allies developed the Agreement for the Prosecution and Punishment of the Major War Criminals of the European Axis and Charter of the International Military Tribunal (IMT), sitting at Nuremberg, which contained the following definition of crimes against humanity in Article 6(c):

"Crimes against humanity: murder, extermination, enslavement, deporta-

135

tion, and other inhumane acts committed against civilian populations, before or during the war; or persecutions on political, racial or religious grounds in execution of or in connection with any crime within the jurisdiction of the Tribunal, whether or not in violation of the domestic law of the country where perpetrated."

The Nuremberg Charter represents the first time that crimes against humanity were established in positive international law. The International Military Tribunal for the Far East, at Tokyo, followed the Nuremberg Charter, as did Control Council Law No. 10 of Germany, under which the Allies prosecuted Germans in their respective zones of occupation. Curiously, however, there has been no specialized international convention since then on crimes against humanity. Still, that category of crimes has been included in the statutes of the International Criminal Tribunal for the former Yugoslavia (ICTY) and the International Criminal Tribunal for Rwanda (ICTR), as well as in the statute of the International Criminal Court (ICC). In fact, there are eleven international texts defining crimes against humanity, but they all differ slightly as to their definition of that crime and its legal elements. However, what all of these definitions have in common is: (1) they refer to specific acts of violence against persons irrespective of whether the person is a national or non-national and irrespective of whether these acts are committed in time of war or time of peace, and (2) these acts must be the product of persecution against an identifiable group of persons irrespective of the make-up of that group or the purpose of the persecution. Such a policy can also be manifested by the "widespread or systematic" conduct of the perpetrators, which results in the commission of the specific crimes contained in the definition.

The list of the specific crimes contained within the meaning of crimes against humanity has been expanded since Article 6(c) of the IMT to include, in the ICTY and the ICTR, rape and torture. The statute of the ICC also expands the list of specific acts. In particular, the ICC statute adds the crimes of enforced disappearance of persons and apartheid. Further, the ICC statute contains clarifying language with respect to the specific crimes of extermination, enslavement, deportation or forcible transfer of population, torture, and forced pregnancy.

To some extent, crimes against humanity overlap with genocide and war crimes. But crimes against humanity are distinguishable from genocide in that they do not require an intent to "destroy in whole or in part," as cited in the 1948 Genocide Convention, but only target a given group and carry out a policy of "widespread or systematic" violations. Crimes against humanity are also distinguishable from war crimes in that they not only apply in the context of war—they apply in times of war and peace.

Crimes against humanity have existed in customary international law for over half a century and are also evidenced in prosecutions before some national courts. The most notable of these trials include those of Paul Touvier, Klaus Barbie, and Maurice Papon in France, and Imre Finta in Canada. But crimes against humanity are also deemed to be part of *jus cogens*—the highest standing in international legal norms. Thus, they constitute a non-derogable rule of international law. The implication of this standing is that they are subject to universal jurisdiction, meaning that all States can exercise their jurisdiction in prosecuting a perpetrator irrespective of where the crime was committed. It also means that all States have the duty to prosecute or extradite, that no person charged with that crime can claim the "political offense exception" to extradition, and that States have the duty to assist each other in securing evidence needed to prosecute. But of greater importance is the fact that no perpetrator can claim the "defense of obedience to superior orders" and that no statute of limitation contained in the laws of any State can apply. Lastly, no one is immune from prosecution for such crimes, even a head of State.

Crimes against Peace

By Steven R. Ratner

C

Crimes against peace, as described by the Nuremberg Tribunal in 1946, are "the supreme international crime, differing only from other war crimes in that it contains within itself the accumulated evil of the whole."

Also known as the crime of **aggression**, crimes against peace formed the first charge against the Nazis in the 1945 Charter of the International Military Tribunal at Nuremberg. The charter defined them as "planning, preparation, initiation or waging of a war of aggression, or a war in violation of international treaties, agreements or assurances, or participation in a common plan or conspiracy [to do so]." Crimes against peace are not war crimes *per se*, which involve unlawful conduct *during* war.

The idea of charging the Nazis with the crime of starting World War II was controversial at the time and has remained so ever since. For the Americans, crimes against peace were the chief offense of the Nazis, and the criminality of aggressive war needed to be enshrined in international law. But starting a war had not been regarded as criminal up to that time. The Kellogg-Briand Pact of 1928, which outlawed war (not too successfully, to say the least), only rendered aggression an *illegal* act for States, not a *criminal* act for which *individuals* could be tried. The French resisted the concept for this reason; the Soviets, for their part, were concerned about criminalizing aggressive war given their invasions of Finland and annexation of parts of Poland. The American view prevailed—though the tribunal's jurisdiction was limited to *Axis* aggression—leading to the conviction of leading Nazis for crimes against peace. Afterward, a fierce debate raged in legal circles as to whether the Allies had applied criminal law retroactively.

Although UN bodies have restated the importance of crimes against peace since World War II, the UN's members—especially Western States—have noted serious obstacles to actually prosecuting individuals. First, a definition of aggression specific enough for prosecutions of governmental officials remains elusive. Second, since wars are typically planned by many people in State bureaucracies, drawing a line of guilt might prove difficult. Third, criminal cases could encompass complex, politically laden factual inquiries ill-suited for courts. While some cases of aggression are as stark as Iraq's invasion of Kuwait, other incidents demand more careful scrutiny.

One clear manifestation of these concerns was the Security Council's unwillingness to give the UN's Yugoslavia Tribunal jurisdiction over this crime. Another was the decision by the States drafting the Rome Statute of the International Criminal Court (ICC) to give the ICC jurisdiction over crimes against peace only if States formally amend that statute to add a definition of the crime and the conditions for the exercise of jurisdiction. States thus seem to say that aggression is a crime in the abstract, but are reluctant to prosecute it. The concept of crimes against peace still has some effect on international law, as States want to recognize the illegality of aggression in the strongest way—by proclaiming that leaders can be held accountable for it. But the dim prospects of actually prosecuting anyone make impunity the norm and crimes against peace somewhat of a dead letter.
(See **crimes against humanity; war crimes**)

Cultural Property and Historical Monuments

By Peter Maass

The mosque was on death row. An execution date had not been pronounced, of course, but the Ferhad Pasha mosque was living on borrowed time when I walked through its front gate in the summer of 1992. Nationalist Serbs controlled Banja Luka and were well on their way to destroying all symbols of Muslim culture, and none was so historic or important as Ferhad Pasha, built in 1583 during the Ottoman Empire.

It was one of the oldest mosques in Bosnia, and it was beautiful, and because of that, it was in greater peril than the handful of frightened Muslims who had just ended an afternoon prayer session. "Yes, I will talk to you," one of them told me. "But please, we must leave this place now." The mosque had survived four centuries of Balkan tumult, but it would be best not to linger in its doomed shadow.

A few months later, on May 7, 1993, people who lived near the mosque were woken from their sleep by an explosion that made the earth tremble under their homes. Antitank mines were detonated under the ancient building's foundations, turning it to rubble, which was carted away to a secret dump. All that was left behind was a blackened patch of ground. The "ethnic cleansers" hoped that destroying the spiritual heart of their community would ensure Muslims would leave their homes and never return. Across Bosnia this was done, as one mosque after another was turned to pebbles and dust. With each explosion, a war crime was committed.

International guidelines protecting cultural property against damage and theft date back to the American Civil War. The carnage of that war led to the 1863 Lieber Code, which gave protected status to libraries, scientific collections, and art works. The code applied only to American troops but influenced a series of international accords leading to the 1954 Hague Convention for the Protection of Cultural Property. The convention's definition of cultural property is fairly broad, including significant architectural monuments, art works, books or manuscripts of artistic or historical significance, museums, large libraries, archives, archaeological sites, and historic

Before and after: In November 1993, Bosnian Croats shelled and destroyed the four-century-old Neretva Bridge in Mostar. It had been used by the beleaguered Bosnians, but its major "offense" was that it was built under Ottoman rule.

buildings, but it only protects them from attack if they are "of great importance to the cultural heritage of every people." The Convention also forbids the use of such sites for purposes that are likely to expose them to destruction or damage (for instance by using a historic building as a command center). However both of these restrictions may be waived for reasons of imperative military necessity.

The convention was reinforced by the Additional Protocols of 1977. Article 53 of the first Protocol (which applies in international conflicts) and Article 16 of the second Protocol (for internal conflict) both prohibit "any acts of hostility directed against the historic monuments, works of art or places of worship which constitute the cultural or spiritual heritage of peoples." It's important to note that the Protocols established protections against the destruction of other types of civilian property not linked to military actions or uses.

The Nuremberg Trials after World War II marked the first time that individuals were held accountable for cultural war crimes. Several Nazi officials were sentenced to death for a panoply of violations that included the destruction of cultural property. Following that precedent, the Yugoslavia War Crimes Tribunal was empowered to prosecute individuals deemed responsible for the "seizure of, destruction or wilful damage done to institutions dedicated to religion, charity and education, the arts and sciences, historic monuments and works of art and science."

Recent years have seen further moves to strengthen the legal regime protecting cultural property. In 1999 a protocol was added to the 1954 Hague Convention that set strict limits on the "military necessity" exception: it could only apply when the property had been made into a military objective, and when there was no feasible alternative that would achieve a similar military advantage. This treaty has so far only attracted a limited number of parties.

An example of the treatment of a building that is indisputably of great cultural significance came in April 2002, when Palestinian fighters took refuge in the Church of the Nativity in Bethlehem. The Israeli army laid siege to the Church rather than attempting to storm it, and in the end a settlement was reached whereby the more senior fighters were flown to Cyprus and others taken by bus to Gaza.

The destruction of the Ferhad Pasha mosque easily qualifies as a war crime. At the time, Banja Luka was under the firm political and military control of Serbs, and there was no fighting in the city or in the area immediately around it. The historic mosque could not be regarded as a military target; the few Muslims who remained in Banja Luka were using it only as a house of worship. Nonetheless, it was destroyed.

Customary Law

By Theodor Meron

Together with treaties, customary law is one of the principal sources or components of international humanitarian law (IHL). It results from a general and consistent practice of States that is followed by them from a sense of legal obligation. The most obvious significance of a norm—a principle or rule—of a customary character is that it binds States that are not parties to the treaty in which the norm is restated. It is, of course, not the treaty provision, but the customary norm with identical content that binds such States. Customary law is important also for filling in matters inadequately covered by humanitarian law treaties. The fact that a norm is customary has also a significance for the applicable rules of interpretation and may have the beneficial effect of limiting the power of States to make reservations or to denounce those treaties of IHL which have a high customary law content. A State cannot opt out of its duty to conform to a general international law. The recognition that an IHL treaty states customary law strengthens the moral claim of the international community for its observance by emphasizing its moral character and deep roots in community values.

The decisions on customary humanitarian law of the Hague Tribunal for the former Yugoslavia are the linear successors to the decisions of the Nuremberg Tribunals. In both Nuremberg and The Hague, the tribunals looked primarily to the belief of States that certain principles are legally binding rather than to the practice of States in reaching their decisions. These decisions were supportive of an expansive view of customary law. Courts and tribunals tend to rely not on battlefield practice but on verbal statements in which States or institutions (for example, UN organs) express support for principles of IHL. Although they adhere to the traditional twin requirements (practice and the psychological belief that such practice is legally binding) for the formation of customary humanitarian law, in effect they weigh statements both as evidence of practice and as articulation of the psychological belief, which in the formation of humanitarian and human rights law is critical. The emphasis on the psychological element helps compensate for scarcity of supporting practice.

How to treat violations continues to be an important question. Both scholarly and judicial sources have shown reluctance to reject as customary norms—because of contrary practice—rules whose content merits customary law status, perhaps because of the recognition that humanitarian principles express basic community values and are essential for the preservation of public order. Even repeated violations are often not regarded as negations of customary law provided they are responded to by protests or condemnations by other States or international organizations, and that the State accused either denies the facts of its questionable conduct or appeals to exceptions or justifications contained in the rule itself.

There is considerable judicial and scholarly support, which is also endorsed by the International Committee of the Red Cross (ICRC), that the rules contained in the four Geneva Conventions of 1949 for the Protection of Victims of War and in the Hague Convention (IV) of 1907 on the Laws and Customs of War on Land (except for administrative, technical, and logistical provisions) reflect customary law. It is also widely recognized that many, perhaps even most, of the provisions, principles, and rules contained in Additional Protocol I to the Geneva Conventions and some, perhaps even many, of the provisions contained in Additional Protocol II reflect customary law. Several rules pertaining to types of weapons, and especially the prohibition on the use of chemical weapons, are regarded as customary.

A declaration of the significance of customary law is incorporated into several IHL treaties, most notably in the so-called Martens clause, named for its drafter, Feodor de Martens, the adviser to the Russian Foreign Ministry at the beginning of the century. First inserted in the preamble of the 1899 Hague Convention II, this provides a minimum threshold of humanitarian treatment by combatants even in the absence of specific treaty language. "Until a more complete code of the laws of war is issued, the High Contracting Parties think it right to declare that in cases not included in the Regulations adopted by them, populations and belligerents remain under the protection and the empire of the principles of international law, as they result from the usages established between civilized nations, from the laws of humanity, and the requirements of the public conscience."

The Rome Statute of the International Criminal Court codifies many rules and principles of IHL as customary criminal law.

In any discussion of customary law, sight must not be lost of the fact that the Geneva Conventions have attained practically universal ratification and that the Additional Protocols have gained many ratifications. For States parties to the IHL treaties, all treaty provisions, no matter whether they reflect customary law or not, are of course binding. In the national law of many countries, however, customary law is a part of the law of the land. As such, it may be invoked by victims of violations of IHL or human rights law.

Customary Law: The ICRC Study

By Burrus M. Carnahan

In 2005, the International Committee of the Red Cross (ICRC) published a comprehensive study of the customary law of armed conflict. Based on ten years of work, the ICRC concluded that this body of law could be summarized in 161 rules. Due to the prestige of the Red Cross, and to the brevity and wide availability of the rules, the study is likely to become a valuable resource for those seeking an accessible summary of generally accepted rules of international law in armed conflict.

The report is published in three volumes, the first volume setting out the rules with commentary on each, and the final two listing the government practices on which the rules are based.

A notable feature of the study is the extensive treatment given to the role of customary law in non-international conflicts, where the reach of treaty law is much more limited than in conflicts between States. The study concludes that 149 out of the 161 rules identified apply in non-international armed conflict.

The ICRC's endorsement of the report gives it authority, but the study has not been endorsed by governments. Although it is likely to be an influential assessment of the current state of customary international humanitarian law, it should not be taken as a definitive codification.

D

Dangerous Forces: Dams, Dikes, and Nuclear Stations

D

By Erich Rathfelder

It was with worried expressions that the people of Omis, a small coastal town on the Adriatic, watched the Cretina River. In that bitter winter of 1993, it seemed as if death and destruction could come roaring down from the river at any time. The citizens of Omis, as well as villagers in the surrounding area, held their collective breath.

The danger of a deluge came from the Peruca Dam, a huge edifice that lay some forty kilometers inland, and that, before the breakup of Yugoslavia, had been part of the country's second biggest hydroelectric complex. Serb forces had controlled it since the beginning of the Croatian War in 1991. Now, Croatian forces were massing for an attack on Peruca and the 641 million cubic meters of water behind the dam represented mortal danger to civilians in the town below.

On January 28, Serb troops had detonated between thirty and thirty-seven tons of explosives in different parts of the dam. Peruca had been shaken to its foundations, but it seemed to be holding. Had its walls been breached, the mass of water would have raced in a giant wave down the river canyon, crushing the villages downriver and completely wiping out Omis.

Fortunately for the people of Omis, a Croatian counterattack was successful. Croatian military engineers reached the dam, opened its sluice gates, and allowed the water level to fall and the pressure to abate. Their action, and that of Capt. Mark Gray, a British officer serving with the United Nations as a military observer, probably saved the lives of between twenty thousand and thirty thousand people. In October 1992, while the Serbs still held Peruca, Gray, on his own initiative, opened one of the sluice gates following heavy rains, thus lowering the water level by six meters.

The Serb military actions were subject to two fundamental principles governing the impact of armed conflict on civilians as well as special rules that apply to "dangerous forces." First, civilians may not be made the direct object of attack. If the aim of the attack on the dam was to wipe out the civilians of Omis it was a grave breach. If it was to cause them under threat of destruction to abandon the area for reasons not strictly related to military necessity or their safety, then the attack was a serious violation.

Even if the attack upon the dam was not undertaken in order to affect civilians directly, if the resulting damage to civilians and civilian objects was not justified by military necessity, and would have been excessive in relation to the concrete and direct military advantages gained through it, the attack would also be a violation of the laws of armed conflict.

In addition, a special set of rules apply in this case.

According to Article 56 of the 1977 Additional Protocol I to the Geneva Conventions, "works or installations containing dangerous forces, namely dams, dikes and nuclear electrical generating stations, shall not be made the object of attack, even when these objects are military objectives, if such attack may cause the release of dangerous forces and consequent severe losses among the civilian population."

On the face of things, it would therefore appear that what the Serbs did was a violation of the laws of armed conflict. However, as with so many prohibitions in international humanitarian law, Article 56 of Protocol I is subject to important caveats. In other words, even so seemingly gross a violation as detonating explosives in a dam that causes severe losses among civilians is not always forbidden to soldiers.

Traditionally, the laws and customs of war allow the destruction of dams and dikes to stop an enemy's advance. And Article 56 does specify three exceptions to the prohibition against attacking or destroying works or installations containing dangerous forces. Where dams or dikes are concerned, the exception occurs when the installation is used for "other than its normal function and in regular, significant and direct support of military operations and if such attack is the only feasible way to terminate such support."

Moreover, not all countries have accepted the provisions of Article 56. The United States is not a party to the first Additional Protocol, and other countries like the United Kingdom and France have entered reservations to the treaty on this point. It is generally accepted, though, that customary law requires that particular care must be taken when attacking such works and installations.

The exceptions to the prohibition would appear not to apply in this instance, since the Croatian forces did not hold the dam and could not be said to have been using it as a military installation. The Serbs also could not claim that destroying the dam allowed them to fend off the Croatian offensive. It would appear, rather, that the Serb attacks upon the dam were a clear violation of the obligation for the Serbs to take "all practical precautions... to avoid the release of dangerous forces."

D

Darfur

By John Prendergast and Colin Thomas-Jensen

D

Reports of war crimes and crimes against humanity in Darfur, western Sudan, began appearing in the Western news media in early 2004. The government of Sudan's counterinsurgency campaign against two Darfur-based rebel groups targeted civilians from the ethnic groups whom the regime suspected of supporting the rebellion. Government security forces and their proxy militias—the Janjaweed—orchestrated a campaign of mass murder, rape, forced displacement, and destruction of livelihood. At least 200,000 people have died in the conflict, and more than 2.5 million have been driven off their lands and into camps for the internally displaced. The international community's failure to protect civilians in Darfur echoed the failure to respond in Rwanda a decade before.

Sudan has been at war with itself almost continuously since independence from Great Britain in 1956. A succession of governments in Khartoum has hoarded the country's wealth and treated its citizens with the utmost contempt. Khartoum's wars against rebels based in Southern Sudan—the Anya Nya rebels from 1955 to 1972 and the Sudan People's Liberation Army (SPLA) from 1983 to 2005—cost at least two and a half million lives. During the course of these campaigns the government honed a counterinsurgency strategy that exploited ethnic divisions by sponsoring ethnically-based militias to attack rebel groups, terrorize and forcibly displace civilians, and intimidate humanitarian workers to force their withdrawal.

Following nearly 20 years of ferocious conflict, a regionally brokered peace process between the SPLA and the ruling National Congress Party (NCP) gathered steam in late 2002 and early 2003. Under intense international pressure—especially from the U.S. administration of President George W. Bush—the two parties met in neighboring Kenya and began negotiating a settlement. However, the two-party negotiating framework posited by the international community left numerous aggrieved populations out of the

A young boy looks over the outer stone wall of his house in northwest Darfur—all that remained after Janjaweed Arab militias attacked the village in August 2004. His family could not flee because they had lost their pack animals in the raid.

equation. The unyielding control of wealth and power by a narrow ruling elite in Khartoum had economically and politically marginalized not only southern Sudan, but most of northern Sudan. Only a genuine devolution of wealth and power from the center to the periphery could have brought stability to the country.

In Darfur—one of the poorest and most neglected regions of the North—peoples of non-Arab origin had for decades engaged in frequent disputes with nomadic groups of Arab origin over scarce natural resources. The government had armed and trained many of these Arab nomads during the 1980s to prevent the SPLA from opening up a new front in Darfur, and throughout the late 1980s and 1990s Khartoum consistently backed Arab groups in increasingly violent, racially motivated conflicts to take land from non-Arab groups.

As the North-South peace talks progressed, frustrated Darfuris rebelled in late 2002. An alliance of Fur, Zaghawa, and Massaleit political leaders and fighters formed the rebel Sudan Liberation Army (SLA) and began attacking government outposts in February 2003. On 25 April, the SLA launched an audacious offensive against Sudanese military installations in El Fashir, the state capital of North Darfur. The rebels bombarded and temporarily captured the airport and the local military headquarters. They destroyed government aircraft, killed scores of government soldiers, captured the local military commander, and retreated into the bush with captured arms and ammunition.

Khartoum was humiliated and the military seemingly in disarray. Many of the army rank and file and numerous commanders were from Darfur, and their loyalty to the regime in a war against their own people was uncertain. But Khartoum's long-time patronage of Arab nomadic groups against their non-Arab rivals offered an easy solution. Darfur's descent into agony followed a grimly predictable blueprint.

The powerful security cabal within the governing NCP cut a land-for-war deal with its tribal allies in North and West Darfur. During mid-2003, Sudanese security services armed and trained Arab militias to attack suspected supporters of the rebellion—namely Fur, Zaghawa, and Massaleit civilians. Driven by ethnic and racial hatreds and the government's promise of state-sanctioned robbery of land and booty, Arab fighters from within Darfur and neighboring countries (notably Chad and the Central African Republic) joined the militias and prepared for war. The government released criminals from jails to join the militias, made cash payouts to its surrogate killers of approximately 100 dollars, and provided them with AK-47 or G-3 rifles, camels, horses, and sometimes uniforms. By September 2003 the systematic destruction of Darfur at the hands of the Janjaweed militias had begun.

Government forces and Janjaweed usually attacked non-Arab villages before dawn. The onslaught often began from the air. Military aircraft—Antonov supply planes and helicopter gunships—would bombard and strafe civilians as they slept. In the chaotic aftermath of aerial attacks, government troops in 4x4 vehicles and mounted units of up to 300 Janjaweed fighters rode through the carnage to murder, rape, and drive villagers from the area. Mass executions and gang rapes were frequent, and attackers looted livestock, food stockpiles, and household goods. They burned houses, schools, mosques and other public buildings. Corpses were dumped into wells to pollute the water supply and farmers' crops destroyed or fed to the growing herds of stolen livestock. By April 2004, the UN reported that coordinated attacks against civilians had displaced more than 860,000 people, including over 100,000 refugees in eastern Chad.

As the Sudanese military and the Janjaweed laid waste to Darfur, the peace negotiations in Kenya between the government and the SPLA lurched forward. The international community was reluctant to intervene in Darfur for fear of losing a long-sought and tantalizingly close agreement in the Khartoum government's war with the South. The U.S., UK, and others already had invested considerable diplomatic and financial resources to push the peace process forward, and Darfur threatened to scuttle the deal and expose the inadequacies of the entire framework for negotiation. In early 2004, Western policymakers decided to first push hard for a North-South peace agreement and then focus on resolving Darfur. This was a monumental miscalculation; the NCP cynically prolonged the talks in Kenya to buy more time for the military solution in Darfur. In January 2004, the NCP's lead negotiator, Vice President Ali Osman Taha, suspended the talks at a decisive moment and announced that he was going on the hajj. While the mediators waited patiently for Taha to return, Darfur burned.

Although some non-governmental organizations documented the atrocities in Darfur throughout 2003, the Western media did not pay close attention to the conflict until early 2004. The Sudanese government effec-

Body of an SLA rebel near Jijira, Darfur, left by the Janjaweed as a warning to others not to fight the government. January 2004.

tively prevented most journalists from traveling to Darfur, but many visited the refugee camps in eastern Chad. Refugees' stories were a catalog of horrors: children thrown into fires, rape survivors branded with scalding iron, and groups of men executed and dumped in ravines. Janjaweed and government troops yelled racial epithets as they marauded through villages; rape victims were told they would give birth to Arab children.

In April 2004, the U.S., the African Union (AU), the government of Chad, and others brokered a "humanitarian cease-fire" between the government, the SLA, and the Justice and Equality Movement (a second rebel group with a small military wing and murky political agenda). The parties agreed to a cessation of hostilities and to allow unrestricted humanitarian access, and the government committed to "neutralize the armed militias." The agreement authorized the AU to deploy cease-fire monitors and troops to protect them. However, both parties systematically violated the cease-fire from the moment it was signed.

Fighting persisted between the rebels and the government, the Janjaweed continued to raid villages with total impunity, and the government blamed the violence on "armed bandits" and "tribal hatreds." While the UN and international humanitarian organizations took the cease-fire as their cue to begin the Herculean task of caring for the growing numbers of internally displaced, the government of Sudan restricted humanitarian access through bureaucratic rules and a cultivated state of continuous insecurity. In the summer of 2004, UN Secretary General Kofi Annan and U.S. Secretary of State Colin Powell traveled to Sudan to demand that the government comply with the cease-fire. The Sudanese government listened politely and signed further agreements to disarm the Janjaweed, but the killing continued apace.

On 9 September, the U.S. government made history when it became the first to accuse another State of committing genocide. During a hearing before the U.S. Congress, Secretary Powell cited a State Department report based on interviews with refugees in eastern Chad and stated that "genocide has been committed in Darfur and that the government of Sudan and the Janjaweed bear responsibility—and genocide may still be occurring." Yet Powell's words were all sound and fury with no real impact on U.S. policy. According to the State Department, the finding of genocide did not impose obligations on the U.S. to halt the massacres. The U.S. hoped that strong rhetoric would stir international outrage and build additional leverage on Khartoum to stop the killings. It didn't work.

Each of us separately visited Darfur in 2004—before and after the genocide declaration—and saw numbing evidence of state-sponsored slaughter. In a ravine deep inside rebel held territory, bodies of fourteen young men were lined up in ditches, eerily preserved by the scorching desert sun. It looked as though they had been lined up and shot in the back or the back of the head: seventeen shell casings resting in the sand indicated how efficient the killing had been. The story the rebels told seemed plausible: the dead were civilians who had been marched up a hill and executed by government forces the previous month. The bodies lay unburied, covered only by a thin layer of dust, so that the rebels could show people like us exactly what happens to people who oppose the government. The rebels asserted that there were many other such scenes.

Riding along the roads in government-held territory was a journey through a depopulated wasteland. Burned villages lined the roads, stolen livestock roamed freely through abandoned millet fields, and every so often a man on a camel with an assault rifle glowered from the side of the road. During a visit to a camp for some 30,000 internally displaced civilians in West Darfur, at least 25 Janjaweed could be seen resting with their camels under a tree next to the makeshift shelters of their victims. The intimidation and fear in the camp was palpable and overwhelming. In one interview after another, Sudanese refugees and internally displaced told us that they would never trust the government to disarm the Janjaweed, and that only an international force could protect them.

While the U.S. declaration may have been intended to galvanize international pressure on the regime in Khartoum, multilateral intervention through the UN was a nonstarter: Sudan had powerful allies in the UN Security Council. China, keen to protect its substantial oil interests in Sudan, and Russia, the regime's main arms supplier, threatened to block strong action. The Sudanese government's cooperation on counterterrorism, the continuing North-South peace talks in Kenya, and a general disinclination to intercede militarily in Africa reduced international will to push for a non-UN intervention, as NATO had pursued in Kosovo.

There to monitor the nonexistent cease-fire, the AU mission in Darfur assumed the international responsibility to protect. With acquiescence from Khartoum, AU member States (including Rwanda) deployed additional troops to increase security in Darfur. However, the AU mission lacked a strong mandate, adequate troop strength to cover a war zone the size of Texas, and the operational capacity to respond to outbreaks of violence and use force to protect civilians. Making matters worse, African policymakers argued that Darfur was an African problem requiring an African solution, dismissed suggestions of increased non-African involvement as meddling in the continent's affairs, and provided the international community with a convenient excuse not to take stronger action to protect civilians.

Meanwhile, the UN Security Council authorized an International Commission of Inquiry to investigate violations of international law in Darfur. The Commission found evidence of serious abuses—including killing of civilians, rape and sexual violence, torture, forced displacement, and destruction of villages and livelihoods—and recommended that the Security Council refer the case to the International Criminal Court. (Contrary to U.S. findings, the commission concluded that the Sudanese government had not pursued a policy of genocide.) Remarkably, the U.S. and China put aside their strong ideological opposition to the Court and the Security Council referred Darfur to the Court in March 2005. However, the Sudanese government prevented Court investigators from visiting Darfur and thus significantly slowed the process of building cases against the people most responsible for the crimes against humanity committed there.

Under intense international pressure, a peace agreement for Darfur was signed in May 2006, but the deal was flawed and incomplete. The Darfur Peace Agreement (DPA) lacked implementation guarantees for disarming the Janjaweed, security arrangements that would encourage the return of displaced people to their homes, and sufficient compensation for the conflict's primary victims, Darfur's civilians. Only one of the main rebel groups—a faction of the SLA led by Commander Minni Minawi—agreed to the terms. Although the Sudanese government had stated that a peace deal would be the trigger for the deployment of a United Nations peacekeeping mission, the handover from the African Union to the UN was not explicit in the DPA and the government quickly reneged.

Rather than peace, the agreement led to further conflict as non-signatory rebel groups realigned (often along ethnic lines) to continue military action. Violence intensified during the summer of 2006 and attacks increased on humanitarian workers, causing even greater hardship for Darfur's displaced population On August 31, the UN Security Council passed a resolution authorizing a UN peacekeeping mission, but weak international efforts failed to gain the consent of the Sudanese government. Yet again, civilians suffered atrocities at the hands of the government, the Janjaweed, and, increasingly, splintering rebel factions.

The absence of punitive action against those who committed crimes against humanity during the first three years of the conflict established a dangerous state of impunity, especially in Khartoum. The NCP's ruling clique saw that it need not fear any consequences for violating signed agreements and Security Council resolutions. While the ICC referral raises hopes that those responsible for crimes of war in Darfur may eventually be brought to justice, the international community's glaring failure to protect the victims will undoubtedly be the conflict's lasting legacy.

(See **courts and tribunals; humanitarian intervention**.)

Dead and Wounded

By H. Wayne Elliott

In 1967 a U.S. Army sergeant in Vietnam posed for a photograph. The photograph, later published nationally, showed the sergeant holding the decapitated heads of two enemy corpses. The soldier was court-martialed and convicted of "conduct prejudicial to good order and discipline." There were other reports of U.S. soldiers cutting the ears and fingers off the enemy dead. Gen. William Westmoreland, commander of U.S. forces in Vietnam, denounced the mutilation of dead bodies as "subhuman" and "contrary to all policy and below the minimum standards of human decency." Not only is the mistreatment of dead bodies "contrary to all policy," it is also a violation of the laws of war.

One of the consequences of war is the death of some of those who get caught up in it. From time immemorial, the proper disposal of the dead has been a military concern. In earlier times the proper disposal of the battlefield dead often had religious overtones. Also, the dead on the battlefield were an immediate hygienic problem. Often, the need to avoid the diseases which could come from the untended dead was enough to force some humane disposal of the bodies. But, the law does not rely solely on the religious practices or the health concerns of the living. The proper disposal of the dead is now mandated by law.

The main obligation to the dead is now found in Article 15 of the First Geneva Convention. The thrust of that article is the need to aid the wounded. However, it also provides that the parties must "at all times, and particularly after an engagement ... search for the dead and prevent their being despoiled." The article also says that "whenever circumstances permit," an armistice should be concluded so as to facilitate the search for the wounded. Of course, while searching for the wounded, the dead would also be found.

The International Committee of the Red Cross (ICRC) Commentary to the Geneva Convention says that the dead must be brought back along with the wounded. One reason for this is that in the highly charged atmosphere of the battlefield, it might not always be possible to determine who is really dead and who is seriously wounded. Another reason is that the laws of war require that an effort be made to identify the dead and to provide a proper burial.

The treatment of the battlefield dead can be divided into two aspects. First, there is a prohibition on deliberate mistreatment of the body, either through failure to treat it with appropriate respect or through mutilation. Second, there is a prohibition on pillaging the dead. These mandates concerning the dead are as much derived from the customary laws of war as from the Geneva Conventions.

The Geneva Conventions take the customary rules further. In Article 16 of the First Geneva Convention, we find an obligation for the party that has the body to send to the other party (usually through a neutral power or the ICRC) written evidence of death. Where the body is identified with the required double identity disk, one half of the disk, along with any personal effects found on the body, is to be sent to the other side.

En route to a burial site, U.S. troops drag the body of a Viet Cong soldier behind an armored vehicle. Tan Binh, Vietnam, 1966.

Article 17 of the First Geneva Convention is concerned specifically with the burial of the battlefield dead. The bodies are to be examined, preferably by a person with medical skills, so as to confirm death. Burial is to be, where possible, in individual graves. The idea is that individual graves would be more consistent with the general requirement that the dead be respected, and also that individual burial would make subsequent exhumation easier. The requirement, however, is not absolute. Climate, sanitation, and hygiene may make mass burial the only proper action. The remaining half of the double identity disk must remain with the body. Cremation is prohibited except where it is based on the religion of the deceased or where imperative reasons of hygiene justify cremation.

Where possible, the burial or cremation is to be done in accordance with the religious rites of the deceased. The bodies are to be grouped according to nationality and the cemeteries mapped in such a way as to make later exhumation easier. This is the core of the Geneva Convention duty to the dead—they are to be treated honorably and their graves protected.

Mutilation of the dead is actually a fairly rare occurrence in well-disciplined armies. This is probably as much the result of a general revulsion at such conduct as from a fear of criminal punishment. However, pillaging the dead is a greater problem. In World War II the U.S. Army prohibited soldiers taking as "war trophies" any item that evidenced disrespectful treatment of the dead. A similar prohibition exists today. Nonetheless, there is a recognized right to search the dead for information that might be of some intelligence value. But private property of the deceased must be safeguarded for later delivery to the deceased's own military authorities.

As this summary indicates, the duty owed to the dead is somewhat subjective. What sort of conduct constitutes disrespect? How can we determine when neglect of the dead has ceased to be mandated by considerations of military necessity and become evidence of the war crime of mistreatment of the dead? There are no hard and fast answers to these questions. However, if the dead are left on the battlefield for some time after the fighting has ended, their very presence is evidence of failure to meet the obligations imposed by law. If the dead are left on the field solely so that they might be seen by journalists or photographed, that is stronger evidence that the threshold of mistreatment is near. If the dead are placed on display as propaganda (dragging the bodies through the streets as occurred in Somalia is a ready example), then the threshold has been crossed and a war crime has been clearly committed.

The laws of war accept that death is an inherent part of war. They also recognize that the disposal of the dead will be given less immediacy than the care of the living.

The *raison d'etre* for protecting and honoring the dead is captured in the inscription on the Tomb of the Unknowns in Arlington Cemetery: "Here Rests in Honored Glory an American Soldier Known But to God." That sentiment is not one peculiar to Americans.

Death Squads

By Jean-Marie Simon

D

They lounged outside police detective headquarters in Guatemala City, wearing mismatched suits and leaning on their machine guns as if they were umbrellas. They were experts in torture, disappearances, and executions. During the Guatemalan military government's undeclared civil war against its own people, which reached its height in the early 1980s, these men, who composed the death squads, terrorized Guatemala.

Indians found dead, their hands tied behind their backs, a sign of the death squads. Santa Cruz de Quiche, Guatemala, 1981.

Death squads were literally called *escuadrones de la muerte* but often were known as *judiciales*, a misnomer, as there was nothing judicial about them.

On Christmas Day, 1980, a *judicial* followed me out of a movie theater and told me I could accompany him either to McDonald's for a Big Mac or to police headquarters. Since the police station was a torture center, where passers-by heard screams coming from the basement, I opted for a brief date with a death squad agent. On another occasion, four heavily armed men in a Bronco Jeep followed two colleagues and me down a deserted street one night. When a friend, a well-connected politician, looked into the matter, he reported that, yes, the men had been after us, but it was just a scare tactic. ("If they had wanted to kill you, you'd be dead," he reassured me.)

Tens of thousands of people died in Guatemala, either in rural massacres conducted by uniformed army troops or, in the cities, in the form of "**disappearances**" at the hands of death squads.

Some were members of the military who donned civilian clothing to carry out the kidnappings. Others, however, were former soldiers, police, bodyguards, or unemployed civilians deputized to do the army's dirty work for pay. *Judiciales* were rural peasants recruited into so-called **civil patrols** whom the army told to denounce their neighbors in return for a gun, some land, some money, or immunity from becoming army targets themselves. For most of them, it was nothing political, just money; if you told a *judicial* you would pay him twice as much to wash cars, he would wash cars instead.

Death squads kidnap and kill because someone in the government or the military commands, sanctions, or condones their behavior. Governments, armed forces, and political organizations have a practical reason to utilize death squads—deniability—but it is rarely plausible.

Death squad executions violate the laws of armed conflict as well as many human rights covenants. A related crime, forced disappearances, is now considered a **crime against humanity** under specific circumstances.

The laws of armed conflict as codified in the four Geneva Conventions of 1949 explicitly prohibit executions without a fair trial. Common Article 3, which applies in internal conflict, forbids "violence to life and person, in particular murder of all kinds, mutilation, cruel treatment and torture" of persons who are not taking part in hostilities. It also forbids "the passing of sentences and the carrying out of executions without previous judgment pronounced by a regularly constituted court, affording all the judicial guarantees which are recognized as indispensable by civilized peoples."

Additional Protocol II of 1977, covering internal armed conflict, states that the court must offer "the essential guarantees of independence and impartiality." The court must inform the accused without delay of the particulars of the offense and provide necessary rights and defense; no one shall be accused except for individual penal responsibility; no one shall be held guilty for a criminal offense which did not exist in law at the time it was committed; those charged with offenses are presumed innocent until proven guilty; anyone charged has the right to be tried in his presence and not to be compelled to testify against himself. Although the protocol is less widely accepted than the 1949 Conventions, Guatemala became a party in 1987.

The Organization of American States in 1994 declared the systematic practice of forced disappearances a crime against humanity, a standard adopted by the 1998 Rome Statute of the International Criminal Court. Human rights covenants, which apply in situations of riots or disturbances but may legally be restricted and temporarily suspended during armed conflict, prohibit the death sentence without a judgment by a competent court.

The situation in Guatemala was clearly an internal armed conflict, and humanitarian law applied. Therefore, the government, army, death squads, and anyone else using force for the government were bound by its terms.

The death squads left very few survivors, and most of these either escaped captivity or were released on the eve of Guatemala's first civilian election in three decades, when the government was eager to bend to foreign demands in exchange for the promise of economic assistance.

Although the army denied any connection to the death squads, no one believed it. Even in Guatemala, where the army was infamous for leaving no witnesses or written accounts of its actions ("We're not Argentina, we leave no survivors," boasted former Army Public Relations Director, Col. Edgar D'Jalma Dominguez, in 1984), it was occasionally indiscreet. When the wife of a trade unionist sought news of her disappeared husband, she was directed to an obscure corner office in the National Palace, where a *judicial* with a black hood over his face recited the details of the kidnapping and torture. (See **due process**.)

Deportation

By Roy Gutman

D

The eighteen-car passenger train drew into the small station at Palic, northern Serbia, halted with a screech, then disgorged the eighteen hundred men, women, and children who had been confined to it for four days. They were inhabitants of the village of Kozluk in eastern Bosnia.

Late in June 1992, two Yugoslav Army tanks rolled into the village center and pointed menacingly at the comfortable houses there. Villagers were offered the choice: leave or have their village destroyed from under them.

The Serbian government chartered this eighteen-car train to take the Muslim inhabitants of Kozluk, Bosnia, to Austria, which refused to accept them. Kept on board for four days, most of them finally ended up deported to Austria—but alive.

After signing away their property to Serb authorities, many walked across the nearby Drina bridge into neighboring Serbia, where border guards told them they could not return to Bosnia. Others boarded buses to the Serbian town of Samac, where they were transferred to the train. The government of Serbian President Slobodan Milosevic had provided the trains of the Yugoslav state railways with the intention of deporting the Kozluk residents to Austria, but so few had travel documents that Hungary refused to allow them transit through to Austria.

Individual or mass deportations are war crimes and crimes against humanity as defined at the Nuremberg Tribunals following World War II, and war crimes under the 1949 Geneva Conventions. If there is enormous loss of life, deportation may constitute genocide, namely the intent to destroy, in whole or in part, a national, ethnic, racial, or religious group, according to legal scholar Alfred de Zayas of Rutgers University.

Deportation was not explicitly banned prior to World War II. The 1907 Hague Conventions omitted mention, because mass expulsions were "generally rejected as falling below the minimum standard of civilization and, therefore, not requiring express prohibition," wrote legal scholar Georg Schwarzenberger.

Hitler's Nazi regime had expelled over 100,000 French from Alsace-Lorraine into Vichy France, and over 1 million Poles from western parts of occupied Poland into the German-run "Government-General of Poland." Germany also deported as many as 12 million non-Germans to work for the German war economy as compulsory labor.

The Nuremberg Tribunal repeatedly condemned the practice of "Germanizing" occupied or annexed territories, that is, transferring in part of the German population, as well as deporting civilians from one occupied region to another or to Germany. It stated that deportations into Germany for purposes of slave labor was "not only in defiance of well-established rules of international law, but in complete disregard of the elementary dictates of humanity."

But the victorious Allies in States taken over by the Communists—Czechoslovakia, Hungary, Romania, Yugoslavia, and East Germany—adopted Nazi practices and expelled some 15 million ethnic Germans to the West after World War II. An estimated 2 to 3 million died as a result.

The Fourth Geneva Convention of 1949 explicitly forbids deportations in conditions of war. "Individual or mass forcible transfers, as well as deportations of protected persons from occupied territory to the territory of the Occupying Power or to that of any other country, occupied or not, are prohibited, regardless of their motive." Also forbidden is the common practice of the occupying power deporting or transferring parts of its own civilian population into the territory it occupies. The convention allows the "total or partial evacuation" of any area where either "the security of the population or imperative military reasons" require, even outside the occupied territory, "when for material reasons it is impossible to avoid such displacement," but the evacuated civilians must be returned to their homes "as soon as hostilities in the area have ceased."

Iraq's deportation of Kuwaitis into Iraq and resettlement of Iraqis in Kuwait was singled out for condemnation by the UN Security Council. Serb "ethnic cleansing" in Bosnia from 1992-1995 also qualifies as a crime against humanity and a war crime. Israel's deportation of Palestinians from occupied territories also violates the Geneva Conventions, in the view of the United States, the UN Security Council and General Assembly, and the International Committee of the Red Cross (ICRC). Israel says the convention has no legal bearing on its conduct in the territories but that it has voluntarily applied the "humanitarian provisions" of its own free will, although without specifying which provisions it has in mind.

The five thousand residents of Kozluk were among the most fortunate of all Bosnian Muslims, for most survived their expulsion. Many families finally made it to Austria where they lived as refugees, and the men returned to fight on the side of the Bosnian government. Their departure was never intended to be a "temporary evacuation."

Detention and Interrogation

By Dana Priest

Shortly after the first CIA paramilitary teams were spirited into Afghanistan's Panjshir Valley in late September 2001 to help topple the Taliban regime, a secretive group of lawyers at CIA and the Justice Department's Office of Legal Counsel began an insurrection of their own. Their aim was to reinterpret long-standing international agreements on the detention and interrogation of prisoners in order to sanction an off-shore CIA prison system beyond the reach of any court, and give the agency's interrogators freedom to extract information from terrorist suspects in nearly any manner they deemed necessary.

The system the CIA put in place was part of what has become the largest covert action program since the height of the Cold War—known at the agency by the initials GST. Its overall purpose is to kill, capture or otherwise neutralize al-Qaeda terrorists. It is wholly separate from the military's counterterrorism programs and has its own distinct rules and legal authorities.

A secret for nearly five years, the CIA's program was acknowledged by President Bush in September 2006, when he announced that fourteen "high-value" terrorist suspects—including the alleged mastermind of 9/11, Khalid Sheikh Mohammed—were being transferred from CIA custody in secret prisons overseas to Guantanamo Bay. President Bush said the people who had been held in the program were "dangerous men with unparalleled knowledge about terrorist networks and their plans for new attacks" and that "the security of our nation and the lives of our citizens depend on our ability to learn what these terrorists know." Having a CIA program for questioning terrorists would "continue to be crucial to getting life-saving information" from any suspects captured in the future, the President added.

Although little beyond the existence of the program has been officially revealed, its broad outlines and the legal arguments used to justify it have become known. The program has its source in two official decisions. First, three days after the attacks of September 11, Congress passed a war resolution authorizing the president to use "all necessary and appropriate force against those nations, organizations, or persons he determines planned, authorized, committed, or aided the terrorist attacks." Congress, in effect, was declaring war against al-Qaeda.

Three days later, on September 17, President Bush signed a classified presidential finding—as required by the National Security Act of 1947—to authorize a covert action program against al-Qaeda. According to the rules governing intelligence operations, covert actions may not violate the U.S. Constitution or U.S. law, including treaties the United States has signed. But they are allowed to violate the laws of the foreign countries in which they take place, according to intelligence experts.

The initial focus of the CIA's counterterrorist program, in the months after September 11, was to kill al-Qaeda leaders and question suspects in order to gain information about a possible imminent second attack on the United States. As years passed without another attack on U.S. soil, the aim of preventing an incipient terrorist operation was overtaken by the desire to acquire knowledge about al-Qaeda's strategic plans, about functioning terrorist cells, about illicit financing and logistics networks, and about the underground flow of potential suicide bombers into Europe, Iraq and elsewhere.

The CIA had no trained interrogators and no facilities to detain suspects when al-Qaeda struck. In the first few months after the attack, as CIA operatives took custody of suspects during the war in Afghanistan, the agency scrambled to find secure and covert locations where they could be held. Initially, prisoners were detained in Afghanistan. Later, prisons were established in several Eastern European democracies, in Thailand, and within the U.S. military's Guantanamo Bay compound in Cuba, according to current and former intelligence officials and other sources. The CIA detention centers in Guantanamo and Thailand were closed down some time ago, and detainees held in the Eastern European prisons were relocated shortly after the *Washington Post* disclosed the existence of prisons there in November 2004.

Intelligence officials argue that in order to gather information from recalcitrant al-Qaeda operatives, the agency needs to be able to hold and interrogate suspects for as long as necessary, without the restrictions imposed by the American legal system or even by the review tribunals established for Guantanamo Bay. About 100 prisoners have gone through these CIA-only "black sites" with approximately 30 prisoners being held at any one time.

It would be illegal for the government to hold prisoners in such isolation in the United States, which is why the CIA placed them overseas, according to former and current intelligence officials and other government sources. These experts said the CIA's internment practices also would be considered illegal under the laws of several host countries, such as those in Eastern Europe, where detainees have the right of access to a lawyer and the right to defend themselves against allegations of wrongdoing. The president's covert action finding, however, allows the CIA to break the laws of foreign countries and to deny the actions if disclosed.

The legality of the secret prisons under international law is highly questionable, according to international law experts and human rights lawyers. The United States claims that its campaign against al-Qaeda is an armed conflict, in which case it would be bound by the customary law of armed conflict; this arguably includes a prohibition on enforced disappearance. If carried out in a widespread or systematic way, either during armed conflict or peace, enforced disappearances are a crime against humanity. Finally, the United States is bound at all times by fundamental norms of human rights, including the right against prolonged arbitrary detention, legal experts say.

The interrogation of suspects held in this secret system proceeded in an improvised way. Teams of polygraphers and psychologists were put together to question alleged terrorists picked up around the world. After the CIA captured the al-Qaeda operations chief Abu Zubaida in March 2002, officials pushed for explicit guidelines that would allow them to use highly coercive methods against so-called "high value detainees." In response to CIA and White House requests, the Justice Department's Office of Legal Counsel issued authorization for a series of "enhanced interrogation techniques."

The EITs include "waterboarding," meant to simulate drowning, "water dousing," soaking detainees with water in cold rooms, prolonged stress and duress positions, liquid diets, sleep and light deprivation, noise and light bombardment, extreme isolation and other measures which are often used in combination with one another.

In his September 2006 speech, President Bush said the procedures used by the CIA were "tough, and they were safe, and lawful, and necessary." However they went far beyond anything that the United States has previously claimed the right to use against captives during war or at any other time. At least some of the practices used would clearly violate the Geneva Conventions,

Satellite image of abandoned brick-making factory (the "Salt Pit") outside Kabul, Afghanistan, 25 January 2001.

but the administration argued that the Geneva Conventions did not protect al-Qaeda fighters picked up in Afghanistan or outside it. In February 2002, President Bush had directed members of the U.S. military to treat detainees humanely—but this directive was deliberately crafted in such a way that civilian intelligence agents were not bound by it.

As a party to the Convention against Torture, the United States is prohibited from using torture at any time. However in a series of internal memos the Bush administration redefined torture in an extremely narrow way. It said to constitute torture, the treatment "must be equivalent in intensity to the pain accompanying serious physical injury, such as organ failure, impairment of bodily function, or even death." For an interrogation technique to rise to the level of mental torture, the Justice Department argued, the psychological harm must last "months or even years."

Although the memo was withdrawn after it became public, a replacement

Satellite image, 17 July 2003. Note the presence of possible new CIA facility.

text said that none of the Justice Department's initial conclusions regarding the legality of specific techniques would be different under the revised standards.

The Torture Convention also bans States from practicing cruel, inhuman or degrading treatment, often referred to as "torture lite." But the administration declared that this provision of the Convention did not apply to the treatment of foreign persons outside the United States. This was an unprecedented interpretation of the law that won little support outside the administration and was disavowed by the former State Department lawyer who had submitted the Torture Convention to Congress in 1989.

To close this loophole, Republican Senator John McCain—a former Vietnam prisoner of war—introduced legislation in 2005 that banned all cruel and inhuman treatment of detainees without any geographical limit. After initially campaigning against the measure, the White House eventually signed it into law in December 2005. However President Bush issued a signing statement that said he would construe the law in accordance with his authority as

Detail of possible new CIA facility, 17 July 2003

Commander-in-Chief. Bush and his lawyers claim that the President has the authority to override statutes if he deems it necessary to national security.

In June 2006, the administration received a further setback when the U.S. Supreme Court issued its decision in the *Hamdan* case. The Court declared that the conflict with al-Qaeda was covered by Common Article 3 of the Geneva Conventions, which forbids cruel, humiliating and degrading treatment of captives. This rule would place greater restrictions on the treatment of prisoners than the McCain Amendment. Following the Court's decision, Congress passed a statute at the administration's request that would limit the enforceability of this part of the Geneva Conventions in American courts.

Beyond the CIA's undisclosed sites, a second tier of prisons exists which are run by foreign security services in their own countries. Experts believe there are at least 70 suspects being housed in them who are thought to have limited intelligence value. For the most part, prisoners were transported by the CIA to these prisons through the process of "rendition." Egypt, Jordan,

Morocco and Afghanistan are among the countries known to hold and interrogate such prisoners, but there are others.

The legal justification for renditions has never been well established or disclosed. Before 9/11, the practice was used to "render" fugitives abroad to justice, meaning into a U.S. or foreign court. These days, however, "extraordinary" renditions are used to transfer subjects into either CIA-run or foreign-run prisons, usually without any legal proceedings. All renditions are done with the consent of the foreign intelligence service involved. There is doubt among some CIA lawyers that this type of rendition is legal.

Under U.S. law and the Torture Convention, the government may not send anyone to a country where he or she is more likely than not to face torture or cruel treatment. The CIA has repeatedly transported prisoners to countries that the State Department has criticized for abusing prisoners in detention.

To comply—at least on paper—with anti-torture laws, the CIA's Office of General Counsel requires a verbal assurance from the foreign intelligence service that the detainee will be treated humanely, according to several recently retired CIA officials familiar with such transfers. Some of these officials say the assurances are ineffective and impossible to monitor. One CIA officer involved with renditions called the assurances from other countries "a farce."

The U.S. war against Iraq stands apart from the rest of America's counterterrorist operations because the administration never denied that the Geneva Conventions applied to all captured Iraqi fighters and civilians. However, either by deliberate military policy or by accident, this distinction was often forgotten in the field. Interrogation tactics approved for use on terrorist suspects in Guantanamo appear to have migrated to Iraq, as did the practice of "ghosting" certain detainees for long periods of time. These tactics were allowed to take hold admist the general chaos and breakdown of discipline within military units that followed the seizure of Baghdad by U.S. and coalition forces.

At the request of the CIA, a number of prisoners were taken out of Iraq in contravention of Article 49 of the Fourth Geneva Convention, which forbids the transfer of protected civilians from occupied territory. One case involved an Iraqi citizen named Hiwa Abul Rahman Rashul, who was captured by Kurdish forces in the summer of 2003 and turned over to the CIA, which whisked him to Afghanistan for interrogation. The Justice Department, however, ruled he was indeed a "protected person" under Geneva. The CIA promptly brought him back to Iraq. But then CIA director George Tenet asked Defense Secretary Donald Rumsfeld not to give Rashul a number and to hide him from the ICRC. Rumsfeld agreed to the request, he said at a news conference a year later. Rashul was then lost in the system for seven months.

Asked to explain the authority under which he complied with Tenet's request or under what authority he could keep Rashul hidden for so long, Rumsfeld responded: "We know from our knowledge that [Tenet] has the authority to do it." In this case, as throughout its counter-terror operations, the administration was purposefully evasive in explaining the legal rationale for the unusual activities it has undertaken. Officials have repeatedly threatened legal action against government professionals and reporters who have brought these activities to the public's attention.

(See **Afghanistan**; **Guantanamo**; **terrorism**.)

Disappearances

By Corinne Dufka

D

The call came around noon on Sunday. "What do you mean, Tita's missing? Who was the last person to see her? Who was she with? Did she go to work on Saturday? What exactly did she tell her mother?" Establishing facts is always a good way to hold back one's feelings in a time of personal crisis.

These were the facts. Tita was Margarita Guzman. Salvadoran citizen. Age: 27. Height: 5'5". Weight: 140 pounds. Hair: Black. Eyes: Brown. No distin-

Civilians in Santiago, Chile, were rounded up and held inside the National Stadium. Untold numbers later disappeared. 1973.

guishing marks. Single mother of two. Employed as a secretary with a social service organization. Last seen wearing blue jeans, a light blue blouse with small flowers, and black pumps, leaving her office at 1:15 pm on Saturday morning, May 4, and heading up Avenida Pablo Segundo.

These things happened. They happened to the poor, to the rich, to the faithful, and it had just happened to my friend Tita. She would never see her children grow big, never light up a room with her sense of humor, never hold her boyfriend again, and never walk the streets of San Salvador as a city at peace. She had disappeared . . . or rather, "been disappeared."

When used as a transitive verb, to disappear means to arrest someone secretly, to imprison and/or to kill them. It has become such a common occurrence in dirty wars ranging from El Salvador and Argentina to Kurdistan and Kuwait that the word seems almost self-explanatory. In international humanitarian law, however, disappearance is complicated for it involves the commission of several separate war crimes including unlawful confinement, failure to allow **due process**, and failure to allow communication between the arrested person and the outside world. It often involves torture and cruel and inhuman treatment, and too commonly it involves murder.

The first stage of a disappearance is capture. Humanitarian law states that State authorities may not make arbitrary arrests, and they must have sound legal bases for taking a person into custody and holding them against their will. The second stage is imprisonment. Additional Protocol II to the Geneva Conventions states that once in custody, a person has the right to humane treatment; the right not to be tortured or otherwise cruelly treated; the right to send and receive letters; the right to due process, including being informed of what he or she stands charged with. A person being detained is presumed innocent, must be granted all the necessary rights and means of mounting a defense—presenting evidence, calling witnesses, and the like—and may not be forced into a confession.

The last stage in a disappearance is murder, or what is sometimes euphemistically referred to as **extrajudicial execution**. Passing and carrying out of a death sentence without the sanction of a regularly constituted court is obviously illegal. The question, though, as in all cases of disappearance and presumed murder is establishing State responsibility. That is both the essence of the task that confronts investigators and the essence of the issue in international law. Not surprisingly, it is the most difficult task as well.

Most disappearances, however, occur in situations other than in international armed conflict—either in internal wars or situations that do not rise to the level of internal conflicts, i.e., disturbances or police actions. Both examples are dealt with in human rights law and the former is addressed in Article 3 common to the four Geneva Conventions. Additionally, the Statute of the International Criminal Court adopted in Rome in 1998 explicitly cites "enforced disappearances . . . by or with the authorization, support or acquiescence of a State or a political organization" as a **crime against humanity** if committed in a widespread or systematic manner.

Try as we did, we never found Tita, nor did we establish with any certainty who had abducted her. We did learn something of her fate, though. Near the Lempa River, outside San Salvador, an old woman stared at her photo for a long time before shaking her head and telling us she was sorry. We tried not to imagine what had happened, but we could not. We'd seen enough of the bodies dumped, sometimes headless and almost always with the clear marks of torture on them, in conspicuous places where passers-by could not avoid seeing them. Rumors from informants who had seen Tita in the hands of the Policia Nacional came and went. But we never found her body, and eventually all of us stopped asking questions except for her little boys, who kept asking why their mother never came home.

Due Process

By Gideon Levy

D

Tarek Burkan was a well-dressed, light-haired Palestinian boy from Hebron, his first mustache growing in. Most of the time I spent with him, he was quiet and seemed calm. Only when I asked him about the circumstances of his detention did he respond openly and aggressively: "Ask the Shabak [the Hebrew acronym for Israel's General Security Service, also known in English as Shin Bet]. Next time I'll throw stones and then at least I'll understand why I'm detained." There was nothing apparently psychotic in this anger of his, just as there is not in the anger of all the administrative detainees, jailed for months and years in Israel without a trial or an explanation.

They are all residents of the territories conquered by Israel in 1967. During the first Intifada, Israel detained thousands; after it ended most were released. Following the outbreak of the Second Intifada the number of detainees again rose to more than one thousand, and in early 2006 Israel was holding over 700 detainees. The number has varied over time, but it is not the number that is significant.

The question is one of principle and it touches on two basic issues: Israel's position among the family of nations and Israel's internal position as a country of law and order in its own right. But the boy Tarek was far removed from all that. I find it hard to believe that he ever heard of the Geneva Conventions, or any other body of humanitarian or human rights law. He is a mentally ill boy whom I met a few years ago in his cell in the Megiddo prison in northern Israel, inside the Green Line. It is a military prison more like a camp than a prison, but its fences are well guarded. As well as Megiddo, administrative detainees are also now held at the Ofer camp in the West Bank and the Ansar 3/Ketziot camp in the Negev desert in southern Israel.

Getting back to the boy, Tarek: several weeks prior to our prison meeting, there was a bad stretch in his illness and he started to be dangerous to himself and his surroundings. He was sixteen years old, had been orphaned from his father when he was one, and hospitalized in the past in a Bethlehem hospital for the mentally ill. Child and adolescent psychiatry expert, Dr. Fahum Tarek, of the Mental Health Center in Tirat Hacarmel, Israel, who examined him at the request of the prison authorities wrote in his statement: "It is almost certain that he suffered [in the past] from paranoid schizophrenia... also during his detention, a psychotic condition with delusional thoughts was suspected." The prison commander admitted that this boy did not belong in Megiddo prison.

Many of the other administrative detainees in Israel do not belong in prison. Among them are young and old, poets and laborers, men and women, Hamas members and left-front members. These are not people who have been charged and convicted of a criminal offence. Instead they are held because they are said to pose a danger to the State of Israel, but in most cases they have not been given a fair chance to argue against their detention, in violation of accepted standards of due process.

Detentions are carried out on the basis of an administrative order, signed by a military commander, but the real responsibility lies with the

Shabak, the omnipotent Israeli security organization. At no stage is there any indictment or trial. Detainees can appeal and have their case reviewed by a judge, but even the appeal process does not meet the minimal standard of due process. Neither the detainees nor their lawyers are given any idea what the evidence against them is—everything is privileged and confidential. No witnesses testify against them, evidence is presented by a Shabak representative to the judge alone. The detainees have no idea when they will be released: every six months they can expect notice that their detention has been extended without any explanation.

There are some whose detention has been extended nine to ten times, and the majority have been jailed for over two years. There are detainees who served court sentences only to find that on the day of their release they were put in administrative detention. Since the signing of the Oslo accords, according to a 1997 report by B'tselem—the Israeli Information Center for Human Rights in the Occupied Territories—some people have been detained for "non-violent political activity and the expression of political opinions." If so, they are political detainees, even if Israel does not accept the definition.

The B'tselem report stated that while Israel claimed to be adhering to general principles of international law governing detention, "rhetorical declarations by officials and judges notwithstanding, Israel severely violates every one of these principles in practice."

Administrative detentions in the West Bank are carried out under order 1229 of 1988. This authorizes military commanders to detain a person for a maximum of six months when there is "a reasonable basis to assume that reasons of regional security or public safety require that a certain person be held in detention." The order fixes no maximum cumulative time, and therefore detention can be extended repeatedly and indefinitely. Even the meaning of the magic words "regional security" and "public safety" is left to the exclusive discretion of the regional military commanders. There is a right to appeal to a military judge against each extension, but the restrictions on hearing the evidence against detainees remain.

The situation is contrary to the natural principles of justice and to several international conventions to which Israel is a party. Israel ratified the International Covenant on Civil and Political Rights in 1991. Its Article 9 states: "No one shall be subjected to arbitrary arrest or detention." Although Israel holds that at the time of and ever since ratification it has been in "a state of public emergency" that requires derogation from Article 9, the power to derogate from (i.e. suspend the application of) the Covenant's rule against detention is not unlimited. Even during emergency situations, the State is required to protect basic human rights as much as possible and every move against them must pass the test of necessity and proportionality. Detention without trial is regarded in human rights law as a preventive measure to be used only in exceptional circumstances; it must not be used as an alternative to criminal proceedings, by holding detainees to punish them for acts they may already have committed.

Administrative detention in the territories is also generally agreed to be subject to the guidelines of the Fourth Geneva Convention of 1949. (Israel disputes the legal applicability of the Convention, but has agreed to respect its humanitarian and customary provisions.) The Israeli government claims that its use of administrative detention conforms to Article 78 of this Convention, which permits detentions due to "imperative reasons of security." However, in this context, the International Committee of the Red Cross (ICRC) Commentary to the Geneva Conventions states that holding people

High-security Prison at Beersheba, 1973.

without trial must be an "exceptional" measure. The commentary notes that according to Article 49, moving detainees to detention sites outside the occupied territories (as Israel does) is prohibited.

Where criminal trials are held, both humanitarian and human rights law set strict rules for how such trials should be conducted. These requirements include: the right to be informed of charges; to be tried without undue delay; to prepare and present a defense; to be assisted by counsel; the right not to be forced to confess, and to be presumed innocent until proven guilty. A similar set of standards is implied by Common Article 3 of the Geneva Conventions of 1949, which applies to non-international armed conflict and forbids "the passing of sentences and the carrying out of executions without previous judgment pronounced by a regularly constituted court, affording all the judicial guarantees which are recognized as indispensable by civilized peoples."

The boy, Tarek, had not heard about any of this. In his cell, he was irate about his detention and, primarily, about the lack of information he had about any of the charges against him. Many comrades who have suffered the same fate, mentally healthier than Tarek, are no less irate. Nonetheless, the real anger and frustration should have been in the State of Israel: in the final historical reckoning, the end result of administrative detention will be that it will affect the jailers more than the detainees. Tarek Burkan was released after serving six months of detention without a trial. His friends and successors in Israel's prisons will also be released one day.

Due Process Rights

According to the International Committee of the Red Cross, these fundamental rules of due process, derived from the Third and Fourth Geneva Conventions, the Additional Protocols, and customary law, apply to anyone detained in connection with armed conflict or occupation:

Civilians detained for imperative reasons of security have the right of appeal, to be decided with the least possible delay, and the right to have their detention periodically reviewed. (In non-international conflict, detainees have the right to challenge the legality of their detention.)
No one may be convicted or sentenced unless he has received a fair trial affording all essential judicial guarantees, including the following rights:
to be tried by an impartial and regularly constituted court;
to be presumed innocent until proven guilty;
to be told—early on and in a language he understands—what he is accused of;
to be given the necessary rights and means of defense;
to be tried without undue delay;
to be able to examine witnesses against him;
to have the assistance of an interpreter, if necessary;
to be tried in his presence;
not to be required to testify against himself or to confess guilt;
to have judgment pronounced publicly;
to be told of his rights of appeal and what time limits there are;
to be convicted only of a crime that he himself committed;
not to be punished more than once for the same act;
to be convicted only for what was a crime at the time of the act in question, and to have a sentence no more severe than the law allowed at the time of the act in question.

E

Environmental Warfare

By Mark Perry and Ed Miles

E **The testimony of George Claxton, a Vietnam veteran who served in Southeast Asia in 1967, reveals just how widely the United States used Agent Orange. "I took showers in the stuff," he says. "We had wooden stalls with a tub overhead filled with rainwater that was tinged slightly orange. We would pull the string hanging in the shower and bathe in it. We knew it was Agent Orange because we saw the planes spraying it on the jungle every day. We didn't think anything of it really and at first we thought, 'Hell, the army is spraying for mosquitoes.' "**

Claxton's experience was not unusual. Between 1965 and 1975, the U.S. military sprayed millions of tons of Agent Orange on the jungles of Vietnam in "ADMs"—airborne "area denial missions" intended to deny cover to the Vietcong and North Vietnamese Army. The strategy worked: large areas of Quang Tri Province along the 38th Parallel and a swath of land in the "iron triangle" of Tay Ninh Province west of Saigon were stripped of all vegetation.

In the wake of Vietnam, there was worldwide concern about the environmental damage caused by U.S. military operations in Southeast Asia. Shortly after the end of the Vietnam War, in 1975, it began to become clear that a disproportionate number of Vietnam veterans were coming down with non-Hodgkins lymphoma and skin sarcomas. The Centers for Disease Control would later determine that the cause of these cancers was the dioxins contained in Agent Orange. The extent of the damage to the natural environment of Vietnam as a result of the spraying was also becoming apparent. While no systematic survey of defoliated areas of Southeast Asia has been conducted, the anecdotal evidence is enormous. Huge portions of Quang Tri and Tay Ninh provinces "look like a moonscape" and remain unsuitable for agricultural use, according to Chuck Searcy, the director of a humanitarian program in Hanoi. And Vietnamese doctors have attested to significant increases in birth defects among people in the affected areas.

The major piece of international humanitarian law prohibiting environmental war was drafted in reaction to what took place in Vietnam, and is contained in two articles of the 1977 Additional Protocol I to the Geneva Conventions. Article 35 states that "it is prohibited to employ methods or means of warfare which are intended, or may be expected, to cause widespread, long-term and severe damage to the environment." This prohibition is spelled out in detail in two sections of Article 55.

The first of these sections involves the protection of the natural environment. "Care shall be taken in warfare," it states, "to protect the natural environment against widespread, long-term and severe damage. This protection includes a prohibition against the use of means of warfare which are intended or may be expected to cause such damage to the natural environment and thereby prejudice the health or survival of the population." The second provision declares that "attacks against the natural environment by way of **reprisals** are prohibited."

Unfortunately, these provisions are more unclear and more ambiguous legally than at least some commentators and activists might have wished.

While they impose the obligation to take precautions, they fall far short of a blanket interdiction against certain methods of warfare that may harm the environment. The use of the expression "long-term" is understood to mean decades, not years, so a considerable degree of environmental harm seems to be tolerable under international humanitarian law.

Some further limitations on the ravages of environmental war were secured by the Convention on the Prohibition of Military or Any Other Hostile Use of Environmental Modification Techniques (ENMOD), which was opened for signature in 1977—again, largely in response to the American use of defoliants in Vietnam—and was ratified by the United States in 1980. This convention is now accepted, along with Articles 35 and 55 of Additional Protocol I, as the clearest expression of international humanitarian law in the field of environmental warfare.

By the terms of the ENMOD, States agree not to "engage in military or other hostile use of environmental modification techniques having

A Vietnamese mother with her two blind daughters, 1980. Their father had been a truck driver on the Ho Chi Minh Trail and had often been soaked with Agent Orange.

widespread, long-lasting or severe effects as the means of destruction, damage or injury." In practice, it remains to be seen whether enough ambiguity has been removed from the law to make these provisions serve as an effective way of preventing the most extreme kinds of environmental attacks. These provisions were not in effect at the time of the Vietnam War, so, obviously, they cannot be applied retroactively to what took place then. Some have argued that the Iraqi government's decision, in the waning days of its occupation of Kuwait in 1991, to set fire to the Kuwaiti oil fields and to purposely dump millions of tons of oil into the Persian Gulf was an instance of such a crime. But since no Iraqi officers were ever indicted or tried for these offenses, the practical impact of the provisions remains unclear.

Kuwaiti Oil Wells

By Robert Block

Dante would have at been at home in Kuwait in 1991. A desert paradise had been transformed into an environmental inferno by a spiteful Iraqi leader.

Across the land more than six hundred oil wells ignited by Iraqi soldiers spewed out orange and red fireballs and roared like untamed beasts. The smoke was so thick and so black that when the winds failed it became midnight at 10:00 A.M. Grease dripped from the skies and soot fell like snowflakes from hell. Everything whose natural color should have been white was a charcoal gray: cats, sheep, and the carcasses of slender-billed seagulls who dropped from the heavens while overflying the country.

The burning oil fields on the Kuwait skyline is perhaps the most enduring image to survive the Gulf War and is also one of the greatest environmental crimes ever perpetrated.

It was Saddam Hussein's final defiant gesture. Defeated but unbowed after the Gulf War, his troops placed explosive charges next to every well they could reach in the Ahmadi, Dharif, Umm Quadir, Wafra, Minagish, and Rawdatayn oil fields. If the entire dispute that led to Iraq's invasion of Kuwait was over oil, then Saddam's attitude appeared to be, "If I can't have it, neither can you."

During the war, the Pentagon issued exaggerated assessments of the oil fires and the deliberate oil spills the Iraqis unleashed, putting Saddam Hussein's acts of ecoterrorism in the worst possible light. Nevertheless the horror of the fires and the ecological damage to the Gulf's fragile flora and fauna from what locals called "Saddam's memorial cloud" were very real.

At the time, John Walsh, a biologist with the World Society for the Protection of Animals, was particularly concerned about dozens of species of migratory birds from Central Asia which traveled over the Gulf. He would brave the heat and the smoke from the burning wells and collect dead birds. After picking up one dead gull, he surveyed the spectacle and wondered aloud: "Is this what the end of the world looks like?"

The Greater Burhan Oil Fields, set afire by the retreating Iraqi troops in 1991, evoke apocalyptic imagery.

Ethnic Cleansing

By Roger Cohen

The life of Hiba Mehmedovic, a Bosnian Muslim, came apart on May 31, 1992, soon after the war in Bosnia began. Three Serbs armed with automatic weapons broke into her home and took away her two sons, Kemal and Nedzad, whom she never saw again. A few weeks later, she herself was forced at gunpoint onto a bus, driven to the front line west of her home town of Vlasenica, and abandoned.

E

She trudged into government-held territory. When I found her, sprawled on the floor of a kindergarten in the town of Kladanj, she was a broken figure emblematic of the war: tearful and terrified, part of a dark tide of Muslims driven from their homes, human flotsam scattered across the floors of empty buildings. Her unseeing eyes spoke of an existence emptied. There were 18,699 Muslims in Vlasenica before the war, about 60 percent of the population; there are none today.

Ethnic cleansing—the use of force or intimidation to remove people of a certain ethnic or religious group from an area—was the central fact of the wars of Yugoslavia's destruction. The practice has a method: **terror**. It has a smell: the fetid misery of refugees. It has an appearance: the ruins of ravaged homes. Its purpose is to ensure—through killing, destruction, threat, and humiliation—that no return is possible.

Yugoslavia, and its Bosnian heart, were bridges. But over four years of war, places of mingling became places of bleak ethnic homogeneity as more than 1.5 million people were shifted in the name of racist ideologies. The single most devastating burst of violence, between April and August 1992, saw Serbs driving more than 700,000 Muslims from an area covering 70 percent of Bosnia.

Such mass **deportation** was not new in this century of ethnic engineering. Greeks out of Turkey; Turks out of Greece; Serbs out of the Fascist Croatia of 1941–1945; Jews out of Hitler's Europe; ethnic Germans out of postwar Czechoslovakia; Palestinians from occupied territories. The waves of forced evictions of ethnic and religious groups have been repetitive, often combining physical removal with devastating violence, or, as in the case of the Jews, genocide.

"Ethnic cleansing" is a blanket term, and no specific crime goes by that name, but the practice covers a host of criminal offenses. The United Nations Commission of Experts, in a January 1993 report to the Security Council, defined "ethnic cleansing" as "rendering an area ethnically homogenous by using force or intimidation to remove persons of given groups from the area." It said ethnic cleansing was carried out in the former Yugoslavia by means of murder, **torture**, arbitrary arrest and detention, **extrajudicial executions**, **rape** and sexual assault, confinement of the civilian population, deliberate military attacks or threats of attacks on civilians and civilian areas, and wanton destruction of property. The Commission's final report in May 1994 added these crimes: mass murder, mistreatment of civilian prisoners and prisoners or war, use of civilians as human **shields**, destruction of **cultural property**, robbery of personal property, and attacks on **hospitals**, **medical personnel**, and locations with the **Red Cross/Red Crescent emblem**.

Perpetrators of such crimes are subject to individual criminal responsibility, and military and political leaders who participated in making and implementing the policy "are also susceptible to charges of **genocide** and **crimes against humanity**, in addition to grave breaches of the Geneva Conventions and other violations of international humanitarian law," the 1994 report said.

International law took up the question of the systematic expulsion of civilians, and the barbaric practices associated with it, after World War II. Article 49 of the Fourth Geneva Convention of 1949 forbids "individual or mass forcible **transfers**, as well as deportations of protected persons from occupied territory to the territory of the Occupying Power or to that of any other country." The actions are grave breaches of the Fourth Convention—war crimes of particular seriousness.

Only the security of the civilian population or "imperative military reasons" may justify **evacuation** of civilians in occupied territory, according to the Fourth Geneva Convention. Additional Protocol II of 1977 extends this rule to civilians in internal armed conflicts. In Bosnia, where the Serbs initially enjoyed overwhelming military superiority, there is no evidence that the forced movement of Muslim men, women, and children was driven by such a consideration. As Pero Popovic, a Serb guard at the Susica concentration camp in Vlasenica once told me, "Our aim was simply to get rid of the Muslims."

Article 49 applies to international conflict. I traveled with enough Serb forces crossing Serbia's border with Bosnia to have no doubt that this was a war organized, financed, and directed from Belgrade. But even if the Bosnian War is viewed as a civil war between Serbs, Muslims, and Croats of the country, the forced expulsions contravene Article 3 common to the four Geneva Conventions, which applies to "conflict not of an international character."

This article states that "people taking no active part in the hostilities" shall always "be treated humanely, without any adverse distinction founded on race, color, religion or faith, birth or wealth." It prohibits "humiliating and degrading treatment" and "violence to life and person, in particular murder of all kinds, mutilation, cruel treatment, and torture."

There is also the Nuremberg Charter to consider. Article 6 defined "crimes against humanity" as including "murder, extermination, enslavement, deportation, and other inhumane acts committed against any civilian population, before or during a war." And Nuremberg made it clear that population transfer is a war crime.

Mrs. Mehmedovic's most precious possession was two photographs of her sons, aged twenty-seven and twenty-five when they were dragged from her house. I took the photographs to Popovic, the Serb guard in Vlasenica, who had recanted. His look of recognition was unmistakable. He told me the two boys had been executed at the Susica camp.

(See **Bosnia; internal displacement; refugees; siege; starvation**.)

A toppled minaret sets the backdrop for a makeshift morgue where the bodies of victims are washed before burial. Bosnia, May 1993.

Evacuation of Civilians from the Battlefield

By H. Wayne Elliott

E

The battlefield is not a place most people want to be. Soldiers are there because of the mission and their duty. Civilians who find themselves on the battlefield are, in most cases, there by accident or at least unintentionally. Wounds, death, and destruction accompany combat. People will be wounded and perhaps killed. Buildings and personal property will be destroyed. What duty is owed by soldiers to those civilians who find themselves caught up in the fight?

A civilian can be defined by who he is not. Generally, a civilian is a person who is not a combatant and does not take a direct part in the hostilities. On the battlefield the soldier is concerned with whether those present are legitimate military objectives, most often called "lawful targets." If they are true civilians, they should not be participating in the fight. If they choose to do so they are subject to being targeted and, if captured, might be brought before a judicial tribunal as an unlawful **combatant**.

Suppose a commander knows there are true civilians in the battlefield area. What obligations are placed on that commander? Must an effort be made to evacuate the civilians? There is no obligation to evacuate civilians from the battle area. At the same time, deliberately endangering noncombatants is a violation of the laws of war. In practice, commanders often avoid the problem of civilians in the battle area by simply giving a warning. This might be accomplished by dropping leaflets, or by making announcements over loudspeakers or radio. At first glance, such a practice might seem unlikely or even blissful. But as a military matter such warnings make sense (unless, of course, surprise is a factor). First, the commander giving the warning is making a demonstrable effort to avoid harming noncombatants. Second, as a military matter, a warning to civilians that they should remove themselves from the area has the propaganda effect of reminding them that their own military force may be unable to stem the advancing forces. Third, most civilians will move toward their own forces and not their enemy. When that occurs, their own forces may well be presented with a major logistical and tactical problem.

The law actually places the burden of protecting civilians most heavily on the force that has some real control over the civilians. Thus, while an attacking force can not deliberately target civilians, neither can a defending force use civilians as some sort of a shield against legitimate attacks.

Suppose that the civilian noncombatants are inside a besieged area, such as Sarajevo during the Bosnian War. Article 17 of the Fourth Geneva Convention does provide that the "Parties to the conflict shall endeavor to conclude local agreements for the removal from besieged or encircled areas" of noncombatants. The word "endeavor" clearly shows that such evacuation is not compulsory. In fact, the commander of the besieged place will tend to want to evacuate the civilian noncombatants because they consume supplies and rations. At the same time, and for the same reason, the commander of a besieging force is not likely to agree that persons who are a drain on enemy resources should be permitted to leave. Whether an agreement is reached or not, civilians cannot be specifically targeted. During the siege of Sarajevo snipers killed individuals who were clearly civilians (school-age children, old people, sick, etc.). In the case of some of those killed at Sarajevo, war crimes were committed—not because the civilians were not evacuated, but because civilians were targeted.

As the force advances, the more general obligations under the Fourth Geneva Convention concerning the occupation of enemy territory might be triggered. When an advancing force becomes an occupying force, the law places that force in the position of an interim government. As such, its responsibilities to the civilian population are much greater and more defined.

The burden when it comes to protecting civilians from the combat effects of war falls on three distinct parties: First, the advancing force, which must make every effort to avoid unnecessary harm to civilians. Second, the defending force, which may well have the best chance at removing civilians

E

Five centuries ago, Jews fleeing the Spanish inquisition found a home in Sarajevo. In 1993, the remnants of the ancient community are bused out of range of Serb shells and snipers.

from the area before it actually becomes the scene of combat. Third, and most important, the civilians themselves. They must avoid participating in the fight. In fact, they should simply avoid, if possible, being in the area where the fighting occurs.

(See **collateral damage**; **ethnic cleansing**; **internal displacement**; **siege**; **transfer of civilians**.)

Executions, Extrajudicial

By Don Oberdorfer

Accompanied by a sudden artillery and mortar barrage and flares casting a metallic glow, two North Vietnamese battalions stormed across lightly defended bridges and lotus-choked moats into the former Vietnamese imperial capital of Hue before dawn on January 31, 1968.

It was part of nearly simultaneous surprise attacks by Communist military forces against nearly every significant city or town in South Vietnam during the lunar new year, or Tet, holiday. The Tet Offensive, as the nationwide attacks would become known, shocked the U.S. government and public into reconsidering and eventually terminating the U.S. military effort in Vietnam.

Hue was occupied for twenty-five days before the North Vietnamese were ousted. During that time, the troops and the political officers who came with them ruled over large parts of the city. One of the central objectives of the occupation, according to a written plan prepared in advance, was to "destroy and disorganize" the administrative machinery that the South Vietnamese regime had established since Vietnam was divided by international agreement in 1954. The effort to root out "enemy" functionaries, according to the plan, was to extend "from the province and district levels to city wards, streets and wharves." The political officers arrived with a carefully prepared "target list" of 196 places, organized on a block-by-block basis, to be given priority attention, including U.S. and South Vietnamese offices and the homes of the officials who worked there, as well as the homes of those who were deemed to be leading or cooperating with their efforts, including foreigners. Once in charge, the occupation forces set about expanding its target lists with the assistance of local sympathizers.

So many were killed. Le Van Rot, the owner of the most popular Chinese soup restaurant in the city, was the government block chief of his area. Four armed men, two from Hue and two from North Vietnam, came to his shop and arrested him, accusing him of being a spy. They bound his arms behind his back with wire and began to tug him toward the door. When he resisted, one of them put a bullet through his head.

Then there was Pham Van Tuong. He worked part-time as a janitor at the government information office. Four men in black pajamas came to his house, calling on him by name to come out of the bunker where he and his family had taken refuge. But when he did come out, along with his five-year-old son, his three-year-old daughter, and two of his nephews, there was a burst of gunfire. All five were shot to death.

Dr. Horst Gunther Krainick was a German pediatrician and professor of internal medicine who had worked for seven years with teams of Germans and Vietnamese to establish a medical school at Hue University. Krainick stayed in his university apartment after the fall of the city, believing he and his wife would not be harmed. Unknown to them, they were on the original target list. On the fifth day of the occupation, an armed squad arrived and put the Krainicks and two other German doctors into a

South Vietnamese police chief Colonel Nguyen Ngoc Loan executes a suspected Viet Cong officer during the Tet Offensive in 1968.

commandeered Volkswagen bus. Their bodies were found later in a potato field, all victims of an executioner's bullets.

The same day, North Vietnamese troops came in force to the Roman Catholic cathedral, where many people had taken refuge from the fighting. Four hundred men were ordered out, some by name and others apparently because they were of military age or prosperous appearance. When the group was assembled, the political officer on the scene told people not to fear; the men were merely being taken away temporarily for political indoctrination. Nineteen months later, three defectors led U.S. soldiers to a creek bed in a double canopy jungle ten miles from Hue where the skulls and bones of those who had been taken away had lain ever since. Those killed included South Vietnamese servicemen, civil servants, students, and ordinary citizens. The skulls revealed they had been shot or brained with blunt instruments.

Altogether, South Vietnamese authorities counted about twenty-eight hundred victims of deliberate slaughter during the Tet Offensive in Hue. The fate of some was known immediately. The bodies of others emerged later from mass graves in nearby jungles or the coastal salt flats. Like those taken from the cathedral, they had been shot to death, bludgeoned, or buried alive.

After Hue was retaken, the South Vietnamese authorities were reported to be guilty of some of the same practices. I learned from a U.S. team that "black teams" of South Vietnamese assassins were sent in to eliminate those who were believed to have aided the enemy during the occupation. On March 14, three weeks after South Vietnam regained control, more than twenty prisoners, including some women and schoolboys, were brought to provincial military headquarters with burlap bags covering their heads and hands tightly wired behind their backs. After being taken into a stone building that was reputed to be a place of execution, all the prisoners disappeared.

It is, of course, unlawful to execute an accused person without giving him a fair trial first. Two bodies of law apply—humanitarian law, which applies in an armed conflict, and human rights law, which applies even where the laws of war do not.

Under international humanitarian law, the sorts of killings that took place in Hue are usually termed "willful killing without judicial process." If the victims are enemy prisoners of war (including accredited journalists and civilian suppliers and contractors attached to enemy armed forces), or medical or religious personnel attached to the armed services, such executions are grave breaches under the Third Geneva Convention. If they are enemy civilians, it is a grave breach of the Fourth Geneva Convention.

The requirements for fair trials of military personnel and civilians are similar. Each accused person has rights: against self-incrimination, against being convicted on the basis of an *ex post facto* law, for being advised of his or her rights, of having the right to counsel, to be told the particulars of the charge, to prepare a defense, to call witnesses, to have an interpreter, and to appeal. "As it is prohibited to kill protected persons during an international armed conflict, so it is prohibited to kill those taking no active part in hostilities which constitute an internal armed conflict," the International Criminal Tribunal for the former Yugoslavia said in November 1998. The key element is "the death of the victim as a result of the actions of the accused." Even when it is unclear whether a situation is an armed conflict, human rights law forbids extrajudicial executions.

(See **death squads**; **disappearances**; **due process**.)

The Camera as Witness

By Alex Levac

On April 13, 1984, four young Palestinians commandeered bus number 300 as it made its way from Tel Aviv to the southern city of Ashkelon, and forced it to Dir el-Ballah, a small town in the northern Gaza Strip which at the time was under Israeli occupation. There the bus was surrounded by soldiers and police. Just before sunrise, after an all-night standoff, crack troops stormed the bus, turning the silent pre-dawn into a delirium of screaming, gunfire, and explosions that lasted several minutes.

With other photographers and reporters who had evaded police road-blocks to get to the scene, I ran toward the noise in the near total darkness. Suddenly, I found myself confronting two men who alternated

A young Palestinian hijacker led away by two Shin Bet officers, who crushed his skull with a rock. The official report read that he was shot during the operation to rescue the bus passengers he was holding hostage. Images of police have been distorted on demand of Israeli censor.

between dragging and propping up a third person. Convinced that he was one of the many passengers rescued from the bus, I snapped just one picture. The two men were on me instantly, demanding that I surrender the film from my camera. With a sleight of hand, I managed to give them an unused roll, and they were on their way.

On the journey back to Tel Aviv, I heard the army spokesman telling Israeli radio that one passenger had been killed, a few had been wounded, and the rest rescued unharmed. He said that two of the Palestinian hijackers had died in the raid and that two others had been captured when the troops stormed the bus. However, an hour later, the next news broadcast reported that all four hijackers had died when the troops stormed the bus. And that version became the official government line.

It wasn't until I developed the film that I realized why the men in the picture, members of the Shin Bet—the domestic security service—wanted my film. The man they were dragging off, I discovered to my astonishment, wasn't a passenger at all. He was one of the hijackers—young, handcuffed to his captors, and very much alive. At least one of the Palestinians had survived the raid. The picture was proof that the security officials had lied. The truth peered out from the eyes of this young Palestinian, bound but living. Here was a man who only a short time earlier had been terrorizing a bus full of passengers and striking fear in the hearts of all Israelis.

The more I looked, the more complete his transformation had become from an abhorrent figure to a pitiful one—a man in need of protection from the two Shin Bet agents guarding him. Moments earlier the agents had been heroes rescuing passengers on a bus. Now, standing on either side of their captive, they were the bad guys. Does the knowledge of impending death shape our judgment? From the moment of his death, the Palestinian became a reflection of our own mortal image. Are we to erase him from our collective memory and let him disappear under a mound of earth, or do we raise his ghost and grapple with his right to live, to be tried, to be a human being?

Every photojournalist wants to make an impact, wants his picture to be worth a thousand words. The power of my photograph of the Palestinian hijacker escorted to his death by his Shin Bet captors is drawn from what the observer does not see but is compelled to imagine—the moment the agents crush the Palestinian's skull with a stone, the moment of death. (See **hostages**.)

F, G

Forced Labor

By John Ryle

Forced labor, like slavery, involves the deprivation of liberty, but differs from slavery in that no claim of permanent right of ownership is made over a person subject to it. International agreements put strict limits on the use of forced labor by the State and prohibit its use by non-State bodies and individuals, but they do not ban it outright.

F

Forced labor is a common feature of modern wars. In Burma (Myanmar), for example, conscription of civilians as unpaid labor for the military authorities is widespread. Typical duties include the construction of roads, barracks, and railways, and porterage for army contingents. Such projects often involve large-scale relocation of populations. In the worst instances, civilians from ethnic minorities in areas of rebel activity have been forced to march ahead

of troops as a human shield against landmines.

In the former Yugoslavia, between 1993 and 1996, forced labor was used by all sides, but most systematically in the Serb-controlled areas of northern Bosnia, where non-Serb minorities under Bosnian Serb control were subject to a "work obligation." Forced labor details were assigned to the front line of conflict; they were also put to work in factories and mines; the work obligation was used as a means of public humiliation for prominent members of minority ethnic groups.

All these practices involve infringements of one or other of the various international agreements that touch on the issue of forced labor. Article 3 common to the four Geneva Conventions of 1949 applies in internal conflicts and requires humane treatment to those who do not take part in hostilities and arguably limits forced labor by imposing minimum standards on it. The Fourth Geneva Convention specifies that, in occupied territory, civilians cannot be compelled to join the armed forces of an occupying power, or to engage in certain kinds of war-related work, such as the production of munitions, and if under age eighteen they may not be forced to work at all.

Chechens accused of collaborating with Russians are forced to labor at digging trenches around Grozny, 1996.

Civilians under military occupation, both in wars between States and, as specified in Additional Protocol II of 1977, in internal conflicts, cannot be required to work longer hours or under conditions worse than the local norm. Civilian internees in a war between States cannot be compelled to work, unless they are medical personnel (who can be required to attend fellow internees) or are employed in administrative, kitchen, civil defense, or other work on behalf of other internees. Enforced prostitution is specifically prohibited in Article 27 of the Fourth Convention.

There are detailed rules in international law for the treatment of **prisoners of war** set out in the Third Geneva Convention of 1949. Most of the restrictions on civilian employment detailed above also apply to them; beyond this, the Geneva Conventions specify that POWs forced to work must be paid a wage, unless their work involves only the maintenance or administration of their place of detention. They cannot be forced to do degrading, unhealthy, or dangerous work. Military officers cannot be forced to work.

In order to determine whether a particular case of forced labor contravenes any or all of the international norms specified above, it will be useful to know the following. First, who is being forced to work: whether they are prisoners of war, women, under the age of eighteen or over forty-five, or members of an ethnic or other minority. Second, the nature of the work and working conditions: who the work is for, the hours and days worked, the distances from home, whether the work is war-related, whether the products are exported, and whether or not they are paid.

Forced labor is also addressed by two conventions of the International Labor Organization (ILO), a constituent organization of the UN. ILO Convention 29 (1930), which was an attempt to tackle the issue of forced labor in European colonies in Africa and Asia, restricts forced labor duties to able-bodied males between eighteen and forty-five, and to those whose absence "will not affect family life in the community." Another ILO Convention, No. 105 (1959), forbids parties from using forced labor as a punishment for expressing political views or as a means to economic development.

The applicability of the ILO Conventions in wartime is limited by the exemption they make for emergencies (including war). But they have nevertheless proved effective in drawing attention to abuses in countries where there are undeclared internal conflicts, such as Burma (which has ratified ILO Convention 29, but not Convention 105). Signatories to ILO Conventions are obliged to submit reports, which are considered by meetings of experts at the International Labor Conference. Outside bodies cannot make official representations at these meetings, but information from human rights reports may be put on the record and governments involved can be asked to respond. Some Western countries have laws banning the import of products manufactured using a conscript labor force. This constraint on trade may be the most effective sanction against many forms of forced labor.

Other international agreements that touch on the issue of forced labor include the UN Convention on the Rights of the Child and the UN Declaration of Human Rights. The UN International Covenant on Civil and Political Rights reiterates the ban on the use of forced labor as a punishment for holding political views, as a means of economic development, or as a form of discrimination against a social group.

Free Fire Zones

By Lewis M. Simons

In the mid-1960s, when I was covering the war in Vietnam for the Associated Press, U.S. commanders were issued wallet-size cards bearing the warning to "use your firepower with care and discrimination, particularly in populated areas." Often, these cards ended up in a pocket of a pair of tropical fatigues, where they remained, ignored, for the duration of the bearer's tour of duty.

F

The intention of the Department of Defense in issuing the cards was to help prevent jittery U.S. soldiers from mistakenly, or intentionally, declaring a suspect village a "free fire zone," then destroying it and its residents. All too often, postmortem investigations revealed that such zones had been peaceful and should not have been assaulted. This type of incident with its attendant hostile publicity—My Lai was perhaps the most infamous, if not necessarily the most egregious—was a recurring nightmare of the military high command and a succession of U.S. administrations.

But the cards only served to accent official naiveté. In reality, U.S. troops in Vietnam seldom knew with any certainty which villages were friendly, siding with the Americans and their Saigon-based allies, and which supported the Hanoi-backed Viet Cong Communist guerrillas.

The practice of establishing free fire zones was instituted because many villages in what was then South Vietnam willingly provided safe haven to Viet Cong fighters. Some, by contrast, were forcibly occupied by marauding bands of guerrillas, who used the villages for cover. Many more were devotedly anti-Communist. Yet the American forces often had fundamental difficulty in distinguishing among any of these villagers. The fact that the guerrillas commonly dressed in black cotton pajama-style outfits, like those worn by most Vietnamese peasants, served only to heighten the confusion.

But despite the GIs' confusion, international law enjoins armies to avoid targeting any but military objectives and assures protection to civilians, in almost any circumstance. Free fire zones as defined by Department of Defense doctrine and the rules of engagement are a severe violation of the laws of war for two reasons. First, they violate the rule against direct attack of civilians by presuming that after civilians are warned to vacate a zone, then anyone still present may lawfully be attacked. The rule prohibiting direct attacks on civilians provides no basis for a party to a conflict to shift the burden by declaring a whole zone to be "civilian free." And second, they violate the rule against **indiscriminate attack** by presuming without justification in the law that warning civilians to leave eliminates the legal requirements to discriminate in targeting its weapons.

Where the protection of the Geneva Conventions does not provide a mantle to civilians is when they take "a direct part in hostilities." There were, of course, occasions when Vietnamese civilians directly attacked U.S. troops, but those which drew the attention of news reporters were overwhelmingly those in which a village was labeled a free fire zone and innocent lives were taken in outbursts of indiscriminate fire and brutality.

Faced with this negative coverage and with severe difficulty in enforcing international laws limiting the imposition of free fire zones, as well as other elements of the rules of engagement, the Pentagon over time added more directives to its pocket cards: a village could not be bombed without warning even if American troops had received fire from within it; a village known to be Communist could be attacked only if its inhabitants were warned in advance; only once civilians had been removed could a village be declared a free fire zone and shelled at will.

According to an article by Maj. Mark S. Martens of the U.S. Army's Judge Advocate-General's Corps and a distinguished graduate of the U.S. Military Academy, Oxford University, and Harvard Law School, all these rules were "radically ineffective." Often they were simply ignored. In some cases, illiterate peasants couldn't understand leaflets dropped to warn them that their villages would soon become a free fire zone. In other cases, hurried, forcible evacuations left large numbers of defenseless civilians behind, to be killed by bombing, shelling, small arms assaults, or burning. "The only good village," went one bit of cynical GI wisdom, "is a burned village."

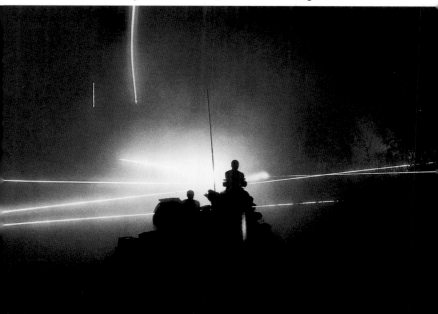

The U.S. Eleventh Armored Cavalry Regiment spray the area in an exercise they call "Mad Minute." Cambodia, 1970.

Ineffective efforts to rein in the GIs' propensity to create free fire zones in Vietnam resulted in a sense among many Vietnamese as well as Americans that U.S. forces were undisciplined. More important, perhaps, the widely touted grand plan to capture the "hearts and minds" of the Vietnamese was immeasurably diminished by the perception—let alone the outbreaks of reality—that Americans did not value Vietnamese lives.

Toward the end of the 1960s, the term *free fire zone* itself was dropped from the U.S. military lexicon in no small part because that doctrine embraced actions that the United States today would regard as illegal. Subsequent U.S. military manuals and rules of engagement, whether for ground, air, or naval forces, tend to track quite closely with the central principle of international humanitarian law on **civilian immunity** and the prohibition on the targeting of civilians.
(See **civilians, illegal targeting of; immunity**.)

Genocide

By Diane F. Orentlicher

Invoked with a frequency, familiarity, and reverence rarely associated with instruments of law, the 1948 Convention on the Prevention and Punishment of the Crime of Genocide has come to embody the conscience of humanity. Yet nearly sixty years after it was drafted, the moral promise of the Genocide Convention has at best been only partially redeemed. While States have belatedly honoured their responsibility to punish genocide, they have shown no corresponding will to prevent it, as the treaty also requires.

Although the Genocide Convention envisages (but does not require) the creation of an international court to punish genocide, forty-five years passed before the first international criminal tribunal was established. Its jurisdiction was limited to crimes, including genocide, committed in the former Yugoslavia since 1991. A similar, more circumscribed, tribunal was created for Rwanda one year later. It was not until September 2, 1998—a half-century after the United Nations General Assembly adopted the Genocide Convention —that the first verdict interpreting the convention was rendered by an international tribunal. On that day the Rwanda Tribunal found Jean-Paul Akayesu guilty on nine counts for his role in the 1994 Rwandan genocide.

In 2002, with the launch of the International Criminal Court, the promise of a permanent international tribunal to prosecute those responsible for genocide was finally met. Genocide is one of the crimes over which the Court has jurisdiction, although its prosecutor has yet to publicly indict any defendants on genocide charges.

If States are slowly and belatedly acting to meet their treaty commitment to punish genocide, the same can hardly be said for the parallel obligation the Genocide Convention imposes to prevent the crime or halt its further progress once genocide is under way. When ethnic cleansing was under way in the Balkans, legal experts in the U.S. government were asked, in the words of a former State Department lawyer, "to perform legal gymnastics to avoid calling this genocide." And as Rwandan Hutu slaughtered hundreds of thousands of Tutsi, the Clinton administration instructed its spokespeople not to describe what was happening as genocide lest this "inflame public calls for action," according to the *New York Times*. Instead, the State Department and National Security Council reportedly drafted guidelines instructing government spokespeople to say that "acts of genocide may have occurred" in Rwanda.

Against the Clinton administration's failure even to call the Rwanda genocide by its name at a time when effective intervention could have saved lives, the administration of George W. Bush forthrightly declared in September 2004 that violence committed by government-supported Arab militias against the black population of Darfur, Sudan, qualified as genocide. Yet the poverty of effective action to stop the violence in Darfur has made it painfully clear that invoking the name "genocide" does not by itself signify a political determination to stop the carnage.

Genocide defined. The definition of genocide set forth in the Genocide Convention is authoritative and has been incorporated verbatim in the statutes of the Yugoslavia and Rwanda tribunals, the International Criminal

Court and several other courts established by or with the support of the United Nations. After affirming that genocide is a crime under international law whether committed in time of peace or war, the 1948 convention defines genocide as "any of the following acts committed with intent to destroy, in whole or in part, a national, ethnical, racial or religious group, as such: killing members of the group; causing serious bodily or mental harm to members of the group; deliberately inflicting on the group conditions of life calculated to bring about its physical destruction in whole or in part; imposing measures intended to prevent births within the group; forcibly transferring children of the group to another group."

In the 1948 convention, then, the crime of genocide has both a material element—comprising certain enumerated acts, such as killing members of a racial group—and a mental element—those acts must have been committed with the specific intent to destroy, in whole or in part, a national, ethnic, racial, or religious group "as such." In its verdict in the Akayesu case,

Rwandan prisoners watch from behind cell bars as government officials try to extract confessions of a genocide from suspects.

the Rwanda Tribunal found that the systematic rape of Tutsi women in Taba Province constituted the genocidal act of "causing serious bodily or mental harm to members of the [targeted] group."

In addition to the crime of genocide itself, the 1948 convention provides that the following acts shall be punishable: conspiracy to commit genocide, direct and public incitement to commit genocide, attempt to commit genocide, and complicity in genocide.

What was left out of the convention is as important as what was included. Although earlier drafts of the convention listed political groups among those covered by the intent requirement, this category was omitted during final drafting stages. Some governments, it appears, feared they would be vulnerable to the charge of genocide if deliberate destruction of political groups fell within the crime's compass.

Also excluded was the concept of cultural genocide—destroying a group through forcible assimilation into the dominant culture. The drafting history makes clear that the 1948 convention was meant to cover physical destruction of a people; the sole echo of efforts to include the notion of cultural extermination is the convention's reference to forcibly transferring children of a targeted group to another group.

In this and other respects the conventional definition of genocide is narrower than the conception of Polish scholar Raphael Lemkin, who first proposed at an international conference in 1933 that a treaty be created to make attacks on national, religious, and ethnic groups an international crime. Lemkin, who served in the U.S. War Department, fashioned the term genocide from the Greek word *genos*, meaning race or tribe, and the Latin term for killing, *cide*.

Although Lemkin's conception included the physical extermination of targeted groups, this was, in his view, only the most extreme technique of genocide. In his 1944 book, *Axis Rule in Occupied Europe*, Lemkin proposed that genocide should be understood as signifying "a coordinated plan of different actions aiming at the destruction of essential foundations of the life of national groups, with the aim of annihilating the groups themselves. The objectives of such a plan would be disintegration of the political and social institutions, of culture, language, national feelings, religion, and the economic existence of national groups, and the destruction of the personal security, liberty, health, dignity, and even the lives of the individuals belonging to such groups...

"Genocide has two phases: one, destruction of the national pattern of the oppressed group; the other, the imposition of the national pattern of the oppressor. This imposition, in turn, may be made upon the oppressed population which is allowed to remain, or upon the territory alone, after removal of the population and colonization of the area by the oppressor's own nationals."

Another four years would pass before Lemkin's crime was recognized in an international treaty, but the legal foundation was laid during the 1945 Nuremberg and other postwar prosecutions. Although the Nuremberg Charter did not use the term genocide, its definition of **crimes against humanity** overlapped significantly with Lemkin's conception of genocide. The term "genocide" was used in the indictment against major war criminals tried at Nuremberg, who were accused of having "conducted deliberate and systematic genocide, viz., the extermination of racial and national groups, against the civilian populations of certain occupied territories in order to destroy particular races and classes of people and national, racial or religious groups." Nuremberg prosecutors also invoked the term in their closing arguments, and it also appeared in the judgments of several U.S. military tribunals operating in Nuremberg.

The comparatively narrow terms of the 1948 convention—in particular, its exclusion of political groups and its restrictive intent requirement—have meant that genocide is a difficult crime to establish. However, a series of decisions by the Yugoslavia and Rwanda war crimes tribunals has helped clarify the treaty's core terms. The tribunals have said that in the absence of direct evidence, genocidal intent can be inferred from such factors as "the scale of atrocities committed" and "the systematic targeting of victims on account of their membership of a particular group." These tribunals have also ruled that defendants can be convicted of certain genocide-related charges without themselves intending the destruction of a protected group if, for example, they knowingly and substantially furthered the commission of genocide by those who were bent on the destruction of a targeted group.

Recent case law has also helped clarify when genocidal intent can be established by virtue of a perpetrator's intent to destroy a protected group "in part." This requirement is satisfied, in the words of the ICTY Appeals Chamber, "where evidence shows that the alleged perpetrator intended to destroy at least a substantial part of the protected group." Applying this standard in the case of Radislav Krstić, who commanded the Bosnian Serb Drina Corps during the infamous Srebrenica massacre of July 1995, an ICTY trial chamber concluded that the intent to destroy the Bosnian Muslims of Srebrenica by killing their men constituted the intent to destroy a substantial part of a national group protected by the Genocide Convention, "the Bosnian Muslims." The trial chamber reasoned, in part, that "Bosnian Serb forces could not have failed to know, by the time they decided to kill all the men, that this selective destruction of the group would have a lasting impact upon the entire group[; they] had to be aware of the catastrophic impact that the disappearance of two or three generations of men would have on the survival of a traditionally patriarchal society." Krstić was convicted of genocide, though the Court's Appeals Chamber later reduced this to a conviction for aiding and abetting genocide.

As noted above, the Genocide Convention imposes a general duty on States parties "to prevent and to punish" genocide. Those charged with genocide are to be tried either in the State where the crime occurred or "by such international penal tribunal as may have jurisdiction with respect to those Contracting Parties which shall have accepted its jurisdiction." By early 2006, the Rwanda war crimes tribunal had convicted 24 defendants of genocide or genocide-related charges. By contrast, a small proportion of those indicted by the Yugoslavia tribunal has been convicted of genocide-related offences.

The operation of these tribunals—along with the ghastly crimes that led to their creation—created a new if modest impetus for genocide prosecutions by national courts. While suspected leaders of the 1994 Rwanda genocide have been prosecuted by the ICTR, over 2700 accused *genocidaires* have been prosecuted before Rwandan courts. A War Crimes Chamber in Sarajevo, which formally began operating in March 2005, has brought genocide-related charges against a number of suspects in connection with the 1995 Srebrenica massacre. In the 1990s and the early years of the 21st century, courts in several countries outside Rwanda and the Balkans, including Germany, Canada, Switzerland, Austria, Denmark, France and Belgium, also instituted genocide proceedings against suspected perpetrators from Rwanda and the former Yugoslavia.

While individuals can be prosecuted for genocide, States can be held legally responsible for breaching their obligations under the Genocide Convention. Parties to the convention can bring a case before the International Court of Justice (which handles disputes between States) alleging that another State party has violated the treaty. But no State turned to the ICJ to enforce the treaty against a State said to be responsible for genocide until 1993. That case was brought by a State that had endured atrocities—Bosnia and Herzegovina—against a State allegedly responsible—the former Yugoslavia—and not by other States determined to enforce the law of universal conscience on behalf of desperate victims beyond their borders. In a controversial judgment rendered on February 26, 2007, the ICJ concluded that Bosnia's legal team had established the occurrence of genocide only in respect of the Srebrenica massacre. But, the Court found, Bosnia failed to prove the Serbian State's legal responsibility for this genocide.

Serbia nonetheless became the first State in history judged to have violated the Genocide Convention. Its failure to arrest and transfer to the ICTY

Ratko Mladic, who was twice indicted for genocide by the ICTY, violated Serbia's treaty-based duty to punish genocide. Serbia was found in violation of another core duty under the genocide treaty—to prevent genocide. In the Court's reckoning, this obligation meant that Serbia should have used its significant influence with the Bosnian Serbs who carrried out the Srebrenica genocide to prevent them from doing so.

Genocide in History

Although the crime of genocide is associated above all with Hitler's Final Solution, this was not the first campaign of extermination that would qualify as genocide. The systematic extermination of Armenians by the Young Turks beginning in April 1915—an episode that loomed large in Lemkin's early thinking about the need to criminalize what he later termed genocide—was the first genocide in the twentieth century. Emboldened by the world's acquiescence in the slaughter of Armenians—over 1 million are estimated to have been put to death—Hitler is famously reported to have reassured doubters in his ranks by asking, "Who after all is today speaking of the Armenians?"

Turning to more recent episodes of wholesale slaughter, at least some scholars have concluded that the Turkish massacre of Kurds in the district of Dersim in 1937-1938, the massacre of Hutus by Tutsi perpetrators in Burundi in 1972, the Khmer Rouge campaign of extermination in the mid-1970s, and the 1988 Anfal campaign against Iraqi Kurds meet the legal definition of genocide.

Among these cases, perhaps none better illustrates the complexities of the 1948 convention's definition of genocide than the case of Cambodia. In view of the magnitude of the carnage there—some 1.5 million out of Cambodia's 7 million citizens are believed to have died as a result of Khmer Rouge policies—there has been a keen desire to affix the term "genocide" to their crimes. Since, however, both the perpetrators and the majority of victims were Khmer, reaching this conclusion has required agile legal reasoning. Some scholars have invoked the concept of auto-genocide, arguing that it is possible to satisfy the 1948 convention's definition even when the perpetrators sought to kill a substantial portion of their own ethnic/national group. Others, more conservatively, have conceded that the vast majority of victims were killed for reasons that may be broadly termed political, but note that certain minority groups, such as the Muslim Cham and Khmer Buddhists, were specially targeted for destruction and argue that at least the crimes against these groups were genocidal. Notably, the jurisdiction of a court established in 2006 to prosecute senior surviving Khmer Rouge leaders, a joint enterprise of the United Nations and the government of Cambodia, includes genocide.

For decades, the dearth of precedents enforcing the Genocide Convention—a grim testament to the international community's failure of will—left experts able to do little more than speculate knowledgeably about whether well-known candidates for the label "genocide" met the legal definition. Today, international tribunals and national courts are gradually clarifying definitional ambiguities and serving notice—however tentatively—that those responsible for genocide may face justice. Still, the very fact that courts are presiding over genocide-related cases stands as a stark testament of a deeper failure: If States have at last begun to meet their obligation to punish genocide, they have barely begun to meet their duty to prevent it in the first place or, at the least, to stop it in its deadly tracks.

Gray Areas in International Humanitarian Law

By Ewen Allison and Robert K. Goldman

A conflict between government forces and rebels can be governed by three sets of rules, and the problem for observers is to determine which applies. Gray areas in humanitarian law revolve around whether a given situation is an armed conflict, and if it is, whether it is internal or international.

G
One concern is how to classify an internal situation falling in the gray zone between peace and war. The line separating particularly violent internal tensions and disturbances from low-level armed conflict may sometimes be blurred and not easily determined. Such situations typically involve riots, isolated and sporadic acts of violence resulting in mass arrests, the use of police, and, sometimes, the armed forces to restore order. The foregoing do not amount to what humanitarian law would call an armed conflict. Instead, they are governed by domestic and human rights law. A gray-zone conflict would actually be armed conflict if, at a minimum, it was protracted and involved armed clashes between government forces and relatively organized armed groups. Determining what counts as protracted and well organized requires a case-specific analysis of the facts.

A second form of internal conflict involves determining if, because of the disintegration of the State, there is any government entity with armed forces capable of quelling civil strife between armed groups from different clans, religions, tribal, or ethnic groups. In a truly anarchic situation with minimal levels of organization, the applicable internal law is Common Article 3, which also applies to government clashes with armed insurgent groups. If, however, there is a conflict between a government and dissident armed forces, and the dissident group is organized under responsible command and exercises territorial control, then Common Article 3 may be supplemented by Protocol II (if the State in which the conflict is taking place is a party to the treaty). To apply Protocol II, at least one of the parties to the conflict must be a government, defined as a generally recognized regime that has a right and duty to exert authority over a population and provide for its needs.

Another gray area involves whether a conflict is internal or international. History has shown that this internal/international distinction is often artificial. For example, troops from a foreign country may fight alongside rebels or government troops involved in internal hostilities. Where such foreign intervention occurs, it may be unclear whether the hostilites are governed by the internal or international armed conflict rules. Such a conflict is called an "internationalized internal conflict." The recent hostilities in Bosnia and Angola are examples of such mixed armed conflicts.

This question is less significant now, thanks to a decision by the International Criminal Tribunal for the former Yugoslavia. In the Dusko Tadic case, the Appeals Chamber found that leading principles of international humanitarian law apply to both sorts of conflicts. Yet these specific principles and rules for international armed confict are not transposed word-for-word into the laws of internal armed conflict. It is, therefore, unclear whether certain provisions apply to both. Generally, the more basic a principle is, the more likely it is to apply across the board.

Finally, a gray area that has been much discussed since September 11, 2001, concerns whether there can be an armed conflict between a State and a terrorist group based outside its borders. The Bush administration has taken the view the struggle against al-Qaeda and its terrorist affiliates is a new kind of global conflict, not contemplated by existing humanitarian law, and not covered by any of the Geneva Conventions. Some analysts have argued that it should be regarded as a form of non-international armed conflict, on the grounds that it is not between two or more States. Many States, while acknowledging the serious threat posed by al-Qaeda and its global affiliates, envision the struggle against these terrorist groups as essentially requiring enhanced international cooperation in law enforcement, intelligence sharing and the like—as well as full compliance with international humanitarian law when this struggle involves armed conflict.

An interview room inside the long-term detention facility at U.S. Naval Station Guantanamo Bay in Cuba. A shackle is attached to the floor. April 13, 2005.

Guantanamo

By Jess Bravin

Shortly before the first American military commissions held since the 1940s were to begin at Guantanamo Bay, Cuba, in August 2004, a handful of journalists was shown round the windowless hearing room where terrorist suspects would stand trial. The escort noted that, per orders from Washington, no film or video camera would record the proceedings. "You won't be seeing this on the History Channel," the officer said with apparent satisfaction.

The contrast, of course, was Nuremberg, where the International Military Tribunal convened within months of Germany's surrender in 1945 to try the surviving leaders of the Nazi regime. Newsreels of those proceedings—now a perennial snippet on cable television—helped cement the moral standing of

the Allied victory, and laid the legal groundwork for hundreds of military trials for lower-ranking Axis officials throughout the European and Pacific theaters.

Guantanamo Bay, the century-old naval base acquired in America's first overseas war, stands at the crosshairs of contemporary thinking on war crimes. For Washington, the interrogation center it opened there in 2002 for men captured in counterterrorism operations was also to be the place where they faced judgment for war crimes, under a new code the U.S. Defense Department drafted to encompass 21st-century terrorism as well as resistance to American forces on the battlefield. To President George W. Bush and his advisors, the enemy that revealed itself on 9/11 was a monstrous aberration lurking outside the existing structure of domestic or international law.

The risk of additional terrorist attacks was too great, officials concluded, to follow rules that evolved in the prior century—and that were inconsistently followed, in any case, by other countries facing terrorist or internal security crises. The risk of mistaken arrest or conviction paled in comparison to the threat, officials concluded, as did the potential damage to America's reputation by disclosure of cruel or inhuman interrogation methods that many scholars considered impermissible under such international instruments as the

Entrance to Camp Delta, Guantanamo Bay, Cuba.

G

Geneva Conventions, the International Covenant on Civil and Political Rights, and the Convention against Torture and Other Cruel, Inhuman or Degrading Treatment or Punishment.

But the aggressive detention, interrogation and prosecution policies the U.S. has pursued there have made Guantanamo a far different metaphor than Washington envisioned. Unlike Nuremberg, now shorthand for international justice, to many around the world Guantanamo symbolizes America's selective adherence to norms of human rights. Whatever history's ultimate judgment, the Guantanamo detention facility marks a watershed in thinking about war crimes: it is perhaps the first major military installation conceived for reasons of legal strategy as well as military necessity. The U.S. government sited its detention operation at Guantanamo because it believed the territory's legal status would limit, if not eliminate, the rights of prisoners held there.

G Guantanamo Bay originally came into American hands after another catastrophic event that seared the American psyche—the February 15, 1898,

Prisoners at Guantanamo are issued an orange jumpsuit and provided halal meals, towels and buckets for water and waste.

explosion of the U.S. battleship *Maine* in Havana harbor, killing 260 sailors. Americans blamed Cuba's colonial ruler, Spain, for the attack, and war ensued. On June 10, 1898, U.S. Marines landed at Guantanamo Bay. Six months later, a defeated Madrid signed a treaty relinquishing remnants of its empire in the New World and the Pacific, setting Cuba on the path to an independence defined and protected by Washington, which won the right to build "coaling and naval stations" at Guantanamo. In 1903, the U.S. formalized the terms with Cuba, placing the 45-square-mile reservation under Washington's "complete jurisdiction and control," while Havana retained "ultimate sovereignty"—an arrangement that could not be terminated without American consent.

Aside from a few incidents after the 1959 Cuban revolution, the swampy inlet receded from American consciousness. During the 1990s, Presidents George H.W. Bush and Bill Clinton used the base to house thousands of Cuban and Haitian migrants interdicted at sea, hoping to prevent them from reaching

American shores where they could claim refugee status. The policy sparked law-suits from immigrant-rights advocates which, while failing to fully clarify the application of treaties and American law at Guantanamo, revealed courts hesitant to second-guess presidential determinations.

The terrorist attacks of September 11, 2001, prompted not only a rapid military response, but an equally vigorous legal offensive by lawyers in the administration of President George W. Bush. The U.S. invoked its right of self-defense against the al-Qaeda network and its sponsors, backed within the week by a resolution of the U.S. Congress authorizing Bush to use "all necessary and appropriate force." In the weeks that followed, as U.S. and allied forces joined Afghan militias to overthrow the Taliban regime and pursue al-Qaeda terrorists, administration lawyers drafted opinions advising that few limits, if any, applied to the powers the president had now asserted. Many of these documents were secret, but on November 13, 2001, Bush made one policy public: a "military order" declaring it "not practicable" to follow U.S. court procedures for foreign prisoners he determined were linked to international terrorism, and authorizing military commissions to try them.

In Afghanistan, indigenous forces such as the Northern Alliance tribal group initially held suspected Taliban and al-Qaeda prisoners, but the U.S. decided it needed to take custody of those it captured or obtained from militias and bounty hunters. On December 27, 2001, Defense Secretary Donald Rumsfeld told a press conference that Guantanamo was the choice.

"Mr. Secretary, we've gotten into trouble every time we've tried to use Guantanamo Bay in the past to hold people, for other reasons," a reporter asked. "Why use it? Why is it the best place?"

"I would characterize Guantanamo Bay, Cuba, as the least worst place we could have selected," Rumsfeld answered. "It has disadvantages, as you suggest. Its disadvantages, however, seem to be modest relative to the alternatives."

Rumsfeld didn't elaborate, but contemporaneous legal opinions, later disclosed, provide some of the explanation. Officials rejected the Pacific Ocean bases at Midway, Tinian and Wake islands after recognizing that they fell within the jurisdiction of the Ninth U.S. Circuit Court of Appeals in San Francisco. Judicial review could "interfere with the operation of the system that has been developed to address the detainment and trial of enemy aliens" if courts examined such issues as prisoner rights under the Geneva Conventions or "whether and what international law norms may or may not apply to the conduct of the war in Afghanistan," wrote Justice Department officials Patrick Philbin and John Yoo. Guantanamo, however, was not formally within any federal court's jurisdiction. While housing prisoners at the base bore "some litigation risk," they wrote, "the great weight of legal authority indicates that a federal district court could not properly exercise... jurisdiction over an alien detained" at Guantanamo.

The first 20 prisoners arrived on January 11, 2002. Even as the manacled prisoners, in blacked-out goggles and orange jumpsuits, were led to their outdoor cells, senior officials in Washington debated whether any laws or treaties covered the men. President Bush settled the question for the Executive Branch in a February 7 order declaring that Geneva applied only between States parties, and therefore al-Qaeda prisoners, agents of a stateless terror network, were excluded. Moreover, while Afghanistan was a State party, the order concluded that forces of the country's *de facto* government, the Taliban, had failed to meet the treaty's criteria for lawful fighting and therefore were categorically excluded from its protection.

The 3rd Geneva Convention provides for case-by-case determinations "should any doubt arise" over a prisoner's status. Under U.S. Army regulations implementing the treaty, a three-officer board is empowered to quickly

G

classify prisoners on the battlefield. Officials told me that providing prisoners even this near-perfunctory process would needlessly dignify the enemy.

Nevertheless, Bush declared, "as a matter of policy, the United States Armed Forces"—which do not include civilian entities such as the Central Intelligence Agency—"shall continue to treat detainees humanely and, to the extent appropriate and consistent with military necessity, in a manner consistent with the principles of Geneva." By the end of February, 300 men were held at Guantanamo. As many as 600 prisoners would be held there at any particular time.

Because of the secrecy surrounding Guantanamo's operations, it has been impossible to assess independently the intelligence produced there. Journalists and dignitaries brought on escorted tours of the prison are not permitted to speak with prisoners, but as evidence of their humane treatment are shown a well-stocked infirmary, copies of the Koran and "comfort items" such as rubber sandals that are provided for detainees, along with fenced yards where they can kick around a ball. The U.S. permits prisoner visits by delegates from the International Committee of the Red Cross, which in general does not speak publicly about its observations. Prisoners have found ways to demonstrate their own views, however, occasionally attacking guards, attempting suicide and launching periodic hunger strikes, which U.S. jailers have frustrated by force-feeding.

Litigation, aggressive journalism, statements of released prisoners and selected disclosures by government officials have revealed other elements of the Guantanamo operation. At various times prisoners have been awkwardly shackled to the floor, deprived of light, subjected to blaring music and sexually humiliated. Officials have continuously wrestled over the degree of force and intimidation that lawfully could be used against defiant prisoners, sometimes out of concern that specific methods potentially could expose interrogators and their superiors to criminal liability.

Within weeks of Guantanamo's designation as a prison site, activist lawyers filed suits alleging that the detentions there were illegal. Those suits initially faltered before judges hesitant to second-guess the president after 9/11, but in June 2004 the U.S. Supreme Court ruled that federal habeas jurisdiction did extend to Guantanamo. The court did not say explicitly what would constitute a lawful detention, however, leaving lower courts to sort the details out.

While continuing to deny the application of the Geneva Conventions, the U.S. government responded to the Supreme Court ruling by convening panels called Combatant Status Review Tribunals, three-officer boards similar to those described in the Army's regulations, to confirm that prisoners belonged there. Prisoners could not see classified evidence on which their detentions were based and essentially could only insist that they were held by mistake; 38 of the 558 prisoners who appeared before the tribunals were released, the Pentagon said. Similar panels, called Administrative Review Boards, were established to hold annual hearings on whether a prisoner had so declined in dangerousness to merit release. Prisoner advocates, however, contended these procedures were inadequate and pursued their lawsuits in federal court.

Those the U.S. approved for release met different fates, often depending on their origin. British citizens returned home to freedom, and even celebrity, as they denounced their captivity. At least 10 released Guantanamo prisoners, the Pentagon has claimed, joined al-Qaeda cells or forces fighting Americans. And others, for complex diplomatic and political reasons, entered an unexpected limbo: the U.S. could find no place to send them.

For instance, several Uighurs, members of a Muslim ethnic group from northeastern China, were held at Guantanamo for months after officials determined they were not enemies of the U.S. and should be released. Treaty obligations, however, prevented returning the Uighurs to China, where they were viewed as disloyal and likely to face retribution. But the U.S. was unwilling to resettle them within its own borders and could find no country prepared to accept them until May 2006, when Albania agreed to receive five Uighurs. They face an uncertain future in a country that, while predominantly Muslim, differs significantly in language and culture.

Meanwhile, the U.S. government struggled to implement Bush's order for military commission trials at the base. Some military lawyers and State Department officials urged procedures that closely followed the existing U.S. Uniform Code of Military Justice, which adheres to the U.S. Constitution and satisfies international legal standards. Senior officials, however, remained convinced that recognizing a defendant's absolute right to examine prosecution witnesses and evidence could force the government to choose between revealing intelligence methods, including the circumstances of interrogations, or forgoing convictions.

Moreover, because the most important al-Qaeda suspects were not initially held at Guantanamo—they, instead, were kept at secret CIA sites even less accessible than the Cuba base—officials could select defendants only from the mid- to low-level belligerents presumed to comprise the inmate population. Further impeding the commissions' effort was the determination that intelligence took precedence over prosecution, with the practical effect that prosecutors were denied access to intelligence files on potential defendants and witnesses. Eventually, officials identified a half-dozen prisoners for trial, a decision President Bush approved in 2003.

Prosecutors selected cases they thought would be relatively simple to resolve, hoping to initiate the commissions with a slew of plea bargains and guilty verdicts. Military defense lawyers assigned to represent the defendants were expected to facilitate the trials by operating within the process conceived by the Pentagon. Instead, the lawyers advised their clients to reject plea bargains and launched a wholesale assault on the legitimacy of the military commission program itself. The prosecution's initial selection of defendants would prove a strategic mistake; rather than an alleged killer or terrorist mastermind whose villainy might justify extraordinary measures, the case that would reach the Supreme Court involved an obscure functionary: Osama bin Laden's admitted driver, Salim Hamdan, who prosecutors alleged also was a bodyguard and confidant of the al-Qaeda leader.

The Pentagon eventually commenced its first military commission hearings in August 2004, but the proceedings soon fell apart. Defense lawyers challenged the impartiality of the panel members, forcing the disqualification of several officers from serving on the commission. Translation errors—immediately raised by defense interpreters and Arabic-speaking observers from human-rights organizations who were invited to attend—marred the hearings. A commission presiding officer, apparently unsure of what rules against self-incrimination applied, silenced a defendant just as he appeared ready to declare his role in al-Qaeda. In November 2004, the proceedings were abruptly halted when a federal judge in Washington ruled the commissions illegal and a violation of the Geneva Conventions.

While legal skirmishing continued, the broader prisoner population at Guantanamo became increasingly restive, and in June 2006 three prisoners succeeded in hanging themselves. A Pentagon official, acknowledging that the prisoner deaths would further damage the U.S. reputation, described the suicides as acts of "asymmetric warfare."

On June 29, 2006, in a 73-page opinion by Justice John Paul Stevens, a slim majority of the Supreme Court painstakingly refuted the legal theories upon which the Bush administration had built its prisoner policies. Viewed narrowly, the court found that the president held no inherent power to establish his own military commissions outside existing law, specifically the Geneva Conventions and the Uniform Code of Military Justice. The president was given the choice of either following the UCMJ or asking Congress to establish an alternative system.

More broadly, the opinion rejected the legal conclusion of Alberto Gonzales, the president's counsel and later attorney general, that Guantanamo prisoners fell outside Geneva. The court found that existing U.S. law required adherence to a Geneva provision known as Common Article 3, which prohibits, among other abuses, "cruel treatment and torture" and "outrages upon personal dignity, in particular humiliating and degrading treatment," while requiring that any trials be conducted by "a regularly constituted court, affording all the judicial guarantees which are recognized as indispensable by civilized peoples." A plurality of justices found that the single charge lodged against Hamdan—conspiracy—was not a valid crime under the laws of war.

Essentially, in its 2004 and 2006 rulings, the Supreme Court ruled that the Guantanamo project had been based on a legal fallacy: that the U.S. president controlled a property outside the jurisdiction of any court, allowing him to operate a detention, interrogation and trial facility where nothing that transpired would ever face review by an independent judge.

Bush administration officials told me they had been so confident in their legal position, they had made no provision should the Supreme Court rule otherwise. Bush himself, however, in the weeks before the court's decision, had begun voicing a hope that someday Guantanamo might be closed. A series of halting steps followed the June decision. The deputy defense secretary issued a directive that Common Article 3 be obeyed, and in September Bush sent 14 "high value" prisoners from secret CIA prisons to Guantanamo, where they would for the first time be visited by International Red Cross delegates and receive other Geneva conditions. Bush said that these prisoners, some of whom allegedly helped plan the 9/11 attacks, should be tried by military commission.

At the same time, the administration proposed legislation that would in large part authorize commissions to operate much as it had originally conceived them, including the power to exclude defendants from their trials and use hearsay evidence obtained through coercion. A month before midterm elections, Congress adopted much of the president's proposal, including a provision purporting to bar all detainee lawsuits asserting claims based on the Geneva Conventions.

In March 2007, the Bush administration concluded its first case before a military commission. David Hicks, an Australian captured in 2001 alongside Taliban fighters in Afghanistan, agreed to plead guilty to providing material support for terrorism, in exchange for nine months in jail, to be served in Australia. Even this conviction was problematic, however; critics noted that Washington was under pressure from Canberra, one of its few remaining allies in the Iraq war, to resolve the Hicks case, which had become an embarrassment to Prime Minister John Howard as he stood for re-election. While the Hicks deal was unfolding at Guantanamo, the new defense secretary, Robert Gates, told a congressional hearing that he believed the offshore prison should be closed. "Because of things that happened earlier at Guantanamo, there is a taint about it," he said.

(See **Afghanistan**; **detention and interrogation**; **due process**; **terrorism**.)

Guerrillas

By Jon Lee Anderson

In 1982, I was standing in a village in Guatemala's central highlands when a unit of armed government troops appeared, pulling two frightened-looking Indian men in civilian clothes held by rope nooses around their necks.

I asked one of them who the men were. "They are subversives," he replied. I asked how he knew that, and the soldier said that the men had been carrying a hunting rifle, and had tried to run away when they were spotted. He drew

The Revolutionary Armed Forces of Colombia (FARC) formed in 1964 as the military arm of the Communist Party, here shown releasing Colombian soldiers they had been holding for three years, June 2001.

his fingers across the front of his throat in a slashing motion. The other soldiers watching our exchange broke out laughing, while the condemned men, seemingly lost in thought, looked fixedly at the ground.

Clearly, no mercy was going to be shown to these men. Whether they were guerrillas or not, however, their treatment was a clear violation of the international laws of war. The Guatemalan Army considered Indians to be subversives, and subversives to be guerrillas; it drew no distinction between civilians and **combatants**. Under international humanitarian law (IHL), guerrillas are included in the category of irregular forces—defined more specifically as fighters who use unconventional methods of warfare, such as sabotage, ambushes, and sniping. There are, however, protections for captured guerrilla fighters even in an internal conflict.

Guerrilla warfare *per se* is not illegal under IHL, but guerrillas must follow the same laws that apply to all regular armed forces.

Like all fighters, guerrillas have different rights depending upon whether the armed conflict is international or internal. Under the Geneva Conventions of 1949, a person fighting in irregular forces, often the kind of fighter we today would regard as a guerrilla, is considered a lawful combatant in an international armed conflict provided that he fights under certain specified conditions. The importance of being a lawful combatant is twofold. First, if captured by opposing international forces (not by his government), he may not be prosecuted or punished for taking part in combat. Second, he must be treated as a prisoner of war under applicable international rules.

In order to be granted the privilege of being a lawful combatant, the fighter must, however, observe four rules:

1. Be commanded by a person responsible for his subordinates; this requirement is intended to ensure that irregular forces have a structure of command and discipline capable of following the laws of war.

2. Wear a distinctive sign or article of clothing visible at a distance in order to indicate that he is a combatant and a potential target who may lawfully be attacked by opposing forces; this provision is for the protection of noncombatant civilians.

3. Carry his weapon openly to indicate his combatant status and to distinguish fighters from the civilian population.

4. Observe the laws of war.

Additional Protocol I to the Geneva Conventions attempted to take into account the realities of guerrilla warfare, in particular the routine practice of concealment among the general population. In a controversial rule, the protocol requires only that a guerrilla combatant in an international armed conflict carry his arms openly just before an attack. The United States has, for a variety of reasons, not ratified the protocol. In this particular instance, the United States believes it represents a step backward in the protection of civilians since it increases the legal ability of guerrilla fighters to expose civilians to greater risk.

Guerrillas in internal armed conflicts are covered by Article 3 common to the four Geneva Conventions of 1949, and more controversially, by Additional Protocol II of 1977, which has not received wide acceptance. Under Common Article 3, insurgents must give humane treatment to captured civilians and government soldiers. Insurgents can punish their detainees for war crimes, but only after giving them fair trials.

Guerrillas too must be humanely treated if captured, but in an internal conflict they do not enjoy any "combatant's privilege." They are fully liable, if captured by their government, to be tried for rebellion, sedition, and for acts, undertaken as guerrillas, such as murder or destruction of property. If a country's domestic law permits, they may be executed provided they are tried and sentenced "by a regularly constituted court, affording all the judicial guarantees which are recognized as indispensable by civilized peoples."

In 1985, I was in Nicaragua traveling with a unit of the CIA-backed Contra guerrillas, who were fighting a campaign against the leftist Sandinista government. "Tigrillo," the commander, had a girlfriend called Marta. One day, I talked to Marta on her own, and she revealed tearfully that she had only joined the Contras after being abducted by Tigrillo's band, along with several civilian men from her village. Accused of being government sympathizers, the men had been hacked to death in front of her; Marta had been spared because Tigrillo found her attractive.

In this case, the Contra guerrillas had violated IHL. Not only had they kidnapped and murdered civilians, they also had kept Marta with them as an unwilling hostage.

Two years later, in the countryside outside the eastern Sri Lankan town of Batticaloa, I visited a base of the Tamil Tigers, a guerrilla group fighting against the predominately ethnic Sinhalese government for an independent Tamil state. During an interview, the Tiger commander, Kumarrappa, ordered his troops to produce a captured "spy." Soon, a tiny, terrified woman with bedraggled hair was produced. Her name was Athuma. Kumarrappa explained that she was to be blown up alive after being tied to a lamppost with explosive wire. Hearing this, Athuma began begging for her life. Kumarrappa listened briefly, smiling, then silenced her by declaring that she would be killed anyway. He waved his hand, and Athuma was led away.

Here, as in Nicaragua, the Sri Lankan guerrillas were in flagrant violation of the laws of war. The civilian woman, Athuma, was to be executed after having been terrorized and mistreated, without benefit of a fair trial. But the Tigers' brutality was matched by the Sri Lankan Army, which roamed the area, torturing and shooting Tamil civilians at will. Tamil suspects who ended up in the local detention camp were often executed and their bodies burned to eliminate evidence. Thus, terror breeds terror.

G

A Maoist rebel of the People's Liberation Army, first brigade, mid division, in the village of Gairigaon, Nepal. February 2005.

As these stories illustrate, visits by an outsider to areas where guerrilla wars and counterinsurgency campaigns are being waged can become bewildering, traumatic experiences. In each place mentioned, I was present as a nonpartisan journalist, but found myself unexpectedly faced with situations where I felt a moral obligation to try to save lives. I had no primer like this one, where the laws are clearly outlined, to help me formulate my arguments more convincingly. It is difficult to know whether men who feel themselves to be above the law can be persuaded by legal arguments, but it is certainly worth a try. In guerrilla wars, where the combatants usually impose their own cruel codes of legality, arguments based on international law probably carry more weight than appeals for compassion.

(See **international vs. internal armed conflict; irregulars; paramilitaries; soldiers, rights of.**)

Gulf War

By Frank Smyth

Attitudes toward international humanitarian norms and law by the belligerents in the Gulf War could not have been more distinct. The U.S.-led coalition commander, Gen. Norman Schwarzkopf, frequently consulted with law of war experts, including members of the International Committee of the Red Cross (ICRC), to ensure that specific military operations would not be seen later as violations. In fact, Schwarzkopf's aides requested so much guidance from the ICRC that its representatives eventually stopped providing it, protesting that they were not legal counsel for the coalition. Iraqi President Saddam Hussein, on the other hand, declined to meet with ICRC representatives.

Of course, the Gulf War was a conventional conflict, and U.S.-led coalition forces enjoyed a great advantage of superior firepower. Though they arguably committed some laws of war violations that contributed to needless civilian deaths, allied forces were able to fight a relatively clean campaign and still win. Saddam Hussein's forces, on the other hand, committed many violations including grave breaches of the 1949 Geneva Conventions and the 1977 Additional Protocol I. Similarly, during the civil uprisings inside Iraq that immediately followed the Gulf War, Saddam disregarded humanitarian norms in crushing them.

U.S. and Iraqi leaders were responding to different considerations in their attitude toward international humanitarian law (IHL). U.S. commanders feared that any perceived violations by coalition troops might undermine the strong support for the war being expressed back home. Elsewhere, they feared that such violations might break up the U.S.-led coalition of twenty-seven countries against Iraq, and, in particular, compel Arab States to withdraw from it. U.S. leaders feared as well that any coalition intervention during Iraq's civil upris-

On the road from Samarra and Nasiriyah, one of the ubiquitous portraits of Saddam Hussein toppled by the bombing of the warehouse behind. Iraq, 1991.

ings might also split the coalition. Saddam, meanwhile, has never demonstrated much concern for Iraqi public opinion, though, during the Gulf War, he did try to appeal to pan-Arab sentiments. Saddam's targeting of civilian population centers in Israel, in particular, was designed to bring Israel into the Gulf War and then, hopefully, split Arab States from the U.S.-led alliance.

Each side in the Gulf War has been accused of violations of IHL; in some cases, the violation is legally clear-cut, while in others experts still debate.

Allied forces destroyed many electrical power stations in Iraq. The attacks adversely affected Iraq's civilian population, as they rendered sewage plants in many civilian areas inoperable and left many hospitals without power. This led some observers like Human Rights Watch (HRW), a private monitoring organization based in New York, to ask whether the attacks violated IHL and in particular the principle of **proportionality**: was the subsequent civilian toll excessive in relation to the concrete and direct military advantage anticipated from the attack?

Coalition forces also launched attacks that killed many civilians, raising questions about **indiscriminate attacks** involving needless civilian casualties. On February 14, for example, a British plane fired a laser-guided missile at a bridge in the Al-Fallujah neighborhood west of Baghdad. It missed and hit a residential area, killing up to 130 civilians. Some observers, including former U.S. Attorney General Ramsey Clark, claim that all such coalition attacks that resulted in Iraqi civilian casualties constitute war crimes. But without evidence that the neighborhood was intentionally, or negligently, targeted or that it was part of a broader pattern of indiscriminate attacks, this incident does not stand either as a grave breach or as a serious violation of the Geneva Conventions.

Another tragedy had occurred the day before, when a U.S. cruise missile penetrated the Ameriyaa air-raid shelter in Baghdad, killing up to three hundred civilians, including at least ninety-one children. CNN broadcast the carnage. U.S. Brig. Gen. Richard Neal in Riyadh later admitted that allied forces had intentionally targeted the shelter. He also said that coalition commanders knew that the shelter had been previously used by civilians in the mid-1980s during the Iran-Iraq War, but that it had since been converted to "a hardened shelter used for [military] command and control." HRW refers to Neal's statements to argue that the attack on the shelter was a laws of war violation. Before they fired at it, allied forces, according to HRW, were obligated, to first warn Iraq that they now considered the former civilian shelter a legitimate military target. HRW added that, in its view, the evidence of the shelter's alleged conversion to a military purpose was insufficient to overcome the presumption that it was still being used by civilians. Other observers, however, including lawyers for coalition forces, disagree. They point out that the shelter had been used solely for civilian purposes several years previously in the Iran-Iraq War, so allied commanders were not obligated to warn Iraq that they now considered the shelter to be a legitimate military target in the Gulf War. Coalition partners, however, have yet to make their evidence public about the shelter's alleged conversion to military use.

U.S.-led forces also killed many civilians when coalition planes, including B-52 bombers, launched heavy strikes in and around the port of Basra. Coalition forces sought to destroy several specific military targets there. Some critics claim coalition forces had resorted to the kind of carpet bombing often seen in World War II, constituting indiscriminate attack, by treating a whole area containing several targets as a single target, in violation of Article 51 of Additional Protocol I. No one disputes that the attacks killed many civilians (though no reliable figures are known) living in residential areas around the port. The question is whether such attacks violated IHL. A U.S. Army spokesman in Riyadh later described Basra as a "military town," which was quartering, among other forces, a strong contingent of elite Republican Guard troops. Lawyers for coalition forces blame Iraq for the subsequent civilian toll. They point out that Iraq was legally obligated to separate military forces from civilians and not to use the latter as a **shield**, and that the presence of civilians around military targets does not render such targets immune from attack. Nonetheless, coalition forces, critics argue, could have used more precise arms, such as cruise missiles or laser-guided weaponry, that might have accomplished the same objective with less **collateral damage** to civilians. U.S. military lawyers have noted in response, however, that the obligation to use more precise weapons systems is qualified by considerations of **military necessity**, including availability and need for their deployment in missions against other **military objectives**. Both HRW and the ICRC concluded the resort to saturation strikes claimed needless civilian lives and damage, but the controversy continues.

G

Even after the U.S.-led coalition liberated their state, Kuwaitis line up at the sports stadium to obtain exit visas. 1991.

Another controversial incident involving coalition forces occurred on the last day of the ground campaign, as an entire column of Iraqi troops was retreating from Kuwait. These troops had not surrendered, making them legitimate military targets. Yet, they put up only minimal resistance, while coalition aircraft dropped Rockeye fragmentation bombs and other antipersonnel arms, killing thousands. The ICRC concluded that the attacks "cause[d] unnecessary suffering and superfluous injury," and that they were tantamount to "a denial of quarter." Many other observers, however, counter that the concept of denial of quarter does not apply to forces that have not surrendered.

The ICRC also singled out some U.S.-led coalition partners for not devoting enough resources to properly register all their Iraqi prisoners with the ICRC or any other "central tracing agency." Saudi Arabia, for one, registered none of its prisoners.

Other forces associated with the U.S.-led coalition as well violated humanitarian norms, though it remains unclear whether the violations took place within the context of an internal or international conflict, and which international norms or laws, therefore, would apply. Following the Gulf War, Kuwaiti authorities committed many human rights violations upon their repatriation. Mobs acting with the blessing of authorities harassed, detained, tortured, and sometimes summarily executed thousands, including Palestinians and others suspected of having supported the Iraqi occupation.

Nevertheless, Iraq is responsible for far more violations of humanitarian norms and laws, as its forces entirely disregarded them throughout the Gulf War and its aftermath. On many occasions, Iraq intentionally targeted civilians, which is a grave breach of the Geneva Conventions. During its occupation of Kuwait, Iraqi troops also harassed, tortured, and sometimes summarily executed thousands of Kuwaitis. Other Iraqi abuses also stand as clear rules-of-war violations. Before the Gulf War, Iraq used civilians, typically foreign nationals, as human shields to seek to protect military targets in both Kuwait and Iraq. In Kuwait, this practice was clearly a war crime under Article 51 of Additional Protocol I, because a state of war and occupation clearly existed with respect to Kuwait. Using foreign nationals as human shields within Iraq before the opening of hostilities between Iraq and the coalition forces is a less clear-cut case. In an unmistakable violation, Iraq, during the war, failed to register coalition prisoners of war with the ICRC. Iraq as well humiliated and tortured some coalition prisoners. (Though one U.S. soldier who was a prisoner of war later admitted that he had abused himself to avoid being shown on Iraqi television.)

Iraqi forces also fired Scud missiles that hit civilian population centers in Saudi Arabia and Israel, an act which some claim was the war crime of directly targeting civilians or indiscriminately attacking population centers. Nonetheless, for these attacks to constitute war crimes, it must first be proven either that Iraq intentionally targeted the civilian centers in order to attack civilians directly or else failed to take measures to insure that military objectives were targeted. Though some of the thirty-seven missiles directed into Saudi Arabia appear to have been aimed at military targets, others appear to have been aimed at cities like Riyadh, the Saudi capital. Most of the thirty-nine Scud missiles fired into Israel and the occupied West Bank seem to have been aimed at cities like Tel Aviv, the Israeli capital. Three questions remain open. Could the missiles Iraq fired at population centers reasonably be shown to have been aimed at legitimate military targets in those cities within the limits of Iraqi technological capabilities? Did anticipated specific and concrete military benefit of such attacks for Iraq outweigh civilian costs (excluding from the calculation the illegal military advantage gained from terror attacks on civilians themselves)? On the other hand, did coalition authorities violate their IHL duties by commingling civilians with military targets in Saudi Arabia? It would appear in fact as difficult to prove illegality in the Scud attacks on Saudi Arabia as it would the coalition attacks on Basra and Baghdad.

But the Scud attacks on Israel would appear to be the most difficult for Iraq to justify, given that coalition forces were not present in Israel, nor was Israel a party to the conflict. Absent some substantial evidence showing that Israel was about to enter the war against Iraq, thus justifying a preemptive military strike against legitimate military targets, the Scud attacks against Israel would appear to have been terror attacks directed against civilians. It is widely acknowledged that Iraq's aim was to draw Israel into the conflict by attacks on its civilian population; although IHL is silent with respect to how a war starts or spreads, Iraq's method appears in this case illegal.

Iraq also committed several acts of **environmental warfare** as part of its military strategy. The ecological impact of the attacks, which provided Iraq

American forces bombed a column of Iraqi troops and civilians as they retreated north. The road became known afterwards as the Highway of Death. Mutla Ridge, Kuwait. March 1991.

with perhaps a slight and only fleeting military advantage, will no doubt be felt for years. During the Gulf War, Iraq released millions of liters of crude oil into the Persian Gulf in an attempt to undermine seawater desalination plants that were being used by coalition forces. Toward the end of the war, Iraq set fire to as many as 950 oil wells, which discharged tons of toxic gases into the atmosphere. To be considered a violation of IHL, such acts must cause the environment widespread, long-term, and severe damage. Experts still disagree whether the above acts meet this threshold.

Iraqi forces committed human rights violations against many of its own citizens, principally in the Shia- and Kurdish-led insurgencies immediately after the end of the coalition-led campaign, which is at least inconsistent with international humanitarian norms. Here U.S. President George Bush also played a key role. On March 1, Bush called upon Iraqis "to put [Saddam] aside" and bring Iraq "back into the family of peace-loving nations." The same day, Shias in southern Iraq began calling for insurrection, while Kurds in northern Iraq rebelled two weeks later; coalition forces stood by as Iraqi troops, backed by tanks and helicopter gunships, decimated the insurgents through scorched-earth campaigns. In many of these attacks, Iraqi forces appear to have made no attempt to distinguish between civilian and military targets. On March 20, in As-Samawah in southern Iraq, Iraqi units advanced behind a human shield of captured Shia women, as they shot Shia men on sight. On March 28, in Kirkuk in northern Iraq, Iraqi helicopter gunships and multiple-rocket launchers dropped a blanket of fire on fleeing Kurdish guerrillas and civilians, again without appearing to distinguish between them. Iraqi Army Special Forces, which led the assault, also summarily executed many Kurdish combatants (as well as *Newsweek* freelance photographer Gad Gross) after capture.

Iraq further violated humanitarian norms and human rights in its treatment of foreign detainees at the Abu Ghraib prison west of Baghdad, where captured journalists were also held. Though captured journalists were treated as prisoners of war, in accordance with Article 4 of the Third Geneva Convention, Iraq generally failed to acknowledge holding them until their release, in violation of the rules of war. At least one journalist, CBS News correspondent Bob Simon, was physically tortured.

Iraq as well violated the human rights of many Iraqi detainees in Abu Ghraib prison. I was detained there along with photojournalist Alain Buu for two weeks beginning about one month after the end of the Gulf War. Though we were not physically harmed, we saw and heard many Iraqis being tortured by prison authorities: hitting a man on the buttocks with a flat board intermittently all night long, while making him crow like a rooster; hosing down a stripped prisoner outside on a cold day, and then stunning him repeatedly with an electroshock weapon; and beating a sixteen-year-old boy, accused of sedition, with rubber hoses. Sometimes we just heard, coming from another cellblock in the prison, the long screams of men in extreme, sustained pain. Some of the violence was perpetrated capriciously by guards; other acts were executed under orders from higher authorities to extract information.

The Gulf War and its aftermath demonstrate the strengths and gaps of international humanitarian norms and law. Though the U.S.-led coalition in some cases at least encroached upon the rules of war, the allies in most cases did make a conscious effort to adhere to them. Saddam Hussein chose to ignore them nearly altogether.

(See **Iran-Iraq War; Iraq.**)

H

Health Care System

By Eric Stover

War directs scarce resources away from health and other human services, and often destroys the infrastructure of these services; it also facilitates the spread of disease. Since the early 1970s, another major threat has emerged for health care systems. Military attacks on medical personnel and medical facilities, though prohibited under international humanitarian law, have reached alarming proportions throughout the world.

One recent example occurred in Kosovo during the Yugoslav government's offensive against ethnic Albanian rebels in the summer and fall of 1998, when troops destroyed tens of thousands of buildings, including health clinics, and displaced hundreds of thousands of civilians who sought shelter in the surrounding mountains and forests. Aid officials estimated that about twenty doctors were arrested by Serbian special police or fled the country and that hundreds of civilians may have died because of the collapse of the health care system. After the assault, a climate of fear descended on the few health care workers who remained in the war zone. Several doctors said that, in spite of their ethical obligations to treat all those in need, they were afraid to provide medical care because it could serve as a pretext for government police to arrest them.

Attacks on medical facilities are prohibited under the Geneva Conventions of 1949 and the 1977 Additional Protocols. These instruments provide that warring factions have an obligation to protect civilians, the **sick and wounded**, combatants who are ***hors de combat***, and medical and religious personnel. All sides in a conflict must protect certain objects from damage, including **hospitals** and other medical facilities, ambulances, and equipment bearing the **Red Cross** or **Red Crescent** symbol that have removed wounded from the field; transport and facilities used by humanitarian and relief agencies; and objects indispensable to the survival of the civilian population, such as crops, livestock, and drinking **water installations**.

But the reality is very different. In contemporary conflict, **medical personnel** and patients are assaulted, abducted, tortured, or murdered. Ambulances can become the target of mortar and sniper fire. **Medical transports** carrying vital medical supplies and food may be shelled or prevented from reaching towns and cities under **siege**. All of these acts may be considered grave breaches of the Geneva Conventions and Additional Protocol I or crimes against humanity. As **refugees** flee to safety, they congregate in makeshift camps where the combination of fatigue, malnutrition, unsanitary conditions, and overcrowding often sends diseases like cholera and measles on a killing spree.

During the 1994 genocide in Rwanda, military and militias known as *Interahamwe* (those who attack together) entered dozens of hospitals and clinics, murdering and maiming patients and staff. One of the most horrific incidents took place in the university town of Butare, where machete-wielding militiamen slaughtered twenty-one children who had been evacuated to a Red Cross orphanage.

During the 1980s, Mozambique National Resistance (RENAMO) guerrillas in Mozambique ransacked over one thousand primary health centers, representing 48 percent of the national total, leaving 2 million people without access to health care.

In Bosnia-Herzegovina, where armed conflict was marked by almost every conceivable violation of medical neutrality, Sarajevo's main medical center, the Kosevo Hospital, was struck by at least 172 mortar shells in 1992 and early 1993. The most flagrant attack on the hospital complex took place in May 1992, when Bosnian Serb forces, at close range, repeatedly shelled the Children's Clinic and the adjoining Obstetrical and Gynecological Hospital, forcing staff to evacuate seventeen newborns (many removed from their incubators and without supplemental oxygen) and thirty-three older children. Nine of the babies later died for want of heat and oxygen.

Even without coming under direct attack, health care systems have to cope with an enormous burden in wartime. Hospitals in or near war zones are usually understaffed and have few, if any, orthopedic surgeons, let alone general surgeons with extensive experience treating blast-related injuries. Patients with mine blast injuries often require twice as much blood as patients wounded by other munitions. Many—if not most—mine amputees will need to be fitted with some kind of prosthetic, which will need to be replaced every three to five years. And after the fighting stops, the pressures continue. Antipersonnel **mines** place a tremendous burden on the health care systems in postwar countries. Victims of mine blasts are more likely to require amputation and remain in the hospital longer that those wounded by other munitions. Unexploded ordinance and small antipersonnel mines strewn along footpaths, rice paddies, riverbeds, and around villages continue to maim and kill the children and grandchildren of the soldiers who laid them.

The other threat to health care systems is disease. Throughout history, conquering armies have not only killed and maimed their enemies, they have brought with them communicable diseases, such as the bubonic plague, tuberculosis, measles, smallpox, chicken pox, whooping cough, mumps, and influenzas, which, when invading a human population without any previous exposure to them, are likely to kill a high proportion of those who fall sick. In the early 1500s, during the conquest of Mexico, millions of Aztec Indians died of chicken pox introduced by Hernan Cortés and his men. Two centuries later, British troops in the American colonies on at least one occasion during the Indian uprising of 1763, known as Pontiac's Rebellion, deliberately sent blankets infected with smallpox to Shawnee and Delaware Indians. During the Revolutionary War, American troops also accused the British of spreading smallpox by forcing infected people out of cities with the design of spreading the disease among American soldiers.

H

Hors de Combat

By Kurt Schork

Iraqi Army troops and Kurdish peshmerga fought several days of pitched battles in and around the city of Sulaymaniyah in October of 1991. By the afternoon of the third day Iraqi resistance in Sulaymaniyah had been reduced to a complex of buildings at the southwest edge of the city. Hundreds of Kurdish irregulars gathered for a final push against the Iraqis, which I witnessed.

Left: Kurdish Peshmerga guerrillas guard disarmed Iraqi prisoners, October 11, 1991, in the north of Iraq. Right: The Kurds slaughtered the prisoners, ignoring the doomed Iraqis' pleas.

After an hour or so of small arms, rocket, and mortar exchanges Kurdish forces mounted an infantry charge across several hundred meters of open field and captured the first line of buildings in the Iraqi position. As the Kurds advanced uphill toward the final cluster of buildings they topped a small rise in the ground, beyond which numbers of Iraqi soldiers lay dead and wounded. Other Iraqi soldiers in that area of open ground made clear they were surrendering by laying down their weapons, kneeling on the ground, and locking their hands behind their heads. Many were crying "Allahu Akbar" (God is Great), pleading for mercy. No further shots were fired from the main building at the top of the rise, where most of the remainder of the Iraqi soldiers were located. In effect, the battle was over.

The Iraqi soldiers I could see were *hors de combat*, that is, "out of combat," and therefore entitled to be protected, not attacked, and treated humanely according to the provisions of international humanitarian law. Article 3 common to the Geneva Conventions of 1949, which governs "conflict not of an international character" such as the Kurdish rebellion in northern Iraq, states: "Persons taking no active part in the hostilities, including members of armed forces who have laid down their arms and those placed *hors de combat* by sickness, wounds, detention, or any other cause, shall in all circumstances be treated humanely."

For those deemed *hors de combat*, the article prohibits "violence to life and person, in particular murder, mutilation, cruel treatment and torture." The ban is absolute. As the International Committee of the Red Cross Commentary to Common Article 3 makes clear: "No possible loophole is left; there can be no excuse, no attenuating circumstances." In an international conflict, violation of this principle constitutes a grave breach.

Instead of accepting the surrender of the Iraqi soldiers, as required by law and as had been the practice in recent fighting around Sulaymaniyah, the Kurds executed them. An Iraqi soldier with no weapon, and with his hands in the air, was shot and killed a few steps from me. Seven unarmed

prisoners kneeling on the ground nearby were shot to death moments later. Individually and in small groups, every Iraqi soldier I saw outside the main building was executed. None had weapons, nor were they resisting or trying to escape.

By the time I reached the main building at least seventy-five Iraqi soldiers had been herded into a large room. None was armed or resisting and many appeared to have been wounded in the fighting before it stopped. These prisoners were also shot and killed. Kurds with Kalashnikovs emptied magazine after magazine into what became a blood-soaked pile of bodies. Some Kurdish noncombatants joined in the slaughter, using blocks of concrete to crush the heads of the Iraqi soldiers who had not yet died of their wounds. Within thirty minutes, all Iraqi soldiers at the location—probably about 125—were dead.

The murder of these Iraqi soldiers was a war crime, judged by even the narrowest definitions of international humanitarian law. Once a combatant "falls into the power of an adversary," is incapacitated, attempts to surrender, or is captured, he is entitled to protection.
(See **quarter, giving no.**)

Hospitals

By Charles Lane

"The guerrillas blew up the hospital."

I still vividly remember the scorching hot day in November 1989 when I heard those words and instantly recognized that there might be a story behind them. I was working as Central America correspondent for *Newsweek*. El Salvador was in the middle of a ferocious nationwide offensive by a Marxist guerrilla group known as the Farabundo Marti National Liberation Front (FMLN). The FMLN had surprised the Salvadoran Army with large-scale coordinated attacks on the capital, San Salvador, and all the major provincial towns across the tiny, Massachusetts-size country. One of the towns they hit was Zacatecoluca, a provincial capital near the country's international airport. Amid the ensuing chaos, both sides charged each other with horrific human rights violations. It was in that atmosphere that I heard the first report of a guerrilla assault on the hospital in Zacatecoluca.

Hospitals, of course, enjoy a special protected status under international humanitarian law. It is a war crime deliberately to attack a hospital or other medical unit, whether civilian or military. It is also unlawful to use a hospital in direct support of a military operation—to convert one wing of the hospital into an ammo dump, for example. (Indeed, hospitals that are misused in this manner lose their legal protection.) Medical personnel in general may not be attacked; but at the same time it is unlawful to use medical facilities, or related equipment such as ambulances, as camouflage or protection for military personnel, or as a shield for military forces.

International humanitarian law is not, however, completely inflexible in how it evaluates **collateral damage** to hospitals that may result from attacks on **legitimate military targets** nearby. The rule of thumb is that if the damage to the hospital is not excessive in view of the direct and concrete military advantages to be gained from attacking the nearby target, then the damage may be considered lawful.

To go back to that hot day in El Salvador nine years ago. I clambered into my beat-up Mitsubishi Montero Jeep and took off down the road for Zacatecoluca. I will never forget the shock I felt when, without warning, a huge explosion erupted from what seemed like only two inches from my right ear. Temporarily deafened, I recovered my other senses enough to realize that an army artillery piece had just been fired from about twenty-five yards away; the Salvadoran military was pouring shells into the hills around Zacatecoluca, in a desultory attempt to deal with the retreating guerrillas.

When I reached the town, I made immediately for the large, modern public hospital not far from the main square. Once inside, I did indeed find that the pediatric ward had been blown to smithereens. Windows were broken, the elevator destroyed, bits of bedding lay strewn about on the floor. And the hospital personnel confirmed to us that the damage had been caused when a guerrilla unit detonated a large bomb in the ward.

End of story? Not quite. The destruction was heavy, but not entirely wanton. There had been heavy fighting that day between the army and the

Traumatized patients in Palestinian psychiatric hospital after Israeli shells hit it during the siege of Beirut, 1982.

guerrillas. Neither side occupied the hospital or attempted to do so, but as the fighting raged among the narrow cobblestoned streets of the town, a few Salvadoran Army soldiers had become separated from their unit and attempted to flee onto the roof of the hospital. The FMLN forces cornered the government soldiers, and, in an attempt to flush them out, decided to detonate an explosive charge in the pediatric ward, the spot nearest to the soldiers' rooftop hideout.

Hence, two crucial legal questions arise: First, were the soldiers a legitimate target for the FMLN? Almost certainly yes. (It could even be argued that the hospital lost its protected status because the soldiers chose to hide themselves there, but their flight onto the hospital roof seemed less calculated than a decision made amid the heat and panic of battle, with no cooperation from the hospital staff, and it would seem perverse to make the hospital pay for that.)

Second, were the FMLN troops within their rights to use an explosive to attack the soldiers, knowing that to detonate it would cause substantial damage to the wing of the hospital where civilian children were treated? I think that in this instance, the answer is also yes—especially in view of the fact that hospital personnel told us that the guerrillas gave them ample warning and permitted them to evacuate all the patients and medical personnel before they set off their bomb.

But it is a qualified yes. The answer, under international law, would ultimately hinge on the question of whether killing or capturing a handful of already fleeing enemy troops really warranted the eminently foreseeable damage to a hospital facility. And that damage was extensive; not total destruction of the entire building, to be sure, but serious enough to force dozens of sick and injured people into a makeshift outdoor clinic. It might reasonably be argued that this level of damage was unwarranted, notwithstanding the FMLN's laudable effort to evacuate the building first. In fact, the FMLN never did capture or kill the soldiers. If humanitarian law was violated, the FMLN theoretically might be required to pay reparations for the damage caused. But there was no evidence of **willfulness** in the legal sense required to constitute individually culpable war crimes.

So I went back to San Salvador and incorporated the Zacatecoluca hospital incident into that week's article. It was true, as I initially heard, that the guerrillas had blown up the hospital. But a close investigation of all the factors that led them to take that action, and of the manner in which they took it, showed that, tragic as it was, the assault may well have fallen into the category of a questionable but lawful military action, rather than that of a major violation of human rights or an individually culpable war crime.

Hostages

By Sean Maguire

"If the bombing starts again we've been told we will die." The chilling words of the unarmed Canadian officer radioed to United Nations headquarters in Sarajevo, just hours after NATO jets had struck a Bosnian Serb ammunition dump to punish noncompliance with UN resolutions.

Now the officer and his colleagues were held by the Bosnian Serbs as human **shields**. The threat to their lives was obvious, though whether they would die at the hands of their captors or as casualties of bombing was unclear.

A hooded Serb soldier guards chained UN peacekeeper held hostage. Bosnia, 1995.

Television pictures showed them chained to the door of a munitions facility and being forced to drive their car to and fro across the air-raid rubble to prevent the planes returning. A forlorn Polish officer was handcuffed outside a radar site while two masked Serb soldiers stood by, shotguns balanced on their hips. The black hoods, which made the guards look like executioners, were to conceal their identities.

Those two Serbs were taking warranted precautions. Indictments for war crimes had already been handed down by the Hague Tribunal, and the Bosnian Serbs knew their actions would be closely scrutinized. Since 1949, the taking of hostages has been forbidden by the four Geneva Conventions. Using prisoners of war or detainees as human shields has been outlawed either specifically or implicitly by clauses that forbid a party from harming those "not actively taking part in hostilities" in its control.

Common Article 3 of the conventions bans the taking of hostages in internal conflicts while the Fourth Convention forbids civilians being taken hostage during times of war. Ignoring these prohibitions during an international conflict is a grave breach of humanitarian law, leaving those responsible liable to international pursuit and prosecution. The conventions also decree that both prisoners of war and civilians should not be "used to render certain points or areas immune from military operations." Civilians get further protection from the 1977 Additional Protocol II to the Geneva Conventions dealing with internal conflicts. It, too, bans hostage taking.

The practice of taking hostages in war has a long pedigree. In the past, it was used to secure the obedience of an occupied people or adherence to the terms of a treaty. The practice was specifically outlawed in 1949 because of the finding at the Nuremberg Trials that existing laws appeared to permit reprisal executions. Under certain conditions an army is still allowed to take **reprisals** for an illegal act by an adversary, but cannot use "excessive" force or execute prisoners of war or civilians.

The International Committee of the Red Cross (ICRC) defines hostages as "persons who find themselves, willingly or unwillingly, in the power of the enemy and who answer with their freedom or their life for compliance with the orders of the latter (the enemy) and for upholding the security of its armed forces."

Disputes about the nature of modern conflicts make it difficult to judge if and how the protections of the Geneva Conventions apply. Should you be hijacked on an international flight, your abductors would not be contravening the Geneva Conventions, which deal with hostages taken by "an authority," but the 1979 International Convention Against the Taking of Hostages, which explicitly outlaws such cross-border criminality.

"Hostages" was the description the UN gave to the four hundred peacekeepers the Bosnian Serbs rounded up from depots and garrisons at the end of May 1995. The ICRC, however, disagreed. It argued that since the UN had ordered air strikes it had become involved in the Bosnian conflict and its personnel were therefore prisoners of war. The ICRC did make plain its horror that once they were forced to serve as human **shields** they were being used as hostages and not treated as prisoners of war. The Hague Tribunal subsequently indicted Bosnian Serb leaders Radovan Karadzic and Ratko Mladic for the hostage-taking campaign and for using UN personnel as human shields.

At the time, unfortunately but unsurprisingly, the Bosnian Serb tactic worked. "I was a kind of insurance policy against NATO threatening to bomb again," said Capt. José Mendez after his release. The Spanish officer spent ten days sitting in the middle of a runway at the main Bosnian Serb air base hoping that NATO would not call the Serb bluff. It did not. The next NATO bombing campaign, which led to the Dayton peace agreement, took place when UN soldiers were no longer vulnerable to capture.

(See **reprisal killings**.)

Humanitarian Aid, Blocking of

By David Rieff

The aid workers who trucked relief supplies from Metkovic in Croatia to the ruined towns and villages of central Bosnia and on to Sarajevo knew they were engaged in a game of humanitarian Russian roulette.

For the fighters, the humanitarian convoys were resupplying their enemies. That made the aid workers enemies as well. "You say you are helping women and children," I heard a Croat fighter say bitterly to an official of the Danish Refugee Council at an improvised checkpoint in western Herzegovina. "You are doing nothing of the sort. You are helping the Muslims."

The Danish official only shook her head. "You're quite wrong," she said. "We are taking no sides; our aid is neutral." The Croat soldier's only response was a bitter laugh.

We waited at the checkpoint for a long time. We would wait for just as long at half a dozen others before we finally arrived in the town of Travnik, controlled by the Bosnian government. The Croats stopped us along the road. The Serbs shelled us from the hills. That was what pushing a humanitarian convoy through was usually like. At the checkpoints, the law counted for little. As the Danish official put it to me, "In this war, not only do the fighters not obey the law, they don't even know what we're talking about when we speak of humanitarian requirements."

And yet the need for **humanitarian interventions** to alleviate the worst of consequences on civilians is one of the few questions about which almost all people outside Bosnia could agree. There was no consensus about the rights or wrongs of the conflict, let alone how to resolve it. But there was real determination to see that humanitarian aid got through, and real indignation when it could not. When the Serbs closed the Sarajevo airport, or convoys were blocked, all outside parties were outraged. Humanitarian aid was supposed to be beyond the politics of the war, beyond all questions of military or psychological advantage. It was something that was unarguably good, and, as such, something that must not be interfered with.

The legal bases for this view were already powerful with the passage of the Fourth Geneva Convention of 1949. It imposed on all its parties the obligation to allow "the free passage of all consignments of medical and hospital stores" and of "all consignments of essential foodstuffs, clothing and tonics intended for children under fifteen, expectant mothers and maternity cases" even to its military adversaries. The 1977 Additional Protocols to the Geneva Conventions further cemented both the obligations of belligerents and the rights of noncombatants. Article 69 imposes on occupying powers the obligation to provide relief supplies to the population of its adversary "without any adverse distinction," to ensure that population's physical survival (it also called for the provision of articles necessary for religious worship). Article 70 requires belligerents to treat offers of relief not as interference in the conflict, so long as the relief effort was "humanitarian and impartial in character," but as a duty imposed by international humanitarian law (IHL).

On the ground, and not only in **Bosnia**, things have been more complicated. In a war of **ethnic cleansing**, the last things fighters want to do is make it possible for the civilian populations of their adversary to remain, let alone be decently housed and fed, or be allowed to worship freely. In so many cases, the violation of IHL was the norm, and respect for it the exception. In northern Bosnia, the Serbs did not provide articles of Muslim religious worship, they systematically blew up mosques. And the more convoys they blocked, the likelier it was that the Muslim population would flee, bringing about the ethnic cleansing that had been the goal of the war in the first place.

The bitter truth was that to stand for international laws governing the free movement of humanitarian aid was to stand against the war aims of the Bosnian Serbs and, to a lesser extent, the Bosnian Croats, and their respective masters in Belgrade and Zagreb as well. For the fighters of the Croatian Defense Council (HVO) to allow a humanitarian convoy into Bosnian government–controlled East Mostar, for example, was to sanction the continued physical presence of Muslims in that part of Bosnia-Herzegovina. And all the killing and destruction had been undertaken precisely with the opposite goal in mind. In this sense, when we who accompanied the aid convoys watched representatives of the United Nations High Commissioner for Refugees (UNHCR) or the private aid groups plead for access, all of us—the aid workers, the fighters at the checkpoints, the civilian beneficiaries, and, of course, the journalists—understood that what was really at stake was the continuation of the war itself. In other words, what in IHL often constitutes a war crime was, for the fighters, the essential tactic of their fight.

But even on strictly legal grounds, the situation was not always clear in a place like Bosnia. The Fourth Geneva Convention and the 1977 Additional Protocols are encrusted with exceptions on the subject of blocking humanitarian aid. That is because the Bosnian conflict is not at all the kind of war either the framers of the convention or the additional protocols had anticipated. Article 23 of the Fourth Geneva Convention states that an army must be satisfied that there are no "serious reasons" for fearing that relief supplies will be diverted from their intended destination and recipients, or that control over distribution will not be effective, or that the enemy will not derive some substantial benefit to its war effort or have its economy shored up. Article 18 of Additional Protocol II emphasizes the "exclusively humanitarian and impartial nature" of all appropriate relief efforts. The guarantee of access comes with the right of belligerents to inspect convoys to see that the aid is what it purports to be and is destined for populations that are entitled to it.

In wars that pit not armies but armed populations against each other, such guarantees are almost impossible to ensure. Fighters on all sides use humanitarian relief supplies for their own purposes, and the laws do not adequately come to grips with the problem of a war in which the distinction between soldier and civilian is unclear, if it exists at all.

It will be a long time before such questions are resolved, for ultimately they are political and moral as much as they are legal. In the Bosnian context, the loopholes in the law making the blocking of aid a war crime could easily be exploited to prevent aid convoys from getting to where the needs are greatest. None of this, of course, is of much comfort to the civilian populations trapped in wars of ethnic cleansing for whom humanitarian aid remains almost the only hope.

Humanitarian Intervention

By David Rieff and Anthony Dworkin

At the height of the siege of Sarajevo, when hundreds of shells were hitting the Bosnian capital every day, many there believed they would not survive. The United Nations airlift, which provided food for many who would otherwise have starved, was constantly being interrupted as Serb forces repeatedly shelled the airport runway. As the months turned into years and the siege was not lifted, it seemed, both to Sarejevans and to many sympathetic foreigners, that either the city would be destroyed or some kind of outside intervention would have to take place.

H

"How can you in the West allow this to go on?" an actress at Sarajevo's National Theater asked in January of 1993. "My teeth are falling out, I'm covered in eczema, I haven't had a bath in months, and I'm a privileged person by the standards of this town. I know no one outside really understands what is going on here; you all think we're savage Balkan people pursuing our ancient ethnic bloodlusts. It's utter nonsense, of course. But even if that's what you think, even if you won't come help us because we have right on our side, why can't you help us for humanitarian reasons? Why can't you just stop the siege?"

Overhead, as if it had been choreographed, a jet screamed through the afternoon sky. It was a NATO fighter on a routine reconnaissance. The actress smiled. "Good timing, wasn't it?" she said. "If it would dive down and drop some bombs, I could have a bath."

She was right about the befuddlement afflicting most people in the U.S. and in western Europe when they thought about Bosnia. Those who believed that the Bosnian government should be aided because it was in the right were always in a small minority, even among those who thought force needed to be used to bring the ethnic cleansing and the siege of Sarajevo to an end. It was more common to hear the argument that what was happening was so horrible that it simply had to be stopped, and that if military means were needed then military means had to be employed. In other words, what was most credible to the vast majority of those who paid attention to Bosnia—even at the height of the slaughter, a small percentage of the Western public—was not a political intervention but an intervention that needed to be undertaken solely on humanitarian grounds.

In the end, when the mass murder of more than seven thousand Muslim men and boys at Srebrenica finally forced the Western powers to act, they did so not out of a political determination to restore a unified Bosnian state but instead out of a version of a humanitarian impulse. The bloodshed and the slaughter, Western leaders finally concluded, could not be allowed to go on.

Humanitarian intervention is at once an immensely powerful and a terribly imprecise idea. No formal legal definition of it exists, but its fundamental premise is that outside powers have the right and, perhaps, under some circumstances, the duty to intervene to protect people in other countries who are being victimized, even if what is taking place is a conflict within a State. Whereas classical interventions are political in character and involve one State either imposing its will by force on another or coming to the aid of another (and thus in no sense challenging the long-standing notion that State sovereignty should be for all practical purposes inviolable), humanitarian inter-

ventions offer a direct challenge to such notions of sovereignty. This is especially true for those interventions directly into the internal affairs of a single State. In a deep sense, they also sidestep considerations of the political rights and wrongs of a given conflict. What matters, from the perspective of the State or group of States contemplating a humanitarian intervention, is the effect a conflict has on civilians.

An example of this kind of thinking was the debate in 1996 over a Canadian proposal for a humanitarian intervention in what was then eastern Zaire to protect the millions of Hutu refugees who were at risk from both the attacks of Tutsi-led Rwandan forces and from the ebb and flow of the Zairean civil war. The Canadians argued that the rights of a civilian population at risk outweighed any other consideration, including the effect that such a humanitarian deployment might have on the political struggle then taking place in Zaire. Those who argued against the deployment in effect were saying that humanitarian needs alone could not justify such outside interference. Many also made the cautionary argument that forecasting the long-term effect of humanitarian military intervention was itself fraught with uncertainty.

As a matter of international law, humanitarian intervention remains purely a matter of the political preferences of the person making the argument. It

UN peacekeepers support a wounded woman during a Serb shelling. Sarajevo, 1994.

seems generally accepted that the Security Council can declare anything it likes to be a "threat to international peace and security," subject not to any genuinely objective constraints of law but only to the political vetoes of its permanent members. Its determinations are shaped by public opinion, international activists, CNN, and the political considerations of Security Council members, as well as by broader, and more principled policies and laws. Within international humanitarian law (IHL), the leap from provisions providing for the delivery of humanitarian relief to military intervention is a long one, but not too long for those politically motivated to do so.

In practice, humanitarian intervention has often served as a justification for States to act in conflicts where there is no domestic support for more straightforward political interventions. The public in North America and western Europe has, for all the talk of compassion fatigue, proved remarkably sympathetic to the use of force to avert or bring to an end a humanitarian disaster. On the other hand, humanitarian intervention has also been a justification for other political motivations. In Rwanda, in 1994, it was commonly assumed that the French humanitarian intervention dubbed Operation Turquoise used the humanitarian imperative as a cover for France's decision to continue to try to influence events in the Great Lakes region of Africa with military force and, more specifically, to save the French-supported, but genocidal, government. And historically, many of the imperial campaigns launched by the European colonial powers in the nineteenth century were justified on humanitarian grounds.

In the mid-1990s, the idea of humanitarian intervention first came to prominence as the brainchild of UN bureaucrats and humanitarian relief organizations who were unable to operate safely in conflict zones. A French humanitarian official, Bernard Kouchner, even popularized the legal theory of the French scholar Mario Bettati of the "right of intervention." By the end of the decade, though, humanitarian intervention had been taken up by a newly ascendant group of statesmen who promoted the claims of moral action in foreign policy. America's Bill Clinton and Britain's Tony Blair led NATO to war with Slobodan Milosevic in 1999 in the face of an escalating campaign of repression against ethnic Albanians in the Serbian province of Kosovo. Tony Blair described the Kosovo conflict as "a just war, based...on values," and it remains the *locus classicus* for humanitarian intervention.

In retrospect, two aspects of the Kosovo war stand out. First, conducted by NATO from the air, it was remarkably cost-free for the intervening forces: no NATO troops lost their lives from enemy action during the conflict. However it can be argued that the cost of NATO's decision not to deploy ground troops was borne at least in part by Kosovo's Albanian residents, victims of a brutal campaign of violence and forced displacement by Serbian forces that escalated dramatically after the war got underway. Kosovo left unclear the question of whether Western public opinion would support similar action if the price in the lives of soldiers and in money grew too high. When, as with the U.S.-led United Nations Operation in Somalia (UNOSOM II), humanitarian interventions entail a tangible cost, pressures to abort them mount quickly and usually become politically irresistible.

The other striking feature of the Kosovo campaign is that it was undertaken without the endorsement of the UN Security Council; Russian and Chinese opposition meant that the United States and its allies could not win a resolution backing the war. Kosovo brought into focus the question of whether the imperative of halting a humanitarian catastrophe was enough on its own to justify intervention under international law. An international commission of experts later said the intervention had been "illegal but legitimate," while other lawyers have cast it as lawful because of the humanitarian emergency it was intended to head off.

For a few years after Kosovo, finding a way to reconcile the humanitarian claim of suffering civilians with the procedural formalities of the United Nations seemed to be one of the central problems of international politics. An influential attempt to change the terms of debate came with the formulation by a Canadian-sponsored commission of an international "responsibility to protect" people facing massacre, and the General Assembly adopted a version of this language at the World Summit in 2005. This gave weight to the idea that the Security Council should act to prevent atrocities, but left unresolved the question of whether States could act on their own if the United Nations was deadlocked. After the American invasion of Iraq, the morality and practical efficacy of armed intervention seem more problematical to many people than they did previously, and the rich world's appetite for humanitarian intervention appears at least temporarily to have waned. However, the continuing victimization of civilians in internal conflicts such as Darfur means the use of military power for humanitarian purposes is likely to retain an enduring appeal, even in these chastened times.

I

Identification

By H. Wayne Elliott

During the American Civil War soldiers rarely wore any sort of identifying disk. Before battle most soldiers would write their name and unit on a slip of paper and pin it to their backs. That simple battlefield expedient sometimes worked. A few soldiers bought ornate engraved pins or metal identification tags from sutlers. The tags had the soldier's name and unit and, sometimes, his hometown. Neither government issued identification disks. The haphazard way in which soldiers were identified probably explains why almost half the Civil War graves in national cemeteries are marked "unknown."

Only a few years later, in the Franco-Prussian War, the Prussian Army issued not only identification disks but required each Prussian soldier to carry an identification card. These cards were called the soldier's *grabstein* (his "tombstone"). Today, the laws of war require that soldiers be identified. In the not-too-distant future we can expect to find electronic disks that would contain a great deal of information about the soldier. DNA coding may mean that there simply will be no more "unknown soldiers." Regardless of the methods used, identification as a lawful combatant and a member of the armed forces is crucial to determining the treatment to be afforded—whether sick, wounded, dead, or captured; whether a soldier, medic, or civilian.

While the military uniform may be circumstantial evidence that the person in it is a lawful **combatant**, the laws of war do not recognize the uniform alone as absolute proof that a person is a member of the military. Status as a member of the military is important. A person who participates in hostilities without being authorized to do so by proper authorities runs the risk of being charged as an unlawful combatant and prosecuted as such. Perhaps more important, a party to the conflict is not obligated to extend **prisoner of war** status to persons who are not lawful combatants. For this reason, armies make every effort to identify those who serve it in combat.

In most armies today soldiers carry identity disks (often referred to as dog tags in the U.S. forces). The disks are referred to in the First Geneva Convention of 1949 in connection with the duty to identify the wounded and the dead. However, the conventions themselves do not mandate that such tags be issued or that the soldier actually carry them. The disks generally have the soldier's name, identifying number, blood type, and religion. These facts would be important considerations in providing proper care in case the soldier is wounded or killed. The disks are primarily intended as a means to aid in the identification of the soldier who, because of wounds or death, otherwise might be unidentified.

Article 17 of the Third Geneva Convention requires that each party to a conflict issue an identity card to persons who are liable to become prisoners of war. The card must include the person's name, rank, identifying number, and date of birth. The card can also include other information as well as the person's signature, fingerprints, and a photograph. The card must be shown by the prisoner on demand, but it cannot be taken away from him. The drafters of the convention required only information that would have no real intelligence value so the captor would have no reason to take the card from the prisoner. If the prisoner has lost the card, Article 18 requires that the detaining (i.e., the capturing) power provide him with another similar card.

The identification card is also important in determining the treatment to be afforded the prisoner of war. The rank of the prisoner of war at the time of capture is on the card and will determine whether the captive is to be treated as an officer or enlisted person. The duties expected of prisoners of war vary with rank, so the card is quite important.

Related to the requirements governing the identification card are the general rules concerning prisoner interrogation. The captive is "bound" to give only his name, rank, date of birth, and serial number when questioned. This requirement is often misunderstood. The Third Geneva Convention, in Article 17, requires that this information be given. The same information is on the identification card, and that card must be shown upon demand. Hence, there is no reason not to provide it when questioned. While this is all the prisoner is bound to give, the captor might ask for more information, including militarily sensitive data. Nonetheless, the POW need not respond with anything more than the four items set out in the Third Geneva

Unknown soldier: In Iran where untrained and unarmed young fighters were deployed in human waves, countless dead were buried without being properly identified. 1986.

Convention and may not be punished or mistreated for failing to do so.

Those who are given an opportunity to observe or talk with prisoners of war should ask to see the identification documents. Not only is the card evidence of the person's status under the laws of war, its absence is evidence that the captor is not in full compliance with the same laws. The presence of the identity disks and the identification card is a ready and visible means of determining some minimal level of compliance with the laws of war concerning prisoners.

(See **dead and wounded**.)

Immunity from Attack

By Emma Daly

Our friend lay in bed, plucking nervously at the gray, bloodstained sheets, her eyes covered by a bandage, her face patterned with glass cuts. "I want to go home," she said vehemently. "I'm terrified of staying in this building."

We could understand her concern: the concrete blocks and curved facades of the Kosevo hospital complex in Sarajevo were scarred by shrapnel marks, bullet marks, and shell craters. Two weeks earlier, two patients had been killed when a shell hit their ward. We could hear the sounds of bombardment in the distance, and, suspiciously close to the **hospital**, the hollow sound of outgoing mortar fire. Hospitals are generally immune from attack under the Geneva Conventions, which grant civilians and civilian objects a high level of theoretical protection in times of war. The **siege** of Sarajevo, however, made a mockery of the humanitarian ideal that the dangers of war should be limited, as far as possible, to the armed forces engaged in the fighting.

The concept of immunity, the rule that certain people and places should be "protected and respected" during wartime, can be dated back at least to 1582, when a Spanish judge suggested that "intentional killing of innocent persons, for example, women and children, is not allowable in war." The Geneva Conventions of 1949 confirmed immunity for civilians, hospitals, and medical staff, and the 1977 Additional Protocols to the conventions state: "The civilian population and individual civilians shall enjoy general protection against the dangers arising from military operations."

The absolute rule is that civilians must not be directly targeted for military attack. Furthermore, some individuals considered especially vulnerable —children under fifteen, the elderly, pregnant women, and mothers of children under seven—are granted special protection and may, for example, be moved to safe zones exempt from attack by agreement of the warring parties. The wounded, sick, or shipwrecked, military personnel who are considered to be *hors de combat*, are protected, as are **prisoners of war**.

Hospitals, both fixed and mobile, ambulances, hospital ships, medical aircraft, and **medical personnel**—whether civilian or military—are also entitled to protection from hostile fire under the Geneva Conventions, provided that structures are marked with a **red cross or red crescent** and not used improperly or near military objectives, and staff are properly protected. Staff include not only doctors, nurses, and orderlies, but the drivers, cleaners, cooks, crews of hospital ships—in short, all those who help a medical unit to function. Some aid workers—for example, Red Cross volunteers treating the sick and wounded on the battlefield—are also covered, as are military chaplains. Other than hospitals, certain other buildings cannot be attacked. Places of worship and historic monuments are protected, as are civilian structures like schools and other objects that are not being used to support military activities. Under the 1954 Convention on Cultural Property important places of worship, historic sites, works of art, and other cultural treasures are likewise protected from attack.

There are exceptions. A school, for example, becomes a **legitimate military**

target if soldiers are based there. With hospitals, the situation is more complicated since they are permitted to keep armed guards on their grounds. But immunity from attack can be lost if the people or objects are used to commit acts that are harmful to one side in a conflict. If the Bosnian Serbs besieging Sarajevo had concluded that government forces were firing weapons from within the Kosevo hospital complex, they would have had the right to fire back—but only if they had first asked the Bosnian government to stop using the hospital as a **shield** and had given them a reasonable period to comply.

Causing harm to an innocent person or object is not always illegal. Civilian deaths and damage are allowed as the result of an attack on a military target, but only if the attack is likely to confer a definite military advantage. Damage to people or objects who are in principle deemed to be immune under international humanitarian law must not be excessive in relation to the expected military gain. For example, breaking the windows of a hospital during an attack on an arms dump five hundred meters away

Ethnic Albanian children look at the bullet holes left after a Serb attack on an Albanian cafe in which one man died and four were injured. Kosovo, 1999.

would not be illegal since the civilian damage would be far outweighed by the military gain.

But keeping legitimate military targets separate from protected civilian sites is hard to do on the ground. Under international humanitarian law, the parties to a conflict are obliged to separate their military from their civilians as much as possible. But the reality is that this can be difficult. In Sarajevo, for example, the territory under siege was so small that to do so was all but impossible. That said, in Sarajevo, as in many towns across Bosnia-Herzegovina, it seemed clear that the besiegers' primary target was civilians. That was one of the reasons why Radovan Karadzic and Ratko Mladic, the civilian and military leaders of the secessionist Bosnian Serbs, were charged with war crimes by the International Criminal Tribunal in The Hague.
(See **civilian immunity; civilians, illegal targeting of; medical transports; proportionality; protected persons.**)

Incitement to Genocide

By Colette Braeckman

"You have to work harder, the graves are not full," urged the voice on the radio. In April 1994, when the genocide started in Rwanda, ordinary people were glued to their receivers. In a part of the world where most people do not have electricity, that's the way information gets disseminated. But in Rwanda that spring the popular radio stations seemed to have only one aim: to incite the Hutu masses to exterminate their Tutsi neighbors.

The most popular station of all was RTLM (Radio Television des Milles Collines), the Thousand Hills Radio Television. It was known for having the best disc jockeys in Rwanda and for its attractive mix of African music, news programming, and political analysis. Founded in 1993 and owned by family members and friends of President Habyarimana, the station preached an extremist message of Hutu supremacy, but many apolitical Rwandans became listeners because of the music it played. In fact, their hearts and minds were being prepared for genocide. When the killing was unleashed on April 6, it became clear what the owners and managers of the station had created—an infernal pulpit from which the message to kill could be disseminated throughout Rwanda.

The incident that triggered the mayhem was the downing of Habyarimana's plane by a missile. Within minutes of the crash, RTLM journalists accused Belgian troops in Rwanda on a UN peacekeeping mission of shooting down the plane. The next morning, ten Belgian soldiers were brutally killed, and not long afterward Belgium withdrew its forces from the UN mission. It was RTLM that gave the signal to begin the massacre of Tutsis and moderate Hutus.

RTLM on April 7 and April 8: "You have to kill [the Tutsis], they are cockroaches..." May 13: "All those who are listening to us, arise so that we can all fight for our Rwanda... Fight with the weapons you have at your disposal, those of you who have arrows, with arrows, those of you who have spears with spears... Take your traditional tools... We must all fight [the Tutsis]; we must finish with them, exterminate them, sweep them from the whole country... There must be no refuge for them, none at all." And on July 2: "I do not know whether God will help us exterminate [the Tutsis] ...but we must rise up to exterminate this race of bad people... They must be exterminated because there is no other way."

The message worked. By July of 1994, when the victory of the Tutsi-led Rwandan Patriotic Front (RPF) put an end to the genocide, up to 1 million Rwandans—mostly Tutsis, but also Hutus belonging to the democratic parties in Rwanda—had been slaughtered. The radios had been all too successful in inciting the genocide.

What they did, which was both to prepare the ground for the killing and encourage listeners to go on killing once the genocide had begun, was, of course, utterly illegal under international humanitarian law, which does not recognize an absolute right to free expression. By definition, most of those killed were civilians, that is, "persons taking no active part in the

Kigali prison. Accused murderers in the 1994 genocide. Rwanda, 1994.

hostilities." In an internal conflict, as stated in Article 3 common to the four Geneva Conventions of 1949, civilians "shall in all circumstances be treated humanely without any adverse distinction founded on race, color, religion, sex, birth, or wealth."

As the rampage spread, the key document became the Genocide Convention of 1948, to which Rwanda became a party in 1975. The convention defines the crime of genocide as "acts committed with intent to destroy, in whole or in part, a national, ethnical, racial or religious group as such." The acts include killing members of the group, causing serious bodily or mental harm, and deliberately inflicting on the group conditions of life calculated to bring about its physical destruction in whole or in part. The convention not only makes genocide itself an international crime but states in Article 3 that "direct and public incitement to commit genocide" is punishable. And in September 1998, an ad hoc International Criminal Tribunal for Rwanda (the ICTR), sitting in Arusha, Tanzania, sentenced Jean Kambanda, the former prime minister, for direct and public incitement to commit genocide, in part for encouraging RTLM to continue its calls to massacre the Tutsis. That same month, the court convicted Jean-Paul Akayesu, the leading civilian in Taba commune, on charges that included the direct and public incitement to commit genocide.

The prohibitions set forward by the Genocide Convention and the precedent set by the ICTR were affirmed in the statute of the International Criminal Court (ICC), which was adopted on July 17, 1998. One hundred and twenty nations approved the Rome Statute, which laid the ground rules for the first international criminal court in history; Article 5 of the Statute listed genocide first among the crimes over which the court had jurisdiction.

The hate-mongering journalists of RTLM stayed on the air until the very last moment of the Rwandan genocide. In July 1994, when the RPF (the Tutsi army that came from neighboring Uganda) defeated the Rwandan army and put an end to the genocide, the RTLM staff took a mobile transmitter and fled to Zaire, together with Hutu refugees. Ferdinand Nahimana, a well-known historian who served as RTLM's director, fled to Cameroon and the Belgian journalist George Ruggiu fled to Kenya. Both were later arrested and delivered to the Arusha tribunal. First condemned, Nahimana launched an appeal but Ruggiu was sentenced to 12 years of imprisonment after having been convicted of incitement to genocide and crimes against humanity.

Indiscriminate Attack

By Roy Gutman and Daoud Kuttab

As Western air forces bombarded Iraqi military targets at the start of the Gulf War, Iraq repeatedly fired SS-1 (Scud) missiles into Israel. Scuds never were known for their precision, but they became even less accurate as a result of Iraq's earlier decision during the Iran-Iraq War to triple the range to 560 miles.

The margin of error was at least two thousand yards, making the missile almost useless for hitting military targets but highly effective in terrorizing

Streetcars pass the ruins of buildings destroyed in the Allied firebombing during World War II. Dresden, March 1946.

the population in an urban area. Of the eleven attacks on Israeli targets, many landed in densely populated residential areas in Tel Aviv or Haifa or in open fields; others were intercepted by U.S.-supplied Patriot antimissile missiles and never came anywhere close to the target. There is no evidence that Iraq made any attempt to aim the Scud missiles at military targets.

The Scud assaults exemplify indiscriminate attack, a defined war crime under the 1977 Additional Protocol I to the 1949 Geneva Conventions. An indiscriminate attack is one in which the attacker does not take measures to avoid hitting non-military objectives, that is, civilians and civilian objects. Protocol I states: "Parties to the conflict shall at all times distinguish between the civilian population and combatants and between civilian objects and military objectives and accordingly shall direct their operations only against military objectives."

An indiscriminate attack also includes using means and methods that, like the Scud, cannot be directed at specific military objectives or whose effects cannot be limited.

Military objectives are limited to "those objects which by their nature, location, purpose or use make an effective contribution to military action and whose total or partial destruction, capture or neutralization, in the circumstances ruling at the time, offers a definite military advantage." Every attack not clearly aimed at a military target is indiscriminate, but some attacks against military targets that cause collateral damage to civilians or civilian objects are also considered as indiscriminate. If the harm to civilians is proportionate to the military advantage expected, the attack, other things being equal, is a legal act of war. If the harm is "excessive in relation to the concrete and direct military advantage anticipated," the attack is regarded as indiscriminate and is prohibited. (Concrete means perceivable by the senses; direct means having no intervening factor.)

Although the United States and several other countries have not ratified Additional Protocol I, this provision is considered to be part of customary law and therefore binding upon all parties to a conflict. Indiscriminate attack has never been specifically banned in internal conflicts, yet this principle carries over as a matter of customary law.

Nearly every army has at some point carried out what today would be described as an indiscriminate attack. Examples include Germany's V-II rocket attacks during World War II, the Allied "strategic bombing" and firebombing of Dresden and Hamburg, as well as the U.S. **carpet bombing** during the Vietnam War. To curb the practice, Additional Protocol I prohibits an attack "by bombardment which treats as a single military objective a number of military objectives located in a city, town, village, or other area containing a similar concentration of civilians or civilian objects."

The point of this provision is to prevent an attacker from treating a whole city that contains not only civilians but also military targets as a single military target. The individual military objectives may still be targeted, with the possibility of **collateral damage** to civilians, but weapons must be aimed individually. What counts as sufficiently discriminate targeting is an important question of interpretation, in light of the physical constraints of weapons systems and the inability even with "smart" weapons to achieve perfect targeting. For that matter, there is not even a requirement that only smart weapons be used.

Even after the protocol came into effect, some of the world's most advanced armies violated the law. Human Rights Watch (HRW) in *Civilian Pawns: Laws of War Violations and the Use of Weapons on the Israel-Lebanon Border* (1996) documented repeated examples of indiscriminate attack during Israel's long-running conflict with the Hezbollah in southern Lebanon. During the 1993 Operation Accountability, the Israeli army targeted Hezbollah members—whether civilians or military—as well as sympathizers and relatives and also shelled whole villages without distinction of specific military objectives. (It should be noted that Israel is not a party to the 1977 Protocol I.)

There were direct attacks on purely civilian targets such as Sidon's wholesale vegetable market, and at one stage Israel warned it would fire on any means of transportation in about twenty villages, turning the region into a **free fire zone**. But Hezbollah, in the period before the Israeli operation, had also fired Katyusha rockets at Israel, hitting no military installations but causing the civilian population to flee south. This, too, was a clear violation of the ban on indiscriminate attacks. Also, Hezbollah issued no warnings and it used weaponry with obvious inaccuracy. In addition, HRW concluded, Hezbollah, in not directing its weapons at military targets, had used weapons to terrorize the civilian population. In essence, what may have started as indiscriminate attack resulted in direct attack, aimed at civilians—also clearly a war crime. The excuse used by Hezbollah, that it was firing in retaliation, made clear that it was attacking civilians by way of **reprisal**.

In 1995 and 1996, Israel and Hezbollah again attacked each other's civilian targets. In Operation Grapes of Wrath in April 1996, there was evidence that Israel had carried out "indiscriminate and disproportionate attacks against civilians in what had become virtual 'free-fire' zones across large swaths of the south" of Lebanon, culminating in the shelling of a makeshift refugee compound at a UN post south of Tyre in which more than one hundred displaced civilians were killed. Israel said Hezbollah had fired mortars and Katyusha rockets from a position three hundred meters from the UN post. Locating military objectives near a concentration of civilians, known as shielding, is also a war crime, and the laws of armed conflict are clear that an attacker is not precluded from attacking a legitimate military target by the proximity of civilians or civilian objects. While acts of shielding did not render the zone immune from attack, neither did they "give Israel license to fire *indiscriminately* into a wide area that includes a UN base and concentrations of civilians," Human Rights Watch correctly noted (emphasis added). The International Committee of the Red Cross (ICRC) one day later issued a statement in which it "firmly condemned" the Israeli shelling at Qana and reiterated there was an "absolute ban" on indiscriminate attacks. However, a senior ICRC official said after an investigation that the real problem here was the fact that the Israeli system was designed to automatically fire back on the source of the original attack. Therefore Israel did not take sufficient precautions in their attack to ensure that it would not result in disproportionate civilian deaths. The UN's military advisor concluded in a May 1996 report that it was "unlikely that gross technical and/or procedural errors led to the shelling of the United Nations Compound." However, he added "it cannot be ruled out completely."

(See **civilian immunity**; **civilians, illegal targeting of**; **legitimate military targets**; **military necessity**; **proportionality**; **shields**.)

Types of Indiscriminate Attack

1. An attack that is not targeted at military objectives. (Damage to civilian property that is actually intended is known as **wanton destruction**, especially if it is wide-scale.)

2. Use of weapons that are not able to be properly targeted.

3. Use of weapons that have uncontrollable effects.

4. An attack that treats an area with similar concentrations of military and civilian objectives as a single military objective.

5. An attack that may be expected to cause harm to civilians or civilian objectives in excess of the concrete and direct military advantage anticipated.

Internal Displacement

By Maud S. Beelman

From a distance, the line of cars and buses that snaked along the rural stretch of northwest Bosnian roadway looked like a traffic jam on that languid August afternoon, as girls in summer white bicycled past fields of cornflower blue. Up close, the terror in the eyes of the people of Sanski Most, the belongings stuffed into satchels and plastic bags, and the police riding shotgun told the real story.

More than fifteen hundred Slavic Muslims were being forced from their homes that day in mid-August 1992 by ethnic Serbs trying to purge northern Bosnia of their neighbor-turned-enemy. The Serbs had even provided city buses to transport those without cars, though the generosity was soon to degrade into a terrifying all-night trek over blood, body parts, and across the front lines. Four months into the war, the UN High Commissioner for Refugees had begun

to realize that the mass movement of civilians in Bosnia was not the chaotic happenstance of war, but rather a calculated, orchestrated transfer of populations aimed at creating ethnically pure areas.

Europe had not seen this kind of mass expulsion of civilians since World War II. Hitler's atrocities across the continent had given rise to the 1949 Geneva Conventions, which include specific protections for civilians. Article 49 of the Fourth Geneva Convention declares that "individual or mass forcible transfers... are prohibited, regardless of their motive."

Those in the Sanski Most convoy, by virtue of being moved to another location in the same country, are regarded under international humanitarian law as internally displaced persons (IDPs). If sent across an international border, it would be a **deportation** and they would be treated as **refugees**.

Additional Protocol II of 1977, which applies in internal conflicts, provides that forced civilian displacement may be undertaken legally only when civilians' very safety or "imperative military reasons" require it. In addition, Article 17 says that civilians cannot be forced from their "whole territory" for reasons connected with the conflict. The article does not say unambiguously

Tents cover the hillside at a camp for internally displaced persons in Tche, Democratic Republic of Congo, where some 20,000 fled amid violent attacks and clashes between rival Hema and Lendu militias. March, 2005.

I

what is meant by "territory." The International Committee of the Red Cross (ICRC) Commentary to the Additional Protocols states that the intent here is to minimize civilian displacement that is politically motivated.

The standard is the same for international or internal conflicts: if civilians have to be moved for either of those two reasons—safety or military imperatives—their evacuations are to be under protected, hygienic, and humane conditions, and as short-lived as possible. None of that applied in the case of Sanski Most, which fell under Bosnian Serb control in the earliest days of the war and saw no fighting for three years until autumn 1995.

International law, therefore, was unambiguous. Article 49 of the Fourth Geneva Convention prohibits the mass transfer of Bosnia's civilians and Article 17 of Additional Protocol II prohibits the expulsions.

Despite IHL, here they were. The daylong journey had descended into the heart of darkness as the convoy turned from the main road onto isolated country paths and made its way through an increasingly hostile gauntlet of Serb soldiers and civilians shouting, "Butcher them, butcher them!" As the sun set, the worst was yet to come. With guns stuck in their faces, the people of Sanski Most were ordered from the buses and their cars, most of which were seized. With what belongings they could carry, they were sent on foot into the darkness through a no-man's-land separating two armies. I went with them.

Old and young, fit and feeble, we trekked along a mountain road that was cratered by mortar impacts, mined on one side, and covered by snipers. In places, the blood was so thick our shoes stuck momentarily to the road, and we stumbled onto chunks of human flesh and other remnants—teddy bears, backpacks, slippers—of those who had gone before. At the front line—a high wall of boulders dynamited from the mountainside—a crippled man was carried over, his wheelchair passed after him. Babies were handed to their mothers. Old men and women, stooped with age, struggled over the rocks to the government-controlled side. The foot journey lasted six hours and covered twelve miles.

By December 1995, just after the Dayton peace accord, at least 1.2 million Bosnians had been internally displaced. Three years later, only a fraction had returned home. "Civilians, not soldiers, were the principal and often intentional victims in the Bosnian conflict. Forced displacement was not just a by-product but an objective of military action and persecution," Sadako Ogata, the UN High Commissioner for Refugees, said at the time.

But three years later, it happened again in the Serbian province of Kosovo, where Serb troops spent much of 1998 crushing an uprising by the 90 percent ethnic Albanian population. As many as 350,000 people had been displaced by September 1998. The majority were women and children.

Not all internal displacements are ethnic cleansing. In Colombia, both sides in the government-rebel conflict have forcibly relocated civilian populations to gain political or economic advantage. Worldwide, there were an estimated 20 to 25 million IDPs in 2005, compared to about 9 million refugees, that is, those forced across international borders.

Legal and humanitarian experts concede existing law is insufficient and weakened by a lack of political will. Interpretations of "imperative military reasons" vary widely, and governments also worry about getting involved in what may be considered the internal affairs of another State. According to Francis Deng, the UN's top representative on IDPs, "Lack of political will is ultimately the issue. Even if you had fine principles, fine laws, but you don't have the will to enforce them, then it's as good as a dead letter."

(See **evacuation of civilians.**)

International Committee of the Red Cross (ICRC)

By Michael Ignatieff

The International Committee of the Red Cross (ICRC) was founded in 1863, the brainchild of Jean-Henri Dunant, a Swiss businessman who had witnessed the Battle of Solferino between France and Austria in 1859 and was shocked by the carnage that resulted from the neglect of the wounded.

Dunant campaigned throughout Europe for a new principle, that wounded enemy soldiers deserved the same medical treatment as troops of one's own nation. Five Geneva notables set up a committee in 1863 with Dunant as its secretary, the nucleus of what was to become the International Committee of the Red Cross, and in 1864, the Swiss government hosted a sixteen-nation international conference to recommend improvements in medical services on the battlefield. Parties to this first Geneva Convention agreed that hospitals, ambulances, and medical staff should be viewed as neutral in conflict and adopted the red cross as the symbol of the medical corps.

From its inception, the ICRC has had a unique and intimate relationship to the Geneva Conventions. Under the 1949 Geneva Conventions and the Additional Protocols of 1977, the ICRC has the mandate to: (a) visit and register prisoners of war, and to deliver mail and food parcels; (b) deliver emergency humanitarian aid to civilians in the midst of armed conflicts; (c) trace missing persons, civilian and military, and reunite them with their families; (d) train armed forces to respect international humanitarian law; (e) extend and develop the Geneva Conventions; and (f) act as go-betweens to secure prisoner exchanges, repatriations, and release of hostages.

The ICRC now has delegations in over fifty countries, just under half of them in Africa. Its annual budget is just over $550 million, most of which comes from governments, chiefly the United States, the European Union, Scandinavian countries, and Switzerland. Its executive committee is entirely Swiss, most of its delegates are still Swiss—though they are recruiting non-Swiss nationals.

ICRC representatives, known as "delegates," work with national Red Cross and Red Crescent societies in the field, and most of their local field workers come from the national societies. Institutionally, however, the ICRC looks on the national societies warily, believing that some of their leaderships are either corrupt or excessively partial to the policies of the local ruling elites.

The ICRC is a unique organization in terms of its legal status under international law, its role in establishing and upholding the Geneva Conventions, and its history and role in bringing relief impartially to civilian victims and the wounded of all nations. These different roles give rise to a unique moral dilemma, whether to denounce publicly the violators of the laws that the ICRC seeks to uphold and develop and that provide the organization its special status, or operate discreetly in order to preserve its ability to cross battle lines, gain access to prisoners, and monitor their treatment. Put more simply, the question is whether the ICRC should speak out—and risk losing access to victims—or keep silent and become complicit in evil.

It is a difficult call, and through most of its history the ICRC has chosen to remain publicly silent. The organization is haunted by its failures. Despite securing initial access to German concentration camps as early as 1935, and despite acquiring unrivaled intelligence about Nazi plans to exterminate the Jews, the ICRC leadership in Geneva failed either to reveal what it knew or to make any public protest. Courageous delegates did save Jews in Hungary and Greece, but the organization did not secure access to the camps until 1945, when it was too late.

This dilemma recurred in July 1992, when ICRC delegates became aware of Serb detention camps in central Bosnia where Muslim prisoners were being starved, tortured, and subjected to summary execution. This time, while maintaining public silence on the matter, local ICRC delegates provided off-the-record corroboration of information journalists had secured from other sources, and thus helped to break the story of the camps.

After the United States began holding prisoners from Afghanistan and

A sign outside the Red Cross (ICRC) compound warns visitors not to bring any weapons inside. Monrovia, Liberia, June 2003.

elsewhere at Guantanamo Bay in 2002, the ICRC was given access to the camp. In October 2003, an ICRC official spoke out against the indefinite nature of the detention regime, which he said was having a harmful effect on prisoners' mental health, though he did not discuss the camp's physical conditions. In November 2004, the *New York Times* published details of a confidential ICRC report on Guantanamo that said some tactics used there were "tantamount to torture." In line with its official policy, the ICRC refused to discuss the report's contents.

As an organization dating back to the middle of the nineteenth century, the ICRC has an immense institutional memory. It visited and transmitted Red Cross messages and parcels for millions of POWs in two world wars; its tracing agency helped reunite hundreds of thousands of refugee families; its delegates have been eyewitnesses to every major armed conflict since 1864, and its expertise in negotiating access to all sides of a conflict is unrivaled.

Independence is its watchword. Officially, its representatives keep their distance from other non-governmental organizations (NGOs) in the field and from the UN. During the Bosnian War, they fought tenaciously to keep their operation separate from UN agencies, refusing convoy escorts from UN peacekeepers, for example, on the grounds that it would compromise their neutrality.

It is an organization which goes by the book—the Geneva Conventions, their clauses and subclauses. This legalistic bias gives their work precision and discipline, but there are other humanitarian organizations (Médecins sans Frontières, for example) that are critical of their cautious, lawyerly neutrality. But the ICRC, like its crusading founder, also plays a central role in campaigns to "civilize" warfare, such as banning blinding laser **weapons** and antipersonnel land **mines.**

Since its creation, the ICRC has been trying to stay true to its mission of being "first in and last out" of any war zone. In the increasingly crowded and competitive field of international humanitarian relief, that helps it stand apart. This has sometimes paid off. During the NATO air strikes in Bosnian Serb territory in August 1995, all the NGOs from NATO countries were evacuated. The ICRC remained and was able to provide humanitarian assistance to the hundreds of thousands of Serb civilians forcibly cleared from the Krajinas by Croat and Muslim forces.

In August 1998, Tomahawk missiles slammed into an Afghan facility the U.S. government said was a terrorist training camp. In the streets of the Afghan capital, Kabul, crowds tried to take over the American embassy; shots were fired at foreigners and two aid workers were killed. The UN evacuated all its personnel from Afghanistan to nearby Pakistan. So did all the NGOs. Only the ICRC remained. Thirty of its delegates stayed on, feeding the war widows of Kabul, keeping the military hospitals open, fitting prosthetic limbs on child amputees, and trying to keep their lines of communication open to all of the factions in Afghanistan's brutal civil war.

The ICRC sometimes pays the price for its staying on. On December 17, 1996, in an ICRC hospital near Grozny, Chechnya, masked assailants scaled the wall of the compound and using pistols fitted with silencers executed six Red Cross personnel in their sleep. On October 27, 2003, a suicide bomber drove an ambulance packed with explosives into the security barriers of the ICRC building in Baghdad, killing two officials and ten bystanders. But the ICRC still tries whenever possible to avoid posting armed guards inside hospitals or as escorts for their convoys.

(See **Red Cross/Red Crescent emblem.**)

I

International Humanitarian Fact-Finding Commission

By Frits Kalshoven

The International Humanitarian Fact-Finding Commission (IHFFC) is an independent, permanent body that owes its existence to Article 90 of Additional Protocol I of 1977. In place since 1991, with its seat and secretariat at Berne, it is at the disposition of parties to armed conflicts that suspect, or are suspected of, serious violations of international humanitarian law (IHL). Although originally created for international armed conflicts, it holds itself capable to function in an internal armed conflict as well; a stance to which no government has objected. The IHFFC considers that it can offer its services to parties to a conflict without having been invited to do so but it will take such a step only if it appears prudent.

I

It is competent to: (1) inquire into alleged serious violations of IHL; (2) facilitate, through its good offices, the restoration of respect for IHL. The IHFFC regards the two functions as not necessarily linked, enabling it to carry out its good offices function independent of any inquiry (and vice versa). This does justice to their somewhat different orientations: while an inquiry into alleged violations may point in the direction of criminal proceedings, good offices may be conducive not just to the restoration of an attitude of respect for IHL but for the other party as well.

States may accept the competence of the IHFFC in relation to other States doing the same, by depositing a declaration to that effect with the Swiss authorities. As of 2006, 69 States have made such declarations—many of them European (including from the former Eastern bloc), and two of the UN Security Council's permanent five, Russia and the United Kingdom. A State's acceptance of IHFFC competence does not bind that State in relation to its opponent or opponents in an internal armed conflict within its territory. The fifteen IHFFC members "of high moral standing and acknowledged impartiality" are elected for five-year terms by the States that have made such declarations. Since the 2006 elections it is composed of ten Europeans (one from Russia) and five from other continents.

For the IHFFC to carry out its functions impartially and effectively requires the consent of the parties involved. This indispensable requirement may at the same time be one of the factors why to this day the IHFFC has remained largely unused.

Frits Kalshoven is a former president of the IHFFC.

International vs. Internal Armed Conflict

By Steven R. Ratner

"The division of world society into national and international is an arbitrary one," in the words of the political scientist John Burton, but a division nonetheless clung to by much of international humanitarian law.

Because the traditional laws of war—and laws of war crimes—concerned only conflicts between States, States accusing each other of violating them or of committing war crimes needed to characterize a conflict as truly international and not internal. Thus, the Geneva Conventions and Additional Protocol I address in nearly all their aspects international conflicts only. They apply in the event of "declared war or of any other armed conflict [between States] even if the state of war is not recognized by one of them," as well as "all cases of partial or total occupation of the territory of a [State], even if the said occupation meets with no armed resistance." The easy cases involve invasion, assault, artillery bombardment, or air raid by one State against another; but the harder cases turn upon the perspectives of the belligerents and States observing the situation.

One such hard case, all too typical these days, is a civil war with foreign involvement or provocation, but without the foreign State's resort to the classic acts of war. What level of such involvement in a case like Bosnia or the Democratic Republic of Congo is enough to trigger the Geneva Conventions? International law offers no precise answers to this question. The International Court of Justice has held that a foreign State is responsible for the conduct of a faction in a civil war if (a) the faction is an organ or agent of the foreign State or (b) the foreign State otherwise orders it to commit certain acts. However, the appeals chamber of the UN's Yugoslavia Tribunal rejected the ICJ's standard in the Tadic case in 1999. It had to determine whether the Bosnian Serb Army was part of the army of Yugoslavia (Serbia and Montenegro), and thus whether the conflict in which Tadic participated was interstate so as to make his atrocities grave breaches of the Geneva Conventions. The Tribunal held that an organized military force belonged to a foreign State if the latter exercised overall control over it, even without issuing specific instructions. It concluded that this was the case for the Bosnian Serb army, and that the conflict in Bosnia during the time of Tadic's actions was thus an interstate war —between Bosnia and Yugoslavia.

The legal consequences of characterizing a conflict as solely internal have been quite significant. First, the Geneva Conventions provide only very basic protections in the event of civil wars through Article 3 common to the conventions. That article prohibits certain flagrant violations of human dignity like murder, torture, ill-treatment, and taking of hostages. Second, Additional Protocol II of 1977, which specifically addresses internal conflicts, provides fewer protections during such conflicts than the Geneva Conventions do for international conflicts. Third, for prosecution of war crimes, the conventions create criminal liability only for violations committed in international armed conflicts.

Nevertheless, recent developments have shown the possibility of prosecuting war crimes in internal conflicts without having to find some sort of linkage to an international war, through reliance on special statutes and customary international law. First, the Rwanda Tribunal statute explicitly gives that court jurisdiction over serious violations of Common Article 3 and Additional Protocol II; second, the Yugoslavia Tribunal has interpreted its Statute to allow for jurisdiction over serious violations of Common Article 3 and other serious violations of the laws and customs of war in internal conflicts; and third, the statute of the International Criminal Court specifically provides for criminality over many acts committed in internal conflicts.

The coherence of these categories has been further challenged during the various military campaigns against suspected terrorists. The U.S. Supreme

Judges at the initial hearing of eight Hutus accused of genocide against the Tutsis. Kigali, Rwanda, April 1995.

Court held in the summer of 2006 that the conflict between the United States and al-Qaeda was regulated at least by Common Article 3. The Court's reasoning was that the Conventions as a whole apply to interstate wars, such as those with Afghanistan and Iraq, while Common Article 3 applies to all armed conflicts that are not between States and thus affords some protections to those caught during such conflicts. If the campaign against suspected terrorists is not viewed as an armed conflict at all, but rather as a law enforcement matter (the view that is most widely held outside the United States) then detainees would be protected under international human rights law.
(see **gray areas in international humanitarian law; guerrillas; paramilitaries.**)

Article 3 Common to the Four Geneva Conventions of August 12, 1949

Article 3, the text of which is repeated in all four Geneva Conventions, is the only part of the conventions that applies explicitly to internal armed conflicts. It has been called a "treaty in miniature," and sets forth the minimum protections and standards of conduct to which the State and its armed opponents must adhere. The protections it spells out are at the core of international humanitarian law. Additional Protocol II of 1977 also covers internal armed conflicts, but it is less widely accepted among States than the 1949 Conventions.

Article 3
In the case of armed conflict not of an international character occurring in the territory of one of the High Contracting Parties, each Party to the conflict shall be bound to apply, as a minimum, the following provisions:

(1) Persons taking no active part in the hostilities, including members of armed forces who have laid down their arms and those placed "hors de combat" by sickness, wounds, detention, or any other cause, shall in all circumstances be treated humanely, without any adverse distinction founded on race, colour, religion or faith, sex, birth or wealth, or any other similar criteria.

To this end, the following acts are and shall remain prohibited at any time and in any place whatsoever with respect to the above-mentioned persons:

(a) violence to life and person, in particular murder of all kinds, mutilation, cruel treatment and torture;

(b) taking of hostages;

(c) outrages upon personal dignity, in particular humiliating and degrading treatment;

(d) the passing of sentences and the carrying out of executions without previous judgment pronounced by a regularly constituted court, affording all the judicial guarantees which are recognized as indispensable by civilized peoples.

(2) The wounded and sick shall be collected and cared for.

An impartial humanitarian body, such as the International Committee of the Red Cross, may offer its services to the Parties to the conflict.

The Parties to the conflict should further endeavour to bring into force, by means of special agreements, all or part of the other provisions of the present Convention.

The application of the preceding provisions shall not affect the legal status of the Parties to the conflict.

Iran-Iraq War

By Jonathan C. Randal

**A quarter century after the outbreak of the war between Saddam
Hussein's Iraq and Iran's Islamic revolutionaries, the terrible lessons it
engendered—and those of Baghdad's two successive conflicts—
bequeathed an ever more freighted legacy of human rights violations.
Indeed the eight-year conflict against Ayatollah Ruhollah Khomeini that
Saddam initiated in 1980—and only barely survived—cast a pall over
the other two wars.**

The second war, to undo Saddam's reckless invasion of Kuwait in 1990, set
Iraq on a collision course with the United States, one of his major, if semi-
clandestine, backers in the first conflict. To whip up support for the fresh
conflict, the United States opportunistically dredged up Saddam's appalling
human rights record which Washington long had conveniently overlooked.

I

By the time the third war started in 2003, Saddam preferred an American invasion and the inevitability of his own downfall to acknowledging Iraq's military weakness in public. For Saddam, maintaining appearances to keep the traditional Iranian foe at bay was more important than allowing international inspectors to discover the inexistence of Iraqi weapons of mass destruction that Washington kept trumpeting to justify its invasion.

If nothing else, thus, for three decades Iraq has served as a locus of hubris, first for Saddam, the erstwhile leader of the would-be Arab superpower, then for the United States, the world's predominant military power in the immediate post-Cold War era. All three conflicts were characterized by massive overconfidence and the first and third wars lasted much longer than their instigators planned. In all these ways, the consequences of the 1980-1988 Iran-Iraq war and the decisions made in regard to it by outside powers continue to be felt.

Yet at the time of the war, realpolitik was thought to justify studied international indifference to the horrors of the conflict, an attitude that contributed to the belligerents' sense of impunity by wittingly tolerating massive violations of humanitarian law, and even likely genocide. Even with the

I

Iranian women in chador practice with pistols in a war little covered by the Western media despite its horrendous casualties. Iran, 1986.

passage of time, such great power accommodation still is hard to stomach, if easily understandable.

Enmity between the two Gulf regional powers existed long before Tehran's Islamic firebrands' threats to export their revolution prompted Iraq's preemptive invasion and eventual international fears of Iranian victory. Strained relations between the neighbors stretch back at least to early Islam's split between mainstream Sunni Baghdad and Shia dissidents in what today is called Iran.

In the decades preceding that first war Washington outfitted the Shah of Iran with state-of-the-art weapons, military bases, and technicians and anointed him de facto gendarme of the Gulf. The Soviets, with smaller British and French inputs, similarly overarmed Iraq. Cold War rivalries dovetailed neatly with arms sales generating easy hard currency earnings to pay for oil. The Gulf then accounted for two-thirds of "free world" imports of crude.

Yet even for the bloodstained twentieth century, the conflict that lasted from

An Iranian soldier: As many as 750,000 were killed in the conflict, the most lethal since World War II.

September 1980 to July 1988 staked out new ground in horror, including the first widespread use of chemical weapons by a government against its own citizens and a meticulously documented campaign of genocide against Iraqi Kurds.

In this, the most lethal conflict since World War II, as many as 750,000 Iranian soldiers and perhaps a third that number of Iraqi troops died on the battlefield. The fighting also provided staggering evidence illustrating systematic disregard for what passes for the rules of warfare—and not just by the belligerents.

For much of its duration, the conflict was construed in many foreign eyes as a curious throwback to World War I's murderous trench warfare, complicated by ideological zeal indecipherable to those unversed in the Middle East's ancient, bloody, and unforgiving history. Never mind that the United States and some Western European states had encouraged Saddam to invade Iran in the first place. But soon the West found the belligerents so equally menacing and unattractive that cynics, personified by former U.S. Secretary of State Henry Kissinger, delighted in both regimes' progressive debilitation.

The "best" outcome was deemed the mutual exhaustion of Ayatollah Ruhollah Khomeini's Iranian Islamic Republic, which was bent on spreading revolution across the Muslim world, and of Saddam Hussein's secular, imitation-Prussian regime in Iraq, notorious for bullying its own citizens and the smaller Gulf Arab oil sheikhdoms. This patronizing attitude provided the five permanent members of the United Nations Security Council with ethically questionable justification for inaction despite binding obligations in the face of repeated and manifest violations of international treaties to which Iran and Iraq and, of course, they were signatories.

The International Committee of the Red Cross (ICRC), neutral guarantor of acceptable warfare's rules known as international humanitarian law, was reduced repeatedly to breaking its customary silence to express explicit exasperation with the belligerents' misbehavior and implicit criticism of the great powers' indulgent complicity with such violations.

This moral abdication in the century's last classic international war soon was taken on board by players in the series of internecine conflicts in Rwanda, Somalia, Liberia, Bosnia, and elsewhere that ushered in the immediate aftermath of the Cold War. That planetary struggle was well into its death throes even as Khomeini "drank the poisoned chalice" and in the summer of 1988 finally accepted the Security Council's cease-fire terms that he had spurned the previous year.

But achieving that outcome required the great powers to abandon the initial splendid isolation of their "plague-on-both-your-houses" approach. Forcing the change were unmistakable signs of Iraqi collapse, which prompted them to provide just enough military aid to keep Iran at bay—and Saddam in the fight. Iraq's brief initial success after invading Iran had quickly crumbled in the face of increasingly resolute Iranian resistance paid for in casualties unacceptable by any but a revolutionary regime.

Eventually backed by all the permanent Security Council members except China, a major international exercise in realpolitik was set in motion after Iran drove the Iraqis back across the international border in 1982 and spurned a multibillion-dollar reparation package in exchange for ending hostilities. That international community's pro-Iraq tilt successfully denied Khomeini's dream of an Islamic Republic in Iraq and of spreading his revolution further afield. Involved was crucial military aid, sometimes overt, more often clandestine, ranging from openly "loaned" French Super Etendard fighter-bombers to covert American jamming of Tehran's radar and furnishing of details from spy satellites that pinpointed Iranian targets. Even so, Iraq barely outlasted Iran. Far from "behaving," just two years after the war an unchastened Saddam invaded Kuwait.

Creating the stalemate to save Saddam from his own folly was not without terrible human cost. The war's free-wheeling cycle of human rights violations multiplied with ever more deadly innovative twists and turns. These violations were regularly denounced by human rights organizations, but to no avail.

Over the years one side or the other, sometimes both, violated the 1949 Geneva Conventions and Additional Protocols of 1977 prohibiting the targeting of civilians and civilian objectives, forbidding the use of children in combat, and protecting prisoners of war, as well as the 1925 Protocol banning the use of chemical weapons.

Countless waves of untrained Iranian boy-soldiers armed only with plastic keys purportedly guaranteeing entry to heaven blew themselves up by the tens of thousands clearing mine fields or died charging into artillery barrages worthy of Verdun or Stalingrad. Iraqi missiles crashed through the night to spread terror among Iranian city dwellers hundreds of miles from the front. Relentless Iraqi and Iranian shelling destroyed each other's cities and towns near the international border.

Particularly troublesome for the ICRC was both sides' penchant for interfering in its usually cut-and-dried procedures. Both Iran and Iraq frustrated the ICRC's tracing of prisoners of war and the identification of the missing and dead, thus enormously complicating postwar efforts to sort out who had survived and delaying repatriation.

Iraq repeatedly complained its prisoners of war were "liquidated," kept incommunicado, or, in the case of Shia soldiers, brainwashed and compelled to join the "Badr Brigades," special turncoat military units organized at Iranian instigation to fight one day for an Islamic Republic in their motherland. The ICRC had trouble with Iran in registering prisoners and persuading Tehran to allow prisoner interviews without witnesses.

Tehran protested that its prisoners in Iraq were prevented from praying together, which Baghdad justified on security grounds. Iraq prevented the ICRC from visiting some twenty thousand Iranians captured starting in 1987.

Even after the fighting ended in 1988, no significant prisoner repatria-

Behind the front lines, weapons, shoes and uniforms of dead or wounded soldiers pile up. Shalamsheh, southeastern Iran, April 1982.

tion took place for two more years despite the cease-fire's provisions for their immediate return and persistent ICRC prodding. (In 1990 Saddam relented to improve relations with Iran as Iraq braced for the U.S.-led coalition to wrest back Kuwait.) When finally some forty thousand men from each side were sent home, the exchanges violated ICRC regulations against such one-for-one prisoner releases.

A decade after the war's last shot was fired, all prisoners were still not back home. But in April 1998 Iran, in a fresh bid to improve relations with the Arab world and break out of two decades of isolation, repatriated some six thousand Iraqi prisoners of war. ICRC officials who visited prisoners of war in Iran reported many of the remaining twelve thousand official detainees looked twenty years older than their actual age. Many had long since joined the Badr Brigade and feared that going home would entail reprisal.

Underpinning Iranian refusal to observe ICRC obligations was not ignorance, as was initially true with Iraq, but the Islamic revolution's rejection of any undertakings by the Shah and his Pahlavi dynasty, which Khomeini had overthrown eighteen months before Iraq started its preemptive war. The ICRC, its rules, regulations, and persistent officials with their claims of objective behavior were all suspect as Western and Christian and disregarded as non-binding on a revolution burning with its own militantly self-righteous vision of universality.

No such ideological explanation easily springs to mind in trying to understand Saddam's rationale for breaking the taboo against using **chemical weapons**, first against Iranian troops, then against his Kurdish fellow citizens. But his decision was in keeping with his long-established penchant for the jugular in punishing anyone who dared cross him. (Gassing Kurds—or the reprisal killing of eight thousand civilian members of Kurdish guerrilla leader Massoud Barzani's tribe in 1983—was all the same to Saddam.) He shrewdly gambled the outside world would tolerate almost anything to stop Khomeini.

An Iraqi colonel captured by Iranians, near Khoramshahr. September, 1982.

After all, during the war Western companies wittingly sold Iraq "dual use" chemicals and equipment for purported "fertilizer" plants, which they knew full well could produce a variety of treaty-banned gases and nerve agents. These weapons long caused problems for UN inspectors tasked with removing them from Saddam's arsenal. (Indeed doubts over Saddam's compliance provided the main casus belli for Washington in 2003.) It strains credulity to believe Western governments were not aware of the dangers of such chemicals before Iraq's occupation of Kuwait in 1990.

But it was only then—with pressure on to demonize Saddam and with their own troops exposed to his chemical weapons—that Western governments overcame their amnesia and started denouncing Iraq's use of these proscribed arms. That sorry scenario was repeated in the American propaganda buildup for the new war in late 2002 and early 2003.

To this day the UN is shielding the Western firms involved. Rolf Ekeus, the former chief UN arms inspector in Iraq, has confirmed privately that the

Security Council cut a deal in 1993 with UN inspectors, Baghdad, and the International Atomic Energy Agency not to reveal the companies' identities.

The desire to avoid responsibility is understandable given the damage those weapons caused. The most publicized example concerned the Iraqi Kurdish village of Halabjah near the Iranian border. Furious that Kurdish guerrillas allied with Iranian revolutionary guards had captured the town, on March 15, 1988, Saddam had it attacked by waves of war planes.

They dropped mustard gas, a World War I favorite, as well as tabun and sarin, both nerve agents developed by the Nazis but never before deployed, and VX, which Iraq was testing for the first time. As many as 5,000 Kurdish civilians died.

For once the obscene effects of chemical weapons were graphically recorded. Iranian helicopters ferried in foreign correspondents, television teams, and photographers. Their reports, and especially images of corpses frozen in Pompeii-like poses in Halabjah streets, shocked the world.

A worker from the Mines Advisory Group, a British-based NGO, prepares a pit for the destruction of mortars. Millions of landmines and unexploded ordnance littered the former front line in the Iran-Iraq war years later. Choman, Kurdistan, 1993.

Halabjah should not have come as the surprise it did. In November 1983 Tehran lodged the first of several complaints with the UN charging Baghdad with using chemical weapons to stop Iranian human-wave infantry attacks. Iraq refused a UN proposal to send experts to both belligerents for on-site investigations.

The 1984 UN report dealing solely with findings on Iranian soil agreed that Iraq had used mustard gas and tabun. But without film and photographic illustration it had little impact. The Security Council issued a wishy-washy resolution that refrained from naming Iraq. The council's rotating chairman condemned the use of chemical weapons in a separate, little-noticed declaration issued in his own name. The council scarcely could have done less.

But even the outcry over Halabjah did not stop Iraq from again using chemical weapons against its Kurds (technically not even a violation of the

1925 Geneva Protocol on chemical weapons, whose virtually toothless provisions had not foreseen wartime use by signatory governments against their own citizens). Indeed Halabjah was not an isolated case. Iraqi documents among millions captured by the Kurds in 1991 establish that in 1987 and 1988 Saddam, in a campaign code-named Al Anfal, used chemical weapons at least sixty times against Kurdish villages.

Iraqi and Kurdish officials agree at least sixty thousand Kurds died in Al Anfal. Saddam continued gassing Kurds even after the 1988 cease-fire. His atrocities against the Kurds were "so grave," noted a UN report, and "of such massive nature that since the Second World War few parallels can be found."

So damning are the Al Anfal documents that human rights lawyers are convinced they constituted a strong case against Saddam for genocide, defined by the UN as the "intent to destroy in whole or in part national, ethnic, racial or religious groups, as such." Human Rights Watch went to enormous effort and expense sifting through 4 million documents and publishing a book marshaling seemingly irrefutable evidence. "It's ridiculous how much there is," remarked a knowledgeable lawyer.

But only governments can bring genocide charges. No state—or coalition of states—volunteered to do so as long as Saddam ruled in Baghdad, apparently for fear of compromising chances for lucrative contracts with Iraq made possible starting in 1997 by the oil-for-food billions Iraq cleverly manipulated. Throughout this period, the United States blew hot and cold, convincing some human rights lawyers that Washington only evinced interest when it exhausted other arguments against Saddam.

Nothing so illustrates the impunity displayed by Saddam as the assessment of his cousin Ali Hassan Majid, who commanded the Al Anfal operations. In 1989 the man Kurds call Ali Chemical justified his repeated use of poison gas by boasting: "Who is going to say anything? The international community? Fuck them!"

Until Saddam's downfall, the only positive result to emerge from the Iran-Iraq war's massive violations of human rights was the revised Chemical Weapons Convention signed in Paris in January 1993. It outlawed use of such weapons, their storage, development, manufacture, transfer, sale, or gift and ordered destruction of existing stocks.

However laudable, the convention came too late for those gassed to death or Halabjah's abandoned and forgotten survivors. British geneticist Christine Gosden visited Halabjah ten years after the attack. Forensic evidence she gathered showed survivors suffering from horrifying genetic defects, skin lesions, respiratory ailments, unusually high rates of aggressive cancers and miscarriages, birth deformities such as cleft palates and harelips, lung disorders, and heart disease.

By the time Saddam and his henchmen were brought to trial in 2005, America's own massive human rights violations in Iraq and the Bush administration's inability to prevent mayhem between Sunnis and Shia made a mockery of the intended moral impact Washington had planned.

Defense lawyers were gunned down, judges changed, and Saddam turned into a semi-martyr in a series of errors culminating in his gruesome hanging orchestrated by a radical Shia faction on December 30, 2006.

One of the most important trials—involving the murder of as many as 180,000 Kurds—staggered on without Saddam. Whether the dozen or so initially planned trials ever occur is open to question. But such is Iraq's torment that the details of Saddam's crimes and foreign powers' embarrassing complicity in enabling them are very likely to be swept away in the maelstrom.

Iraq

By Thom Shanker

The insurgency in Iraq took root during the American-led invasion and emerged full-blown just weeks after President Bush declared "Mission Accomplished" in May 2003. It became an irrevocable part of the political and military landscape on Aug. 19, 2003, with the bombing of the United Nations headquarters in Baghdad, which killed 22 people, including the chief of mission, Sergio Vieira de Mello.

The bombing was a signature **terrorist** act, designed to undermine the image of a U.S.-dominated coalition that could transform shock-and-awe military might into a calm and successful postwar management of the public order across the nation. It led quickly to the withdrawal of many of the international officials and non-governmental organizations helping with

Iraq's reconstruction, and all but destroyed the international community's ability to provide humanitarian aid.

The murder of international civil servants serving under the blue-and-white flag of the United Nations was yet more proof—if any was needed—that in modern conflicts of a terrorist, insurgent or sectarian nature, nothing and nobody is shielded by the internationally recognized laws designed to keep war within agreed limits.

But another image has come to stand just as starkly as an emblem of gross disregard for the laws of armed conflict during the war in Iraq.

Abu Ghraib prison west of Baghdad will forever be a symbol of abusive behavior by American military jailers. Responding to the nascent insurgency, the U.S. military arrested thousands of Iraqis and put them under the control of overstretched and under-trained military police based in Saddam Hussein's former political prison. Photographs of Army guards smiling, and one giving "thumbs up," as their Iraqi detainees were humiliated, degraded and harmed, came to replace the video of jubilant Iraqis toppling Saddam Hussein's statue as the most-remembered image of the war.

Although the Bush administration used various arguments in its efforts to rally support for the invasion—Saddam Hussein's alleged links to

I

U.S. tanks in Western Iraq. 2003.

al-Qaeda and suspected arsenals of unconventional weapons most prominent among them—the White House statements always carried a patina of
international legal rationale: The goal was to punish a tyrant who flouted a
series of United Nations resolutions and had been responsible for decades
of **crimes against humanity** in the mass executions and gassing of his own
citizens. Thus, while President Bush's "global war on terror" was the central
justification from political Washington, even the war's earliest critics
acknowledged that Saddam Hussein was a wrongdoer who should, at some
point, be held to account.

Any examination of the laws of war as applied to Iraq should divide
the conflict, much as the military did, into two periods. The first was the
build-up to war and the relatively brief period of major combat operations
that began with air strikes on Baghdad and tanks breaching the berm in
Kuwait, and ended with the capture of Baghdad and the toppling of the
Saddam Hussein regime. The second was the lengthy, complicated and

An elderly man killed in the fighting between U.S. forces and the Mahdi militia is
covered with his own cloak by a Najaf resident on the wrecked outskirts of the old
city. August 2004.

bloody fight that pitted coalition forces and a newborn Iraqi government
against Sunni insurgents, foreign terrorists and radical Shiite militias—and
the effort to quell sectarian conflict between Sunnis and Shiites.

The rush to Baghdad exemplified the modern way America fights wars,
with its emphasis on deploying the smallest troop levels possible, and
compensating with precision munitions, heavier firepower, more far-reaching communications and an emphasis on refined targeting to limit
collateral damage to civilians and civilian infrastructure. "Speed kills," was
the motto of Gen. Tommy R. Franks, the wartime commander, and the
rapidly moving offensive certainly proved his doctrine—at least for the
goal of capturing Baghdad.

The Iraqi capital fell in less than 30 days, certainly with minimum casualties for coalition forces and limited civilian casualties, as well. And even in

advance of the air attacks and ground invasion, the American military dropped leaflets urging Iraqi soldiers to go home and not be killed.

But a strategy nicknamed "Baghdad First," which called for the military to rapidly sweep past population centers in order to topple the pillars of power in the Iraqi capital, left large swaths of the country completely ungoverned, a vacuum filled by lawlessness and then insurgent and sectarian violence. The pressure from Washington to keep troop levels low, plus decisions to disband the Iraqi army and toss Ba'athist Party members from government jobs, meant that there were too few troops to impose order over an escalating number of disenfranchised, angry and well-armed Iraqis—even though the Fourth Geneva Convention requires occupiers to ensure public order and safety. History will no doubt write that an effective military campaign plan to oust the Saddam Hussein regime foundered on insufficient attention to, and failed efforts at, planning for the post-invasion **occupation** and stabilization effort.

Resistance fighter gives a guided tour of house damaged during the fighting with U.S. Marines in Fallujah. April 2004.

Even before the regime of Saddam Hussein was driven from power, Ba'athist Party loyalists had scattered throughout the country, and officially sponsored but locally commanded bands of **irregulars**, called Fedayeen Saddam, harassed American combat troops and lines of supply to dramatic effect.

These forces wore no uniforms with fixed and distinctive insignia; they hid among the population; they did not carry arms openly; they answered to no chain of command that followed the laws of war.

And they were in the vanguard of a changing conflict in which conventional warfare morphed into insurgency vs. counter-insurgency, and then again transformed into sectarian conflict, Sunni vs. Shiite, with all the hallmarks of civil war.

The anti-coalition forces avoided traditional military engagements and instead chose tactics that included the most **perfidious** ways of fighting:

263

Abu Ghraib prison, Iraq. 2003.
hiding among the civilians, inviting American attacks that would kill and wound innocents; fighting from protected sites; planting roadside bombs targeted at military convoys yet that killed **indiscriminately**; and car bombings of civilian locations for maximum death, disruption and dismay.

The anti-coalition campaign was designed for mass terrorizing of the population, and so included abductions, torture, and the dumping of bodies to sow fear and disorder and foster yet more rounds of sectarian violence. Insurgents who kidnapped coalition military personnel flagrantly violated the rules protecting prisoners of war established in the Third Geneva Convention.

One technique favored by U.S. adversaries was to fight from within mosques, sites that are protected under international law, in hopes that images of American forces counter-attacking these revered religious locations would stir even greater anger on the Arab street.

The use of religious sites as cover for military actions is in most circumstances a violation of international law and always forfeits their protection, yet coalition forces, as well, were required under those same tenets of international humanitarian law to calibrate their response to what was proportional; in other words, to counter a sniper in a minaret, a commander may not order his forces to shell the entire mosque compound.

The mosque as battleground took a most dramatic turn in February 2006, with the bombing of the Golden Mosque in Samarra, a revered Shiite holy site. In retrospect, the conflict in Iraq clearly morphed on that day from one in which the Sunni insurgency was the greatest threat to stability to one in which the country risked sliding into Sunni vs. Shiite sectarian chaos, and civil war.

The war in Iraq also elevated a new arsenal into the military lexicon, as Improvised Explosive Devices, or IEDs, killed and wounded more American troops than any other weapon. Built from artillery shells, plastic explosives and even flammable liquids, these devices were buried in roadways, hidden inside animal—or even human—carcasses or inside garbage cans, and planted on the undersides of bridges—and then detonated by remote control when military convoys drove past. Massive car bombs also were given a name in this category, VBIEDs, or vehicle-borne improvised explosive devices.

IEDs are designed to inflict the maximum pain, often being packed with shrapnel and nails. Dating back to the Hague Rules of 1907, armies are required to avoid using **weapons** that cause unnecessary suffering beyond what is required to disable enemy fighters.

In particular within Baghdad, death squads loyal to various sectarian leaders, and some even alleged to be under the control of partisan officials within the various Iraqi ministries, carried out kidnappings and executions. These were in clear violation of Common Article 3 of the Geneva Conventions, which applies during internal conflict or **civil war** and outlaws "violence to life and person, in particular murder of all kinds, mutilation, cruel treatment and torture." (It need not be noted that such kidnappings, torture and murder are outlawed by Iraqi domestic laws, even though such behavior against political enemies was a tool of the Saddam Hussein regime while in power, as well.)

As the war dragged on, a series of incidents in which American forces killed Iraqi civilians in questionable circumstances resulted in international anger, and courts martial.

The alleged massacre of Iraqi civilians at Haditha generated global public attention and outrage, and crystallized concerns about the way some American forces interpreted their rules of engagement.

Four United States Marines were charged under the Uniform Code of Military Justice with murder in the killings of 24 Iraqi civilians—at least 10 women and children were among them—in the insurgent-plagued Sunni village of Haditha, northwest of Baghdad, in November of 2005. Another four officers had been charged with dereliction of duty by failing to ensure that the incident was properly reported and investigated.

The shootings that killed two dozen Iraqis, most of them unarmed, occurred after a military convoy was struck by an IED, killing a Marine lance corporal. Over the next several hours, the Marines attacked several homes, killing those inside, including one man in a wheelchair. The Marines also shot men in a taxi at the scene.

The Marines said they were following standard rules of engagement in a hostile area. They said the IED had been detonated by someone in the near-by houses, and that their convoy then had come under fire. Marines said they had spotted a man with a weapon fleeing one of the houses.

Even supporters of the Marines' actions were hard-pressed to say their behavior did not go well beyond legal norms of **proportionality**, in which military response cannot be excessive when viewed in light of its expected utility. They may have further violated the law of war by failing to take the required steps to properly identify the target, in particular as grenades were thrown blindly into rooms to clear them of potential adversaries. Therefore, they may have violated the law by not striving to minimize collateral damage.

The treatment of Iraqi detainees captured in sweeps designed to quell

American Marines check a building after being fired on by a sniper. Fallujah, 2006.

the insurgency has left a similar scar on the United States' reputation.

A high-level, independent panel that reviewed the abuses at Abu Ghraib prison, led by James R. Schlesinger, a former defense secretary, attributed the "acts of brutality and purposeless sadism" to a cascading series of failures that stretched from the prison upward through the chain of command.

The panel called for improvements in the training of military police and intelligence officers, with focus on guaranteeing that behavior remained in keeping with American jurisprudence, approved doctrine of the armed services and the United States' interpretation of the Geneva Conventions.

Senior Pentagon leaders failed to offer clear guidance on what techniques were allowed for interrogating prisoners, the review found, allowing military jailers and intelligence officers to believe they were allowed to put detainees in stress positions, to use dogs to induce fear and employ other harsh techniques.

Perhaps most significantly, the Schlesinger panel found that the response to the growing and tenacious insurgency in Iraq—employing harsh interrogation techniques in an effort to find "actionable intelligence" to thwart the adversaries—had actually damaged the ability of the United States to obtain intelligence and protect national security.

Irregulars

By Ewen Allison and Robert K. Goldman

The term *irregular* is often used to describe a combatant who belongs to a paramilitary group, militia, volunteer corps, organized resistance movement, or rebel force. Irregulars are frequently part-time combatants who do not wear a uniform or carry arms openly when on active duty. However, irregulars can also be part of a country's armed forces, as they are in Switzerland, where the army is composed almost entirely of uniformed militias.

Irregular is not necessarily a synonym for **guerrilla**. Guerrillas are fighters distinguished by their use of tactics such as ambushes, sniping, and sabotage. Irregulars might not use such tactics at all, while regular armed forces often do.

In internal armed conflicts, the most important characteristic of irregulars is that they prefer to blend into the civilian population and thus, often, endanger civilians as government forces will destroy or otherwise punish entire villages or towns in an attempt to neutralize rebel irregulars.

Partisan is commonly used to describe irregulars who resist the occupation of a country by a foreign power—for example, French Maquis in World War II. Partisans might operate inside or outside occupied territory.

In international conflicts, irregulars may be considered lawful combatants, entitled to prisoner of war status if they adhere to certain standards. These include that they: distinguish themselves from the civilian population (i.e., look like combatants); carry weapons openly during engagements or deployments; be commanded by a responsible officer and, generally, be expected to comply with international rules relating to armed conflict. Failure to meet these standards can lead to trial and punishment for hostile acts. (**Mercenaries,** within the legal definition set forth under the 1977 Additional Protocol I, are not entitled to prisoner of war status.)

In internal armed conflict there is no prisoner of war status and the government is free to try its armed enemies for treason or other violent acts. Each trial, however, must be in a "regularly constituted court, affording all the judicial guarantees which are recognized as indispensible by civilized people" according to Article 3 common to the Geneva Conventions of 1949.

J

Journalists, Protection of

By William A. Orme, Jr.

In the vicious civil conflicts and undeclared cross-border battles that are increasingly the norm for full-blown shooting wars, few combatants are aware that the Geneva Conventions afford special protections to journalists. It might be prudent for a reporter in such situations to keep a Kevlar-coated copy of the Geneva Conventions in the left breast pocket since the protective powers of international treaties are based on the assumption that the combatants will observe international law.

The laws of armed conflict stipulate that journalists play a unique and essential role in wartime. A century ago war correspondents ran the risk of being shot as spies. Though this can still happen today—the 1998 killing of an Iranian journalist by Taliban militiamen being just one recent case in point—the executioners at least now face the possibility of internationally sanctioned punishment.

The spirit and the letter of international humanitarian law are clear. When accredited by and accompanying an army (or, to use the modern terminology, when "embedded" with military forces) journalists are legally part of that military entourage, whether they see themselves that way or not. This has been the legal practice at least since the early nineteenth century. If captured by opposing forces, they can expect to be treated as prisoners of war. The Geneva Conventions say so quite unambiguously, equating war correspondents with "civilian members of military aircraft crews" and other integral, albeit nonuniformed, participants in the greater military enterprise.

As prisoners of war, such journalists have the right not to respond to interrogation (though notebooks and film may legally be confiscated by military personnel). Absent evidence of atrocities outside their roles as war correspondents, they are not to be treated as spies.

The 1949 Geneva Convention regulations were tailored for the accredited uniformed war correspondent, who could be viewed

J

by the enemy as part of the military entourage. Though clearly not a soldier, the correspondent was still performing an officially sanctioned role in an organized military force. To the extent that tradition or prudence dictated by-the-books treatment of noncombatants or prisoners of war, the correspondent presumably benefited.

Those days are largely gone. The fear of being taken prisoner can still be quite real in Iraq or Chechnya or the Afghan highlands, but the potential captors might well not be conversant with international humanitarian law. Being held hostage by guerrilla forces or a renegade pariah regime today is a qualitatively different (and usually more frightening) experience than being an Axis or Allied prisoner of war in the 1940s. In the early 1960s many correspondents and combat photographers still wore army-issue fatigues. A decade later the Vietnam press corps stood conspicuously apart from the fighting force in dress, political perspective, and even national loyalties.

The position of "unilaterals"—journalists working in conflict zones who are not directly accompanying the armed forces—was addressed in the First Additional Protocol of 1977. Article 79 of Protocol I makes clear that journalists "engaged in dangerous professional missions" independent of the armed forces retain the status of civilians, with the protections that involves: they may not be directly targeted unless they take a direct part in hostilities. To make it clear that they have a professional reason for being on the battlefield, they "may obtain an identity card," though this is not obligatory. The

The camera of Japanese photographer Taizo Ichinose is preserved as a relic in a family shrine in Kyushu, Japan, 1996. Ichinose escaped injury when he lost this camera in an ambush.

Red Cross Commentary to the Protocol warns that non-embedded journalists act at their own risk if they get too close to a military objective or if their clothing too closely resembles that of combat personnel.

The rights that accredited journalists enjoy in wartime today were won in their respective national political cultures. In the final analysis, field commanders tolerate the presence of the press because of the political power and legal protections the press has acquired in their own local arenas. Some reporters may feel that to demand special protection under international humanitarian law is to invite special regulation under such law. Regardless, the protection is explicitly stated in law. In many instances accreditation comes with the territory; it is the only way to get access to the military transportation needed to cover the conflict, or to the official briefings (where it is often explained that what has just been seen firsthand may not have in fact happened and the real story is what was not seen by reporters).

But journalists roaming around the wilder conflicts of the world are forced to live instead by the Dylan dictum: to live outside the law you must be honest. Never pretend to be what you are not or deny being what you are unless your life depends on it. Carry a camera, but never a gun. And keep that dog-eared copy of the Geneva Conventions in your breast pocket until after the shooting stops.

J

Journalists in Peril

By Frank Smyth

Three weeks after the Gulf War ended, we entered northern Iraq with Kurdish guerrillas who were fighting Saddam Hussein and traveled 150 miles south to Kirkuk on the front line between rebel and government forces. Though writers working for dailies and network crews had already come to Kirkuk and left, I and two photographers working for weeklies, Alain Buu and Gad Gross, along with our armed Kurdish guide, Bakhtiar Muhammed Abd-al-rahman Askari, elected to stay. We all naively thought Saddam would soon be overthrown.

Everything changed on March 28, just after dawn. Thousands of Kurds—guerrillas and civilians—were still in the city. Incoming artillery and tank shells shook the ground, first claiming the life of a young girl on her bicycle. "This is Saddam Hussein!" yelled one man who knew her. "Mr. Bush must know." Soon several small helicopters broke the sky. They opened up with machine guns, as the guerrillas returned fire with antiaircraft guns. I saw Kurdish guerrillas carrying two surface-to-air missiles. The incoming shells were becoming more accurate, and tanks were closing in on the town. By about noon, the smaller helicopters were joined by four or five helicopter gunships. Glistening like angry hornets, they fired machine guns and unloaded seemingly endless volleys of exploding rockets. The gunships provided crucial air cover for dozens of advancing tanks. Several multiple-rocket launchers dropped a blanket of fire on fleeing guerrillas and civilians.

The four of us took shelter behind a wall of bulldozed earth. My bravado began crumbling like dirt. A tank appeared over a hill. Gad and Bakhtiar ran toward some small houses. Alain and I dove into a ditch. We were separated through the night while Iraqi soldiers camped around us. We heard them talking, walking, peeing—even opening cans of food. I turned off the alarm on my watch and tried to control my breathing. When I get nervous, I take quick, short breaths. But Alain's blood pressure dropped from the stress, and he soon began sleeping. I woke him to stop his snoring. The temperature, too, dropped in the night. We couldn't allow our teeth to chatter, either.

Embracing each other like lovers to stay warm, we stayed in the ditch for over eighteen hours. I watched an ant colony at work below, and envied each bird passing above. Shortly after sunrise, Alain and I heard a commotion coming from the houses. It sounded like some people had been captured. Within minutes, we heard one short automatic rifle burst. It was followed by a scream and then broken by another burst that ended in silence. A blanket of terror descended upon us. We both feared that it had been Gad screaming.

I began to silently panic, as my imagination went back in time. I felt like a small boy who had agreed to play a deadly game of hide-and-seek with some of the bigger kids in the neighborhood. But they had severe rules, which I had foolishly agreed to in advance: "If we catch you, we kill you." I never thought I'd get caught. Now... I imagined myself, still as a kid, trying to talk my way out of it, and, according to my own reasoning, failing every time.

From within the ditch, Alain and I looked out in opposite directions, hoping that if we were seen, we might have a chance to surrender. An hour later, Alain jumped up with his hands held high and yelled "Sahafi" (journalist). "What are you doing?" I said, though it was already too late. Alain said that a soldier had seen him. I forced myself up and followed him. Soldiers with raised rifles threatened to kill us. One drew his finger sardonically across his neck. But a military intelligence officer, who seemed to be newly arrived on the scene, intervened. He reassured us that we would not be killed, even as he ripped a pendant of the Virgin Mary off Alain's neck.

He brought us to some other military officers with different uniforms who were army special forces commanders. They told us about Gad. He had "killed himself," said one, because "he had a gun." Another officer showed us Gad's camera bag and press tags, which were stained with blood. We were certain then that Gad and probably Bakhtiar had been summarily executed after being captured. The army commanders said in both English and Arabic that they wanted to kill us, too. But the military intelligence officer insisted that we be transferred to a military intelligence unit for interrogation. He saved us.

We underwent many blindfolded interrogations, and were later brought to Baghdad and imprisoned. During one particularly severe interrogation, I was accused of being a CIA agent, while Alain was later accused of being a French intelligence agent. Though treating us as prisoners of war, Iraq failed to report our captures to the International Committee of the Red Cross. Nevertheless, after eighteen days, on the last night of the Muslim holy period of Ramadan, Saddam released us. But Iraqi authorities kept Gad's camera bag. His remains have yet to be recovered.

Jurisdiction, Universal

By Françoise Hampson

Can an American be tried before American courts for speeding on the roads of France? When considering whether someone can be convicted, it is necessary to consider not only the conduct in question, but also which courts have jurisdiction. The most common basis of jurisdiction is territorial (i.e., the courts of the place where the action took place), but some legal systems, mainly civil law ones, also recognize jurisdiction based on nationality (i.e., French courts can try French citizens in some cases for criminal conduct outside France). International law also permits a State, in some circumstances, to exercise criminal jurisdiction on other bases. In some cases, the courts of any State may try an individual. This is called universal jurisdiction.

In October 1998, Gen. August Pinochet, the former Chilean dictator, was arrested by British authorities at the request of a Spanish prosecutor. In a landmark ruling, the House of Lords decided that Pinochet could not claim immunity as a former head of state for acts of torture committed after the ratification of the Torture Convention by Britain, Chile and Spain, and was therefore liable to extradition. However, the British government stopped extradition proceedings on grounds of Pinochet's health and returned him to Chile. The most important completed prosecution under universal jurisdiction is probably Spain's conviction of former Argentine naval officer Adolfo Scilingo for **crimes against humanity** in April 2005.

Only the most serious offenses are, in international law, subject to universal jurisdiction. A State has primary jurisdiction over these offenses, but whether or not an individual will be tried depends, among other things, on whether the domestic law of the State allows for trial of such crimes. The most serious offenses subject to universal jurisdiction include serious violations of the laws and customs of war, crimes against humanity, and, since the ruling of the International Criminal Tribunal for the former Yugoslavia (ICTY) in the case of Tadic, violations of Article 3 common to the four Geneva Conventions of 1949, applicable in non-international armed conflicts.

In addition, certain treaties provide for universal jurisdiction, such as the UN Convention against Torture. Surprisingly, the **Genocide** Convention is not in this list, though any State may assert universal jurisdiction. It provides for territorial jurisdiction or jurisdiction to be exercised by an international penal tribunal. Generally, treaties which provide for universal jurisdiction require the State to try the suspect or to extradite him/her to stand trial elsewhere.

One category of behavior is subject to a special regime. Grave breaches of the Geneva Conventions of 1949 and Additional Protocol I of 1977 are defined within the treaties and can only occur in international armed conflicts. Every State bound by the treaties is under the legal obligation to search for and prosecute those in their territory suspected of having committed grave breaches, irrespective of the nationality of the suspect or victim or the place where the act was allegedly committed. The State may hand the suspect over to another State or an international tribunal for trial. Where domestic law does not allow for the exercise of universal jurisdiction, a State must introduce the necessary domestic legislative provisions before it can do so. That is not enough; the State must actually exercise jurisdiction, unless it hands over the suspect to another country or international tribunal.

Jus ad Bellum/Jus in Bello

By Karma Nabulsi

Under international law, there are two distinct ways of looking at war—the reasons you fight and how you fight. In theory, it is possible to break all the rules while fighting a just war or to be engaged in an unjust war while adhering to the laws of armed conflict. For this reason, the two branches of law are completely independent of one another.

Jus (or *ius*) *ad bellum* is the title given to the branch of law that defines the legitimate reasons a State may engage in war and focuses on certain criteria that render a war *just*. The principal modern legal source of *jus ad bellum* derives from the Charter of the United Nations, which declares in Article 2: "All members shall refrain in their international relations from the threat or the use of force against the territorial integrity or political independence of any State, or in any other manner inconsistent with the purposes of the United Nations"; and in Article 51: "Nothing in the present Charter shall impair the inherent right of individual or collective self-defense if an armed attack occurs against a Member of the United Nations."

Jus in bello, by contrast, is the set of laws that come into effect once a war has begun. Its purpose is to regulate how wars are fought, without prejudice to the reasons of how or why they had begun. So a party engaged in a war that could easily be defined as unjust (for example, Iraq's aggressive invasion of Kuwait in 1990) would still have to adhere to certain rules during the prosecution of the war, as would the side committed to righting the initial injustice. This branch of law relies on customary law, based on recognized practices of war, as well as treaty laws (such as the Hague Regulations of 1899 and 1907), which set out the rules for conduct of hostilities. Other principal documents include the four Geneva Conventions of 1949, which protect war victims—the sick and wounded (First); the shipwrecked (Second); prisoners of war (Third); and civilians in the hands of an adverse party and, to a limited extent, all civilians in the territories of the countries in conflict (Fourth)—and the Additional Protocols of 1977, which define key terms such as *combatants*, contain detailed provisions to protect noncombatants, medical transports, and civil defense, and prohibit practices such as indiscriminate attack.

There is no agreement on what to call *jus in bello* in everyday language. The International Committee of the Red Cross (ICRC) and many scholars, preferring to stress the positive, call it international humanitarian law (IHL) to emphasize their goal of mitigating the excesses of war and protecting civilians and other noncombatants. But military thinkers, backed by other scholars, emphasize that the laws of war are drawn directly from the customs and practices of war itself, and are intended to serve State armies. They commonly use the more traditional rubric, the laws and customs of armed conflict or more simply, the laws of war.

(See **aggression; crimes against peace; just and unjust war; war crimes**.)

275

Just and Unjust War

By Karma Nabulsi

Doctrines of what constitutes a just war developed out of Roman law, religious encyclicals, military theory and practice, modern political theory and philosophy, as well as international law and jurisprudence. The roots in Western thought can be traced to classical moral, legal, and historical sources and include the scholastic tradition as well as the medieval notions of chivalry and honor. A critical debate in the United States over participation and conduct in the Vietnam War revived just war theory in the West among secular philosophers and Christian thinkers.

The debate was an attempt to determine whether U.S. participation in the war was unjust in origin or in the way it was being fought. Distinctly different but significant notions of just and unjust war arose in Communist theories on the "people's" war against fascism in the 1930s and 1940s, "national liberation" struggles against colonial powers after World War II, and "holy war" in modern Islam, for example, during the Iran-Iraq war. "Jihad" has become a cliché for the struggle of radical Muslim forces against mostly Western powers.

The criteria for engaging in a just war, first summed up by Dutch philosopher Hugo Grotius in the seventeenth century and drawing on older, medieval Catholic theologians, consist of seven elements: (1) that there be a *just cause*; (2) that there is a *right authority* (legitimate sovereign) to initiate the war; (3) a *right intention* on the part of the parties using force; (4) that the resort to force be *proportional*; (5) that force be a *last resort*; (6) that war is undertaken with *peace as its goal* (not for its own sake); (7) and that there be a reasonable *hope of success*.

More recently, the term *just war* has been largely replaced by the term *legitimate use of force*. The principles of just war today are contained in the United Nations Charter, which reaffirms the inadmissability of the acquisition of territory by force. Although conquest was legally prohibited in Europe in the mid-nineteenth century, European powers compensated by engaging in conquests abroad. Within Europe there remained a branch of thought, largely Prussian, which continued to argue that the principle of conquest—might is right—provided ample cause for a just war. This school of thought lost all legitimacy as a result of World War II.

Today, a just war is commonly understood to mean one that is fought in self-defense, as authorized in Article 51 of the UN Charter. This is the one principle that has been clearly defined and consistently emphasized throughout the history of just war theory. The United Nations General Assembly also has set out a comprehensive and strict definition of illegal **aggression** and justified self-defense.

A non-Western, indeed predominantly anti-Western, school of thought on just war thinking—the doctrine of national self-determination—arose out of the struggles for colonial emancipation. The United Nations went some way toward endorsing this doctrine through General Assembly resolutions of the 1960s. In 2003, supporters of the U.S. attack on Iraq claimed that it would be a just war, but their claim was widely disputed.
(See **crimes against peace; jus ad bellum/jus in bello**.)

L

Legitimate Military Targets

By Gaby Rado

Six months before it ended, the war in Bosnia was brought home to the foreign television journalists in the form of an enormous rocket that exploded in the courtyard of the Sarajevo television building. Fired from a Bosnian Serb stronghold, the explosive—actually a gravity bomb strapped to rockets—destroyed the offices of two international television agencies as well as the European Broadcasting Union. Most of the wounded were foreign journalists.

Faridoun Hemani, a Canadian friend employed by Worldwide Television News, was filmed walking around with blood pouring down his face, trying to guide others out of the building. "We heard something hit the TV station, but it didn't sound like a big deal. Then suddenly, everything came falling

down on us," recalled Margaret Moth, a brave CNN camerawoman who had lost most of her jaw in a sniper assault two years earlier and had gone back to work in Sarajevo.

Unbeknownst to most television reporters, radio and television stations can sometimes qualify as military objectives under the laws of war, as can other infrastructure, communications, and energy targets. All these facilities become legitimate targets when they are put to military use. (For the same reason, military-industrial and military research sites are also military objectives.) Journalists *per se* are not a legitimate target, but if they are wounded while visiting or working in a legitimate target, it is considered collateral damage.

The definition of a legitimate target is central to the laws of armed conflict. Additional Protocol I, Article 52, defines a legitimate military target as one "which by [its] nature, location, purpose, or use makes an effective contribution to military action and whose total or partial destruction, capture or neutralization, in the circumstances ruling at the time,

Only the central tower survives the persistent Serb shelling of the offices of **Oslobodjene,** *an independent Sarajevo newspaper that continued publishing from a bunker underneath the ruins.*

L

offers a definite military advantage." Any attack requires that it be justified, in the first place, by military necessity. However, no object may be attacked if damage to civilians and civilian objects would be excessive when compared to that advantage.

Although not all States are party to Additional Protocol I, its rules on targeting are accepted as customary law.

Legitimate military targets include: armed forces and persons who take part in the fighting; positions or installations occupied by armed forces as well as objectives that are directly contested in battle; military installations such as barracks, war ministries, munitions or fuel dumps, storage yards for vehicles, airfields, rocket launch ramps, and naval bases.

Legitimate infrastructure targets include lines and means of communication, command, and control—railway lines, roads, bridges, tunnels, and canals—that are of fundamental military importance.

Legitimate communications targets include broadcasting and television stations, and telephone and telegraph exchanges of fundamental military importance.

Legitimate military-industrial targets include factories producing arms, transport, and communications equipment for the military; metallurgical, engineering, and chemicals industries whose nature or purpose is essentially military; and the storage and transport installations serving such industries.

Legitimate military research targets include experimental research centers for the development of weapons and war matériel.

Legitimate energy targets include installations providing energy mainly for national defense, such as coal and other fuels, and plants producing gas or electricity mainly for military consumption. Attacks on nuclear power stations and hydroelectric dams are generally, but not always, prohibited by the laws of war.

One of the major problems in differentiating legal from illegal or criminal acts of war concerns apparently civilian objectives that may have a use by the military. Most buildings used by civilians in peacetime are protected under international law. Article 52 of Additional Protocol I states, "In case of doubt whether an object which is normally dedicated to civilian purposes, such as a place of worship, a house, or other dwelling or a school, is being used to make an effective contribution to military action, it shall be presumed not to be so used."

It is a war crime to attack willfully anything that is not a legitimate military target. On the other hand, incidentally causing damage to a protected person or object is not always a war crime. Although the categories listed above indicate facilities typically regarded as legitimate targets, attacking forces are still obliged to meet the test of whether predictable harm would be proportional to the military advantage. Given that it is a balancing test which must often be performed under condition of imperfect information, commanders customarily have latitude to exercise their judgment. Still, if the harm is "excessive in relation to the concrete and direct military advantage anticipated," it is a war crime.

Levée en Masse

By Karma Nabulsi

The *levée en masse,* or mass uprising, has acquired something of a mythical status in the history of war. The Red Cross representative at the negotiations that produced the Geneva Conventions of 1949 said that they had "practically never occurred"; whereas in countries such as Poland, popular and long-lasting national uprisings took place with great regularity throughout the nineteenth century. Napoleon made increasing use of *levées* as a means of national defense when the combined armies of the Allies entered French soil. Warsaw in the early days of the Nazi invasion during World War II is a more modern example.

The term *"levée en masse,"* which first became an international legal term at the Brussels Conference in 1874, must be distinguished under the laws of war from an insurrection by a people against its own national government. The *levée en masse* is defined as taking place against foreign troops either invading or occupying a country, restricting the definition to one involving national self-defense. It refers especially to situations in which the populace spontaneously takes up what weapons it has and, without having time to organize, resists the invasion.

Those who join in a *levée* may under certain circumstances claim the **combatant**'s privilege, that is, the right to fight the enemy. Captors may not prosecute combatants for their hostile acts but must grant them **prisoner of war** status upon capture. (They may be prosecuted, however, for other crimes and for disciplinary infractions.) The privilege is normally reserved for members of a country's armed forces, including partisans.

There are several conditions for obtaining the combatant's privilege. The *levée en masse* may be undertaken against foreign troops only when and where they invade the country. Participants must carry their weapons openly and respect the laws and customs of war. Once territory has become occupied, civilian resisters can be punished by the occupying power.

Even after effective occupation of territory, members of the armed forces who have not surrendered, organized resistance movements, and genuine national liberation movements may resist the occupation, but they must distinguish themselves from the civilian population, or at least carry their weapons openly during attacks and deployments. Any direct involvement by civilians in these hostilities would be unlawful.

Indirect support to the resistance movement, such as providing information or nonmilitary supplies, would be lawful under international law but is likely to contravene security laws passed by the occupying power, in which case those responsible would be liable to trial and punishment or to undergo restrictions on their freedom of movement. Even in that event, they would be entitled to the protection of the Fourth Geneva Convention, and collective action against them would be unlawful.
(See **soldiers, rights of.**)

Limited War

By Peter Rowe

A State may make it clear, by what its leaders say or by its actions, including unilateral declarations or bilateral agreements, that it is fighting a limited war. By this it may mean that it wishes to engage its enemy only within certain defined territory, or that it does not seek to persuade any other State to take part in the conflict as an ally, or that it does not intend to use certain weapons at its disposal, or that it intends only to destroy a certain type of military infrastructure, such as radar installations.

The armed conflict between Great Britain and Argentina in 1982 could be described as a limited war in the sense that Britain had the capability to strike at mainland Argentina but chose not to do so. No other State was involved and Britain for its part limited the conflict to the Falkland/Malvinas Islands and a belligerency zone that Britain declared around it, the purpose being to distinguish neutrals from enemy combatants. Had a Royal Navy warship come across an Argentinian warship in the Pacific during the time of the conflict, it would probably not have attacked it.

International humanitarian law (IHL) applies as soon as an armed conflict occurs, even if a state of war is not recognized by any of the combatant nations. Thus, once an armed conflict occurs, the intensity or the scope of the conflict is irrelevant. The same obligations are owed by the combatants engaged in it as are owed in any other form of armed conflict between States. It follows that the concept of limited war, like **total war**, although of great importance for understanding the behavior of parties in wartime, is not a legal term within IHL.

In practice, however, a limited war may be intended to be of short duration. As a result it may be considered impracticable to build prisoner of war camps. Prisoners of war may therefore be repatriated during the conflict, an event which took place during the Falkland conflict in 1982. With modern weapon systems, a State may have the capacity to strike with very accurate weapons at prime **military objectives** without any other military action being necessary. The capability of the attacked State to respond may, in consequence, be nonexistent or very limited, and the object of keeping the conflict limited can be achieved.

In all of these situations, IHL applies.

M

Mass Graves

By Elizabeth Neuffer

You could smell the mass grave at Cerska long before you could see it.

The sickly, sweet smell of the bodies came wafting through the trees lining the dirt track up to the grave. The killers had chosen their spot well, an obscure rise off a rutted road few needed to travel.

Investigators with the International Criminal Tribunal for the former Yugoslavia (ICTY) had discovered the grave. And the stench that hovered in the air indicated they were exhuming it, collecting evidence for war crimes cases.

The corpses were dressed in civilian clothes. They had gunshot wounds to the back of their heads. Their decaying hands were bound behind their back. These men and boys, forensic experts at the scene said, had been gunned down in cold blood.

The Cerska grave is one of several exhumed in Bosnia that help explain the fate of approximately seven thousand Bosnian Muslim men and boys from Srebrenica, who disappeared after Bosnian Serb forces overran the UN safe area in July 1995. Bosnian Serb leaders asserted that Srebrenica's men, wielding arms, were killed in combat.

The grave proved otherwise.

Individual and mass graves provide vital evidence to war crimes prosecutions, especially those involving **extrajudicial executions** and targeting of civilians. Forensic experts over the last thirty years have worked to exhume and examine graves in Argentina, Guatemala, El Salvador, Honduras, Ethiopia, Mexico, and Iraqi Kurdistan. Exhumations in Argentina, for example, helped show that many of the thousands of civilians who disappeared during the juntas had been executed; that forensic evidence was presented during the 1985 trial of nine Argentine generals, five of whom were later convicted.

In recent years, forensic teams have exhumed mass graves in Rwanda and the former Yugoslavia, some of the largest graves yet discovered. Evidence from the exhumations are a key part of many war crimes cases. For example, evidence from graves like Cerska, combined with witness testimony, would be part of the case against former Bosnian Serb leader Radovan Karadzic and army commander Gen. Ratko Mladic. Both men have been charged with war crimes, genocide, and crimes against humanity.

To prove genocide or crimes against humanity in the case of Srebrenica, prosecutors would have to show that Bosnian Muslims were deliberately targeted for mass executions. Forensic evidence can help establish that the dead in a mass grave are Bosnian Muslim civilians and that they were executed.

Mass graves themselves can be a violation of international law. The Third and Fourth Geneva Conventions and Additional Protocol I contain provisions governing the proper burial, identification, and registration of those killed in war. Prisoners of war, for example, must be "honorably buried" in graves that bear information about them.

From top to bottom, victims of the fall of Srebrenica in the mass grave at Pilice Collective Farm; view of the mass grave at Ovcara where the Serbs murdered patients and staff from the hospital in Vukovar; forensic scientists Dr. Clyde Snow and Bill Haglund and their team examine the mass grave at Ovcara. 1996.

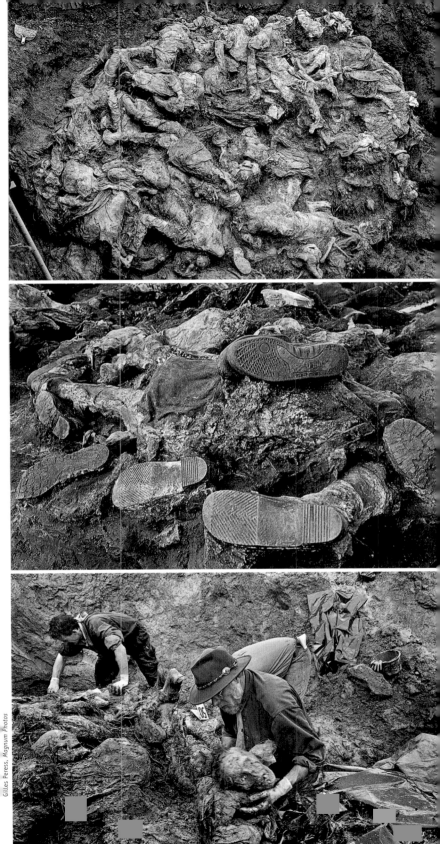

But the right to exhume a mass grave or to halt tampering with a grave is not clear under international law. UN General Assembly resolution 3074, adopted in 1973, calls for States to cooperate in war crimes investigations. Articles 32 and 33 of Additional Protocol I require parties to search for missing persons after hostilities end, and otherwise assist in finding out their fate. But an individual country does not have to allow suspected mass graves to be examined.

Not all mass graves contain victims of war crimes or atrocities. Some may hold the bodies of hurriedly buried combatants. Witnesses and survivors will help identify which grave is which. Even then, the mass grave may not be obvious.

Experts often comb through a field or forest to find a mass grave. They will look for abrupt changes in vegetation to indicate recent burial activity, or changes in the texture and color of earth. Depressions or mounds are another sign digging has recently taken place.

Reporters who come across what they believe to be a mass grave should not interfere with it. Mass graves are often mined or strewn with unexploded ordinance. Disturbing a grave might also compromise the evidence it contains. Do not try to excavate, or collect anything protruding from the grave. Only photograph the grave and mark its location on a map.

Mass graves can be easily tampered with and the evidence they contain lost forever. It is important to exercise judgment about whom is notified of a suspected mass grave. Two starting points are the International Committee of the Red Cross (ICRC) and the UN High Commissioner for Human Rights. The Boston-based Physicians for Human Rights, which sends forensic teams to examine graves around the world, is another. Once forensic experts arrive on the scene, they will conduct their search with an archaeologist's precision. Each part of the human skeleton—some two hundred bones and thirty-two teeth—has its tale to tell.

A forensic team will begin by probing the grave, often with a metal rod, seeking to test its consistency and detect the smell of dead bodies. Once investigators have dug down to the level of bodies, they will sift the earth for shreds of evidence and dust off each body. Bodies are carefully examined before being removed. Valuable evidence can include blindfolds, bullets, and bonds that will indicate how a victim was killed. Jewelry or papers help with identification.

The science of determining the cause of death is complex. An expert examining a bullet wound can determine where a person was shot, the range of the shooting, and the angle at which the bullet entered—all clues to whether someone was executed or not. Identification is the next step. Experts rely on witnesses, who may know who is in which grave. Accurate dental records help make a match between a body and a missing person. DNA testing can also be used to help identify victims.

Success varies. In Rwanda, identification is almost impossible, due to a lack of records and the vast size of graves. But experts were able to identify most of the two hundred bodies exhumed from Ovcara, Croatia, thanks to a list of who was in the grave. They were far less successful with the Cerska grave, because of the number of people who have gone missing.

But grieving mothers and wives still hope they will succeed. "Bring his body to me," said Hatidza Hren, a Bosnian Muslim searching for her husband. "I will recognize his bones."

(See **disappearances; medico-legal investigations**)

Medical Experiments on POWs

By Sheldon H. Harris

According to the Hippocratic oath, it is the duty of medical personnel not only to heal the sick and offer comfort to those beyond healing but also to do nothing knowingly harmful to a patient. But beginning in the 1930s and continuing throughout World War II, the Japanese medical profession as a whole, and, most particularly, medical staff attached to the Japanese military routinely committed atrocities, subjecting prisoners of war, noncombatants, and political and common criminals alike to hideous medical experiments.

Although the Imperial government had pledged to treat prisoners of war (POWs) with care and respect, prisoners were treated brutally while medical treatment for sick prisoners was either nonexistent, or, at best, primitive, apathetic, or indifferent. The consequences of this policy of mistreatment are revealed by a comparison of mortality rates in Japanese POW camps with those in Europe. The death rate in Japanese camps was at least 27 percent. In Europe the figure was roughly 4 percent.

Graver still was the decision on the part of the Japanese medical establishment as Japan's army conquered a wide swath of territory in the Pacific and on the mainland of Asia in 1942 to treat POWs and conquered peoples as prime candidates for human experimentation, as well as substitutes for the animals traditionally used for medical training purposes. Captives, both military and civilian, were strapped to gurneys, vivisected without anesthesia, injected with scores of different pathogens, or used in demonstrations of surgery techniques.

In one instance in the Philippines, several prisoners were used to teach neophyte Japanese physicians the art of surgery. A number of healthy males were taken into a field, forced to lie down on a sheet, had masks placed over their noses, and were anesthetized. The victims were then cut open as the senior surgeon demonstrated "proper" techniques to his students. When the lesson was over, one of the surgeons would shoot the patients, since they were no longer useful for teaching purposes.

In another incident in China in 1942, a senior surgeon conducted an "operation exercise" for the benefit of the young doctors and other medical personnel attached to his unit. This surgeon injected an anesthetic into the lumbar region of a healthy patient. When one of the observers questioned the surgeon as to whether he was going to disinfect the needle he was using for the injection, the surgeon replied, "What are you talking about? We are going to kill him."

Captured American airmen were frequently subjected to vivisection experiments. In July of 1944 on Dublon Island in the South Pacific, a surgeon used American POWs for a particularly ghastly experiment. Eight POWs were subjected to tests in which tourniquets were applied to their arms and legs for periods up to seven and eight hours. Two of the men died from shock when the tourniquets were removed. They were then dissected and their body parts were tested for various maladies. Their skulls were saved as souvenirs by the principal surgeon. In another episode in May and June of 1945, eight American airmen were vivisected at Kyushu Imperial University, one of Japan's most prestigious medical schools. Lungs were removed from two of the prisoners. Other victims had their hearts, livers, and stomachs removed. Still others, their brains and gall bladders. Of course, none of the eight survived.

These are only a few examples from what was a systematic pattern of medical atrocities. From 1942 until Japan's surrender in mid-August of 1945, Japanese physicians and support staff performed hundreds of similar experiments. Many hundreds, if not thousands, of test subjects died. But few of the perpetrators were ever brought to justice, and many enjoyed distinguished careers in postwar democratic Japan.

No Japanese government has ever acknowledged the guilt of these physicians, although the laws of armed conflict completely prohibit such crimes and did so during World War II, even before the passage of the 1949 Geneva Conventions. The 1906 Hague Convention, which Japan had ratified before hostilities broke out, provides that "officers, soldiers, and other persons officially attached to armies, who are sick or wounded, shall be respected and cared for, without distinction of nationality, by the belligerent in whose power they are."

At the Nuremberg Tribunals following World War II, medical experiments were declared a crime against humanity. The Geneva Conventions of 1949 defined medical experiments on POWs and protected persons—that is, civilians under the control of an occupying force—as a grave breach, and the 1998 Rome Statute of the International Criminal Court stated that medical experiments are war crimes, whether they occur in an international armed conflict or an internal one. It defined the crime as: "Subjecting persons who are in the power of an adverse party to physical mutilation or to medical or scientific experiments of any kind which are neither justified by the medical, dental or hospital treatment of the person concerned nor carried out in his or her interest, and which cause death to or seriously endanger the health of such person or persons."

(See **biological experiments**.)

Medical Transports

By Michael Ignatieff

When is a helicopter an ambulance and when is it a gunship? The line is sometimes not as clear as it seems.

The Russian-built Mi-17 helicopter shuttling through the ground fire above Freetown in 1997 made up to fifteen sorties a day. Sometimes it was airlifting troops, ammunition, fuel, and food to the Nigerian troops who were dislodging Sierra Leone's military junta and reinstating Tejan Kabbah, the country's elected president. But sometimes, it was also carrying doctors and medics, plus "casvacs"—casualty evacuations. It came under continuous fire. Is firing on a casvac a violation of the Geneva Conventions? If the Mi-17 had been downed and the casualties killed, would that constitute a violation of international humanitarian law (IHL)?

According to the Geneva Conventions, the mere fact that transports are carrying casualties does not entitle them to protection. It all depends whether the helicopter carries a clear **Red Cross** or **Red Crescent emblem** and whether, when flying over enemy territory, the pilots file a flight plan beforehand with the combatants and keep to the altitudes, departure, and arrival times stipulated on the plan. If these conditions are not followed, or if the chopper is used for hostile purposes, it is a legitimate target, whether or not there are wounded on board.

It's not hard to see why. How are ground troops supposed to tell the difference between the Mi-17's resupply and its casvac sorties? In the Sierra Leone case, the Mi-17 didn't carry a Red Cross marking. In any case, if it had done so, it would have contravened the provisions of the Geneva Conventions outlawing the use of aircraft for the transport of weapons and matériel.

Detailed rules applying to aircraft are spelled out in Articles 24 to 31 of the 1977 Additional Protocol I on International Armed Conflict. This prohibits the use of medical aircraft to gain any military advantage over an adverse party and allows the adverse party to the conflict to force the plane to land for inspection. If the aircraft is in conformity with the rules, it should fly on "without delay." In the event of a violation, it may be seized, although the sick, the wounded, and medical or religious personnel among its occupants are to be treated as protected persons. Medical air transports are allowed only to carry light weapons for self-defense as well as the small arms and ammunition of the sick or wounded. They cannot be used to collect or transmit intelligence data or carry equipment for such purposes or even to conduct searches except by prior permission.

The rules applying to ambulances or other ground vehicles are straightforward. Like **medical personnel**, they "may in no circumstances be attacked," but must be "respected and protected," according to Articles 35 and 19 of the First Geneva Convention of 1949. They also should be marked with the Red Cross or Red Crescent emblem. They are subject to inspection and lose their protection, subject to a prior warning and a reasonable time limit, if they are used to commit acts harmful to the enemy that are outside their humanitarian duties.

Whether the niceties of the convention *can* apply in messy cases like Sierra Leone is another question. The convention implies that States, military

M

hierarchies, and chains of command have clear lines of responsibility. None of these were present in Sierra Leone. The Mi-17 wasn't owned by a State, but by a private British company—Sandline International—providing **mercenary** aid, on a cash basis, to President Kabbah, with the British government allowing it to be refueled and serviced on British warships in Freetown's harbor, while hiding behind official denials of involvement.

Sierra Leone belongs to a family of ethnic conflicts where the Geneva Conventions are honored more in the breach than in the observance. Even when medical transports *are* clearly marked with a Red Cross and are obviously carrying only casualties and medical personnel, they are often attacked. The worst recent case was in Rwanda in 1994, during the genocide, when gangs pulled victims out of Red Cross ambulances and finished them off.

Journalists traveling in Red Cross ambulances, hospital ships, and medevac helicopters cannot be sure that they will be protected. In theory, Additional Protocol I, Article 79, requires that journalists be treated as civilians. In theory, journalists can hitch a ride in Red Cross and ICRC vehicles, providing, of course, they do not carry weapons, and they are prepared to sign an insurance waiver. In practice, nonmedical personnel often attract suspicion at inspections and checkpoints. Are they spies? Are they military personnel in disguise? Military inspection of Red Cross transports is allowed and the presence of nonmedical personnel can be used as an excuse to impound, seize, or attack. Indeed, the presence of anyone other than the sick, the wounded, or the medical or religious personnel tending them is prohibited on medical aircraft. The rule of thumb is to get authorization on paper from the ICRC or from local combatants to travel. Also remember the insurance waiver. Anyone who climbs on board their Land Cruiser should make sure someone back home has arranged insurance coverage—if they can find a company willing to write a policy!

M

Medical Personnel

By Eric Stover

International humanitarian law specifically prohibits military attacks on medical personnel and units. The Fourth Geneva Convention specifies in Article 20 that "Persons regularly and solely engaged in the operation and administration of civilian hospitals... shall be respected and protected." Other articles forbid the destruction, closure (whether temporary or permanent), or knowing interruption of the supply of food, water, medicines, or electricity to civilian hospitals and clinics. Article 19 notes that protection of civilian hospitals and mobile or permanent units may be forfeited if "they are used to commit, outside their humanitarian duties, acts harmful to the enemy."

Physicians and other health workers remain protected under IHL so long as they identify themselves as medical personnel; respect principles of medical ethics, including medical confidentiality; provide care to all victims on the basis of need, without discrimination of any kind; and do not bear arms, with the exception of light weapons for self-defense. A physician or health worker who undertakes nonmedical functions during an armed conflict cannot claim the protection of the rules of war. Dr. Che Guevara, in his political and combatant roles in Bolivia during the 1960s, could make no claims to any of the protections defined by medical neutrality. Nor could the Bosnian Serb leader Radovan Karadzic, a psychiatrist.

Medico-Legal Investigations of War Crimes

By David Rohde

As a dozen photographers and reporters anxiously awaited the team's first move, John Gerns, a forensic investigator, calmly hoisted a six-foot-long, T-shaped iron rod from a pickup truck. Gerns and a team of investigators from the International Criminal Tribunal for the former Yugoslavia (ICTY) had finally arrived in a pastoral meadow in Lazete, Bosnia.

Hurem Suljic, a fifty-two-year-old Bosnian Muslim, had told investigators he had narrowly survived the mass execution of hundreds of Bosnian Muslims here by Bosnian Serb soldiers in July 1995. Nine months after the executions allegedly occurred, a kaleidoscope of wildflowers had sprouted above what Suljic said was a mass grave.

Standing at the edge of the meadow, Gerns used his body weight to slowly drive the prod into the ground. Pausing a moment to catch his breath, he gently pulled the stake from the earth and did something that baffled many of the journalists. Gerns sniffed the tip of it. The forensic investigator, the journalists were later told, was checking the soil for the smell of decomposing human flesh.

The Lazete exhumation was the final stage of a medico-legal investigation, an inquiry into a death that can be carried out in peacetime or war. In most criminal justice systems, when an individual succumbs to a violent or suspicious or unattended death, a medico-legal investigation is conducted to probe the circumstances surrounding their demise.

The investigation begins with the accumulation of ante- and post-mortem evidence. When it is completed, a legal document is produced, mainly a death certificate that identifies the deceased and, as far as possible, the cause and manner of death.

Medico-legal investigations can also be inquiries into the possible use of torture or chemical weapons. Experts may examine former prisoners or detainees for signs of torture or refugees who have survived chemical weapons attacks.

In Lazete, the deceptively placid meadow presented war crimes investigators with an opportunity to triangulate different types of evidence—in this case, to prove whether or not the commander of the Bosnian Serb Army was responsible for a mass execution.

Hurem Suljic, who survived the massacre by hiding under the body of a fellow prisoner, had given investigators a sworn statement that he had witnessed Bosnian Serb Army commander Gen. Ratko Mladic overseeing the Lazete executions. Investigators found landmarks near the meadow, such as a school and railroad tracks, that matched Suljic's statement. But investigators needed to find bodies and determine the victims' cause of death to corroborate his account.

William Haglund, an American forensic anthropologist, led the team that day. The investigators, as with most peacetime medical inquiries, included experts from various disciplines such as pathology, radiology, anthropology, archaeology, and odontology.

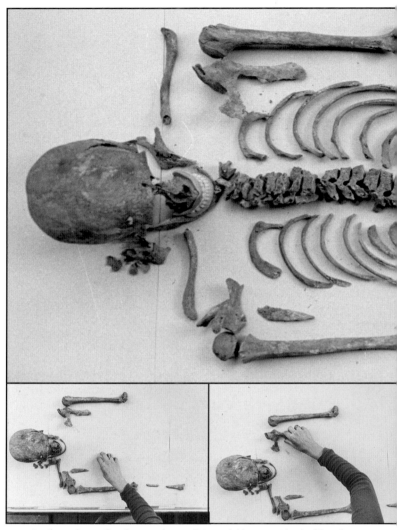

As the exhumation began, journalists quickly grew tired of its slow, painstaking pace. Investigators first mapped out the meadow and photographed it before digging. Whenever a bullet casing, bone, or body was found it was carefully labeled, photographed, and placed in a plastic bag. Just as in a civilian murder investigation, evidence, no matter how overwhelming, can be thrown out or discredited in court if collected improperly.

Investigators, if they are conducting a proper inquiry, should follow the "Manual on the Effective Prevention and Investigation of Extra-Legal, Arbitrary and Summary Executions," also known as the "Minnesota Protocol," adopted by the UN in 1992. The manual details how every step of a medico-legal investigation, from gathering antemortem evidence, such as medical records and X-rays, to conducting autopsies, should be carried out.

The findings in Lazete and other mass graves in the hills surrounding Srbrenica proved damning. One hundred and sixty-four bodies were exhumed from the graves. Many of the victims had their hands tied behind their backs and wore blindfolds. Religious artifacts and other objects found on their

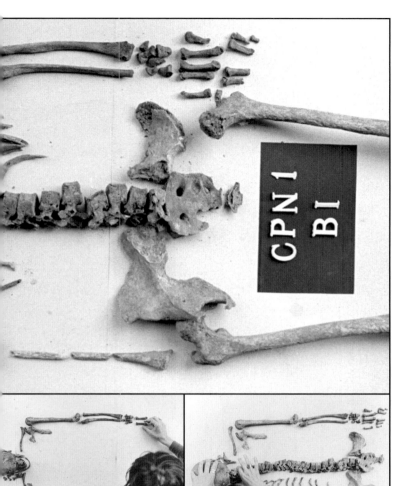

An Argentine forensic expert displays the remains of one of the victims of the
1981 massacre in El Mozote, El Salvador. November, 2003.

bodies indicated they were Bosnian Muslims.

Suljic's account had been corroborated, but the most chilling piece of evidence was a snapshot found in the shirt pocket of one of the victims. A smiling woman, apparently the victim's wife or girlfriend, stared out from the tattered photo. A bullet had torn through the center of it.

Mercenaries

By Elizabeth Rubin

Colonel Roelf was an Afrikaner who as a soldier and trained assassin spent his adult life suppressing black African liberation movements for the apartheid-era South African defense forces. Yet when I met him in the spring of 1996 in Sierra Leone, the black African civilians whose homes he had liberated in the midst of a brutal civil war said they regarded him as their savior.

Roelf was in Sierra Leone with Executive Outcomes (EO), a private mercenary army composed of former South African soldiers, which had been hired by the government to end the war. "We want to help African countries to neutralize their rebel wars and not depend on the UN to solve their problems," Roelf told me one afternoon in the remote diamond region where he and his fellow mercenaries had set up their hilltop military base. "We are something like the UN of Africa, only with a smaller budget." When some Sierra Leonian women stopped by to request protection for a soccer game down by the river because rebels were still roaming the bush, Roelf promised to help. "I am the ombudsman here," he said. Roelf was in fact more of an independent marshal hoping to enlarge his bank account with diamonds. And he was clearly attempting to dress up his mercenary operation with the language of international peacekeeping. But the village chiefs didn't care whether Roelf was a mercenary, an Afrikaner, a UN peacekeeper, or what, so long as he continued to protect the people with his soldiers and helicopter gunships.

Between 1991 and 1995 Sierra Leone descended into a state of violent anarchy with both rebels and renegade government soldiers waging a war of terror against civilians—torching villages, hacking people to death, or chopping off their hands, feet, and genitals. The international community had little inclination to get involved. The United Nations had seen enough humiliation with Somalis dragging dead American peacekeepers through the streets of Mogadishu, the Bosnian Serb Army taking United Nations peacekeepers hostage, and Rwandan *genocidaires* killing Belgian blue helmets. So the young Sierra Leonian military president turned to the international market and hired Executive Outcomes. They agreed to destroy the rebels and restore law and order in return for 15 million dollars and diamond mining concessions. Within a year EO stabilized the country enough for the population to line up for its first presidential elections in twenty-eight years.

EO belongs to the burgeoning industry of private security companies that have entered the theater of war in the last two decades offering to do what the United Nations cannot—take sides, deploy overwhelming force, and fire preemptively for a hefty fee. As Roelf's corporate employer back in South Africa stresses, unlike the mercenaries of yore, the company will only work for "legitimate governments." Nevertheless, EO also fits the definition of mercenaries in international humanitarian law—any person who is not a national of a party to the conflict and who is promised material compensation in excess of that paid to his employer's armed forces.

International laws concerning the status of mercenaries and the use of them by warring parties are extremely murky due to the changing political atmosphere in which they have been drafted. Mercenarism is perhaps the second-oldest profession. Back in the days of Italian city-states even the Pope contracted *condottieri* to hire outside soldiers for defense. In the seventeenth- and eighteenth-centuries the Swiss were renowned for their free-standing battalions hired out to other European countries. It was not until this century, during the turbulent period of decolonization in Africa, that mercenaries gained notoriety as bloodthirsty dogs of war wreaking havoc with the sovereignty of weak, newly independent African States. Such freelance guns-for-hire are accountable to no nation-state and no international laws. They will work for the highest bidder regardless of the cause and are rightly regarded as destabilizing agents. After all, they have no stake in the country's future and as long as war continues, so do their salaries.

So, in 1968, the United Nations General Assembly and the Organization of African Unity established laws against mercenaries, making the use of them against movements for national liberation and independence punish-

Belgian mercernary Marc Goosens, killed in an attack on a Nigerian bunker, is carried away by Ibo soldiers. Biafra, 1968.

able as a criminal act. In 1977, the Security Council adopted a resolution condemning the recruitment of mercenaries to overthrow governments of UN member States. The 1977 Additional Protocol I to the Geneva Conventions, in Article 47, stripped mercenaries of the right to claim combatant or prisoner of war status in international armed conflicts, thus leaving them vulnerable to trials as common criminals in the offended State. It also left the definition of mercenaries, in the view of many critics, dangerously subjective and partly dependent upon judging a person's reasons for fighting.

The United Nations Charter, however, also declares that nothing shall impair the inherent right of individual or collective self-defense if an armed attack occurs against a UN member. With the proliferation of low-intensity internal conflicts around the globe and the reluctance on the part of member States to intervene militarily, States and even humanitarian operations may, in the future, rely more on private security companies. So did Sierra Leone violate international standards by using mercenaries? Or was it practicing its right to defend against State collapse?

Depending on how you tally the gains for Sierra Leone, there was some truth to Roelf's claims. EO's intervention allowed over 300,000 refugees to return home. To keep the same number of people in squalid refugee camps in neighboring Guinea was costing the international aid community about $60 million a year. Furthermore, the civilians trusted EO much more than they'd ever trust their own unreliable soldiers to keep order. On the other hand, the new civilian government owed millions to a company of South African mercenaries and was wholly dependent upon them to stay in power. As it turns out, the World Bank ordered the bankrupt civilian government to terminate their contract with EO. With no reliable national army or peace-keeping force, the country slid back into violent disarray. A year later, rebels and rapacious government soldiers overthrew the government and ruled by terror. The cycle didn't end there. About eight months later, a British company related to EO launched an assault with a Nigerian force and threw out the junta, causing a tremendous political scandal in London. A peace agreement signed in 1999 failed, and it took the intervention of the British Army to stabilize the situation and finally put an end to the war.

At the heart of the debate about mercenaries and security companies is the question of whether it is possible to make a distinction, in legal terms, between good and bad mercenaries. Would Sierra Leone have been better off if EO were employed on a semipermanent basis? What to make of the Serb and Croat soldiers—formerly enemies—who were hired by Zaire's dictator, Mobutu Sese Seko, to stanch a popular revolution? Or the Romanian and South African snipers paid by the Bosnian Serbs to kill Bosnian civilians during the siege of Sarajevo? Perhaps the time has come to modify the laws and the definition of mercenaries. International law experts have suggested that by affording mercenaries the status and hence the rights of combat-ants, they would be more likely to abide by their obligations as combatants. Perhaps. Perhaps not. Others suggest a law requiring security companies to be registered with national governments. This would at least make the com-panies accountable to a government licensing body, which would require such companies to abide by international laws. Despite the fact that States are likely to use these private companies as covers to engage in unpopular foreign policy, this may be the best possible means of control.

While Executive Outcomes is not the most savory form of crisis inter-vention, it was hard to argue with the words of Sam Norma, the Sierra Leonian deputy defense minister, who said to me back in April of 1996, "Our people have died, lost their limbs, lost their eyes and their properties for these elections. If we employ a service to protect our hard-won democracy, why should it be viewed negatively?"

(See **private military firms**.)

Military Necessity

By Françoise Hampson

Military necessity is a legal concept used in international humanitarian law (IHL) as part of the legal justification for attacks on **legitimate military targets** that may have adverse, even terrible, consequences for civilians and civilian objects. It means that military forces in planning military actions are permitted to take into account the practical require-ments of a military situation at any given moment and the imperatives of winning. The concept of military necessity acknowledges that even under the laws of war, winning the war or battle is a legitimate considera-

British forces assault the outside wall of a technical college, behind which Iraqi forces had taken up positions and were launching rocket-propelled grenades. Basra, Iraq. March 2003.

tion, though it must be put alongside other considerations of IHL.

It would be overly simplistic to say that military necessity gives armed forces a free hand to take action that would otherwise be impermissible, for it is always balanced against other humanitarian requirements of IHL. There are three constraints upon the free exercise of military necessity. First, any attack must be intended and tend toward the military defeat of the enemy; attacks not so intended cannot be justified by military necessity because they would have no military purpose. Second, even an attack aimed at the military weakening of the enemy must not cause harm to civilians or civilian objects that is excessive in relation to the concrete and direct military advantage anticipated. Third, military necessity cannot justify violation of the other rules of IHL.

Moreover, the action in question has to be in furtherance of a military, not a political, goal. This poses obvious problems of characterization. Is persuading the enemy to surrender a military or political goal? Is "persuading" the enemy to surrender by aerial bombardment a military or political goal?

What constitutes a military objective will change during the course of a conflict. As some military objectives are destroyed, the enemy will use other installations for the same purpose, thereby making them military objectives and their attack justifiable under military necessity. There is a similarly variable effect on the determination of **proportionality**. The greater the military advantage anticipated, the larger the amount of **collateral damage**—often civilian casualties—which will be "justified" or "necessary." This flexibility also appears with regard to the prohibition of the use of weapons that cause "superfluous injury or unnecessary suffering." The greater the necessity, the more suffering appears to be justified. Thus, even in the Advisory Opinion on the Legality of the Use of Nuclear Weapons the majority of judges in the International Court of Justice in The Hague left open the possibility that a State might be able to justify its use of **nuclear weapons** where the very survival of the State was under serious threat.

State practice recognizes that judgments about military necessity often require subjective evaluations with incomplete information on the battlefield and imperfect knowledge of where the failure to take action might lead. For this reason, great discretion has always been attached to commanders' judgments, especially those made under battlefield conditions. Rarely, if ever, is the judgment of a field commander in battle—balancing military necessity and advantage—subject to legal challenge, let alone criminal sanction. An exception would be when the method of warfare used by the commander was illegal *per se*, and therefore not covered by the claim of military necessity.

In some cases, there is a presumption that certain actions are unlawful; it was not possible to prohibit them in absolute terms but they are unlawful unless justified by "imperative military necessity." This qualification of "absolutely necessary" or "for reasons of imperative military necessity" puts a significant burden of proof on those invoking the exception. Examples include the Fourth Geneva Convention, which restricts the internment of protected persons and the transfer or deportation from an area of occupied territory; Additional Protocol I, which would normally prohibit a scorched-earth policy but which allows it in exceptional circumstances in national territory; and Additional Protocol II, which normally prohibits the **internal displacement** of the civilian population.

In the course of hostilities, these rules impose significant restraints on the conduct of law-abiding forces, but those forces may be able lawfully to invoke military necessity where their very survival or the requirements of winning the conflict are at stake.

(See **civilian immunity; civilians, illegal targeting of; immunity; indiscriminate attack; military objectives; property; willfulness**.)

Military Objectives

By Hamilton DeSaussure

The term *military objective* is often used to describe the overall plan of a given mission: to take a certain hill, to reach a river, or to bring back hostages. In the more narrow sense, a military objective can refer to a specific target for neutralization or destruction. The laws of war use the term in the latter sense: to identify and attack a locality, facility, or enemy personnel that under the circumstances constitutes a **legitimate military target**. Certain potential objects or individuals clearly are unlawful targets. For example, any direct attack upon the civilian population, or upon any places, localities, or objects used solely for humanitarian, cultural, or religious purposes such as hospitals, churches, mosques, schools, or museums are immune. On the other hand, such **immunity** is lost if they are used or employed for enemy military purposes. There is always a presumption in favor of the immunity. Additional Protocol I to the Geneva Conventions of 1949 provides "in case of doubt whether an object which is normally dedicated to civilian purposes, such as a place of worship, a house or other dwelling or a school, is being used to make an effective contribution to military action, it shall be presumed not to be so used."

At one time, over a century ago, the laws of war set forth a simple rule as to what constituted a military objective. It was a fort or fortified place and adjacent towns assisting in their defense. This definition soon became obsolete at the beginning of the twentieth century as firepower increased the range of destruction and aircraft became an instrument of war that penetrated deep into enemy territory. The concept of the "defended place" was substituted for forts and fortified places at the two Hague Peace Conferences, which codified the laws of armed warfare just prior to World War I. Of course, what constituted a defended place was far more indefinite and variable than what qualified as a fort or fortress. The average person can identify a fort, but when is a town or city defended? Is it defended if it contains no military installations or armed forces and has no strategic military value but remains within the protective zone of an air defense unit which covers hundreds of miles of territory? The term defended place became as outmoded as the so-called fortified place with the advent of World War II and the increased capabilities of aerial and artillery firepower to attack the industrial infrastructure of war.

There was an intergovernmental attempt after World War I to specify what constituted legitimate military objectives by enumerating categories of legitimate targets. The rules proved too restrictive and no belligerent nation cited them as precedent in subsequent conflict. It became easier to list those categories of personnel and places that were not legitimate objects of attack than to define those that were. However, the wholesale destruction and killing wrought by mass aerial bombing in World War II made it imperative to redefine the scope of the military objective. The systematic destruction of urban areas city block by city block and the attack on the morale of the enemy population, which was sanctioned by both Allied and Axis bomber forces, brought forth many outcries for more humane rules of armed conflict. The destruction of the city of Dresden, killing as many as 100,000 civilians in one coordinated attack by British and U.S. bombers in two days in February

1945, reflected the lack of any meaningful definition of the military objective. In the Far East, firebomb attacks alone in the space of a few months killed eighty-four thousand civilians and destroyed many homes and urban facilities. This was before the holocaust of the atom bomb. While these events occurred in a high-intensity global conflict they demonstrated the urgent need to update and codify the laws of armed conflict and clearly state what could and could not be a legitimate target for hostile attack.

The contemporary rule defining military objects is found in the Additional Protocol I of 1977. Article 52 limits attacks to places, localities, facilities, structures, and "objects which... make an effective contribution to military action *and* whose total or partial destruction, capture or neutralization, in the circumstances ruling at the time, offers a definite military advantage." However, the rules provide specific immunity for certain individuals and localities. First, the civilian population must never be the object of attack, making it clear that morale or terror-bombing tactics are clearly a war crime today. Civilian objects used for peaceful purposes, are also protected. But the new rules go further by providing that in cases of doubt whether certain objects normally used for civilian purposes are being used to help the military mission, thereby losing their protection from attack, a presumption shall be made that it is not so used. Second, Protocol I also outlaws **carpet or area bombing** tactics. It provides that it is unlawful to bomb "as a single military objective a number of clearly separated and distinct military objectives located in a city, town, village, or other area containing a similar concentration of civilians or civilian objects." This is a useful and humane rule that eliminates the territorial or mass-bombing attacks so frequently resorted to in World War II, and to a lesser degree in the Vietnam conflict.

The enormous fire-raising attacks by U.S. forces over large urban areas in Japan in 1945 and the devastation wreaked city by city in Europe throughout World War II would be regarded today as flagrant violations of the modern rules and clearly prohibited by the Additional Protocols regardless of the nature or intensity of the conflict. Many contemporary writers of the laws of war consider that the size and scope of the conflict affect the scope of the military objective—that is, as nations devote more of their resources to the war effort and become more heavily committed to a successful conclusion, economic activities such as transportation, supply, and communications normally used only for civilian purposes may become legitimate targets. This is true but still would never today justify expansion of the legitimate target to include the civilian population or civilian areas as such.

Third, Protocol I also provides that any loss of civilian life incidental to the attack on legitimate military targets must be reduced to what is absolutely necessary to accomplish the mission. It would be indiscriminate and unlawful to cause civilian casualties that are excessive under the circumstances. The military target itself always must be identified and individually singled out for attack within the limits of available technology and weapons. Precision guided munitions (PGMs) were used in successful Vietnam air campaigns, such as Linebacker I and II, and made a critical impact on the United States's successful prosecution of Operation Desert Storm. Where there is a high concentration of civilians, it is imperative to use PGMs, as opposed to "dumb bombs," when available and subject to military necessity.

Military operations in the Gulf War in 1991 demonstrated the precision with which military targets could be hit without injury or disruption of the civilian population. Tomahawk cruise missiles disabled power plants and missile sites and destroyed military headquarters in Baghdad with minimum loss to civilians and civilian structures. F-117 stealth fighters and F-111 fighter-bombers were able to "thread" laser land-guided bombs through areas as small as doorways and air vents with surgical accuracy. The introduction of PGMs and high technology systems for spotting targets makes it even more necessary to isolate the target from the civilian population and dwellings. One air force writer has pointed out that while it would often take forty-five hundred sorties dropping nine thousand gravity bombs (presumably weighing about two thousand pounds each) to destroy a target in 1940–1945, one F-117 on one sortie could take out a precision target with the use of a PGM in the Gulf War. The circular error probable (CEP) or range of the possible hit is now measured in feet, rather than in miles.

Of course PGMs are expensive, not always available for certain missions even to the technologically superior force, and often should be conserved for a later phase of the battle. However the operational decisions on their use cannot obscure the fact that state-of-the-art military combat has forever changed what and how much civilian loss is permissible. An operational decision to use gravity-driven weapons when more precise munitions are available can make the attack excessive and unlawful if civilians are killed who would have been spared with the use of more accurate weapons.

Therefore, the loss of civilians, even deliberately located in and around a military target must clearly be shown to be absolutely necessary. Additional Protocol I specifically stipulates that feasible precautions in minimizing civilian loss includes the choice of weapons as well as the means and methods of attack. For example, bombing a military headquarters facility in a densely populated city would never justify the use of unguided bombs if PGMs were available to the striking force and if it appeared that innocent civilians within the vicinity would be injured or killed. However, the defending force cannot deliberately use civilians as a shield for its own military operations, for instance by moving them into a critical command and control center. An example of this principle is Iraq's use of the Amirya bomb shelter during the **Gulf War**. The United States attacked it, killing between two hundred and four hundred civilians, causing some to allege a violation of the laws of war. The fact that civilians are used as a shield does not cause them to lose their normal protection. This means that the attacking forces should nonetheless make particular efforts to avoid or at least minimize their injury or death.

In armed conflicts between two States where only one armed force has high-technology weapons systems, the humanitarian rules do not change. Each force is judged by the capabilities it possesses to defend itself or launch an attack. The high-technology State cannot rely on the lack of PGMs by its enemy to justify its own resort to less than its own state-of-the-art weaponry. At the same time, the defending force must use all means available to avoid attacks on, or excessive incidental damage to, the civilians when it launches its own defense or attack.

The military commander planning or executing the attack cannot be the final arbiter of whether the loss of civilian life and property is reasonably proportionate to the attack's military advantage. Only by the independent assessment of non-participating entities or organizations can the strict rules for the limitation of unnecessary suffering and destruction be upheld.

In the final analysis, the loss of any civilian life or property as a result of an armed attack, regardless of the level of the war, or the intensity of the particular planned mission, must clearly be shown to have been unavoidable with the use of the most precise weapons available to the attacking force. (See **proportionality; military necessity**.)

Mines

By John Ryle

Indiscriminate use of landmines became widespread during the post-Cold War era. Cheap, effective and easy to transport, mines were increasingly used in internal conflicts as a means to control and terrorize civilians, in addition to their conventional military use as an area denial weapon.

In 1997, after a worldwide campaign, 122 governments signed a ban on anti-personnel mines in Ottawa, Canada. Commonly known as the Mine Ban Treaty or the Ottawa Convention, it comprehensively prohibits the production,

A man searches for landmines while a woman cultivates the land as it is cleared. Luena, Angola, 1995.

stockpiling, transfer, and use of antipersonnel mines. It obliges States party to it to clear mines they have laid and to make provision for their victims. By 2006, 151 States had ratified the convention. But major mine producers such as the United States, Russia, China, India, and Pakistan have not signed. The treaty has two other limitations: it does not cover antitank mines, and non-State actors—rebels and insurgent groups—cannot be party to it.

Although the United States has announced self-imposed controls on the transfer of mines, the U.S. and other nonsignatories are legally bound only by the pre-existing Protocol II of the Conventional Weapons Convention of 1980 (Prohibitions or Restrictions on the Use of Certain Conventional Weapons That May Be Deemed to Be Excessively Injurious or to Have Indiscriminate Effects), which is widely agreed to be vague and unenforceable.

Some legal specialists, however, have argued that all mines are unlawful under international customary law, which prohibits the use of weapons that are by their nature indiscriminate.

N,O

Nuclear Weapons

By Burrus M. Carnahan

For over fifty years, the legality of nuclear weapons has been one of the most emotional and intellectually divisive issues in the laws of war. Eminent experts in international law can be found on both sides of the question.

Those supporting the legality of nuclear weapons argue that such weapons can be used in accordance with the laws of war. The United States government, for example, has for thirty years claimed that it recognizes the

following legal principles as applying to the use of nuclear weapons: that the right of the parties to a conflict to adopt means of injuring the enemy is not unlimited; that it is prohibited to launch attacks against the civilian population as such; and that distinction must be made at all times between persons taking part in hostilities and members of the civilian population to the effect that the latter be spared as much as possible.

Supporters of nuclear weapons argue that the actual practice of States is a more primary source of international law than theoretical legal principles. They note that the five original nuclear powers (United States, Soviet Union/Russia, United Kingdom, France, and China) have deployed nuclear weapons for decades, and have openly claimed the legal right to use these weapons in self-defense. (In 1998, India and Pakistan also openly claimed

A photo of the ruins of Hiroshima, signed by men of the Enola Gay's crew: Pilot Colonel Paul Tibbets Jr., Bombardier Major Thomas W. Ferebee, and Navigator Captain Theodore J. Van Kirk.

the right to nuclear weapons.) It has also been pointed out that the 1968 Treaty on the Non-Proliferation of Nuclear Weapons (the NPT) expressly recognizes the legal right of the five original nuclear powers to possess nuclear weapons. Over 170 countries are parties to the NPT.

Those opposing the legality of these weapons include a number of non-governmental organizations (NGOs) as well as some governments. They tend to base their arguments on the general humanitarian principles underlying the laws of war. For opponents, the vast destructive power of nuclear weapons makes a mockery of efforts to protect hospitals, the sick and wounded, civilians, and others as required by these humanitarian principles. Civilians may be spared "as much as possible" in a nuclear war, but in practice, they believe, it will be possible to spare very few. The civilian casualties and environmental damage will inevitably be disproportionate to the value of the military targets that nuclear weapons destroy.

In 1994, several NGOs opposed to the use of nuclear weapons convinced a majority of the United Nations General Assembly to ask the International Court of Justice at The Hague for an advisory opinion on the legality of nuclear weapons and their use. Under the UN Charter, the General Assembly is authorized to request such an opinion from the court on any legal question. (The United States opposed adoption of the resolution but was outvoted.) The court's opinion, delivered on July 8, 1996, illustrates how deeply divided the international legal community is on this issue. The fourteen judges then sitting on the court split evenly on whether nuclear weapons could ever be lawfully used in accordance with the laws of war. In that situation, the president of the court is allowed to cast a second vote to break the tie. By this procedure, the court gave the General Assembly the following ambiguous advice:

"[T]he threat or use of nuclear weapons would generally be contrary to the rules of international law applicable in armed conflict, and in particular the principles and rules of humanitarian law;

"However, in view of the current state of international law, and of the elements of fact at its disposal, the Court cannot conclude definitively whether the threat or use of nuclear weapons would be lawful or unlawful in an extreme circumstance of self-defense, in which the very survival of a State would be at stake."

The Court's narrowly-adopted compromise has something for both sides of the debate. Anti-nuclear activists can take comfort in the conclusion that nuclear weapons could rarely be used in a manner consistent with international humanitarian law, while those who believe nuclear weapons to be legitimate can point to the exception for cases where a State's survival is at stake. Perhaps for this reason, in the decade since the Court's decision, a consensus appears to have developed in favor of the Court's approach to the legality of nuclear weapons. In its massive report on Customary International Humanitarian Law, published in 2005, the International Committee of the Red Cross (ICRC) had no difficulty concluding that use of chemical and biological weapons was absolutely prohibited. As to nuclear weapons, however, the ICRC referred to the Court's opinion and concluded that it was "not appropriate to engage in a similar exercise" at this time. In effect, the ICRC deferred to the Court as a superior authority on international law.

Occupation

By George Packer

In the first weeks after the fall of Baghdad in April 2003, Iraqis would stop Americans on the street and ask who was in charge of the country. No one seemed to know. The Iraqi leadership had vanished, and the institutions of the state had collapsed.

The Iraqi exile politicians returning to Baghdad imagined that power would be handed quickly to them, but they were a contentious group with dubious backing inside the country. The American military, which had led the drive to overthrow the regime of Saddam Hussein, was now standing back, unwilling to intervene to stop the rampant looting and impose civil order. The civilian reconstruction group, under retired Army Lieutenant General Jay Garner, had no practical or legal authority and few assets to run the state. They saw themselves as liberators and were hesitant to assert themselves as rulers of Iraq. At a meeting in late April at the Baghdad convention center between coalition administrators and Iraqi notables, a tribal sheikh stood up and asked, "Who's in charge of our politics?"

"You're in charge," Garner replied. There was a collective intake of breath among the Iraqis in the room. An American official at the meeting later told me, "They were losing faith in us by the second."

By the middle of May, Garner had been replaced by L. Paul Bremer III, who had the status of presidential envoy and the legal backing of United Nations Security Council Resolution 1483, which acknowledged that the United States, the United Kingdom, and their coalition allies were the de facto occupying powers of Iraq. Thus began the troubled, year-long life of the Coalition Provisional Authority. Where Garner had tried in his laid-back way to ease a rapid transfer of power to the Iraqis, Bremer acted as if he was in charge. In the words of one C.P.A. official, the "arrogance phase" of the chaotic early days, with its rosy assumptions, had given way to the "hubris phase" of a heavy-handed occupation. The C.P.A. eventually issued dozens of legal orders, with the goal of remaking Iraq into a free-market democracy.

At least some of those orders were of doubtful validity under international law. The 1907 Hague Regulations and the fourth Geneva Convention of 1949 define the position of an occupying power in carefully delimited terms, as place-holder and caretaker rather than as a normally functioning government. Occupation brings with it a balanced set of responsibilities and prerogatives. According to Article 43 of the Hague Regulations, it is the duty of an occupying power to "take all the measures in his power to restore and insure, as far as possible, public order and safety, while respecting, unless absolutely prevented, the laws in force in the country." To promote public order, or to ensure its own security, an occupying power can repeal or suspend local laws, and introduce its own regulations (for instance by regulating the press or limiting the right of assembly). If it is necessary for imperative reasons of security, it can intern people without trial, though this must be done according to a regular procedure with a right of appeal and regular (ideally six-monthly) reviews. Domestic courts must be allowed to function wherever feasible, enforcing those local laws that have not been suspended, and the occupying power can also establish its own tribunals to enforce its penal regulations, so long as no one is sentenced without a fair trial.

Occupiers are also obliged to look after the welfare of the civilian population, ensuring as far as possible that it has adequate food, water and medical treatment. The Red Cross and other humanitarian relief groups must be allowed to operate and distribute supplies if the occupying power cannot meet the needs of civilians itself. It is forbidden for an occupying power to transfer civilians out of occupied territory, or to transfer its own civilian population in.

All these rules apply from the moment an occupying power actually controls a body of territory, even if it does not acknowledge the title of occupier.

The laws of armed conflict allow some scope for occupying forces to alter the legal systems of the countries they control, but envisage that such measures be limited to those with short-term consequences. However at least since World War II there has been a contrasting strain of thought, arguing that transformation of the political system in place before occupation may in some cases be not only permitted but desirable. Even as the fourth Geneva Convention was being negotiated, the United States and its coalition part-

ners were engaged in the complete remaking of Germany and Japan. In practice, the international community has been willing to accept such "transformative occupation" through endorsement by the United Nations Security Council, where it is aimed at promoting fundamental human rights or the principle of self-determination. The occupation of Iraq has tested the limits of this emerging consensus.

The military occupation of Iraq allowed public order to collapse and was never able to restore it, while the C.P.A.'s ambitions went far beyond merely administering Iraq until sovereignty could be returned. Order Number 39, which opened the Iraqi economy to foreign investment and allowed for foreign ownership of Iraqi assets, imposed just one of many far-reaching changes in Iraqi law. C.P.A. officials pointed to language in Security Council Resolution 1483 that instructed the authority to "promote the welfare of the Iraqi people" and provide "economic reconstruction and the conditions for sustainable development."

But the C.P.A.'s project was ideological, not just administrative: the radical transformation of Iraq. If it had paid more attention to "the welfare of the Iraqi people," and less to the vision of the Republican administration

Baghdad women line up at a gasoline distribution center under the watch of U.S. army troops, May 2003.

0

in Washington, the C.P.A. would not have tried to privatize state-owned industries in a country where employment ran well over fifty percent. And if they had taken their responsibilities under the Geneva Conventions more seriously, American commanders would have resisted the pressure from their civilian bosses to use coercive interrogations in the effort to snuff out the insurgency. The result of this failure was the scandal of torture at Abu Ghraib, the single worst mark against the Coalition Provisional Authority. The laws of occupation don't merely serve to protect the rights of the occupied—they also protect the perception of the occupier.

Pushing the envelope of international law was not the occupation's core problem. Whether or not its authority was legal, it was increasingly perceived by Iraqis as illegitimate. This perception had at least as much to do with the chaos and incompetence of the C.P.A.'s rule as it did with the original invasion. When I met Bremer at his office at the Republican Palace in the secure Green Zone, he told me that the closest historical precedent for his job was that of the allied military occupiers of Germany and Japan after World War II. This was a misleading analogy, and it helped to explain the C.P.A.'s many mistakes. Those postwar occupations were legitimate, in the eyes of the world and of the defeated nations. General Douglas MacArthur could write the constitution of Japan in a way that even Bremer couldn't force an American draft constitution down Iraqi throats. Whatever his legal authority, MacArthur had the power of the moral victor. The measure of the C.P.A.'s illegitimacy in the eyes of Iraqis lay in the rising number of attacks against foreign soldiers and civilians during the year of the formal occupation. Some Iraqis voted with roadside bombs and Kalashnikovs; others stood aside and refused either to join in the reconstruction or to resist it. By June of 2004, when Bremer was signing a flurry of last-minute legal orders before the transfer of sovereignty, Iraqis had definitively rejected the occupation, and very little of the C.P.A.'s efforts survived the restoration of self-government. Bremer and his aides flew home, and Iraq returned to itself.

In his memoir "My Year in Iraq," Bremer describes a dark moment in which he concluded that the Americans in Iraq had become the worst of all things, "an incompetent occupier." The only justification for a prolonged occupation by a foreign power, such as the world hadn't seen since 1945, was a practical one: that post-Saddam Iraq was too shattered and divided to govern itself. Only an occupation that was able to reconstruct the country and usher in genuine self-rule could have overcome all the counts against America in Iraq. From the beginning, the occupiers had to navigate between two imperatives: to exercise enough control that Iraq stood a chance of succeeding, and to yield enough control that Iraqis cooperated with the project. In the end, the C.P.A. accomplished neither.

(See **detention and interrogation; due process; Iraq.**)

P

Paramilitaries

By Christiane Amanpour

In April 1992, Zeljko Raznatovic (a.k.a. "Arkan") arrived with his uniformed militia in the east Bosnian town of Bijeljina to begin a campaign that came to be known as "ethnic cleansing."

The town was practically undefended, and his forces set up roadblocks, arrested civilians, and went house to house seizing others. One witness saw three people get their throats slit at a checkpoint. Another saw a woman shot as she was eating burek, a cheese pastry. When Arkan was done, twenty thousand Muslims had either fled, been transported to camps, or were slaughtered.

Arkan headed a paramilitary group called the Serbian Volunteer Guard, later known as Arkan's Tigers. A paramilitary force is a legal armed formation

P

that is not integrated into a regular armed force. The term "paramilitary," which is not a legal term, covers militias, volunteer corps, and even police units taking part in armed conflict. They qualify as lawful **combatants** under international law as long as they are under responsible command, carry distinctive signs, carry arms openly, and obey the laws and customs of war.

Like other legal combatants, paramilitaries, if fighting in an international conflict and captured, are to receive the protections of the Geneva Conventions accorded to all prisoners of war. They are to be treated decently like anyone else detained because of the conflict, that is, protected from the dangers of war, given all the food and medical care needed, and allowed outside contact through the International Committee of the Red Cross (ICRC). Like any other force, they cannot be tried for the mere act of taking part in hostilities as combatants, but can be interned as POWs until the conflict stops. But paramilitaries, like anyone else, may be tried for war crimes they commit.

Notwithstanding their often legitimate military functions, paramilitaries are routinely deployed by governments to preserve plausible deniability and

Ron Haviv, VII

One of Arkan's "Tigers" kicks the head of one of two women they have just shot. The women had run to the aid of the dead man also murdered by the paramilitaries.

P

to cloud the issue of command and control. Too often, paramilitaries provide a cover for governments intent on violating international law. They also protect political leaders from direct responsibility for war crimes. But their activities are sometimes controlled under public law, and they often operate in subordination to the regular army.

In the former Yugoslavia, paramilitary forces were the primary agent of criminal violence, murdering unarmed men, women, and children, raping and pillaging, and instituting a campaign of terror with the goal of forcing all non-Serbs out of territories that historically were ethnically mixed. As officially recognized armed formations, they are indisputably subject to international law for their role in alleged war crimes, crimes against humanity, and genocide.

A series of decrees established the role of paramilitary troops as the former Yugoslavia began to disintegrate. In August 1991, Serbia issued a decree regulating the enlistment of volunteers in the territorial defense, a paramilitary formation, which allowed volunteers to take part in maneuvers and training, thereby acquiring arms. In December 1991, the rump Yugoslav government established "volunteer" forces as an adjunct to the Federal Army. Arkan, a soccer promoter and café owner, was a close political associate of Serbian strongman Slobodan Milosevic. Already by that autumn, Arkan, with the help of a recruitment campaign in the state-owned media, had begun rallying unemployed soccer hooligans and criminals and training them at army facilities.

Arkan thus did not operate as a free agent; on more than one occasion he even took command. UN investigators determined that Arkan's forces worked in coordination with the Federal Army in eleven municipalities in Bosnia, and in three of those municipalities, including Bijeljina, Arkan was reported to be the leader of the joint operation to seize cities and expel their native populations. In Zvornik, at the start of April 1992, Arkan issued the ultimatum to surrender and then called in the army to begin the shelling. His trained army of killers and commandos moved into town in Federal Army vehicles. In black woolen caps and black gloves cut off at the fingers, they combed the city with prepared lists and assassinated leading Muslims.

Three years later, Milosevic referred to the volunteers as "bandits and killers." He said in an interview they amounted to "only a couple thousand" troops, and "were totally marginal in that war." The UN Commission of Experts said upward of twenty thousand paramilitary troops took part in the war and played a central role in the mayhem.

As for Arkan, he was indicted by the Yugoslav war crimes tribunal on charges of genocide, war crimes and crimes against humanity, but before he could face trial he was gunned down in Belgrade in January 2000.

Parlementaires

By Ewen Allison

In late July 1995, after pounding the town of Zepa for days with artillery, rockets, and machine guns, Gen. Ratko Mladic, commander of the attacking Bosnian Serb forces, accepted the town's surrender. Mladic had earlier demanded that the town surrender all men of fighting age as prisoners of war, and promised to escort all women, children, and elderly to government lines and safety. Despite the pleas of Zepa's mayor, Mehmed Hajric, NATO and UN forces refused to intervene. Finally, Mayor Hajric took a white flag in hand and went to Mladic to negotiate the surrender of Zepa. He and three companions were seized by the Serbs and imprisoned in the neighboring town of Rogatica. Shortly thereafter the Bosnian forces took Zepa.

After fifteen days of imprisonment, Hajric managed to escape. However, according to the Hague Conventions on Land Warfare of 1899 and 1907, which remain in force and are considered part of conventional international humanitarian law, Hajric enjoyed a special protection. He had the status of parlementaire and could not, without reason, be arrested and detained.

A parlementaire is a person who is authorized by one party to a conflict to speak with another party to the conflict, and who travels under a white flag. Hajric met both requirements—he had the authority to appoint himself as negotiator, and did, in fact, carry a white flag.

Although the rules on parlementaires evolved during earlier centuries and were codified in the Hague Conventions, they apply today. A parlementaire may be accompanied by a flag bearer, an interpreter, and a trumpeter or drummer. The commanding officer to whom a parlementaire is sent is not required to meet him and may take measures to prevent the parlementaire from spying.

Significantly for Hajric's case, a parlementaire may not be directly attacked, and almost always has the right not to be arrested, detained, or executed. A parlementaire loses these rights if he abuses his mission—by spying or committing a hostile act. Even if accused of such abuses, he retains the right to a fair trial and humane treatment.

Hajric, however, had done nothing amiss. His detention was unlawful.

P

Perfidy and Treachery

By David Rohde

They had fled from Srebrenica, the world's first UN-declared civilian safe area, after it had fallen to the Bosnian Serbs on July 11, 1995, and the tales several dozen of these Bosnian Muslim men told were chillingly consistent.

The Dutch UN peacekeepers and the NATO jets the UN Security Council had promised would protect Srebrenica had put up scant resistance. The men knew that they were earmarked for death and they had fled, joining a three-mile-long, single-file column of fifteen thousand mostly unarmed men trying to make their way across thirty miles of enemy territory to reach Bosnian government lines. Over and over again along the line of march, hundreds had been killed in a series of well-planned ambushes by Bosnian Serb forces. After that, Bosnian Serb soldiers wearing stolen UN uniforms and driving stolen UN vehicles announced over megaphones that that they were UN peacekeepers and that they were prepared to oversee the Bosnian Muslims' surrender and guarantee they would not be harmed.

Disoriented and exhausted, many Bosnian Muslims fell for the lie. It was only after they had surrendered that they discovered their fatal mistake. For in surrendering, they were going to their deaths. Those whom the Serbs got their hands on were killed by firing squad.

Srebrenica was the worst massacre in Europe since World War II. The shock at what took place there was so great that to separate war crimes from entirely licit military actions seemed, and in many ways still seems, almost obscene. And yet from the point of view of international humanitarian law, the ambushes the Serbs sprang on the fleeing Bosnians were legal ruses soldiers can employ in wartime. Investigators for the International War Crimes Tribunal for the Former Yugoslavia said the fact that many of those in the retreating column were Bosnian government soldiers made the column a military threat and thus a legitimate target. In legal terms, the Bosnian Serb ambushes did not lull the Bosnian Muslims into a false sense of protection under international law, rather they led them to miscalculate the nature of the threat.

What was entirely criminal was the Bosnian Serbs' use of UN emblems and matériel to lure the fleeing Muslims to surrender—a clear example of a war crime. The prohibition in modern times against what is alternatively called "perfidy" and "treachery" goes back to the American Civil War. But the definitive statement banning the kind of deceptions the Bosnian Serbs engaged in on the roads out of Srebrenica can be found in Articles 37, 38, and 39 of the 1977 Additional Protocol I to the Geneva Conventions.

Article 37 of Protocol I states that "acts inviting the confidence of an adversary to lead him to believe that he is entitled to, or is obliged to accord, protection under the rules of international law applicable in armed conflict, with intent to betray that confidence, shall constitute perfidy." And Article 38 explicitly prohibits the use of "the distinctive emblem of the United Nations, except as authorized by that organization." It also prohibits the "improper use of the distinctive emblems of the **red cross**, **red crescent** or red lion," which, if used perfidiously, is a grave breach.

The difference between perfidy and treachery is the difference between wrongful deception and betrayal. Perfidy is making someone believe a falsehood, while betrayal involves an act that actually harms the person. In international law, treachery and perfidy are used interchangeably.

Other examples of perfidy are feigning to negotiate under a flag of truce or surrender, feigning to be incapacitated by wounds or sickness, and feigning of civilian, noncombatant status. Article 39 prohibits the use of flags, military emblems, insignia, or uniforms of the opposing side at the time of an attack in order to protect or impede military operations.

But the protocol states explicitly that ruses of war are not prohibited. A ruse is an act that is intended to mislead an adversary or to "induce him to act recklessly" but which infringes no rule of armed conflict and does not attempt to gain his confidence by assuring protection under law. Camouflage, decoys, mock operations, and misinformation are all permitted ruses. An example of a legal ruse was when U.S. forces gathered at sea during the 1991

The remains of a Bosnian from Srebrenica who may have surrendered to Serbs treacherously disguised as UN peacekeepers. Pilice, 1996.

Gulf War to trick Iraq into thinking an amphibious assault was imminent; the attack eventually came by land.

During the recent Iraq War, insurgent fighters were reported to have used perfidious tactics on many occasions, including feigning surrender or injury, using civilian cars and taxis as car bombs, and using an ambulance packed with explosives to attack the ICRC headquarters in Baghdad in October 2003.

In the case of the Muslim men of Srebrenica, the textbook definition of perfidy, which is actually extremely narrow, was all too tragically fulfilled. The Bosnian Muslims who surrendered did so because they were tricked by the Serbs into believing they were in the presence of UN peacekeepers. This was not a ruse, which is legal in warfare, but treachery pure and simple, and it cost thousands of people their lives.

The killing of all those who surrendered, who were ***hors de combat***, is, of course, the gravest breach of all.

Persecutions on Political, Racial, or Religious Grounds

By William Shawcross

Just before Christmas 1975, I drove east from Bangkok a couple of hundred miles to Thailand's border with Cambodia. It was some eight months since the Khmer Rouge Communists had won power in Cambodia, defeating the U.S.-backed government of Gen. Lon Nol.

Since then the Khmer Rouge had expelled all Westerners (and most other foreigners), emptied all the towns of people, and embarked on a radical Maoist experiment to return the country to an autarchic preindustrial age.

The only witnesses of the terror which this plan involved were those refugees who had managed to make it to the Thai border. (Those who reached Vietnam were kept silent by the Vietnamese Communists, still at that stage allied to the Khmer Rouge.)

The refugees I met in a United Nations High Commissioner for Refugees (UNHCR) camp at the border town of Aranyaprathet all had horrible tales to tell. They spoke of Khmer Rouge cadres beating babies to death against trees, of any adult suspected of ties to the old regime being clubbed to death or shot, of starvation and total lack of medical care, of men with glasses being killed because they were "intellectuals." It was absolutely clear to me that these refugees were telling the truth. History shows that refugees usually do. Less clear at that time was why the Khmer Rouge were behaving in such an atrocious way.

The killing continued and even intensified over the next three-and-a-half years. No intervention was attempted to stop it. When U.S. Senator George McGovern proposed a military intervention in the name of protecting humanity, he was mocked.

At the end of 1978, after perhaps 1.5 to 2 million of the 7 million people in Cambodia had died, the Khmer Rouge were overthrown by their erstwhile Vietnamese allies. Hanoi installed instead a client Communist regime. Its policies can in no way be compared to those of the Khmer Rouge, but it was a brutal one-party system nonetheless.

In 1980 I visited Cambodia and was taken to a mass grave outside Phnom Penh where victims of the Khmer Rouge terror were buried. These people had been clubbed to death; their hands were still tied, the skulls were bashed in, and some of the bones still had putrid flesh clinging to them.

I had heard about such mass graves since childhood—my father was the chief British prosecutor at Nuremberg and one of my earliest memories is of listening to recordings of his speeches for the prosecution. In one he quoted the terrible atrocities seen at a grave in a place called Dubno. The images of families of all ages herded towards pits where SS men smoking cigarettes were waiting to shoot them made a lifelong impression on me. Obviously I had hoped never to see such sights myself. But in Cambodia I did.

For many years following the overthrow of the Khmer Rouge no real effort was made to bring the Khmer Rouge leaders to justice. In summer

1979 the Vietnamese staged a show trial of the leaders in absentia—it was a farce. Since then there has been no successful effort to bring the Khmer Rouge to justice, in part for political reasons.

The question is with what precise crimes they should be charged. Since the majority of their victims were other Cambodians, the **Genocide** Convention on its face probably does not apply to the majority of these killings, and this has been the predominant view within the international legal community until recently. However, there is prima facie evidence that they assaulted in particular such ethnic and religious groups as the Cham, the Vietnamese, and the Buddhist monkhood. These attacks would probably meet the standard in the Genocide Convention of action with an "intent to destroy in whole or in part" these groups.

Crimes against humanity have been linked to armed conflict, whether internal or international, but there is an expanding body of opinion which suggests that under international law this need not always be so and that large-scale killings can constitute crimes against humanity even in the absence of armed conflict. The International Tribunal for the Former Yugoslavia has ruled that crimes against humanity need have no link to armed conflict, and the 1998 Rome Statute of the International Criminal Court makes no reference to a link. A State Department study in 1995 concluded that the Khmer Rouge could be tried for crimes against humanity, and the United States and other governments attempted unsuccessfully in 1998 to bring Pol Pot to trial shortly before his death.

The Khmer Rouge's systematic murder, extermination, unacceptable forced labor, torture, forcible transfers of population—all provide prima facie evidence of massive persecutions. A prosecution of the Khmer Rouge for crimes against humanity would likely feature charges of persecution as well as extermination and murder at its center. Nuremberg and subsequent tribunals determined the following acts to constitute elements in persecution: deprivations of the rights of citizenship, to teach, to practice professions, to obtain education, and to marry freely; arrest and confinement, beatings, mutilation, torture, confiscation of property; deportation to ghettos, slave labor, and extermination; plunder and destruction of businesses as a means of terror or related to other violence; deprivation of fair trial rights; a collective fine, seizure of assets, creation of ghettos, forcing the wearing of yellow stars, boycott of businesses, preaching hatred, and incitement to murder and extermination.

The 1998 Rome Statute for the International Criminal Court includes persecution among listed crimes against humanity and defines it as "the intentional and severe deprivation of fundamental rights contrary to international law by reason of the identity of the group or collectivity." The statute proscribes "persecution against any identifiable group or collectivity on political, racial, national, ethnic, cultural, religious, gender, or other grounds that are universally recognized as impermissible under international law, in connection with any other act referred to in this paragraph [on crimes against humanity] or any other crime within the jurisdiction of the court." A crime against humanity, according to the statute, must be committed as part of a "widespread or systematic attack."

Even though it is thirty years since they were overthrown and further abuses have since been committed against the Cambodian people, the crimes of the Khmer Rouge are without parallel. Peace and justice go hand in hand. There is still no real peace in Cambodia; one reason is that a culture of impunity has developed there as a result of the total lack of accountability.

Nuremberg embodied the rhetoric of progress. The judgment of Nuremberg was grasped, in Rebecca West's words, as "a sort of legalistic prayer that the Kingdom of Heaven should be with us."

It was predictable that that prayer would not be fulfilled. But even when the prescriptions laid down at Nuremberg are ignored as cruelly as they have been in the last fifty years, they have not been forgotten.

In the case of Cambodia, justice has been long denied, but by the middle of 2006, after long arguments between the Cambodian government and the United Nations, a Tribunal was at last under way. Just how effective it could be was open to question. The Tribunal has been given a $56 million budget, and the enabling legislation stated that it would only try the most senior leaders and "those most responsible" for crimes committed during the Khmer Rouge years in power.

Whether justice will eventually be served, even in part, is still very uncertain. Many of "those most responsible," notably Pol Pot himself, have already died. Others have been protected by the present Cambodian government, many of whose members had originally been Khmer Rouge cadres and which is now notoriously corrupt and given to its own extralegal behavior. There is little reason for confidence that any interventions by the government will assist due process. If it continues to try to control

A reclining Buddha overlooks the skeletal remains of murdered Cambodians discovered near a temple by the Vietnamese when they occupied Sisophon in 1980.

the proceedings for political reasons there is a danger that the rationale for the Tribunal would collapse. Certainly, arguments over its conduct will continue. When the trials finally begin, denial and memory loss will no doubt prevail and the process may leave the Cambodian people more confused than they already are. It is unlikely to end the culture of impunity which exists within Cambodia today. But it is probably true to say that unless even a limited attempt is made to bring to justice some representatives of one of the worst crimes against humanity in recent history, Cambodia would have absolutely no hope of coming to terms with its past and therefore building a better future.

(See **courts and tribunals**.)

P

Pillage

By Thomas Goltz

Pillage has been a feature of nearly every conflict fought since ancient times. But rarely has it been carried out with such ruthless efficiency as in the war between Abkhaz separatists and the new government of Georgia in 1992 and 1993. One reason the conflict exploded into open war was the stunning amount of pillaging carried out by the Mkhedrioni, a quasi-State militia led by warlord Jaba Iouseliani, and the National Guard, commanded by Tengiz Kitovani.

The "White Knights" and National Guard requisitioned entire airplanes to haul their heisted televisions, radios, refrigerators, carpets, and chairs out of the Abkhaz capital of Sukhumi. The Abkhaz paid the Georgians back in spades when they managed to drive not only the Georgia "defense" forces from the territory in late September 1993, but also the vast majority of the Georgian population living in the area. Anything left behind became fair game for seizure—cars, appliances, the contents of kitchen pantries, everything.

Although the practice of pillage in conflict has been prohibited for nearly a century, few countries and cultures are exempt from the charge. The 1907 Hague Convention states: "The pillage of a town or place, even when taken by assault, is prohibited." Prior to the Hague Convention, pillage was widely accepted as justified after assault, to compensate for the risks and losses from that method of conquest. In practice, it was often hard to distinguish between pillage after assault and requisitioning of food from peasants to sustain the army. The advent of new methods of food preservation, including canning in the nineteenth century, meant armies could carry their supplies, allowing limits to be placed on both requisitioning and pillage.

Requisitioning—the taking of "necessities" from a population for the use of an army of occupation—is legal, however. Requisitioning must be ordered by the local commander, must be proportionate to what the area can provide, must take the needs of the population into account, and should be of such a nature as not to require the population to take part in military operations against their own country. Requisitioned goods shall "as far as possible, be paid for in ready money; if not, their receipt shall be acknowledged." However, goods possessed by the enemy's armed forces are "subject to the laws and customs of war," that is, they may be seized as booty.

The 1949 Geneva Conventions reduce the ban to three words: "Pillage is prohibited." The requisitioning of food or medical supplies is permitted only for their use by the occupation forces and administrative personnel, and then "only if the requirements of the civilian population have been taken into account." The conventions also require that fair value be paid for requisitioned goods, and set out specific restrictions on requisitioning medical facilities.

Although the ban on pillage is most often observed in the breach in contemporary conflict, matters were worse before the law was codified; Europe's great museums testify to the grand scale of pillaging during wars of the past centuries. In many of the wars following the end of the Cold War, pillaging turned into a principal feature of the conflict. The Iraqi Army pillaged Kuwait as it departed that country under the pressure of Operation Desert Storm in early 1991, and Serb paramilitaries stripped Croatia and

Bosnia-Herzegovina of all movable privately owned goods, fencing them in Belgrade and Novi Sad.

Not every expropriation is pillage. Not long after the Azerbaijan Army retook control of northern Karabakh in the summer of 1992 and put down the secession in that part of the Armenian enclave, I watched Azeri oil tankers pull up to the storage vats of brandy in occupied towns, drain the contents into the trucks, and drive away. The drivers told me that the brandy was to be sold for the benefit of widows and orphans, but in fact it was often used to fuel military vehicles. Not far from this scene, horse-drawn carts, piled high with refrigerators, stoves, and diverse plumbing fittings, trundled slowly through the countryside, carrying the contents from smoldering villages toward markets elsewhere.

The fortunes of war shifted, and nine months later, after ethnic Armenians had seized the Azeri province of Kelbajar, a British colleague visiting Stepanakert, the self-proclaimed capital of the breakaway province, came

Two television sets that were looted and later abandoned in the middle of the desert by Iraqi soldiers in their haste to reach the safety of their own country. Kuwait, 1991.

upon a large "used refrigerator and television" market. The Armenians began the systematic removal of window and door frames as they went house to house in occupied Azeri cities such as Agdam, Fizuli, and Zangelan.

Decanting the brandy, especially when it was being used by the fuel-starved Armenians was probably not pillage. Most likely it was public property, and the Azeris could claim to be the State. A State has the right to declare a state of emergency or martial law and requisition goods needed to sustain the civilian population. Indeed, if used in the war effort, as it was to fuel tanks, the seized brandy was legitimate war booty.

The refrigerators and televisions, windows and door frames, on the other hand, are undoubtedly a case of pillage, for they were stolen from private civilian homes and not requisitioned by proper military procedures for any proper military purpose. The rule of thumb is that in an international conflict, any goods seized without proper procedure have been pillaged; in an internal conflict, to determine whether an army has pillaged, it is important to find out first whether the goods are private or State property. If the internal party has a claim to being the government of the region, then it has a claim to the goods owned by the State.

Poisonous Weapons

By Gwynne Roberts

Shaho was nine when the Iraqi Kurdish town of Halabja was chemically bombed by the Iraqi Air Force in 1988.

He still vividly remembers the planes overhead, the clouds of gas smelling of fruit, and then fleeing for his life to Iran. Within weeks, Shaho began to suffer back pains and over the next few years he lost the ability to stand or walk. His condition is known as scoliosis, severe curvature of the spine. He has no doubt what caused it.

"Before the chemical attack, I was perfectly healthy," Shaho told me when I visited Halabja a few years ago. "I am certain that poison gas caused my illness. My mother lost her sight at the time, and I've got gradually worse ever since." He spends each day at home lying on his mattress, turned every thirty minutes by his devoted sister to avoid bedsores. His family has gone deep into debt to try to find a cure—without success. (Although research into the effects of nerve and mustard gas on the human body is limited, such agents are known to cause disorders in a range of tissues in addition to the brain and spinal cord and may thus be responsible for abnormal growth of cells in bone.)

Nizar, in his late twenties, also from Halabja, is hardly able to walk and crumbles to the floor after a few paces. He bursts into tears. "I can't even go to the toilet on my own," he says. "Please help me. I am afraid of ending up in bed forever." He too was gassed and he lay unconscious for two days. The gases, which smelled of apples, attacked his nervous system, and over the years he has gradually lost control of his muscles. Both cases link severe neurological damage to **chemical weapons**.

In one way both were lucky—they, at least, survived the bombardment. The battle for Halabja began on March 15, 1988, when Kurdish rebels and Iranian Revolutionary Guards, equipped with chemical warfare suits, moved into the town, driving out Iraqi units in heavy fighting. Townspeople were then stopped from fleeing Halabja and forced by the invaders to return to their homes. This tactic was to cost thousands of lives.

The chemical attack began a day later at 6:20 p.m. and continued sporadically over three days. Wave after wave of bombers—seven to eight in each wing—attacked Halabja, a town of eighty thousand, and all roads leading to the surrounding mountains. They dropped a cocktail of poison gases: mustard gas, the nerve agents sarin, tabun, and, according to a well-informed East European chemical weapons specialist, cyanide. Clouds of gas hung over the town and the surrounding hills, blotting out the sky and contaminating the fertile plains nearby.

The townspeople had no protection and the chemicals soaked into their clothes, skin, eyes, and lungs. At least five thousand, and probably many more, died within hours. Many were poisoned in the cellars where they had sought refuge—trapped by gases that were heavier than air. It was the largest chemical attack ever launched against a civilian population.

On the road out of the town, an estimated four thousand were killed near the village of Anab as they attempted to flee to Iran. Many flung themselves into a pond to wash off the chemicals but died within minutes. Their corpses lay undisturbed for months, deadly toxins from their bodies seeping into the earth and reportedly contaminating the water table.

Some survivors fled into Iran, where they live to this day. Others who escaped to nearby Kurdish towns returned to Halabja and now live in the very homes where scores of close relatives perished. They complain that mortar dust still causes skin lesions and eye soreness, even though international experts say any contamination has long since disappeared.

Until relatively recently, evidence of the attack still littered the hills around Halabja, empty chemical shells with Russian markings standing upright in the ploughed earth like grotesque mushrooms. Casings were stacked in local scrapyards, and even used as flowerpots by Halabjans.

Local people are convinced that the chemicals blighted the lands around Halabja, once the most fertile region in the Middle East. Farmers say that agricultural output dropped dramatically in the years after the attack. Pomegranate orchards dried out, and other fruit trees became unproductive.

Iraqi forces killed this Kurdish man and child with poison gas in Halabja, 1988.

They complain that the chemicals also caused mutations in plant and animal life. The town has been visited by plagues of locusts for the first time in living memory. According to a local surgeon, snakes and scorpions became more poisonous after the attack, up to twenty people dying from lethal bites each year, a tenfold increase in the region.

But these chemical weapons left behind an even more frightening legacy. According to Christine Gosden, professor of medical genetics at Liverpool University, who accompanied me to Halabja, these poisons have genetically damaged the local population.

After the Iraqi Army withdrew from the region after Desert Storm in 1991, Halabja was shunned by the outside world and ignored by the international aid agencies. Its inhabitants, however, continue to live a total nightmare—their health has been irreversibly damaged in the attack, as well as that of their children and their children's children.

During our visit, we were literally overwhelmed by people exhibiting a variety of serious irreversible medical conditions ranging from aggressive cancers, neurological damage, and skin diseases to heart-rending disfigurements and severe psychiatric disorders. Surgeons have grown used to removing bullets from people unsuccessful in their attempts at suicide.

Professor Gosden, working with doctors in the area, compared the Halabja rates of infertility, congenital malformations, and cancers with those of an unexposed population from a city in the same region. She found that, ten years after the attack, the frequency rates were three to four times higher. Most worrisome of all, she discovered that more and more children were dying each year of leukemia and lymphomas. Their tumors were more aggressive than elsewhere, and there was no chemotherapy or radiotherapy available.

"The situation is a genetic time bomb which is exploding into future generations," she said. "It is far worse that I could have ever imagined."

In Halabja, Iraq, a Kurdish guerrilla inspects an unexploded chemical bomb from the 1988 attack that killed 5,000 Kurds. May 1991.

Shaho's case exemplifies the need for further research. Scoliosis may seem an unlikely side-effect of chemical weapons, but Dr. Gosden points out that the human bone structure is not static; in fact our entire skeleton is replaced each year. Other bone disorders such as osteoporosis can lead to the shrinking of the skeleton, while cancer can cause severe Dowager's hump and the weakening and fractures of bone.

Halabja is certainly a medical catastrophe. There is also little doubt in the minds of Halabjans who is responsible: Saddam Hussein and the western companies which supplied Iraq with the chemical precursors and hardware to manufacture the gas.

The attack happened during the final stages of the Iran-Iraq conflict and the Iraqis were in clear breach of the 1925 Geneva Protocol banning the use of "asphyxiating, poisonous, or other gases, and of all analogous liquids." The attack also violated the 1899 and 1907 Hague Regulations, which ban the use of "poison or poisoned weapons."

Their deployment against civilians, however, puts this crime onto another dimension. Iraq has not ratified the 1977 Addition Protocols to the Geneva Conventions protecting civilians during combat. But in this case, the Hague Regulations of 1907 are applicable. They stipulate that any force bombarding a populated area has to take precautions to minimize incidental damage. It is clear that no such precautions were taken.

Halabjans allege that western governments were also to blame because they turned a blind eye on the illicit trade in chemicals and equipment needed for Iraq's weapons program. Khomeni's Iran seemed a more pressing problem at the time. Halabja remains a sensitive issue for many western governments because such allegations, if proven, could damage national interests. Keeping the names of these companies secret still seems to be a priority.

In 1993, the United Nations reached a formal agreement with the Iraqis not to reveal the names of companies which had supplied the regime with chemical precursors. Nine years later, just before the recent Iraq War, Saddam supplied the UN and the International Atomic Energy Agency (IAEA) with a 12,000-page weapons declaration identifying all of them. However, this was kept secret and never officially published,

In the meantime the Halabjans grow increasingly angry. They complain about unemployment, poor roads, inadequate housing and health care, a pressing problem with thousands suffering from respiratory illnesses, cancer and other diseases. The economic boom evident in much of Kurdistan has passed Halabja by.

Halabjans' feelings erupted on March 16, 2006, when protesters destroyed the local monument erected in memory of the gas victims. It sent shock waves across the region.

Townspeople were unhappy that top officials, both Kurdish and foreign, visit the town, and cite it as justification for the war against Saddam, promptly forgetting their offers of help to its afflicted population as soon as they leave. They also say that whilst Saddam's associates may have to answer at their trial in Baghdad for their crimes against Halabja, those who provided the regime with the tools to launch the attack will escape without penalty.

"Those who are suffering need a lot of money to get treatment in western hospitals," said Abdel Qader, a survivor of the 1988 attack who heads the Halabja Chemical Victims' Society. "We want to see those who helped Saddam punished and our rights restored."
(See **Iran-Iraq War**.)

Prisoners of War

By H. Wayne Elliott

Winston Churchill, himself a former prisoner of war, once wrote,
"Prisoner of War! That is the least unfortunate kind of prisoner to be, but it is nevertheless a melancholy state. You are in the power of your enemy. You owe your life to his humanity, and your daily bread to his compassion. You must obey his orders, go where he tells you, stay where you are bid, await his pleasure, possess your soul in patience."

Yet, in spite of the problems incumbent with the status of a prisoner of war, Churchill believed that being a prisoner of war is the "least unfortunate kind of prisoner to be." Churchill understood that with the status of "prisoner of war" come some legal protections. The prisoner of war is not considered a criminal. He is to be treated in a humane fashion. His wounds and illnesses treated. His captivity regulated by a code of rules which are intended to pro-

tect the prisoner during captivity. Today those rules are found in the Third Geneva Convention of 1949, also known as the Geneva Convention on Prisoners of War (GPW).

At one time in history persons captured by the enemy in war enjoyed no protection. The captive might be treated as a slave of the person who captured him or, if less "lucky," simply be executed. Of course, if the captive had some level of importance, he might be ransomed. And for the ransom system to work the captive really needed to be protected from harm. Still, whatever protections existed were not found in any formal legal documents. Beginning in the nineteenth century there was a series of international conferences which aimed at setting out the rules in a formal code or treaty. By World War II some forty countries had agreed to the 1929 Geneva Convention on POWs. The experiences of World War II led to the adoption of the Third Geneva Convention in 1949.

The Convention sets out a system of basic safeguards for those who fall within its parameters. Some of the benefits of being held as a POW may appear to be more than is deserved. These include advances of pay, maintaining financial accounts, access to canteens, or the receipt of musical instruments. Other requirements are more substantive. POWs must be properly housed and fed. They must receive appropriate medical care and be given the opportunity to

Suspected Viet Cong are led roped together to a prison camp. Vietnam, 1967.

P

correspond by mail with their families. The protections of the Convention are only available to those who fall within its definitions.

So who is entitled to the protections of the Convention? Who is a prisoner of war? The indiscriminate attacks of September 11, 2001, and the capture of some of those either involved with the attacks or fighting to shield those who were have focused attention on the issue. Are these captives legally entitled to be treated as prisoners of war? And what of those captured in the war in Iraq?

The Geneva Conventions apply in all cases of "declared war or of any other armed conflict" between two or more States that are party to the treaties. Thus, it seems obvious that the Geneva Conventions apply to the conflicts in Afghanistan and in Iraq. However, that does not mean that every person held is entitled to the protections of the POW Convention, nor that the status of a prisoner of war serves to immunize a captive individual from punishment for criminal activities.

The Bush administration announced its policy on captives from

Processing of a Taliban combatant, Bagram Air Force Base, Afghanistan. New Year's Day, 2002.

Afghanistan in February 2002. It drew a theoretical distinction between al-Qaeda fighters and members of the Taliban forces. Since al-Qaeda was a non-State group, the conflict between the United States and al-Qaeda was outside the reach of the Geneva Conventions, the White House said. By contrast, since the Taliban were the de facto armed forces of Afghanistan, the Geneva Conventions did apply to the conflict between the U.S. and the Taliban. However, according to the White House, the Taliban forces did not meet the criteria set out in the Third Geneva Convention for attaining POW status. Therefore, in practice, all detainees from Afghanistan were "unlawful combatants" who did not deserve the privileges of prisoners of war.

Nevertheless, the White House proclaimed, the prisoners would receive "many POW privileges as a matter of policy." Included in the listed privileges which would be extended to the detainees held at Guantanamo were appropriate Muslim meals, opportunities to worship and correspond and send mail, subject, of course, to the security needs of the facility and the U.S. government. This limitation on the right of correspondence is permitted by Article 76 of the Convention.

As far as al-Qaeda is concerned, the decision to deny its members POW status seems perfectly acceptable. Al-Qaeda is little more than a criminal conspiracy directed against the western world. However, the decision to deny prisoner of war status to captured Taliban fighters has been more widely questioned.

To receive the protections of the POW Convention, detainees must fall into one of a set of specified categories. The first category is "members of the armed forces of a Party to the conflict." (Also included in this category are members of "militias or volunteer corps forming a part of such armed forces.") The Convention leaves it up to a State to decide who falls within its "armed forces." However, the general rule is that the force must be under responsible command, and be subject to an internal disciplinary system

Russian soldiers captured by Chechen fighters during the failed Russian assault on Grozny, being held at the Presidential Palace, December 1994.

which enforces compliance with the laws of war. Some experts also believe that there is an implicit requirement that forces wear distinguishing uniforms and carry their weapons openly.

A second category of people entitled to the protections of the Convention are those who are "members of other militias... belonging to a Party to the conflict..." However, to be covered the "other militias" are explicitly required to comply with the four conditions set out above. This provision was added to the Geneva Conventions in 1949 to cover partisan groups, such as those that had fought against the Axis powers in World War II.

Finally, some people who are not themselves combatants are entitled to prisoner of war status, if they are "persons who accompany the armed forces without actually being members thereof." This provision covers civilian contractors, as well as "embedded" war correspondents. To be covered the captive must be operating with the authorization of the armed force which they accompany. That force must also issue an identity card to the person accompanying the force.

If there is any doubt about whether an enemy fighter captured during armed conflict is entitled to POW status, Article 5 of the Convention authorizes a special tribunal to rule on the matter. These so-called "Article 5 Tribunals" are administrative bodies and not criminal courts.

Going back to the war in Afghanistan, the members of Taliban forces who were captured during the conflict there might be seen as belonging to the first category. However, the administration argued that even if the Taliban comprised the armed forces of Afghanistan, it did not comply with the laws of war. Because the Taliban as a whole was therefore disqualified from claiming POW status, the administration argued, there was no need to hold special hearings to determine eligibility in each individual case.

An important difference between prisoners of war and other detainees is that POWs are immune from prosecution for lawful acts of war. They may however be prosecuted for war crimes, as long as they are tried according to the same procedures as would be used in domestic proceedings against soldiers from the country holding them. (The treaty also provides that even if a prisoner of war is convicted he retains the benefits of the Convention.) By contrast, other detainees may face prosecution for acts like killing an enemy soldier, which could be charged as murder under the domestic law of the State involved.

Another significant obligation imposed by the POW Convention is that all prisoners should be released and repatriated "without delay" after the end of active hostilities, unless they have been sentenced for war crimes or are facing trial. This is also true of other captives held in connection with an international armed conflict. In the case of Afghanistan, it can be argued that the war between the United States and Afghanistan ended after the installation of the Karzai government, and that the fighting that continues in the country is now an internal conflict with outside forces participating on the government side. Therefore it seems that detainees from Afghanistan should be returned to the custody of the Afghan government, and the United States is reportedly negotiating with the Afghan government to arrange such a transfer.

In the case of Iraq, the picture is somewhat different. People captured in Iraq who were part of the armed forces of Iraq clearly were POWs, and the U.S. government recognized this. Saddam Hussein was held as a prisoner of war by coalition forces before being put on trial by the Iraqi authorities for violations of international law. However, the establishment of the new government of Iraq in 2004 could be seen as marking the end of the legal conflict between America and Iraq. As in Afghanistan, the fighting in Iraq after this date should probably be seen as an internal conflict. There is no provision for POW status in internal conflicts, and Iraqis who continue the fight by attacking the U.S. forces in Iraq can be prosecuted for their acts either by the Iraqi government for violations of Iraqi law or by the U.S. for certain violations of American law. Several Iraqis have been prosecuted in Iraqi courts for offenses directed against the coalition forces. Although the United States continues to detain suspected insurgents in Iraq, it does so with the consent of the country's sovereign government and on the basis of a UN Security Council resolution, rather than as a participant in an international conflict.

A POW may well be the "least unfortunate" kind of prisoner. But not every captive is a POW. The goal of the law here is to make compliance with the law a prerequisite for the protections of the Convention. In short, those who violate the law should expect fewer protections from it.
(See **combatant status**; **due process**; **soldiers, rights of**.)

Prisoners of War, Non-Repatriation of

By Mark Huband

Mustapha Sirji swayed from one foot to the other. The towering mud walls of the Martyr Mohammed Lasyad Prison rose around us out of the Algerian desert.

Forgotten by the country that had sent him to war, he had spent, by the late 1990s when I met him, over twenty years locked in a desert jail which

Moroccan POWS were held by the Polisario Front for more than 20 years, among the longest-held POWs in the world. The last were freed Aug. 18, 2005. Photo from near Tindouf, Algeria, April 2002.

echoed with the sound of prayers as the burning sun sank beneath the barren Sahara outside.

"I ask the others if I am a human being here, or if I am an animal," he said, his eyes glazed. "We are Muslims. We believe in God. We pray. We are not rocks. We are living in this inferno. We are the forgotten victims of this drama. We have our lives to live. I have lost my youth. We have lost our families. Every time we receive letters somebody has died. How long is this going to go on? Please, will somebody notice us?"

Mustapha Sirji and his comrades were among twenty-three hundred Moroccan soldiers taken prisoner by the Polisario Front, a guerrilla army that fought for more than fifteen years to establish an independent state in the former Spanish colony of Spanish Sahara. Spain actually granted independence in 1975, but within days neighboring Morocco occupied the mineral-rich region. And the war that cost Mustapha Sirji his freedom began.

The conflict reached a stalemate a long time ago, and there has been no fighting for many years. The Polisario withdrew to small strips of territory along Western Sahara's eastern and southern borders, and across the border, in neighboring Algeria. But in the absence of a settlement of the underlying dispute they took their Moroccan prisoners with them, and efforts to arrange their release were repeatedly frustrated.

Five prisons in the Tindouf region of Algeria were home to the Moroccan POWs. The Mohammed Lasyad Prison, said to be the most decent of the five, was a large sandy courtyard surrounded on three sides by a twenty-foot wall. On the fourth side was a rocky outcrop. Dome-shaped huts lined the wall, built by the prisoners themselves. The courtyard was where the five hundred men did what they had been doing every day for twenty years: praying and playing football.

"Nobody really wants to talk with you," Mustapha Sirji told me. "We have had a few visitors before—some people brought food—but they leave and we never hear from them again. They all say they will raise our case with the outside world. But they never do, and so we are left alone again. Forgotten again."

Under international humanitarian law, the continued imprisonment of Mustapha Sirji and his comrades was a grave breach, that is, a war crime. Article 118 of the Third Geneva Convention of 1949 states that prisoners "shall be released and repatriated without delay after the cessation of active hostilities." The obligation is restated in the 1977 Additional Protocol I, which lists the "unjustifiable delay in the repatriation of prisoners of war or civilians" as a grave breach; this means there is **universal jurisdiction** over violations. The obligation on any side holding prisoners to arrange for their prompt release and repatriation does not depend on a formal peace treaty having been signed, although a belligerent is entitled to make sure that its adversary has genuinely stopped fighting and does not intend to resume the conflict; otherwise, repatriating prisoners would be analogous to reinforcing the enemy's army. If that risk is not present, under international law the duty to repatriate is clear. Prisoners, however, do have the right, in the view of the International Committee of the Red Cross (ICRC), to refuse forcible repatriations. Such situations arise where a change of government in the POW's home State might make return dangerous.

That was not the situation of the Moroccan POWs. They were desperate to go home. And yet, despite the fact that a cease-fire between Morocco and the Polisario Front was agreed to in September 1991, the Moroccan prisoners of the Polisario languished in camps like Martyr Mohammed Lasyad Prison, just as Iranian prisoners spent years in detention in Iraq after the end of the Iran-Iraq war.

Finally in the early years of the new century the plight of the Moroccan prisoners was resolved. In response to diplomatic initiatives involving several countries, the Polisario held a series of prisoner releases, culminating in the return of the final group of POWs to Morocco in August 2005. At the same time a peace proposal was developed at the United Nations that called for an interim period of self-rule in Western Sahara followed by a referendum. The Polisario ultimately accepted a version of the plan as a basis for negotiations, but Morocco rejected it and the political stalemate continues.

Private Military Firms

By P.W. Singer

"They shoot people, and someone else has to deal with the aftermath. It happens all over the place. These guys run loose in this country and do stupid stuff. There's no authority over them, so you can't come down on them hard when they escalate force." Thus Brigadier General Karl Horst, deputy commander of the U.S. 3rd Infantry Division, described the challenge of private military firms. Horst's unit was responsible for security in and around Baghdad. Between May and July of 2005, he tracked at least a dozen shootings of civilians by private military contractors.

When we think of war and who fights it, we imagine a world of men in uniform, warriors fighting for their country, motivated by the ideals of patriotism. The reality of warfare in the 21st century is far different. The wars of today are fought by men, women, and even children. They fight for organizations that range from terrorist groups to drug cartels and are motivated by causes that range from religion and ethnic grievance to the good old-fashioned profit motive.

Within this witches' brew of 21st-century challenges to humanitarian law, one of the more notable, but least understood, developments has been the newly emergent global trade in hired military services, better known as the "privatized military industry." In this new industry, firms are supplying not the goods of warfare, but the services of war, substituting many of the professional functions of the traditional state military.

Privatized military firms (or PMFs) are corporate bodies that specialize in selling military skills. First emerging in the 1990s, firms in the industry have performed every task that militaries used to monopolize: conducting tactical combat operations, strategic planning, intelligence, operational and logistics support, troop training, technical assistance, etc. While soldiers for hire certainly have a lengthy historic pedigree, extending from the free companies of the Hundred Years War, the Condottieri of the 1500s, and the army of von Wallenstein in the Thirty Years War, to "Les Affreux," of the 1960s Congo, PMFs take the trade into the 21st century. Organized as business entities and structured along traditional corporate lines (many even have public stock and boards of directors), they represent the corporate evolution of the mercenary trade.

These PMFs range from small consulting firms, comprised of retired generals, to immense transnational corporations that can do everything from provide hundreds of armed commandos to supply the logistics for entire military operations. These firms presently operate in over fifty countries, from rich states like Saudi Arabia to poor states like Sierra Leone. Even the U.S. military, arguably the most powerful armed force in history, has become one of the prime clients of the industry. The U.S. Defense Department entered into over 3,000 contracts with U.S.-based firms in the period from 1994 to 2002, estimated at a contract value of more than $300 billion.

These numbers boomed in the Iraq War that started in 2003. With American forces over-extended by poor planning, by 2005, over 80 firms were operating in Iraq, employing more than 20,000 private, non-Iraqi personnel to carry out what would have been military functions in the past (tens of thousands of additional civilian contractors provided reconstruction and oil services). To put this into context, the private military industry has contributed more forces to Iraq than the rest of the U.S.-led coalition combined (meaning President Bush's proclaimed "coalition of the willing" was really more of a "coalition of the billing"). With these greater numbers came greater costs. By October 2006, at least 359 foreign contractors had been killed in Iraq and as many as 3,000 had been injured. Again, such numbers are more than the rest of the coalition combined and, indeed, are more than any single U.S. Army division.

The result is that private military firms have become indispensable to major and many minor military operations. But they have also brought new challenges. For example, some of the most controversial aspects of the Iraq war also involved PMFs. These included the allegations of war profiteering that encircled Vice President Dick Cheney's old Halliburton firm, the brutal killing of Blackwater employees at Fallujah by Iraqi insurgents that was cap-

Employees of a European private military firm are pictured on either side of an Iraqi "choof" or watcher, stationed every fifth kilometer along a major oil pipeline. February 2004.

tured on TV and the widespread fighting—and lawsuits—that followed, and the role of CACI and Titan contractors working as military interrogators and translators at the Abu Ghraib prison. Outside of Iraq, private militaries have been involved in everything from a "rent a coup" scandal in Equatorial Guinea to allegations of civilian killings in Colombia.

These private military employees operate in the military domain, but they are not part of the military and remain outside the military chain of command. They are civilians, yet by the military tasks they take on, they are not simply innocent bystanders or noncombatants accompanying the armed forces, as civilians are usually conceived of. In legal terms, civilians do not have the right to take a direct part in hostilities. They are entitled to use force only in self-defense or to prevent crimes. The distinction is not always easy to draw, given the chaotic circumstances of modern conflict and the breakdown of formal frontlines, and in many cases PMF employees operate in a grey area—as when heavily armed contractors are hired to escort convoys through insurgent territory, or when contractors serve on naval warships.

But perhaps even more worrying is the problem of controlling and regulating private contractors' actions in a warzone where normal peacetime codes of conduct are inapplicable and the local law has collapsed. Contractors sometimes lack proper training or appropriate rules of engagement, and are not subject to military systems of accountability to enforce these anyway. As civilians, they cannot be court-martialed by State militaries. Some States (including the United States) have passed laws giving domestic courts jurisdiction over crimes committed by military contractors overseas, but implementation of such laws has been completely absent, and they do not take account of what is a globalized marketplace, with most employees operating extra-territorially. So in reality they have proven mythical. After three years of operations in Iraq, not one PMF employee had been charged with any crime, which means the market either found 20,000 perfect angels in the midst of a warzone or the gap was letting crimes go past.

With little effective way of enforcing law at the international level (given the limited reach of the new International Criminal Court), this leaves an incredible vacuum in the law that can mean crimes go unpunished. The lack of definition also means that PMFers lack legal protections if captured by the enemy. Indeed, as Phillip Carter, a legal writer and former U.S. Army officer, has noted, "Legally speaking, they [military contractors in Iraq] actually fall into the same grey area as the unlawful combatants detained at Guantanamo Bay." At the same time, there is little in the law to define such basic corporate practice questions as to who can work for private militaries, what rules they should operate under, and who private militaries can work for. To put it bluntly, a circus faces more regulation and inspection than a private military firm.

The confluence of military and business interests represented by the private military industry is a defining change in both warfare and politics. Privatization in the military space, as in all other realms, is not necessarily a terrible thing. It carries both advantages and disadvantages. These must constantly be weighed and mitigated through effective policy and smart business sense. Still, there has to be a certain amount of discomfort at the corporatization of war. Dwight Eisenhower, warning of the "military-industrial complex" back in the 1950s, could never have imagined it would go so far. (See **mercenaries**.)

Property, Civilian, Destruction of

By Amira Hass

Three architectural styles of buildings and two types of ruins dip among plump, round-cheeked cactuses and elegant almond trees, densely filling a mellow valley before climbing, scattered, over the hill slopes. These buildings tell the story of Beit Mirsim, a Palestinian village just touching the southern part of the Green Line (the 1948 armistice border between the West Bank/Jordan and Israel). They tell not only the story of destruction by the victorious Israeli Army, but also of the continuing effects of the Six-Day War of 1967 on people's lives.

There is also a subtext to be read here: that of the persistent Israeli urge to "clear" Palestinians away, to make them "move eastward," and leave forever their childhood landscapes. And there is the other side of this coin: Palestinian resilience.

During the Six-Day War, an Israeli Army unit ordered the villagers of Beit Mirsim to evacuate their homes, which were situated hard by the Jordanian border. Half of the village's agricultural lands had already been lost to Israel after the war of 1948, and this time the villagers had refused to leave the hills overlooking the village. To this day, the villagers can recall clearly how, in a matter of hours, the valley was filled with the heart-breaking sounds and scenes of explosives tearing away their homes made of big, heavy stones, with arched windows and doors. Israel's Defense Forces (IDF) destroyed houses in several villages adjacent to the Green Line or in the eastern Jordan Valley. Only in Beit Mirsim and a neighboring village did people return.

The laws of armed conflict permit the deliberate destruction of property under certain circumstances. Article 52 of the 1977 Additional Protocol I to the Geneva Conventions sanctions such attacks, but only on "those objects which by their nature, location, purpose or use make an effective contribution to military action and whose total or partial destruction, capture or neutralization, in the circumstances ruling at the time, offers a definite military advantage." This provision establishes the standard for assessing when military forces are entitled to make a direct attack on ostensibly civilian objects and property for the purpose of destroying them.

In the view of the villagers of Beit Mirsim, their homes neither offered the IDF's Jordanian adversaries definite military advantages nor impeded Israel's own military plans in that particular sector. In their view, the destruction of their homes had little to do with concrete military advantages at the time. They believe their homes were destroyed in order to cause them to leave the zone permanently, not just for the duration of the battle. The destruction of homes in order to persuade the civilian population to flee permanently violates the laws of armed conflict.

It is not known whether Israeli commanders at the time of the destruction would have agreed that it served no concrete military purpose. As a general rule, however, under battlefield circumstances, in which concrete military advantages must be weighed against **collateral damage**, under conditions of uncertainty and imperfect information, and often with great

Without any warning or explanation, the Israel Defense Forces razed the Bedouin hamlet of Wad al Amaher. July 2001.

speed, there has been great hesitation to second-guess the judgment of commanders who must make this determination.

Since it is anything but clear that the destruction of Beit Mirsim offered definite military advantage to Israeli forces, it can be argued that what the Israelis did was a grave breach of the Geneva Conventions and Additional Protocol I. According to the Hague Conventions of 1899 and 1907—which the Israeli Supreme Court has ruled applies to the West Bank and the Gaza Strip—it is illegal "to destroy or seize the enemy's property, unless such destruction or seizure be imperatively demanded by the necessities of war." They also state that "private property... must be respected."

Even if there was a military justification for the demolitions, they would still have had to comply with the rule of **proportionality**, which says the harm caused to civilians must not be excessive in relation to the military advantage anticipated from the attack.

Another legal basis for evaluating the destruction of houses at Beit Mirsim is the Fourth Geneva Convention, which expressly forbids destruction of civilian property under conditions of occupation except as justified by **military necessity**. Israel states that the *de jure* applicability of the Fourth Convention is "doubtful" and since 1967 it applies the "humanitarian provisions" of the Fourth Convention to the occupied territories, without specifying which provisions. No other country recognizes Israel's selective interpretation of the 1949 Conventions. The Fourth Convention holds that "extensive destruction and appropriation of property, not justified by military necessity and carried out unlawfully and wantonly" is a grave breach.

Nonetheless, the issue at Beit Mirsim, as in any instance of what seems

Ibrahim, 11, in front of his house which was targeted by the Israel Defense Forces'
artillery in the middle of the night before. Gaza Strip, July 2001.

at first glance like a possible case of destruction, is that of military necessity. And because commanders can always make such a claim that the
exigencies of war compelled them to act as they did, enforcing prohibitions
against destruction of enemy property will always be problematic, and their
claims of military necessity, or, for that matter, their entirely legal wish to
pursue military advantage, will be difficult to refute.

Military necessity or no military necessity, the people of Beit Mirsim are
tenacious about their homes and village. They were so persistent about staying there that in 1967 Defense Minister Moshe Dayan personally went to
negotiate with them.

"General Dayan came to speak with us," recalled Abu Sherif, now seventy. "At last he agreed that we build one room, in place of each demolished
house. We told him: 'But General Dayan, one room is not enough for a family
of ten.' And he replied, 'We hope that things will improve and that with the
course of time you will be able to build more.'" The second architectural generation was then born: tiny one-room constructions, made of smaller stones.

After the 1993 Oslo agreement between the Palestine Liberation
Organization and the Israeli government, villagers began building once
again—without waiting for redeployment of Israeli troops or Israeli building
permits which never come. They built a third generation of houses, spacious,
ugly-looking, made of naked concrete. In the course of 1997, fifteen of the
thirty families still living there received orders to stop "illegal" construction
and demolish their own houses. One was blown up—smashed, gray concrete
blocks, a broken tap, cramped and twisted black iron bars which crawl
upward out of the rubble. Construction was then stopped.

Proportionality, Principle of

By Horst Fischer

The principle of proportionality is embedded in almost every national legal system and underlies the international legal order. Its function in domestic law is to relate means to ends. In armed conflict, the principle is used in two distinct ways.

First, it is used in *jus ad bellum* to judge the lawfulness of a military campaign undertaken in self-defense. According to a long-standing principle of customary law, any use of armed force by a State in self-defense must be both necessary and proportionate, meaning that the use of force must be limited to the neutralization of the attack against which the State is defending itself. For example, in its 2005 decision in the case of the *Democratic Republic of Congo v. Uganda*, the International Court of Justice ruled that Uganda's seizure of airports and towns deep inside Congolese territory "would not seem proportionate to the series of transborder attacks it claimed had given rise to the right of self-defense."

Secondly, the principle of proportionality is used in *jus in bello* to determine the lawfulness of an armed attack against a military objective that causes civilian casualties. Proportionality provides a standard for assessing when a strike against a target that is itself legitimate is nevertheless disallowed because of the likely degree of **collateral damage**, i.e. civilian casualties or damage to civilian objects. The U.S. attack on the al-Amiriyah bunker in Baghdad in 1991, which was aimed to destroy a military target but cost many civilian lives, is a case in point. If the bunker was a military objective in which civilians were sheltering, the principle of proportionality would come into play and determine if an attack against it was lawful.

As formulated in Additional Protocol I of 1977, attacks are prohibited if they "may be expected to cause incidental loss of civilian life, injury to civilians, damage to civilian objects, or a combination thereof, which would be excessive in relation to the concrete and direct military advantage anticipated." This creates a permanent obligation for military commanders to consider the likely results of the attack compared to the advantage anticipated. The target list has to be continuously updated as the conflict develops with special attention given to the safe movement of civilians. The attack on the al-Amiriyah bunker might have been illegal, if—which has never been proved—the United States did not follow carefully enough the movement of the civilians seeking shelter in Baghdad.

Some States ratifying Protocol I have stated that the concrete and direct military advantage anticipated from an attack can only be considered as a whole and not from isolated or particular parts of the attack. Article 85 defines an **indiscriminate attack** undertaken in the knowledge that it will cause excessive damage to the civilian population as a grave breach and therefore a war crime. The principle is hard to apply in war, still harder after an attack has occurred. But grossly disproportionate results will be seen as criminal by all belligerent parties and the world community.

"Terror attacks" and attacks which directly target civilians and civilian objects are prohibited in all cases, and the principle of proportionality does not come into play.

P

Protected Persons

By Heike Spieker

In international humanitarian law, individuals are accorded a range of "protections" from the effects of hostilities. Individuals accorded such "protections" are called "protected persons" within the specified limits of protection given them by international humanitarian law. They fall into several distinct categories. Historically the first group of individuals protected by international treaties were combatants and not civilians. Early treaties dealt with the treatment of the wounded, protections for medical personnel and facilities, and humane conditions for prisoners of war.

In 1949, the four Geneva Conventions enunciated the first comprehensive set of rules protecting combatants and noncombatants in international armed conflicts. The first three conventions referred to the protection of combatants and related personnel—wounded and sick in the field; wounded, sick, and

shipwrecked at sea; and prisoners of war—and the fourth to the protection of civilians. A combatant in simplest terms is a member of an armed force—a person who takes an active part in hostilities, who can kill, and who, in turn, is a lawful military target. A combatant can acquire the status of a protected person under a number of circumstances—for example, if captured or wounded.

The four conventions require that protected persons be humanely treated "without any adverse distinction founded on race, color, religion or faith, sex, birth or wealth, or any other similar criteria." Protected persons may not be willfully killed, injured, or used for medical experiments. Captured and detained persons must be given the food, clothing, shelter, and medical and spiritual care they require. No one may be deprived of the right to a fair trial. Protected persons may not be tortured, coerced, used as human shields or face collective punishments.

The conventions do allow for some distinctions. They provide that "women shall be treated with all the regard due to their sex," and that female prisoners of war have treatment equal to that given men. The Fourth Geneva Convention also provides that women be protected against "rape, enforced

Civilians are to be given general protection against dangers arising from military operations and from direct attacks against them as well as indiscriminate attacks. Sarajevo, outside the Academy of Fine Arts, 1992.

prostitution, or any form of indecent assault." Additionally, it establishes "particular protection and respect" for groups of individuals such as the wounded and sick, expectant mothers, aged persons, children, ministers of religion, and medical personnel.

The Fourth Geneva Convention further divides protected civilians into three categories: aliens in the territory of a party to the conflict, persons in occupied territory, and internees. These three groups are provided with protections that vary according to membership in one group or another, but all must be given the basic protection codified in Article 27: respect, protection, and humane treatment under all circumstances.

Additional Protocol I of 1977 supplies an ingredient missing from the Fourth Convention. Specifically, Article 51 states that any civilian "enjoys general protection against dangers arising from military operations" and forbids direct attacks against them as well as so-called indiscriminate attacks, which do not distinguish between civilians and combatants. Additional Protocol I also elaborates on Fourth Convention provisions that relief actions be undertaken if a civilian population is not adequately provided with the basic supplies essential to its survival. In addition some groups of people are granted special protection, such as children, women and journalists.

Civil Conflicts: The first explicit treaty provision covering protected persons in non-international armed conflicts—often called internal armed conflicts or civil conflicts—is found in Common Article 3 of the 1949 Geneva Conventions. The basic principle is to require humane treatment without adverse discrimination. It prohibits violence to life and person, the taking of hostages, and outrages upon personal dignity. The article calls for basic judicial and procedural guarantees and imposes an obligation to collect and care for the wounded and sick.

This principle of humane treatment under all circumstances is further developed in the 1977 Additional Protocol II, which extended to internal armed conflict many of the rules found in Protocol I and the 1949 Conventions. Protocol II covers the civilian population, both as a group and as individuals; the essence of the protection is the prohibition against making civilians the object of attack. Attacks are prohibited against dams, dikes, and nuclear power stations if they may result in severe civilian losses. Also banned are attacks on objects necessary for the survival of the civilian population. Additionally, terrorism and starvation of civilians are prohibited as methods of combat. So is forced displacement, unless undertaken for security or imperative military reasons. Relief operations are to be undertaken when the civilian population is suffering "undue hardship." An important caveat is that technically Protocol II applies only to internal armed conflicts in States that have ratified it, and only once the conflict has reached a certain threshold of intensity. Thus Common Article 3 is the applicable law for most instances of non-international armed conflict.

(See **civilians**, **illegal targeting of; hors de combat; sick and wounded**.)

Q,R

Quarter, Giving No

By John Burns

The ancient name for Sri Lanka, Serendip, long ago passed into English as the word "serendipity," meaning "the making of pleasant discoveries by accident." Lying off the southeastern coast of India, the island earned its name from European mariners who found on this lush, gentle island a sanctuary from the forbidding vastness of the Indian Ocean.

It has been a harsh irony of the past two decades that Sri Lanka, with its white beaches and scented uplands, has become synonymous with one of the world's most violent and merciless conflicts. In two separate civil wars, one still continuing and the other ended by the unremitting harshness of government forces in the early 1990s, at least 100,000 Sri Lankans have died. In a population of 19 million, the losses have been compared to those suffered by France and England in the century's two world wars. Even more horrifying, many thousands of the dead were slaughtered not in battlefield combat, but as a result of a take-no-prisoners tactic adopted by all sides.

In one of the wars, the Sri Lankan forces, representing the island's Sinhalese Buddhist majority, are fighting the Liberation Tigers of Tamil Eelam, who want a separate State in the north and east of the island for the predominantly Hindu Tamil minority. The second conflict, within the Sinhalese community, was between the government and the ultra-leftists of the Janatha Vimukthi Peramuna (JVP), which paralyzed large parts of central and southern Sri Lanka in 1988 and 1989. Prisoners who live to tell the tale have been a rarity in both conflicts.

The war between the government and the Tamil Tigers, with origins that go back to a savage outburst of anti-Tamil rioting that broke out in 1983, reached a cataclysmic moment in the small hours of July 19, 1996, at a remote spot in the northeast of the island in the bloodiest battle of the conflict. Desperate to regain the initiative after the loss six months earlier of their stronghold in the Jaffna Peninsula at the extreme north of the island, the Tamil Tigers attacked a strategic base of the government forces at Mullaitivu, a coastal outpost southeast of the peninsula.

Attacking from sea and land, waves of Tiger fighters, many of them young boys and girls barely into their teens press-ganged into suicide squads known as the Black Tigers, overran the base. By dawn, at least six hundred Tigers were dead, along with thirteen hundred government soldiers, the highest single casualty toll in the history of the conflict. After the Tigers withdrew, a relief column of government forces found not a single government soldier still alive.

The wounds of many of the dead, some clutching white flags of surrender, indicated they had been shot dead or blown apart by grenades at close range; hundreds of others appeared to have been herded together, doused with gasoline, and burned to death. What occurred at Mullaitivu, it seemed, was less a battle, at least in its concluding stages, than a massacre.

A distinguishing feature of the Sri Lankan fighting, and a cause of acute concern to international humanitarian organizations like Amnesty International and the International Committee of the Red Cross (ICRC), has been the rare occasions when the opposing forces have taken—or acknowledged having taken—prisoners. Fighters on both sides who have dared to speak candidly to human rights investigators and reporters have admitted that the rule, sometimes explicit in battle orders, more often understood, was that no enemy combatants were to be left alive.

Where prisoners have been taken, as often as not it has been to serve the ends of propaganda, not humanitarian concern, as when government forces have captured Tiger fighters as young as eleven and twelve and taken them to remand homes in Colombo where foreign television crews have been invited to film them as proof of the Tigers' use of children in combat. At times when they have sought respite from government military pressures, as they did with a six-month cease-fire that they later abrogated in 1994-1995, the Tigers have also held and exchanged prisoners.

But overall, the Sri Lankan fighting has been a chilling demonstration of the survival of a practice going back to the earliest recorded wars—a practice that became known as "giving no quarter" to an enemy (a phrase that literally

Soldiers patrol for mines and radio-controlled bombs in Mutur, Sri Lanka, June 2006.

meant denying shelter, but which came to mean denying the right of survival).

Although ancient history contains examples of generals ordering troops to spare soldiers defeated in battle, and even of attempts by early lawgivers to punish those judged too brutal with the enemy, modern efforts to ensure humane treatment of enemy fighters date back to the American Civil War, when President Lincoln, in 1863, promulgated what became known as the Lieber Code, a codification of the laws of armed conflict, which expressly forbade Union troops to give no quarter.

A conference in Brussels in 1874, attended by European powers in the aftermath of the Franco-Prussian war, eliminated what had been a major loophole in the Lieber Code, the so-called great straits provision, which allowed a soldier or a fighting unit to eliminate survivors of battle when their "own salvation" made taking prisoners impossible.

In 1949, the execution or elimination of defenseless soldiers was defined as one of the grave breaches of the laws of international armed

347

conflict in each of the four Geneva Conventions. In 1977, Additional Protocol I to the Geneva Conventions gave in Article 40 what many legal scholars regard as the most authoritative definition of the principle.

The article provides, among other things, that "a person who is recognized or who, in the circumstances, should be recognized to be *hors de combat*, shall not be made the object of attack." The article defines *hors de combat* as including those "in the power of an adverse party"; those who clearly express "an intention to surrender"; and those who have been "rendered unconscious or otherwise incapacitated by wounds or sickness" and are therefore incapable of defending themselves. In internal conflict, Article 3 common to the four Geneva Conventions binds parties to treat "humanely" soldiers who have laid down their arms, and those made *hors de combat* by sickness, wounds, detention, or any other cause.

In Sri Lanka, despite numerous assurances over the years, neither the government forces nor the Tamil Tigers seems to have cared that the practice

Mass grave from an attack on a bus, killing 64 civilians. The government blamed the LTTE, but the Tamil political organization denied responsibility. June 2006.

of eliminating defenseless enemy soldiers is a grave war crime. While a cease-fire agreed in 2002 led to a respite in the fighting and thus in violations of the law, major military operations were resumed in 2006 and followed a similar pattern to before. On the battlefield in Sri Lanka, it seems, there will continue to be no quarter given by either side, until one side or the other prevails in the war.

(See **executions, extrajudicial**; **protected persons**; **soldiers, rights of.**)

Red Cross/Red Crescent Emblem

By Christian Jennings

For the seven Burundian soldiers, the fire instructions and target designation were simple. The ambush party lay in the tall elephant grass at the side of the road in northern Burundi's Cibitoke Province. They were waiting for two white Toyota Land Cruisers, clearly marked on the hood, side panels, roof, and rear doors with the internationally recognized emblem of a red cross on a white background.

Ten minutes and dozens of Kalashnikov rounds later, one of the Land Cruisers was lying bullet-riddled in the ditch, and the three International Committee of the Red Cross (ICRC) delegates traveling inside were dead, one of them beheaded; but the second vehicle had managed to escape.

The attack on two vehicles from the ICRC on June 4, 1996, on the road between the Burundian villages of Rugombo and Mugina, was one of the most blatant contemporary violations of the symbol of the Red Cross. Subsequent investigations both by journalists present in Cibitoke that day and by the ICRC have established that the Swiss delegates were targeted specifically.

Article 38 of the First Geneva Convention of 1949 establishes the red cross on a white background as the emblem of the medical services of the armed forces. All permanent medical personnel or chaplains are required to wear it, as a waterproof armband on the left arm, and are entitled to display the flag. It is also the emblem of the Red Cross and Red Crescent Movement, the National Societies, the ICRC, and the International Federation of Red Cross and Red Crescent Societies. Their personnel can use the symbol at all times.

The Red Cross "is the emblem of the Convention, and therefore an emblem of protection. It allows its bearers to venture onto the battlefield to carry out their humanitarian tasks," the ICRC said in its Commentary on the Additional Protocols of 1977. The nature of the symbol as a "protective emblem" means that an attack on vehicles and individuals carrying that emblem is a serious violation of the Geneva Conventions and a war crime.

The protection applies as well in internal conflicts. Additional Protocol II of 1977, which governs internal armed conflict, specifies in Article 12 that the "distinctive emblem shall be respected in all circumstances."

All indications were that the Burundian military specifically targeted the two ICRC vehicles because of the nature of their humanitarian activities in the country: at the time of the incident, the ICRC was the only humanitarian organization working in Cibitoke. Its staff was consequently witness to massive abuses of the civilian population by both the Tutsi military and Hutu rebels, including mass killings, forced displacement and rape. Also, as the army claimed, "they were feeding the rebels."

The incident raises doubt whether the Red Cross or Red Crescent emblem provides any form of protection to its bearer in the complex ethnic and national conflicts that have proliferated on the African continent. The characteristic of such conflicts is a multiplicity of factions, dominated by militias or warlords who show no respect for international humanitarian law. Incidents of abuse of the emblem abound. An ICRC transport plane was fired on in Zaire in 1996 as it brought in a mobile hospital to Uvira. One antiaircraft round actually hit the center of the Red Cross emblem on the fuselage. During the Rwandan genocide of 1994, Tutsis were on occasion dragged from Red Cross ambulances and slaughtered by Hutu extremists.

A different but equally serious war crime is the abuse of the Red Cross emblem. The Geneva Conventions and Additional Protocols state that the emblem "may not be employed" except to protect medical units and establishments, and using it to deceive someone into thinking he is safe and then attacking or capturing him constitutes "perfidious use" and is a grave breach if it is intentional and causes the death of or serious injury to an adversary. Transporting weapons in a vehicle marked with a Red Cross is thus a grave breach. In Kosovo in June 1998, refugees fleeing to Albania reported that Serb forces fired at them from helicopters bearing Red Cross markings, also a grave breach.

The ICRC is still struggling over how to address another abuse: when an

Ambulances with Red Cross markings, loading casualties in the village of Qana, were attacked by an Israeli helicopter gunship on July 23, 2006. Civilians and Red Cross paramedics were among those wounded.

International Red Cross society takes a lead role in committing war crimes, particularly unrecognized national societies. During the war in Bosnia, Ljiljana Karadzic, the wife of political leader Radovan Karadzic, who has been indicted for genocide, ran the Bosnian Serb Red Cross. That organization—unrecognized by the ICRC—was involved in the ethnic cleansing of non-Serbs and ran at least one concentration camp, at Trnoplje, near Prijedor, where internees were killed, tortured, and raped.

The Red Cross emblem has aroused controversy for almost as long as it has been around. First adopted in the 1864 Geneva Convention, the red cross on a white background was formally described in the 1949 Geneva Conventions as intended to be a "compliment to Switzerland," formed by reversing the Swiss federal colors: a white cross on a red background. Turkey, asserting that Muslim soldiers found the cross offensive, unilaterally began using a red crescent in 1876, and this was accepted in the 1929 update of the Geneva Convention along with the now unused "red lion and sun" for Iran. Israel sought approval of the red shield of David, a six-pointed star, at the 1949 Conference that produced the current Geneva Conventions. ICRC officials feared it would lead to a flood of new national and religious symbols and already had requests for recognition of the red flame, shrine, bow, palm, wheel, trident, cedar, and mosque. One delegate suggested a red heart. All such proposals were rejected for fear that abandoning a universally recognized symbol would endanger human lives. The ICRC did not officially recognize societies that used unauthorized symbols: from the red shield of David to the green cross of the Cruz Verde, a renegade national society set up in El Salvador in 1980.

However in December 2005 a diplomatic conference of signatory countries to the Geneva Conventions formally adopted a 3rd Additional Protocol approving the adoption of a new Red Crystal emblem. The emblem was chosen for its neutrality—it has no national, religious or cultural connotations, although national societies can incorporate existing symbols within the Crystal's center. Following the adoption of the Red Crystal, the Israeli national society, the Magen David Adom, and the Palestinian Red Crescent Society were recognized by the ICRC and admitted into the International Federation.

The ICRC withdrew its expatriate staff from Burundi after the killing of its delegates in 1996. The Burundian military led an inquiry into the ambush, and immediately blamed Hutu extremists. Those who allegedly took part in the ambush say that the Burundian military officer who led the official inquiry also set up the ambush. After long discussions with the Burundian government, the ICRC resumed operations in the country in 1999.

Refoulement

By David Rieff

"We cannot return to Rwanda," the young man in the sweat-stained Denver Broncos T-shirt told me earnestly. "We are Hutus, you see, and were we to do so we would surely be killed."

It was a hot day in the early fall of 1994, and we were standing on the grounds of the cathedral in the center of Goma in what was then eastern Zaire. So great was the crush of people that it was hard to hear everything he was saying. And his friends constantly interrupted him. "We can't be sent back," one of them declared. "That would be immoral. We would be killed." "Not just immoral," a third young man added, "it would be illegal. A UNHCR [United Nations High Commissioner for Refugees] official told us that only this morning. We cannot be sent back. That would be refoulement."

There was a hush after the word was uttered. It was this prohibition against refoulement, which means the forced return of a person to a country where he or she faces persecution, that provided for these destitute Hutus their only possible protection against being killed. Defeated on the battle-field, decimated by the cholera epidemic that had exacted a fierce toll from them when they had first arrived from Rwanda, they had discovered the saving grace of **refugee** law, and repeated its provisions like a mantra.

"We are refugees. We cannot be made to go back home," the young man said. "Would you be willing to return to Rwanda if you were in our place?"

The answer to that was easy enough, but the reasons were far more complicated than the refugees wanted to admit. Of the more than 2 million people who fled Rwanda in the aftermath of the genocide of the spring and early summer of 1994 in which between 500,000 and 1 million Tutsis and liberal Hutus were killed, tens of thousands (at a conservative estimate) were either soldiers and officials of the defeated Hutu regime. Many thousands more had been caught up in the frenzy of killing and were guilty of murdering their Tutsi neighbors. But hundreds of thousands of others had played no role in the genocide including thousands of children, many born in the UNHCR-administered refugee camps.

Separating those who were not entitled to refugee status from those who were was an impossible task for UNHCR officials, whose experience lay more in trying to secure the protections refugees are entitled to under international law than in separating legitimate refugees from soldiers who had crossed the border, or from criminals who had committed crimes in Rwanda and whose return there would have been an act of justice, not a violation of international law. The United Nations Convention Relating to the Status of Refugees and its 1967 Additional Protocol stipulated that refugees could not be returned to a place where they faced persecution. But surely its architects had never imagined a situation like the one that occurred in Goma.

Previously, most instances of refoulement involved individuals fleeing across an international border, or, in some cases, moving on to a third country, and claiming that, were they sent home, they would face persecution. An Iraqi Kurd arriving at the Frankfurt airport and being sent home, a Haitian making her way to Miami in a leaky boat and being towed back to Port-au-Prince by a U.S. Coast Guard cutter—these are the instances of refoulement over which international law has some intellectual and moral purchase. In this context, it is possible to talk about the requirements for what constitutes "persecution" within the meaning of the refugee convention; in practice, these requirements differ in interpretation from country to country, but in principle any person who can legitimately claim refugee status is protected from refoulement. Only when a person ceases to be a refugee does the rule against refoulement cease to apply. The real debate is when a refugee gets the right. Are illegal aliens covered? Some countries believe they are; others do not. Does a person have to enter a country officially to get refugee status and the accompanying protection against refoulement? Again, the opinions of international lawyers and governments differ.

What became clear in Goma was that in instances of mass migration — where children and murderers arrive in a great mass, and separating them is neither easy nor safe—the law is very hard to use, and harder still to use appropriately. Nobody in those camps wanted to return to Rwanda; many had

Attacks by the Tutsi-led Rwandan military break the stranglehold of the Hutu militia on the camps in the Congo, and a flood of Hutu refugees begins the long journey home to Rwanda. 1997.

killed before, and there was no reason to suppose they would not kill again.

For UNHCR, it was better to err on the side of maintaining its protection mandate and the prohibition against refoulement than to send back people who feared persecution in a Rwanda where power had changed hands; even if doing so meant, in practical terms, allowing mass murderers to claim the rights of innocent refugees. For those who wanted the Rwandan crisis to be brought to a close, and saw in the refugee camps little more than a safe haven for those who had perpetrated the genocide and their dependents, the prohibition against refoulement seemed like madness.

For two years, UNHCR's view prevailed. Then, the Rwandan Army struck at the camps. Most refugees were forced back across the border. It was an unhappy solution to a problem for which legal definitions of refugee status and legal prohibitions against refoulement only serve as poor guides.

Refugees, Rights of

By David Rieff

Two emblematic figures, the exile and the refugee, loom large in our consciousness at the beginning of this new century as at the end of the last. Vast refugee flows have become a feature of the contemporary world. Part of this can be attributed to the fact that it is easier to cross borders now than it was, say, 150 years ago. People have always wanted to move away from danger zones; today, whatever the risks, they have the means to do so. As a result, when Hurricane Mitch devastated Honduras in 1998, many predicted that within a matter of months Honduran refugees would pour into the United States.

The Honduran refugees were fleeing a natural disaster and, as such, were something of an anomaly, since refugees from natural disasters constitute only a small percentage of the 34 million refugees and displaced people in the

R

world. When most people think of refugees they usually think of the victims of political repression, as in East Timor, religious persecution, as in Tibet, or of civilians fleeing a war zone in which they have become the targets, as in a dozen conflicts from the Democratic Republic of Congo to Kosovo.

Of course, there is nothing new about repression, and the question of whether war has grown more barbarous in the twentieth century remains a controversial one. Those who, in the aftermath of World War II, devised the international humanitarian law (IHL) on refugees seemed to have believed that it had. So do those who have spent time in such killing zones as Bosnia, South Sudan, and the Great Lakes region of Africa. There, civilians are more often than not the preferred targets of the belligerents, and every villager caught in these maelstroms is, when viewed in a certain light, a potential refugee.

Perhaps this is why Sadako Ogata, the United Nations High Commissioner for Refugees, once observed that "refugees are the symptoms of the ills of an age"—our age. In almost every crisis that has plagued or baffled us since the end of the Cold War, from Tajikistan to Burundi, the refugee issue has been at the center. There has been no escaping it, and, it seems, no resolving it.

This is not because of an absence of laws, but, rather, a lack of imple-

Carrying her meager household possessions a refugee woman scans the skies for attacking war planes. Tigre, Ethiopia, 1985.

R

mentation. Indeed, if the political will of the powerful nations of the world matched the legal protections that already exist for refugees, many of the cruelest tragedies of the last part of the twentieth century might have been greatly diminished. A raft of treaties passed in the aftermath of World War II, and, half a century later, the accumulating weight of customary law guarantees refugee rights. Unlike in the case, say, of internally displaced persons (the distinction is that a refugee is a person who crosses an international border), refugees enjoy a wide array of rights and protections including the right to certain kinds of legal aid and material assistance. Compared to what should be, the situation of refugees in the world today is appalling; compared to what it would be without IHL, it is at least not hopeless. The most important laws concerning refugees are the Fourth Geneva Convention of 1949, the 1977 First Additional Protocol to the Geneva Conventions, and the 1951 UN Convention Relating to the Status of Refugees. The Geneva Conventions required a certain humane standard of treatment for civilians who do not enjoy diplomatic status. The Fourth Convention granted refugees the right not to be returned to the country where they faced danger or could legitimately claim that they would be subject to religious or political persecution. Additional Protocol I extended the standard for civilian protection set in the 1949 Geneva Conventions to include all civilians regardless of their nationality.

The UN Convention Relating to the Status of Refugees defines who refugees are and how they are to be treated. For the most part, the guarantees the convention grants are the basic human rights outlined in other international legal instruments. Refugees are not to be returned to the place where they face persecution, nor, except on grounds of national security, are they to be expelled without due process. They are not to be treated as illegal aliens (a key right, particularly in Western Europe and North America where the authorities routinely try to claim that people claiming refugee status are really economic migrants). Their right to move about in their country of asylum is not to be unnecessarily restricted, and they are to be given identity papers if they do not have them.

In a world awash in refugees, where people in rich countries feel overwhelmed by the press of economic migrants, legal and illegal, and where people in poor countries in areas adjacent to conflict zones have neither the resources nor the expertise to deal with vast refugee flows (2 million Rwandan refugees crossed the border into Zaire in less than a week in the summer of 1994), this has meant that where refugees have been concerned, the situation has grown more and more difficult. In particular, the burdens on the main international organization charged with protecting refugees, the Office of the UN High Commissioner for Refugees, have become excruciating. More generally, the gap between the law and realities on the ground is greater in the area of refugee rights than almost any other. Perhaps that gap is an emblem of failure. But many refugee advocates say that it gives us the means actually to make the ideals of refugee protection a reality, whereas if no such body of law existed, and the idea of protection had not been enshrined within it, the situation would be even more dire than it is.

(See **internal displacement; refoulement; victims, rights of.**)

Reprisal

By Frits Kalshoven

When a belligerent party is hurt by conduct on the part of its adversary that it regards as a grave breach or systematic encroachment of the laws of armed conflict, one possibility is to retaliate by means of an action that itself violates the same body of law. While recourse to such retaliatory action can be arbitrary and in total disregard of any constraints, rules of customary law have developed in the past that provide the limits within which retaliation could be regarded as a legitimate reprisal. The main elements of this customary "right of reprisal" are: subsidiarity (failure of all other available means), notice (formal warning of the planned action), proportionality (the damage and suffering inflicted on the adverse party not to exceed the level of damage and suffering resulting from its unlawful conduct), temporary character (termination of the reprisal when the adversary stops violating the law).

A reprisal may be "in kind" (violating the same or a narrowly related rule of the laws of armed conflict) or "not in kind" (violating a nonrelated rule). In either case, the reprisal need not and usually cannot be directed against those persons on the adverse side who are responsible for the unlawful conduct, and hence tends mainly to affect people who are "innocent" of that conduct. Also, the adversary often regards an alleged reprisal as a plainly unlawful act that in turn justifies reprisals, leading to a spiral of increasingly serious damage and suffering.

These features have led to a trend to ban reprisals wherever possible. As a result, all four Geneva Conventions of 1949 categorically prohibit reprisals against the persons and objects they are designed to protect. Likewise, Article 20, which concludes the part of Additional Protocol I of 1977 on the wounded, sick, and shipwrecked, prohibits reprisals against the persons and objects protected by that part.

While these bans are generally accepted as entirely justified, the provisions in Articles 51 through 55 of Additional Protocol I prohibiting reprisals against civilians and civilian objects are highly controversial, and some States have entered reservations to their treaty ratifications. A recent example of a reserving State is the United Kingdom, which has formulated its reservation in terms that would permit it to undertake customary "in kind" reprisals.

Additional Protocol II of 1977 is silent on the matter of reprisals. This should not however be interpreted as a right for parties to an internal armed conflict to resort to retaliatory action; the better view is that essential requirements of humanity accepted for international armed conflict apply by way of analogy in internal armed conflicts as well.

(See **protected persons; reprisal killings.**)

R

Reprisal Killings

By Kenneth Anderson

In 1944, following the Allied landings at Normandy, French resistance partisans began operating openly and on a large scale against German forces. Organized into the French Forces of the Interior (FFI), they were in contact with the Allied command and the Gaullist Provisional Government of France, although they operated under command independent from those forces. By wearing insignia visible at a distance, carrying their arms openly, operating under responsible command, and adhering to the laws of armed conflict, the FFI qualified as combatants as defined by the 1929 Geneva Convention.

The Germans, however, did not recognize the FFI as legal **combatants**. They took the view that, following the 1940 armistice, France was no longer at war with Germany, and so its citizens in the FFI were criminals, not combatants. The FFI for its part claimed that the Franco-German armistice had been breached and hostilities had resumed. By their reasoning, French forces fighting according to the 1929 rules had to be granted combatant rights, including prisoner of war status for captured fighters. Because Germany did not view the FFI as legal combatants, it killed numbers of them out of hand, by summary execution. On the day after the Normandy landings, for example, the Germans shot fifteen partisans captured at Caen.

As the scale of fighting in France increased, the German claim that the armistice and its terms were still legally in place became unsustainable. Nevertheless, the German forces continued to execute FFI fighters, even though Charles de Gaulle's Provisional Government protested on behalf of the FFI and threatened reprisals. By late summer 1944, many German soldiers had surrendered to the FFI, and the FFI was in a position to act. When it became known to the FFI that the Germans had executed eighty partisans and planned to execute more, the FFI announced that it would carry out eighty reprisal executions. The International Committee of the Red Cross (ICRC) sought to intervene and obtained a postponement pending an agreement by the Germans to grant the FFI legal combatant status. After six days without a German response, the FFI executed eighty German prisoners. It appears that no further FFI fighters were executed after that.

Reprisal is a legal term in international humanitarian law (IHL) describing a particular kind of retaliation. To be a reprisal, it must be undertaken for the purpose of forcing, or inducing, enemy forces to cease their own violation of IHL. It is a self-enforcement of the laws of war, for reprisal is undertaken not in retaliation or punishment, but rather to force the other side to stop its violation. For this reason, a reprisal is technically an action that, if done on its own, would constitute a violation of IHL. When, however, it is done for the purpose of forcing an adverse party to cease violating IHL, it may become a legal act, providing all the legal criteria are met. Moreover, an act of reprisal, to be a reprisal and not mere retaliation, must be proportionate to the violation of IHL committed by the other side.

Today, reprisal has almost entirely disappeared from the canon of IHL. Even assuming that the German position on the legality of FFI combatants was wrong, the 1929 Geneva Convention specifically outlawed precisely this

German soldiers surrender to Free French forces in Paris. August 25, 1944.

kind of reprisal using prisoners of war. Each successive revision of IHL treaties has put additional categories of combatants and civilians beyond the reach of reprisal actions. The 1949 Geneva Conventions extend the prohibition from prisoners of war to those civilians protected by the Fourth Geneva Convention, and Additional Protocol I of 1977 specifically extends the protection to civilians of any kind as well as to "civilian objects." Perhaps the only circumstance in which IHL today still permits reprisal actions, if at all, is as a response to the use of illegal methods or weapons against combatants. The trend, clearly, is to outlaw reprisal under all circumstances.

The FFI killings of the German soldiers, although effective in stopping the German summary executions, were plainly a violation of IHL as then in force, and would certainly be a violation of IHL and a grave breach of the Geneva Conventions and Additional Protocol I today.

(See **protected persons.**)

Rwanda

By Mark Huband

The term *genocide* is used widely and sometimes loosely, but what took place in Rwanda in April and May of 1994 was the third unquestionable genocide of the twentieth century. As defined by the 1948 Convention for the Prevention and Punishment of the Crime of Genocide, it consists of certain acts "committed with an intent to destroy, in whole or in part, a national, ethnical, racial, or religious group as such." In Rwanda, somewhere between 500,000 and 1 million Tutsis and moderate Hutus, who fit the convention's definition of a national group, were murdered.

The planning of this **genocide**, which was important legally because it established the clear intent of its architects to commit the crime, had become

R

known to the United Nations well before it took place. The Rwandan government's effort in 1993 to carry out a census in which all Rwandans had to state their tribe had been followed by a slaughter of Tutsis in the northern part of the country. This would prove to be a macabre dress rehearsal for the genocide of 1994.

In the interim, the Rwandan president, Juvenal Habyarimana, signed a peace accord in Arusha, Tanzania, with the Tutsi-led Rwandan Patriotic Front (RPF) that was intended to end the country's four-year civil war. Whether President Habyarimana sincerely intended peace, or more likely, viewed it as a pause in which to finalize plans to exterminate the Tutsis, will probably never be answered conclusively. What is clear is that he was restructuring the Hutu-dominated national administration to put extremists in positions of authority—extremists whose main goal was to conspire to launch a final, genocidal strike against the hated Tutsi minority.

On April 6, 1994, President Habyarimana flew back from Tanzania after a meeting on the peace process. As Habyarimana's plane attempted to land in the Rwandan capital, Kigali, it was shot down by extremist members of the

This Hutu man was too sympathetic to the Tutsis, according to the Interahamwe militia, who slashed his head with a machete.

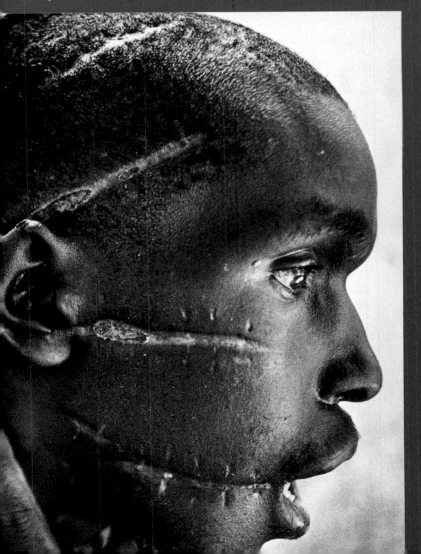

president's own party. They were, in any case, quite ready to sacrifice him since they believed he had conceded too much to the RPF in the peace agreement, even if only temporarily.

Habyarimana's death served as the pretext to launch the genocide. Rwanda's national radio as well as a number of private stations relayed instructions to the death squads, the so-called Interahamwe (the name, in Kinyarwanda, means "those who fight together"), and ceaselessly urged the killers to step up their slaughter. The Rwandan armed forces backed up the Interahamwe in those areas where the killers encountered resistance from Tutsi civilians. Prepositioned transport and fuel permitted the death squads to reach even the most isolated Tutsi communities.

Other genocides—the Turkish slaughter of the Armenians, the Nazi extermination of Europe's Jews and Gypsies—took place largely in secret. Rwanda was different. There was a United Nations peacekeeping force on the ground in Rwanda. Its members stood by and watched as the killings took place. The rest of the world watched on television as Rwanda exploded.

I recall a young woman pleading silently through the terror in her eyes as she was led to her death past French UN troops. The French were guarding foreign evacuees fleeing the Rwandan capital in an open truck, and a government militia had ordered the convoy to halt on a muddy road near the city's airport. The UN troops waited obediently, saying it was "not our mandate" to intervene. Beside them in a compound, two men were kneeling in silence as the militiamen crushed their heads with clubs, then cut their throats. The woman knelt beside them. Within less than a minute her head was all but severed. Then the convoy was allowed to move on.

The world's governments not only knew what was occurring but were complicit. Article 1 of the Genocide Convention binds its signatories to act to prevent as well as to punish genocide. The fact that the UN knew the genocide was being planned and, presumably, communicated this knowledge to member-States, and the fact that once the genocide began nothing was done, makes what took place in Rwanda in 1994 more than a crime. It was an event that shamed humanity.

It is clear by now that far from having been caught unawares, the great powers were intent on obscuring the reality of what was taking place in Rwanda. When the Security Council met, it was decided that the representative of Rwanda—of the government that was committing the genocide— would be allowed to make a statement. For all practical purposes, the council's main concern appears to have been to debate for as long as possible the question of whether a genocide was taking place.

There were thousands of examples of the State's role. At the Nyarubuye Catholic Mission in eastern Rwanda, I happened upon Leoncia Mukandayambaje, a survivor, sitting outside her hut among the trees. She had fled here when the local mayor, Sylvestre Gacumbitsi, had given the local Tutsi population special passes to allow them to reach the large brick complex. After grouping them there, he arranged for two truckloads of murderers to be sent.

In school rooms, in cloisters, in corridors, and in doorways, the 2,620 victims covered the floor in a carpet of rotting death. Leoncia was saved by her baby daughter, whom she held close to her while the murderers hacked both with machetes. Her daughter's blood covered her. The murderers assumed both mother and child were dead.

Unhallowed ground: A rotting corpse outside the parish church of Nyarabuye offers a grim foretelling of the thousand more slaughtered inside by Hutu militia.

By the time the UN Security Council had finally concluded what was plain from the start—that a genocide had indeed been taking place—it was too late to do anything for the people of Rwanda. To have admitted this earlier would arguably have bound the parties to the Genocide Convention, among whom were all the permanent members of the Security Council, to intervene and bring the mass murder to a halt. The council, on May 26, did eventually find that a genocide was taking place. By that time, half a million had died. Secretary-General Boutros-Ghali's acknowledgement was too little, too late.

He was still ahead of U.S. Secretary of State Warren Christopher. From the beginning of the slaughter, the U.S. government had prohibited its officials from using the term *genocide*. Finally, on June 10, Christopher relented, reluctantly and with bad grace. "If there is any particular magic in calling it genocide," he conceded, "I have no hesitancy in saying that."

There was magic, all right, in the sense that using the term would have bound the United States and other governments to act. By the time Christopher made his grudging concession to reality, it was too late, which may have been the idea all along.

The complicity of the so-called world community in the Rwandan genocide should not, of course, obscure the fact that the principal responsibility for the crime lies with its Rwandan architects. Apologists for the Rwandan authorities insisted at the time that the killings were unfortunate by-products of a renewal of the civil war. Later, Hutu extremists justified the killings as acts of self-defense against Tutsi aggression. Such arguments stood reality on its head. Almost all the victims in the spring of 1994 were killed as part of a government-inspired campaign of extermination, not as casualties of the subsequent fighting between the Rwandan Army and the RPF.

According to the provisions of the Genocide Convention, the government was guilty on all counts of the Convention's Article 3: genocide, conspiracy to commit genocide, direct and public **incitement** to commit genocide, and complicity in genocide. Members of the government had used its administration to organize the slaughter and, equally grave, incited the Hutu civilian population to kill their Tutsi neighbors and even, for intermarriage was common in Rwanda, to kill Tutsi spouses and relatives.

After the slaughter was over, an international tribunal was established to bring the guilty to book, to try them under international humanitarian law and under the provisions of the Genocide Convention. By 2006, the Rwanda tribunal had convicted 28 people for their part in the genocide, seven of whom had their cases under appeal. Doubtless, such trials are better than nothing. At least, in the Rwandan case, there will not be total impunity. But trials are a poor substitute for prevention, and the one thing that is clear is that the Rwandan genocide could have been prevented had the outside world had the will to do so. The facts were plain. The legal basis for intervention was there. It was courage that was lacking.

(See **Congo, Democratic Republic of**; **courts and tribunals**; **United Nations and the Geneva Conventions**.)

Safety Zones

By Adam Roberts

The sieges or bombardments of Leningrad, Dresden, Hiroshima, Vukovar, Sarajevo, and Srebrenica caused huge civilian losses and suffering. However, most attempts to devise schemes to protect particular places from the horrors of war have had limited success.

Safety zones is an unofficial term covering a wide variety of attempts to declare certain areas off-limits for military targeting. The Fourth Geneva Convention of 1949 and Additional Protocol I provide for three main types: hospital zones, neutralized zones, and demilitarized zones. These treaty arrangements require consent between belligerents, depend on complete demilitarization, and do not specify any arrangements for defending the areas. They have been used only occasionally.

In post–Cold War conflicts, the UN Security Council or other bodies rather than belligerents have proclaimed safety zones ad hoc. Such areas have been variously called "corridors of tranquillity," "humanitarian corridors," "neutral zones," "protected areas," "safe areas," "safe havens," "secure humanitarian areas," "security corridors," and "security zones." Two motivations have been the safety of refugees and the prevention of massive new refugee flows. Military activity has generally continued within the areas. Unlike self-declared "**undefended towns**," safety zones are not envisaged as being open for occupation by the hostile power.

In northern Iraq after the 1991 Gulf War, the Western powers, having encouraged an abortive Kurdish uprising, established a safe haven enabling some 400,000 Kurdish refugees who had fled to the Turkish border to return. UN agencies subsequently took charge.

The UN Security Council established six safe areas in Bosnia-Herzegovina in 1993 to protect the inhabitants of six towns from Bosnian Serb forces besieging them, but it never defined the geographical limits or its commitment to protect them. The Serbs complained the Bosnians were using these zones to launch attacks against them; yet the zones could not have been neutralized because the inhabitants were unwilling to entrust their security to international forces. In July 1995 UN troops watched as Bosnian Serb forces conquered the safe areas of Srebrenica and Zepa and committed appalling atrocities.

Three-quarters of the way through the 1994 genocide in Rwanda, the Security Council decided on the establishment of secure humanitarian areas, but no country provided troops. Instead, when the worst of the killing was over, the council authorized France to establish by force a zone that ultimately provided refuge for Hutus who had organized the genocide, casting further doubt on the idea.

Overall, safety zones have saved many lives, but establishing them, preventing military activity in them, and protecting them from external assault is difficult and demanding. Safety zones rarely provide an enduring haven from the horrors of war.

(See **evacuation of civilians**.)

Sanctions

By Tom Gjelten

Children die because hospitals cannot get the medicines required to treat them. Factories close and unemployment soars because manufacturers cannot import the supplies and materials they need or export their finished products. Basic foodstuffs are so expensive that the average family can no longer afford to eat well. Can the imposition of sanctions against a nation under some circumstances be a war crime?

Had the argument not been made so often by such disreputable world figures as Saddam Hussein and Slobodan Milosevic, the question might be taken more seriously. When a State—or a group of States—refuses to trade with another country, it is the civilian population in the targeted country that suffers the most. Inevitably, sanctions inflict harm on innocent people, and in extreme cases they may violate international humanitarian law (IHL)

Sanctions arise in a variety of ways. Article 41 of the United Nations Charter authorizes the Security Council to decide on "measures not involving the use of armed force... to give effect to its decisions... These may include complete or partial interruption of economic relations and of rail, sea, air, postal, telegraphic, radio, and other means of communication. and the severance of diplomatic relations." International embargoes against Rhodesia, Libya, Haiti, Iraq, and Yugoslavia were enacted under this provision. Alternatively, sanctions can be ordered by a regional organization, as the European Union did in the Yugoslav case. They can also be imposed unilaterally by one country against another, as in the example of the U.S. trade embargo against Cuba.

A more important distinction is whether the sanctions were imposed or enforced during wartime by one or more of the warring parties. IHL does not apply in the absence of armed conflict. This means that "nonbelligerent" sanctions, including those against Cuba, Libya, Haiti, Rhodesia, and Yugoslavia, may be opposed on moral or political terms but normally cannot be considered war crimes. Supporters of economic sanctions may even justify them as an alternative to military action.

In the case of Iraq, the United States and other countries applied sanctions before launching the 1991 Gulf War, in an effort to force the Iraqi regime to withdraw from neighboring Kuwait, which it had invaded in August 1990. But the imposing countries, including the United States, continued to enforce the sanctions in wartime, so they had to conform to IHL.

The 1977 Additional Protocols to the 1949 Geneva Conventions prohibit any wartime measure that has the effect of depriving a civilian population of objects indispensable to its survival. Article 70 of Protocol I mandates relief operations to aid a civilian population that is "not adequately provided" with supplies. Article 18 of Protocol II calls for relief operations for a civilian population that suffers "undue hardship owing to a lack of supplies essential for its survival, such as foodstuffs and medical supplies." Such provisions establish the legally permissible limit of sanctions, though their definition is subject to interpretation. The UN embargo against Iraq exempted "humanitarian" aid, but critics said the sanctions still caused excessive suffering.

Other provisions of IHL similarly restrict the scope and bite of economic

S

sanctions. Article 33 of the Fourth Geneva Convention (on the protection of civilians in wartime), for example, prohibits "collective penalties." The International Committee of the Red Cross (ICRC) Commentary on the conventions interpreted this provision as prohibiting "penalties of any kind inflicted on persons or entire groups of persons in defiance of the most elementary principles of humanity, for acts that these persons have not committed."

Supporters of sanctions may defend the measures against this restriction by arguing that they do not constitute **collective punishment** because they target governments, not people, and that **collateral damage** to the civilian population is unintended and unfortunate. In the case of Iraq, however, that argument was undercut when U.S. officials suggested that the sanctions were intended to create hardship conditions in the country and thus encourage the popular overthrow of the government.

Sanctions imposed under nonbelligerent conditions must normally be judged on the basis of moral or political considerations rather than legal

Iraqi woman collects her monthly food ration of grain and soap at a state-run food distribution center in Basra, Iraq, after the UN imposes what U.S. National Security Advisor Samuel Berger calls "the most complete embargo of any country in modern times." May 2000.

ones. The U.S. National Conference of Catholic Bishops has argued that "sanctions can offer a nonmilitary alternative to the terrible options of war or indifference when confronted with aggression or injustice." But some political philosophers disagree, arguing that aggressively applied sanctions, even in the absence of armed conflict, may be considered a form of **siege** and are objectionable on the same grounds. From this perspective, sanctions run the risk of becoming a form of war against civilians, waged by governments unwilling to expend the blood or treasure necessary to attack an enemy regime directly.

Sexual Violence

By Thom Shanker

She gave her name as Marijanna, but it really is Mirsada, and she said very little after arriving at the hospital in August of 1992, when the conflict in Bosnia-Herzegovina was only a few months old and the brutality of the shifting front lines still veiled stories of mass rape.

With the passing weeks, though, the pale-skinned, brown-haired girl—half Croat, half Muslim—spoke of being imprisoned with her mother and two dozen other women in the basement of a municipal hall in her home town of Teslic, in north-central Bosnia. Her jailers, Bosnian Serb irregulars, raped her and the others and forced them to have sex with uniformed Bosnian Serb troops deploying through the area. She and her mother each had to watch as the other was gang-raped three times a day, every day, for four months. Mirsada was released only when she became visibly pregnant, and her jailer-rapists said, "Go bear our Serbian children." By the time she crossed the front and found medical care in Croatia, the fetus was too developed to be safely aborted. As she sat in the maternity ward of Zagreb's Petrova Hospital, she kept a palm over her stomach. In her womb was ever-growing evidence of the ever-expanding horror of the Bosnian war. Mirsada was seventeen.

Rape as a spoil of combat can be found throughout history, as far back as the oral recounting of Mediterranean warrior-kings attributed to Homer, but today rape and other forms of sexual violence have become a strategic weapon of war and terror. Through the ages, the practice of seizing women as war booty, hardly different than cattle and corn, may have been superseded by the rise of a Judeo-Christian tradition and the development of customary laws of war in the West, but those laws had scant impact on public acceptance of rape as a natural, if unfortunate, by-product when men took up arms for battle. This worldwide shrug, in effect saying that rape is an unavoidable part of the battlefield, caused initial stories from Bosnia to be viewed as unremarkable by citizens in the West (who were confused by the war itself) and discounted by politicians in the West (lest public alarm at atrocities force them to action). It was not until victims like Mirsada came forward and foreign correspondents confirmed the archipelago of sex-enslavement camps and uncovered a program of systematic mass rape that the world took notice, and arguments could be raised that the rapes constituted crimes against humanity and were elements of a premeditated program of genocide.

Rape has been considered a war crime for centuries, and punishable as such. In 1474, Sir Peter von Hagenbach was convicted by an international military tribunal on charges of rape during a military occupation. He had been appointed by Duke Charles the Bold of Burgundy to govern the Austrian town of Breisach, and his brutal tools to subdue the town included pillage, murder, and rape. During the American Civil War, the Union Army operated under a general order prepared by Francis Lieber and signed by President Lincoln in 1863 that made rape a capital offense. In the twentieth century, rape was included—in increasingly explicit terms—in various treaties regulating the conduct of war, starting with Article 46 of the

S

regulations annexed to the 1907 Hague Convention. It ensures respect for "family honour and rights"; the prosecution relied on this provision when it brought war crimes charges relating to the pandemic rape of Nanking, China, in the post-World War II trial before the Tokyo Tribunal.

The history of modern warfare has shown, though, how little formal and customary laws of war have been observed—and how rarely they have been enforced. The Soviet Army raped its way across Prussia and into Berlin in the final days of World War II, yet Moscow's military judges took a victor's place of honor on the bench at Nuremberg. In fact, the founding statute of the International Military Tribunal in Nuremberg made no specific reference to rape, relying on language prohibiting inhumane treatment to encompass rapes committed by Nazis. And the companion tribunal in Tokyo phrased its provision for war crimes jurisdiction in highly general terms, "namely, violations of the laws or customs of war."

From the postwar period, Article 27 of the Fourth Geneva Convention of 1949 clearly states that "women shall be protected against any attack on their honor, in particular against rape, enforced prostitution, or any form of indecent assault." Again rape was referred to as a crime against honor or dignity, not a crime of violence. Article 27 applies to international conflicts, and in the early months of the Bosnian War, the world community tied itself in knots arguing whether the conflict was a civil war within a constituent republic that was attempting to illegally secede from Yugoslavia, or whether the conflict was an international war of aggression, inspired and abetted by Belgrade, the capital of Serbia, against the newly sovereign state of Bosnia-Herzegovina.

This debate mattered not to the question of rape as a war crime. Civilians in noninternational conflicts are protected by Article 3 common to the four Geneva Conventions of 1949. Although rape is not explicitly mentioned, the prosecutor at the International Criminal Tribunal for the former Yugoslavia brought sexual assault charges under Common Article 3, citing its provisions on cruel treatment, torture, and outrages upon human dignity, in particular, humiliating and degrading treatment. Civilians in both international and noninternational conflicts are given further protection under the 1977 Additional Protocols to the Geneva Conventions. Additionally, the appeals chamber of the Yugoslavia tribunal has held that the Common Article 3 establishes minimum guarantees for all armed conflicts. Thus, serious violations of its provisions in international, as well as internal, armed conflicts would be considered war crimes.

In the lengthening shadow of the Yugoslav conflict, it is clear that rape and other forms of sexual violence are also a war crime when committed against men. For example, Dusko Tadic, a Bosnian Serb, was convicted among other things of violating Common Article 3, as incorporated into the statute of the Yugoslavia tribunal under the heading "violations of the laws or customs of war," for his role in the incident during which one detainee at Omarska was forced to bite off the testicle of another. In the Celebici case, three defendants were convicted for various forms of sexual violence against both men and women. The court also specified that if the prosecutor had indicted one accused for "rape" instead of "cruel treatment" when forcing two male detainees to perform fellatio on each other, it would have convicted on rape instead of the more obscure cruel treatment. The Yugoslavia tribunal also convicted Anto Furundzija, a Bosnian Croat paramilitary leader, of torture by means

A 70-year-old woman describing how she was beaten and raped by young soldiers on her farm in Kalungwe, South Kivu province. Democratic Republic of Congo, 2005.

of rape, when a colleague orally, vaginally, and anally raped a Bosnian Muslim woman while Furundzija verbally interrogated her. In the Furundzija case, the first United Nations war crimes trial to focus exclusively on rape, the tribunal carefully chose gender-neutral terms in defining the elements of rape committed against "the victim," whether man or woman.

But the most groundbreaking decision on gender-related crimes was rendered by the Rwanda tribunal, when Jean-Paul Akayesu was convicted of not only rape as a crime against humanity, but also rape as an instrument of the genocide in Rwanda. In addition, the tribunal convicted Akayesu for inhumane acts for several instances of forced nudity. The above cases represent some of the most pioneering jurisprudence in successfully prosecuting gender-related crimes.

Thus, rape can be prosecuted as a war crime as a grave breach under Article 147 of the Fourth Geneva Convention, as a violation of Common

S

Every Wednesday for many years Kim Sun Duck, 76, and other Korean former comfort women picketed the Japanese Embassy in Seoul seeking a public apology and reparations.

Article 3, and as a violation of the laws or customs of war. Rape has successfully been prosecuted as rape, as a form of torture, a means of persecution, and indicia of enslavement, among other crimes. It is now indisputably regarded as a serious crime of war, crime against humanity, and instrument of genocide.

The statute establishing a permanent International Criminal Court, adopted by the United Nations diplomatic conference in Rome on July 17, 1998, grants jurisdiction to prosecute rape, enforced prostitution, sexual slavery, forced pregnancy, enforced sterilization, and other forms of sexual violence of comparable gravity. (The Yugoslav and Rwanda tribunals have noted that other forms of sexual violence include forced marriage, forced abortion, forced nudity, sexual mutilation, and sexual humiliation.) The crimes can be prosecuted whether during war or peace, if of a widespread or systematic nature. The ICC Statute also recognizes gender related persecution and trafficking in women and children. Thus, in the past 14 years, since the Yugoslavia tribunal was established in 1993, the progress on gender-related crimes has been unprecedented.

In Bosnia, as in virtually all contemporary wars, rape was a weapon of combat, a mighty instrument of terror and destruction. After Mirsada gave birth to a healthy, nine-and-one-half-pound girl, she refused to see the baby. The Zagreb maternity staff, mostly Catholics not expert in Muslim names, called the newborn Emina, after a romantic but sad poem by a favorite Bosnian poet. On the second day after the birth, the nurses noticed that Mirsada was not in her room, nor in the ward, nor anywhere on the hospital grounds. She never contacted the hospital again. Mirsada, though, is not seeking justice against her attackers. Her name does not appear on the roles of witnesses to be called at The Hague, nor is she among those who have contacted victims-rights attorneys bringing separate civil lawsuits against the architects of ethnic cleansing and genocide in Bosnia.

Sexual Violence: Enslavement

By George Rodrigue

In June 1996, the International Criminal Tribunal for the former Yugoslavia (ICTY) issued an indictment against eight Bosnian Serb soldiers for the enslavement and rape of Muslim women in the eastern Bosnian town of Foca during 1992 and 1993. The entire indictment focused exclusively on various forms of sexual violence committed against women and girls in Foca, and it represented the first sexual slavery prosecution in any international criminal proceeding. In the indictment, among other charges, members of the Serb military police were accused of enslaving and repeatedly torturing and raping one fifteen-year-old girl over the course of eight months.

The girl's story was all too typical of the kind of practices that went on throughout the Bosnian war, as in other conflict situations. In July 1992, with at least seventy-two other Muslims, she was held captive in the Foca high school. For a time, she was raped every night by one or more soldiers. The attacks continued after she was moved from the school to Foca's Partizan Sports Hall. And after that, when she was taken to a house that served as a Serb military brothel, she was turned into a servant as well as a sex slave, washing the clothes and cleaning for the soldiers who were raping her. According to the indictment, her captors eventually sold her for five hundred deutsche marks to two soldiers from Montenegro.

Victims' statements indicate overwhelmingly that what happened to this particular girl in Foca was anything but unique. Multiple witnesses, interviewed separately, described "rape camps" throughout Bosnian Serb-controlled territory, as well as a far smaller number of camps run by Croatian and Bosnian government forces. The Foca indictment eventually went to trial against only three accused in what is known as the Kunarac case, as they were the only indictees who had been apprehended and turned over to the tribunal. Eventually, all were convicted of torture, rape, and enslavement for sexual violence. The rape and enslavement as crimes against

humanity counts were used essentially to prosecute the crime of sexual slavery ("sexual slavery" was not explicitly listed as a separate crime in the ICTY Statute, although it is now listed as a specific crime in the Statute for the International Criminal Court.)

This was by no means the first time the world was confronted with systematic rape and enslavement of women. The 100,000 Asian "comfort women" enslaved in Japanese military brothels during World War II provide perhaps the ghastliest twentieth-century example. Other postwar courts convicted soldiers of the war crime of "enforced prostitution": a Netherlands tribunal in Batavia convicted Japanese military defendants who had enslaved thirty-five Dutch women and girls in comfort stations for war crimes including rape, coercion to prostitution, abduction of women and girls for forced prostitution, and ill-treatment of prisoners. These principles have been reaffirmed in the 1949 Geneva Conventions and the 1977 Additional Protocols. It

A teenage girl who was forcibly taken as a "wife" by a commander while in a militia is seen through a curtain as she visits the local hospital to be checked for sexually transmitted diseases. Goma, Democratic Republic of Congo, March 2005.

should be noted that "forced prostitution" and "sexual slavery" are both listed in the ICC Statute as crimes against humanity and war crimes. ("Forced prostitution" was included in the ICC Statute largely because of it is explicitly listed in earlier treaties. The elements of these two crimes are quite similar and the vast majority of survivors vehemently reject any reference to prostitution, however forced, and assert that the term sexual slavery more adequately describes the crime committed against them.)

Under certain conditions, the kinds of practices that took place in the so-called "comfort stations" during World War II, and with the sex-slave camps in Bosnia, may constitute the crime against humanity of enslavement when they are committed as part of a widespread or systematic attack

375

against a civilian population. In the "comfort women" context, women and girls were systematically held for sexual use for the Japanese soldiers with an aim of providing these soldiers with relatively easy and safe sexual access during the war. In the Bosnia context, as in many other conflict situations, women and girls of the opposing side were targeted for various forms of sexual violence, including sexual slavery, in large part in order to terrorize and demoralize the enemy. Sometimes, the women are held and repeatedly raped in order to get them pregnant; other times, more selfish purposes may be behind the sexual enslavement. Thus, in the two situations, the targeted group and purposes were different, but the result— females being held and repeatedly raped by male soldiers—was essentially the same.

It should be noted that **slavery** is an international crime, whether or not it is linked to a combat environment. The Slavery Convention defines slavery as "the status or condition of a person over whom any or all of the powers attaching to the right of ownership are exercised." The ICC Statute similarly defines enslavement as the exercise of any or all of the powers attaching to the right of ownership over a person, and the Statute emphasizes that this includes the exercise of such power in the course of trafficking in persons, in particular, women and children.

The legal basis for prosecuting those responsible for rape, enslavement, enforced prostitution and sexual slavery has long existed, even if prosecutions have not always been robust. The post-Cold War environment of ethnic conflict, as well as the establishment of the International Criminal Court and other international or part-international tribunals may lead to more cases being brought to court. For example, the Special Court for Sierra Leone has issued two indictments against senior commanders charging them with rape, sexual slavery, and forced marriage. Forced marriage, broadly considered a more intimate form of sexual slavery (typically a woman or girl is used by one combatant instead of many) will be prosecuted explicitly for the first time in this court. Whether as the charges involve rape and enslavement, sexual slavery, or forced marriage, depending on the specific facts, these prosecutions are finally redressing a common but long-ignored wartime abuse.

Sexual Violence: Systematic Rape

By Alexandra Stiglmayer

Although the phrase "systematic rape" was widely and correctly used to describe certain forms of the sexual crimes committed against women during the war in Bosnia-Herzegovina, there is no specific crime of "systematic rape" under international law.

But proving that rape is widespread or systematic is important for establishing a **crime against humanity.** To be convicted of rape as a crime against humanity, it is not necessary to prove that rape itself was widespread or systematic, but instead that the attack was widespread or systematic, and rape was one of the acts that formed part of the attack, The systematic character of certain rapes may also help establish the stringent intent requirement for the charge of **genocide**.

The systematic pattern of rapes in conflicts around the world might also be relevant in establishing the criminal responsibility of superior officers for sexual assaults committed by subordinates. For example, under the statute of the Yugoslavia Tribunal, a commander can be prosecuted for rapes committed by his subordinates if he "knew or had reason to know that the subordinate was about to commit such acts or had done so and the superior failed to take the necessary and reasonable measures to prevent such acts or to punish the perpetrators thereof." High-level military or civilian leaders can be held individually responsible for rape crimes committed by others if they ordered, encouraged, aided and abetted, or otherwise facilitated the crimes. When rape is systematic or widespread, especially when notorious or committed over a period of weeks or months, silence of leaders can be regarded as approving of or acquiescing in the rape crimes.

Women in conflict zones are frequently raped to humiliate and degrade, as part of a program to terrorize, to drive away the unwanted ethnic "other," to boost the military's morale, to demoralize the males associated with the raped women. Rape is regularly committed as part of a broad, systematic— even strategic—campaign to destroy a targeted group, and this destruction is explicitly or implicitly encouraged by authorities, sometimes even ordered.

High-, mid- and lower-level actors in future wars will have to take note of some of the historic judgments rendered by the Yugoslav and Rwanda tribunals. In Arusha, for example, Jean-Paul Akayesu, mayor of Taba commune, was found to have encouraged and even ordered Hutu militia and even civilians to commit rape and other acts of sexual violence against Tutsi women, as well as to kill Tutsis outright. The Rwanda Tribunal held that the rape of Tutsi women "was systematic and was perpetrated against all Tutsi women and solely against them." The trial chamber concluded that if done with intent to destroy a protected group in whole or in part, "rape and sexual violence constitute genocide in the same way as any other act," and that Akayesu had systematically targeted Tutsi women to contribute to the destruction of the Tutsi group as a whole. It explained that sexual violence "was a step in the process of destruction of the Tutsi group—destruction of the spirit, of the will to live, and of life itself." On September 2, 1998, Akayesu was convicted of rape as a crime against humanity and as part of the genocide.

S

Shields

By Robert Block

The world saw human shields on television when, in the events preceding the Gulf War, the Iraqi government seized foreign nationals in both Iraq and Kuwait and held them at strategic and military installations. This is a most obvious case of using civilians as hostages or human shields to attempt to prevent an attack.

International humanitarian law (IHL) prohibits parties to conflict from using civilians to shield military objectives or military operations from attack. But armies and irregular forces use innocent civilians as human shields in conflicts all over the world. Often, they do it in a manner that, unlike Iraq's blatant example, is not instantly recognizable.

Two such cases occurred in the aftermath of the **Rwandan genocide** in mid-1994, when more than 1 million people fled to Zaire and lived in the

S

squalor of refugee camps. Some did not go back because of their role in the slaughter by an extreme nationalist Hutu regime of as many as 1 million ethnic Tutsis and moderate Hutus. Others feared that Rwanda's new pro-Tutsi rulers would be unable to distinguish the guilty from the innocent who fled Rwanda in the final days of that country's civil war. But many others wanted to take a chance and go home where they had families and fertile land. They were not allowed to. Although considered **refugees** by the international community, they saw themselves as prisoners of those who ran the camps.

"We wanted to come back to Rwanda, but in the camp there were people who stopped us. They had guns and machetes and they threatened us with death if tried to come back," she said. "They told us that one day we would all go back together by force and they set up military bases among us to attack the enemy."

A Salvadorian policeman uses an ice cream vendor as a human shield during a skirmish with demonstrators in San Salvador.

Indeed, between August 1994 and November 1997, the remnants of the armed forces of Rwanda and the dreaded Interahamwe militias still loyal to the defeated extremist regime of President Juvenal Habyarimana used the refugee camps in Zaire as a staging ground and launchpad for attacks into Rwanda. The extremists would stage raids into Rwanda from the camps and then seek refuge back there, using the refugees as shields from counterattacks. When the camps were broken up by a combined force of Rwanda's new Tutsi-dominated army and Zairean rebels, proof emerged of plans for a massive military invasion of Rwanda from the refugee camps.

Under international law, parties to a conflict must keep military assets as far as possible from concentrations of civilians. It is also a crime of war to use any civilians as a human shield. According to Article 51 of the 1977 Additional Protocol I to the 1949 Geneva Conventions: "The presence or movements of the civilian population or individual civilians shall not be used to render certain points or areas immune from military operations, in particular in attempts to shield military objects from attacks or to shield, favor or impede military operations."

The second example occurred in 1997. Zairean rebels fighting to over-throw the government of dictator Mobutu Sese Seko often complained that when they approached groups of Rwandan refugees who were then fleeing Zaire's civil war, they were often fired upon by armed elements hiding among the civilians. This fact was in turn used as an excuse by the rebels to indis-criminately attack refugee areas, often massacring hundreds of women, children, and elderly—clearly illegal under IHL.

Some cases are not so cut-and-dried.

One such incident took place in El Salvador in March 1984. Under attack for its appalling human rights record, and unable to convince the world that it was waging a righteous struggle against Communist insurgents, El Salvador's military was searching for an incident to bolster its case before upcoming elections.

The army's prayers appeared to have been answered one Monday evening outside the small town of San Antonio Grande when rebels of the Farabundo Marti National Liberation Front (FMLN) attacked a train traveling from the town of San Vicente in the west of the country to the capital, San Salvador.

The railway line cut though the heart of guerrilla territory. Trains plying this route were regularly fired upon or blown up. But these were always cargo trains, usually carrying supplies for the military or the businesses of the army's wealthy patrons—clear military objectives. This time, however, the train was full of civilian passengers.

Eight people, including women and children, were killed and dozens wounded. Here at last was the "proof" of what the Salvadoran Army had con-tended all along: that its enemies were war criminals with no regard for human life. An attack that does not distinguish between **military objectives** and civilians is a war crime.

The foreign press was summoned to the site the next morning by the Salvadoran military. Inside the train, the bodies of two men, four women, and a child were lying in a pool of congealed blood underneath wooden seats on the floor of a railway carriage. They had been left where they fell, untouched for fifteen hours so reporters could broadcast the guerrillas' deed to more dra-matic effect.

Outside, a young woman was on her knees, rooted to a spot where she had collapsed. She was bent over the body of a small boy, resting her head on the back of one hand, while the other clutched at her breast as if trying to tear her own heart out. She wailed, pleading to God for her little son's life while damning the guerrillas. Her cries went out over the airwaves as well.

This, an army spokesman announced with enthusiasm, was proof of the barbarity of the guerrillas. But upon talking to survivors another picture, different from what the Salvadoran Army wanted us to believe, began to emerge.

According to the engineer, the rebels had brought the train to a halt after two mines went off on the track. The rebels had then demanded the surrender of a detachment of soldiers and five thousand rounds of ammunition that were in the last car. The soldiers had refused and a firefight ensued. Surviving passengers said that when the FMLN attack intensified the soldiers had taken refuge in their carriage, shooting at the attackers while hiding behind the civilian passengers for protection. It was then that people were killed.

Not wanting the bodies of its troops to be seen lying alongside those of civilians in a passenger carriage, the army removed the soldiers' corpses long before journalists arrived.

Despite the survivors' story it is unclear whether the soldiers had rushed

Hutu refugees in Kibeho camp plead with UN soldiers for protection. Over 4,000 Hutus were killed earlier in the day during an operation by the Tutsi-led Rwandan army to clear the camp. The tragedy left over 1,000 children orphaned.

S

to the passenger area to use civilians as shields—clearly a war crime—or fled to that particular car because they thought it was the best place to take cover, thereby committing no violation of law.

Whatever the truth, in the television propaganda war for the hearts and minds of the world, it was the guerrillas of FMLN and not the Salvadoran Army who lost sympathy points that day.

(See **hostages**.)

Sick and Wounded

By Eric Stover

The Geneva Conventions of 1949 recognized that **"military necessity"** has its limits and that **combatants**, as well as civilians, who are wounded or held as prisoners of war ***hors de combat*** should not be military targets and should be treated with dignity at all times. The conventions also specify that both civilians and combatants who are sick and wounded should be treated equally, and that neither should be given differential treatment.

The sick and wounded, Article 12 common to the First and Second Geneva Conventions of 1949 states, "shall be treated humanely and cared for by the Parties to the conflict in whose power they may be, without any adverse distinction founded on sex, race, nationality, religion, political opinions, or any other similar criteria. Any attempts upon their lives, or violence to their persons, shall be strictly prohibited; in particular, they shall not be murdered or exterminated, subject to torture or to biological experiments; they shall not willfully be left without medical assistance and care, nor shall conditions exposing them to contagion or infection be created."

History is replete with the accounts of sick and wounded combatants and civilians who have been physically and psychologically abused by their captors. One of the most horrific accounts of the abuse of prisoners during World War II took place in a Japanese-run germ warfare factory on the Manchurian Plain. Japanese doctors at the secret facility injected captured Chinese and Korean soldiers, many of whom had been wounded in battle, with bubonic plague, cholera, syphilis, and other deadly germs to compare the resistance to disease of various nationalities and races. Hundreds of prisoners of war died as a result of the **biological experiments** and hundreds more were killed by the Japanese when they fled the laboratory.

During the siege of the eastern Croatian city of Vukovar in November 1991, troops with the Yugoslav People's Army (JNA) and Serb irregulars removed hundreds of patients and staff from the municipal hospital and executed them at the end of a ravine on the Ovcara collective farm, nine kilometers south of the city. Five years later, forensic investigators, assembled by Physicians for Human Rights (PHR) and the International Criminal Tribunal for the Former Yugoslavia (ICTY), exhumed two hundred bodies from a **mass grave** on the Ovcara farm. Some of the bodies were dressed in smocks and white clogs, garb common to hospital employees in Europe. Other bodies bore signs of previous injuries: a thigh bandaged in gauze or a broken arm set in a plaster cast and sling. A pair of broken crutches lay on top of one body. Another had a catheter dangling from its pelvis. By May 1998, the forensic scientists had identified ninety-one of the bodies. The ICTY, in the meantime, had indicted the former major of Vukovar, Slavko Dokmanovic, and three JNA officers—Mile Mrksic, Miroslav Radic, and Veselin Sljivancanin—for the massacre on the Ovcara farm.
(See **medical experiments on POWs**.)

A badly burned woman was tagged "VNC," Vietnamese Civilian. Wounded were usually automatically deemed "VCS," Viet Cong Suspect. Vietnam, 1967.

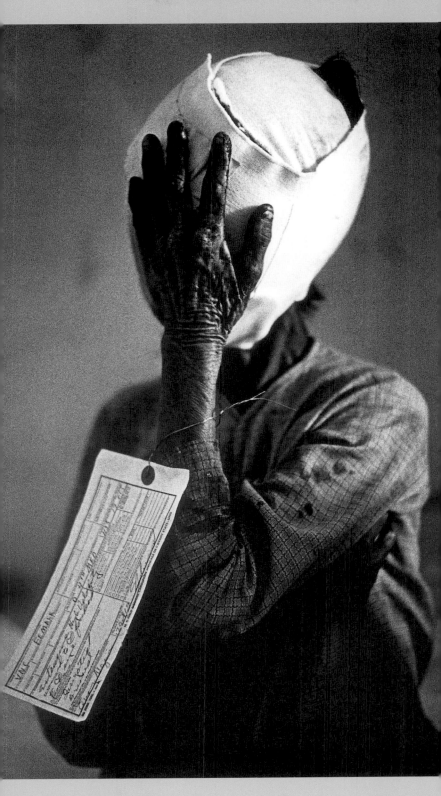

Siege

By Tom Gjelten

For centuries, armies have tried to capture cities by surrounding them, blocking access roads, and then bombarding the encircled territory until the townspeople, or their defenders, give up. Constantinople was besieged at one time or another by the Persians, the Arabs, the Bulgars, and the Russians. The siege of Leningrad (St. Petersburg) during World War II lasted 872 days and resulted in the deaths of more than a million civilians.

Fifty years later, it was Sarajevo's turn. In May 1992, the Bosnian Serb Army, having failed in an attempt to overrun the city, closed all roads leading in and out of Sarajevo, blocked commerce, and began to pound city neighborhoods with artillery and sniper fire from all directions. Human rights groups, relief agencies, and some governments said the Serb war tactics around Sarajevo subjected the city to a siege, immorally and illegally.

Under international humanitarian law (IHL), siege is not prohibited *per se*. The capture of an enemy-controlled city is a legitimate military aim, and army commanders have often seen siege as less costly than the alternative—fighting house to house, street by street. Historically, a key element of siege warfare has been to reduce a town's defenses and force its surrender by cutting off its vital supplies and leaving the population, civilian and military alike, to starve. Cruel as this tactic is, the laws of war permitted it at least until the end of World War II, under the rationale of **military necessity**.

The last revision of the U.S. Army field manual on the law of land warfare, for example, informed commanders that civilians who are fleeing a besieged city can, as an "extreme measure," be turned around and forced back into the city for the specific purpose of "hastening its surrender." Implicitly, this principle permitted the deliberate **starvation** of the civilian population, if only as a means of demoralizing the city's armed defenders. Under pre-World War II Hague Regulations, "undefended" cities could not be bombarded, but siege tactics are normally used against defended places, so this prohibition did not exclude sieges.

The laws pertaining to siege warfare, however, have changed radically in the post-World War II era. Though the word "siege" is never mentioned as a

Serb snipers shoot and kill a sixteen-year-old cyclist. Sarajevo, 1993.

term of law, the Additional Protocols of 1977 impose restrictions on warfare that, if enforced, would effectively make siege illegal. Besieging forces are not allowed to target civilians or starve them "as a method of warfare," and relief agencies are authorized to provide aid to needy populations.

The most important limitations are the rules regarding "objects indispensable to the survival of the civilian population," including food and **water supplies**. The Fourth Geneva Convention of 1949 upheld the traditional view that an army may legally block food or other relief shipments into a besieged city if the aid would result in more goods becoming available to the local military forces. But Article 54 of the First Additional Protocol contains an absolute ban on the starvation of civilians as well as forbidding the destruction of foodstuffs, crops, livestock and drinking water supplies that a civilian population relies on for sustenance. This provision may require a besieging force to allow relief supplies to enter a besieged city, even if some of the supplies will inevitably be shared with the defenders. A besieging army is also forbidden, for example, from destroying a city's drinking water supply.

Comparable rules are found in the Second Additional Protocol, applicable in internal conflict. Even when the protocols do not apply, prohibitions on the starvation of civilians are now widely seen as part of customary law. In addition, rules against the deliberate targeting of civilians would apply during sieges as at other times.

In Sarajevo, officials of the United Nations Protection Force (UNPROFOR) questioned whether the city was genuinely besieged, since Serb forces occasionally allowed UN relief convoys to pass into the city. Comdr. Barry Frewer, the UNPROFOR spokesman, summarized the official view while briefing journalists in July 1993: "The Serbs have encircled the city," he acknowledged. "They are in a position to bring force to bear on the city. You call it a siege. We say they are deployed in a tactically advantageous position."

The dispute was both ridiculous and irrelevant. No word other than "siege" as effectively described the city's condition, and in any case the terminology did not resolve the question of whether Serb military actions were lawful. The critical issue was whether the means of Sarajevo's continued encirclement violated IHL. Some parts of the war record leave little doubt. Indiscriminate shelling of residential areas is clearly illegal. Serb army commanders had modern artillery, a clear line of sight toward their Sarajevo targets, and three years of practice. UN military observers regularly reported deliberate civilian targeting by Serb gunners.

The attacks on Sarajevo prompted war crime indictments against Serb commanders judged responsible for firing "on civilian gatherings that were of no military significance." In December 2003, the Yugoslav war crimes tribunal convicted Major General Stanislav Galic, commander of the Bosnian Serb army unit around Sarajevo from 1992 to 1994, of the war crime of conducting a campaign of terror against the civilian population of the city, and of the crimes against humanity of murder and inhumane acts. He was sentenced to twenty years' imprisonment.

Might some army find a way to besiege a city without violating IHL? The limits have been tested by Taliban forces in Afghanistan, Hutu rebels in central Africa, and by Russian forces in Chechnya. Lawful or not, siege warfare remains as popular as ever.

Slavery

By E. Benjamin Skinner

In 1999, slavery was eliminated from Sudan by the stroke of a pen. For five years, UN Special Rapporteur Gáspár Bíró had chronicled the recrudescence of government-sponsored slave raiding in the North-South war, the longest in Africa's history. The response of the UN Human Rights Commission, at the request of the government of Sudan, was to replace all references to "slavery" in UN documents with the term "abduction."

For Aweng Deng Nyal, seized in a militia raid in 1991, the news that the slaves of Sudan had been emancipated would have come as a surprise. That is, if she ever heard it. Driven by famine, Aweng had sought food from a southern garrison town. As part of a government strategy to depopulate Dinka areas on the frontline of the war—"to break the backbone of the rebellion," in the words of the Sudanese Defense Minister Ibrahim Suleiman Hassan—a group of government-backed Arab murahileen horsemen intercepted Aweng, shot her husband, cut her brother's throat, bound her hands, and dragged her north. For nine months, Yah'ia Muhammed—the man whom she had watched kill her family—forced Aweng to farm his land. She slept fenced in with cattle and, once a day, was given a cupful of boiled sorghum to eat.

In the course of the civil war, Murahileen militias captured over ten thousand Southern Sudanese like Aweng. Most became textbook slaves, raped and forced by violence to work for no pay. A survey by the Rift Valley Institute in 2002 established the identities of over 10,000 southerners abducted in this way.

That enslavement is a **crime against humanity** is axiomatic. Along with piracy, genocide and torture, it is a crime of **universal jurisdiction**. Today there are more slaves in the world than at any point in human history. But "slavery" is a word that blurs at the edges, into indentured labor, debt bondage and human trafficking. Large numbers are held in debt bondage on the Indian subcontinent. Millions are forced into prostitution or agricultural work. Are they slaves? In terms of ethics, yes. In international law, not necessarily.

The Slavery Convention of 1926 defines slavery as "the status or condition of a person over whom any or all of the powers attaching to the right of ownership are exercised." It defines the slave trade as including "all acts involved in the capture, acquisition or disposal of a person with intent to reduce him to slavery" and "all acts involved in the acquisition of a slave with a view to selling or exchanging him." A Supplementary Convention adopted in 1956 addresses debt bondage and serfdom, which it characterizes as "institutions and practices similar to slavery." Parties to the Conventions are required to prevent and suppress the slave trade and eliminate slavery and similar practices "progressively and as soon as possible."

Today, as in the past, enslavement and bondage are often forms of commercial exploitation, bred by chaos—as in Bosnia, Kosovo, Transnistria and Nepal. Sometimes, it is a means to terrorize local populations, as when the Lord's Resistance Army forced children to take up arms in Uganda. The twentieth century saw the rise of a new, focused use of human bondage. Since Armenia in 1915, slavery and forced labor emerged alongside genocide as a method of erasing cultures.

The Nazis used several million Jews as forced laborers in World War II. The Khmer Rouge in Cambodia destroyed urban culture by forcing city dwellers into rural labor camps. In Bosnia Serbian forces established camps where Bosnian Muslim women were forced to have sex with non-Muslim men, with the aim of breeding Muslims out of Bosnia. And in Sudan, as Aweng Deng discovered, successive governments in Khartoum abetted northern Arab militias to revive the practice of slave raiding that the British had stamped out after the reconquest a century earlier.

Slavery is as old as war. Since antiquity slaves have been the spoils of battle. But the nineteenth century saw the crumbling of the ideological justification for the "peculiar institution" as it was known in the United States. The first codification of the laws of war—the Lieber Code promulgated by President Lincoln during the American Civil War—contained a provision against enslavement. The Geneva Conventions of 1949 do not specifically forbid slavery, but its prohibition is implicit in other rules. The

S

These boys from south Sudan's Bahr El Ghazal region were abducted and forced into slavery by northern militia. They have now been returned as part of a redemption deal and will be released. Wunrok, Sudan, 2001.

second Additional Protocol of 1977 includes a ban on slavery in civil wars. The prohibition of slavery is also regarded as a rule of customary law applicable in all conflicts. The statute of the International Criminal Court lists enslavement and sexual slavery as crimes against humanity.

But the UN's antislavery efforts have not been robust. Member States demonstrated little appetite for projecting force in order to stop slavery and slave-like practices that occurred during civil wars. And when international criminal courts handed out indictments after wars ended, charges of slavery were few and flimsy.

On March 1, 2006, in his last appearance before the International Criminal Court (ICC), Slobodan Milosevic accused the Kosovo Liberation Army of "white slave trading." The charge was true and also hypocritical, since it was on Milosevic's watch that the Serbian army had established the internment camps where the forced labor and killing of Bosnian Muslim men and the mass rape of Bosnian Muslim women took place. But no high Serb official has been convicted of enslavement.

Take the case of Milorad "Mico" Krnojelic, the director of the notorious KP Dom concentration camp in the Bosnian town of Foca. Mico oversaw the illegal imprisonment—and in many cases torture, murder and enslavement—of over 760 Muslim and other non-Serb civilians. Mico's guards forced dozens to work, under threat of solitary confinement or worse, on the front lines.

The International Criminal Tribunal for the former Yugoslavia (ICTY) charged Mico with enslavement of the prisoners. While Mico was sentenced to fifteen years for murder and torture, and while other Serb officers were convicted of enslavement, prosecutors failed to prove he gave the orders, and he was acquitted of slavery charges.

The international criminal justice system faced another challenge when former Liberian president Charles Taylor was transferred for trial in The Hague. Between 1998 and 1999, rebels sponsored by Taylor brought chaos to neighboring Sierra Leone. Massacres and amputations sparked international outrage, but forced conscription, forced labor and sexual enslavement were equally destructive atrocities. Boys were forced to bear arms. Girls were captives in sex slave camps. In some cases, their ordeals continued for years.

In 2003, Taylor was charged with enslavement and sexual slavery, crimes against humanity under the Statute of the Special Court for Sierra Leone. With his trial due to start shortly, his conviction is far from certain.

Back in Sudan, one day in 1992, Yah'ia Muhammed's elderly mother, a humane woman who often cried when she saw her son beat the slaves, brought Aweng some water. "My son is going to kill you today," she said. "He is bringing in fresh slaves who will work harder."

Aweng ran to a neighboring village. There, when Muhammed's overseers came looking for her, a free Dinka family hid her under a plastic sheet in their mud and straw tukul. When the war ended eleven years later, she was finally able to return to her smashed home in southern Sudan, where I found her in May 2003. In Sudan, slave-raiding ended with the peace agreement in the North-South war. But thousands of abducted people are still held in bondage. Sudan, like every other country in the world, is a signatory to the international conventions on slavery; and slavery is a crime under Sudanese law. Complicity at the highest levels of the government and the military-security apparatus is clear. But no one in Sudan has ever been charged with enslavement, let alone convicted.

(See **child soldiers, sexual violence: enslavement**.)

S

Soldiers, Rights of

By Peter Rowe

Soldiers have rights, insofar as they are members of the armed forces, as defined in international humanitarian law (IHL). They are known as **combatants** and have the right to participate directly in hostilities. This means, in practical terms, that combatants are entitled to attack enemy forces, kill or injure them, and destroy property as part of military operations—activities that if done not in wartime or not by combatants would all be criminal behavior. Thus, if captured, combatants must be treated as prisoners of war under the Third Geneva Convention of 1949 rather than as criminals, because as combatants they are legally entitled to fight.

It is up to a State to determine by its own law, however, who is a member of its armed forces. This has particular significance for the determination of when reservists, common in many countries, become members and thus combatants within the meaning of IHL. Once a person is a member of the armed forces of a State it is irrelevant whether that State describes the duties that he/she is to perform as combat or noncombat duties, or whether the members of the armed forces are conscripted or are volunteers. It is also irrelevant whether the State describes those armed forces as special forces, commandos, presidential guards, or by any other name. Where, however, a State incorporates its armed law enforcement agencies (such as its police force) into its armed forces, it must notify the other party to the conflict, for the simple reason that such bodies would not normally be considered to be part of the armed forces of a State, and so not liable to attack as combatants. Certain armed formations in certain states, such as **paramilitaries**, may or may not be members of the armed forces within the meaning of IHL, depending on how the State's own law treats such paramilitary forces.

According to the 1977 Additional Protocol I to the Geneva Conventions, States are under an obligation not to recruit **child soldiers** under the age of fifteen into their armed forces and to take all feasible measures to ensure that children do not take a direct part in hostilities.

The definition of combatants beyond those who fight for the regular armed forces of a State is regulated by IHL.

IHL treats all combatants alike, except for two distinct classifications. One distinction is between officers and other ranks, and is relevant only to certain obligations imposed upon the capturing State in respect to prisoners of war, such as the prohibition against forcing officers to work. The second distinction, between commanders and others, is extremely important since commanders have specific duties placed on them by Additional Protocol I to ensure that their subordinates are aware of their obligations under IHL and to suppress any breaches of these obligations. In addition, commanders are required to prevent any such violation if they have become aware that their subordinates are going to breach IHL. In this way, a commander has **command responsibility** for the actions of his subordinates, even though he may not directly have ordered the violations.

Captured combatants are entitled to be treated as prisoners of war even if it is alleged that they have committed war crimes. In certain conflicts State leaders have declared that captured air crew are "war criminals" and are not to be treated as prisoners of war. This is contrary to IHL, although a

S

Vietnam combatant.

State is entitled and has the right to investigate war crimes, even those alleged to have taken place among POWs. In internal armed conflict, insurgents are not entitled to POW status under the Third Geneva Convention or Additional Protocol I since the conflict is not international. Accordingly, they may be tried for sedition, treason, rebellion, murder, or other crimes under the domestic law of their State; nonetheless, under Article 3 common to the four Geneva Conventions, and notwithstanding that they may be tried by their State, they retain certain minimal protections under IHL, and in particular, may not be summarily executed and must receive the benefit of a regular trial.

(See **prisoners of war; protected persons.**)

Starvation

By Marita Vihervuori

At the main Serb checkpoint outside Sarajevo, the big Human to Human aid convoy stood stalled in its tracks. Sweating profusely, a uniformed Serb fighter pushed a wheelbarrow full of goods taken from one of the vehicles into the cellar of the house he and his comrades were using as a guardroom. Nearby, other Serb fighters were stacking cartons of the seized aid into a minivan.

Their commander was unapologetic. "According to the orders of the authorities of the Republika Srpska, 30 percent of the supplies in all aid convoys must be turned over to us."

In fact, the Human to Human convoy was one of the few private aid convoys that ever made it to Sarajevo. But not intact. After losing 30 percent of its cargo at the first checkpoint, it was stripped of still more in the Serb-controlled suburb of Ilidza. In the end, only the flour and macaroni made it into the city.

Staff of the United Nations High Commissioner for Refugees (UNHCR) in Sarajevo were well aware that the Serb forces besieging the Bosnian capital were seizing humanitarian aid intended for civilians within the city. They should have been; more often than not, they were allowing the Serbs to take 30 percent of the goods UNHCR itself was bringing in as well. Under international law, the Serbs had every right to inspect all food and medical supplies being brought through their lines into government-controlled territory in order to satisfy themselves that the relief was destined for noncombatants rather than the Bosnian Army. They did not have the right to siphon off the food. **Pillage** is a war crime in an international conflict and a prohibited act in an internal conflict.

Starvation of civilian populations as a method of warfare is prohibited in both international or in internal conflicts, a prohibition stated explicitly in the two 1977 Additional Protocols to the Geneva Conventions. Yet a military force controlling the flow of relief supplies over routes or into territories it controls is under no obligation to do anything to support the military forces arrayed against it. The tension between these two positions has given rise to a complex series of rules that are difficult to implement without the use of force by the international community. The International Committee of the Red Cross (ICRC) takes the position that the fear of diversion to combatants provides no legal justification for refusing passage. But its position is not widely shared.

Humanitarian aid for civilians, under Article 23 of the Fourth Geneva Convention, enjoys the right of free passage through battle lines if intended for "children under fifteen, expectant mothers and maternity cases," and a broader exemption can be made when all or part of the civilian population in occupied territory is "inadequately supplied." Because of a very real military concern that the goods might be used to supply enemy armed forces, "inadequately" is understood in a strict sense.

It is, moreover, prohibited under Article 54 of Additional Protocol I to destroy "objects indispensable to the survival of the civilian population," including foodstuffs and their production, drinking water, and irrigation works, or to undertake actions "which may be expected to leave the civilian population with such inadequate food or water as to cause starvation or force its movement." Whether this prohibition on destruction of such objects extends to a positive obligation to allow their entry to provide for populations at risk of starvation is not clear from Article 54 but might be implied from subsequent provisions on relief operations.

If civilians in a conflict are not adequately provided with supplies, then under Article 70 of Protocol I "relief actions which are humanitarian and impartial in character and conducted without any adverse distinction shall be undertaken, subject to the agreement of the Parties concerned in such relief actions." Short of conditions requiring supplies essential to the survival of the civilian population, relief operations are subject to agreement of the parties.

In an internal armed conflict, if the civilian population is suffering "undue hardship" due to a lack of food or medical supplies "essential to its

A victim of an endless civil war where the government was widely accused of using starvation as a weapon. Sudan, 1998.

S

survival," relief actions "which are of an exclusively humanitarian and impartial nature" and conducted "without any adverse distinction" shall be undertaken subject to the the consent of the State involved.

Although the United States is not a party to Additional Protocols I or II, it supports the prohibition of starvation as a means of warfare.

It was in large measure because of the ambiguity in the law—the tension between **military necessity** and the obligation of all sides in a conflict to allow in articles needed to prevent starvation or the threat of starvation, so as to force civilians to flee their homes—that the United Nations and private relief groups in Bosnia were so vulnerable to the kind of blackmail I witnessed at the Serb checkpoint.

If allowing the Serbs to take 30 percent of the relief supplies meant that they would let in the other 70 percent when, strictly speaking, their obligation to do so was not ironclad, it was better to give in. Or so most aid groups reasoned. The alternative might very well have been to allow the most vulnerable groups—the very old and the very young, in particular—to starve. And more widespread starvation, which the humanitarian effort did manage to stave off in Bosnia, remained a possibility almost to the end of the war.

In Bosnia the signals were far from clear. The UNHCR and other agencies realized early on that it remained open to question whether the Serbs were obligated to allow aid through. Directives from the UN Security Council required as much, but realistically, they also knew they were incapable, as the law required, of preventing some of the aid from flowing to the Bosnian Army. Whatever the legal niceties, in all wars, the army eats first.

These were some of the reasons they acted as they did—another was that there was no will on the part of the UN or the great powers to push the aid through by force. Thus, trying to buy off the fighters seemed preferable to insisting that relief operations had to proceed in an absolutely uncompromising way.

S

Famished children at the gates of a feeding center in Somalia, a result of warfare among clans following the overthrow of President Siad Barre in 1991. Baidoa, Somalia, 1992.

"We could not let all those people die," was the way one UNHCR official in Zagreb put it at the time, "so we closed our eyes to many things." Loopholes in the law as well as realities on the ground had a lot to do with that decision.
(See **humanitarian aid, blocking of; siege; water supplies and works, destruction of.**)

T

Terrorism

By Anthony Dworkin

Since September 11, 2001, terrorism has emerged as the biggest security concern across much of the world. It has also become a kind of talisman whose invocation seems to absolve those fighting against it from previously unchallengeable legal and moral restraints. The use of terrorist tactics of unprecedented destructiveness by al-Qaeda and a network of associated groups is a frontal assault on the values of humanitarian law, and has at the same time created a crisis within the law, undermining acceptance of its core principles by the world's pre-eminent military power.

Al-Qaeda declared war on America long before 9/11. It was in August 1996 that Osama bin Laden first proclaimed a jihad against "the Americans occupying the land of the two holy places." "I'm declaring war on the United States," he confirmed to an interviewer from ABC News two years later. In one respect there was nothing surprising in this choice of language. Armed groups labelled as terrorists by the States against which they fight have regularly aspired to the status of warriors engaged in a legitimate contest and sought to dignify their campaigns of violence with military trappings. However in this case al-Qaeda was able to muster the resources and organizational skill to bring off an attack whose impact was on a scale similar to interstate conflict, half a world away from the group's base.

The suicide hijack-bombings of September 11 killed close to 3,000 people, brought down the tallest buildings in New York and inflicted serious damage on the Pentagon. The United Nations Security Council implicitly, and NATO explicitly, characterized them as an armed attack that gave the United States a right of self-defense under the UN Charter. Within a day, President Bush had announced a "war on terrorism" that he later said would be fought "wherever terrorists hide, or run, or plan." This conflict, according to a subsequent White House directive, ushered in a new paradigm that required new thinking in the law of war.

Terrorism is a concept that does not have a recognized and agreed legal meaning. Because the word is not merely descriptive but normative, it tends to become a place-holder for those forms of political violence that the speaker regards as most illegitimate. The most authoritative recent definition is in the 2004 Report of the UN High-Level Panel on Threats, Challenges and Change, which refers to terrorism as "any action... that is intended to cause death or serious bodily harm to civilians or noncombatants, when the purpose of such an act, by its nature or context, is to intimidate a population, or to compel a Government or an international organization to do or abstain from doing any act." This statement dismisses the idea that attacks on civilians may be raised above the level of terrorism if they take place as part of a campaign of resistance to occupation. However it also excludes attacks against military targets by non-State groups (such as al-Qaeda's attack on the American destroyer *Cole* in Yemen in 2000) from the sphere of terrorism and so would be regarded as incomplete by some people.

The UN Panel proposed its definition as the basis for a comprehensive

Remains of the World Trade Center, New York City, September 2001.

international convention banning terrorism—something that has long been under discussion at the United Nations—but the idea was not endorsed by the 2005 UN World Summit, as some developing countries insisted on preserving an exclusion clause for national liberation movements. Nevertheless, the actions associated with terrorism are already prohibited under a wide variety of international and domestic laws. Acts of terror when committed by non-State groups are generally crimes under the law of the country where they take place, and are most often prosecuted as such. For instance, Ramzi Yousef, who masterminded the 1993 bombing of the World Trade Center, was convicted in a New York court and sentenced to life imprisonment without parole. In addition, in recent decades, there have been 13 international conventions directed at specific acts identified with terrorism, including the 1979 Convention on the Taking of Hostages and the 1997 Convention against Terrorist Bombings.

Terrorist actions committed in the context of armed conflict are violations of international humanitarian law. One rule—stated in Article 51 of the first Additional Protocol of 1977 and Article 13 of the second Additional Protocol—specifically addresses the psychological effects that terrorism aims at, by prohibiting "acts or threats of violence the primary purpose of which is to spread terror among the civilian population." This provision is a reminder that—for all the debate about whether terrorism as a concept is necessarily limited to non-State groups—national authorities and regular armed forces can also carry out acts of terror.

In addition, treaty and customary law contains rules against the deliberate **targeting of civilians**, the launching of **indiscriminate attacks**, and the taking of **hostages** that are binding on all participants in both international and non-international armed conflicts. The prohibition on **perfidy** would ban attacks that rely on the attacker using the appearance of a civilian to avoid suspicion (as with most suicide bombs). In addition, wholesale acts of violence or systematic campaigns directed against a civilian population as an organizational policy might qualify as a **crime against humanity**.

As a method of fighting, terrorism represents the ultimate form of asymmetrical warfare, in which an armed group tries to neutralize the greater strength of its opponent by avoiding conventional battles in open terrain. Like guerrillas, terrorists fight with stealth; indeed there is some overlap between the two categories, and groups like the FLN (Front de Libération Nationale) during the Algerian war of independence against the French in the 1950s or the Tamil Tigers today in Sri Lanka combine elements of both approaches. But terrorism, as generally understood, does not involve an attempt to capture and hold territory, or to attack military targets for anything other than symbolic purposes. For these reasons campaigns of terror that are divorced from any broader military struggle have traditionally been seen as a form of crime, not warfare.

The uniqueness of the Bush administration's response to September 11 lay in invoking the notion of war to claim sweeping powers against al-Qaeda suspects, while at the same time denying the protection of the laws of war to America's supposed enemies. U.S. officials argued that the traditional prerogatives of war—the right to detain hostile fighters without trial or target them without warning—were necessary and appropriate, but that the restraints embodied in the Geneva Conventions, the Additional Protocols and customary law were not applicable against such an unconventional and dishonorable foe. By their actions, al-Qaeda's fighters had placed themselves outside the law and could be treated as military necessity required: this was the moral and legal intuition to which American policies appealed for justification.

But the administration's position—based on arguments developed largely by civilian officials, often in the face of strong opposition from senior uniformed lawyers and State Department experts—relies on an extraordinarily narrow and anachronistic picture of international law. It may have been true in earlier centuries that irregular fighters were entirely at the mercy of their enemies, but since World War II a complex set of international rules has been developed that builds on a vision of essential human dignity to offer some fundamental protections to individuals in all circumstances. These rules are found in Common Article 3 of the 1949 Geneva Conventions, in Article 75 of the first Additional Protocol, in human rights instruments like the Convention against Torture, and in customary law. They enshrine principles of humanity and due process and are not in any way dependent on a reciprocal commitment from the individual protected by them to respect similar values himself. The decision of the U.S. Supreme Court in the *Hamdan* case in June 2006, ruling that Common Article 3 applied at a minimum to American military operations against al-Qaeda, recognized this point.

Whether or not the fight against them is characterized as an armed conflict, suspected terrorists are entitled to baseline protections (for instance against cruel and degrading treatment or improper trials) in all situations. What about the Bush administration's claim that the existence of a "war against terrorism" allows the United States to target enemy combatants or detain them indefinitely? As stated, the phrase is legally meaningless, since the notion of war has historically been restricted to conflicts between States and there cannot be a war against a method of fighting. More cautious and lawyerly administration officials speak instead of an armed conflict against al-Qaeda and affiliated groups.

Even this claim is open to question. For an armed conflict to exist there must be protracted armed violence between two or more organized groups, and it is by no means clear that those conditions hold in the case of the United States and al-Qaeda (as distinct from the geographically limited conflict against the Taliban in Afghanistan that the U.S. launched in October 2001). More importantly, it is also not clear that the traditional prerogatives of warring parties—to target or detain enemy combatants—would automatically carry over into such an unconventional conflict, if it existed. Fundamental human rights principles forbidding arbitrary killing and prolonged arbitrary detention are now generally agreed to apply in time of war as well as peace. As armed conflict moves ever further from the traditional model of uniformed troops confronting each other on the field of battle, these human rights principles are likely to assume increasing importance in our understanding of what is permissible. In a conflict that may have no definite end, and where there is enormous uncertainty about who is taking part in hostilities on the other side, it does not seem compatible with these norms to seize or target anyone you assert to be an enemy combatant without independent oversight.

The Bush administration's reluctance to acknowledge these principles has obscured the continuing relevance of international law and threatens its authority. In the long run, however, concern over the excesses of the "war on terror" may force a new awareness that the overlapping legal regimes that apply to the use of armed violence contain no gaps and operate across more of a continuous spectrum than has previously been recognized.

(See **detention and interrogation, international vs. internal armed conflict.**)

Torture

By Nicole Pope

Ferhat is a broken man. Short and squat, with jet black hair and a bushy mustache, he looks healthy and strong as a bull, yet the life has gone out of his dark eyes.

This man in his thirties cannot sleep at night because he is afraid of the dark. He loses his temper when his four young children play loudly, because their screams remind him of the nightly cries he heard from his cell. He speaks in a monotone voice, his rasping accent revealing his Kurdish origins. At times overcome by emotion, he just stops, stares at his shoes, and shakes his head to push back the images that still haunt him, years after he was tortured in an interrogation center in Istanbul.

Like many others from Turkey's mainly Kurdish southeast, Ferhat (not his real name) was caught up in the conflict that tore his region between 1984 and 1999. Over thirty-five thousand people died and hundreds of thousands of villagers, Ferhat and his family among them, were forced to leave their homes when they were burned down by the army in an attempt to deny supplies and logistical support to the guerrillas living in remote mountainous areas.

Ferhat was not a fighter, but he was a member of a legal pro-Kurdish party that was viewed with great suspicion by the Turkish authorities and was later closed down by the courts. Arrested on two occasions in 1993 and in 1994, Ferhat was charged with "aiding and abetting an illegal organisation", but refused to confess to a crime he says he did not commit, despite extensive physical and mental pressure. At the end of his first trial, he was acquitted. There was no evidence against him other than a denunciation obtained from another prisoner under similar circumstances.

Ferhat's case took place in the context of what was considered an internal conflict, even if the Turkish Army often crossed the border into northern Iraq in pursuit of Kurdistan Workers Party (PKK) militants. While a State is entitled to suppress an insurrection as well as detain and prosecute rebels, torture is universally prohibited. "No exceptional circumstances whatsoever, whether a state of war or a threat of war, internal political instability or any other public emergency, may be invoked as a justification of torture," states the 1984 Convention for the Prevention of Torture and Inhuman or Degrading Treatment or Punishment.

The Convention, to which Turkey is a party, defines torture as "any act by which severe pain or suffering, whether physical or mental, is intentionally inflicted on a person," when the agent responsible is "a public official or other person acting in an official capacity." The treaty lists reasons for inflicting pain or suffering that are associated with torture: obtaining from the detainee or a third person information or a confession; punishing him for an act that he or a third person has committed; intimidating or coercing him or someone else; or for reasons based on discrimination. Pain and suffering arising only from "lawful sanctions" is not prohibited under the Convention.

In addition, torture during armed conflict is specifically prohibited by international humanitarian law, whether the conflict is international or internal, and no matter whether the victims are soldiers who have laid down their arms, civilians, or rebels. The prohibition exists in customary law and in treaties. The Geneva Conventions of 1949 include torture of protected persons (sick or wounded members of the armed forces, prisoners of war, or civilians in the hands of the enemy) among the grave breaches which States are obliged to enforce through criminal prosecution. The first Additional Protocol prohibits torture as well as humiliating and degrading treatment of any detainee, as does Common Article 3 of the Geneva Conventions in non-international conflicts.

The International Committee of the Red Cross study of customary international humanitarian law says that the use of "torture, cruel or inhuman treatment and outrages upon personal dignity, in particular humiliating and degrading treatment" against any person is forbidden in all armed conflicts.

In all these cases, the law makes a distinction between torture, which is often used to force information out of a suspect, and inhumane treatment, which attacks a person's dignity, but the line between the two is often blurred. Indeed, revenge and hatred, as much as the need to obtain a confession, often drive the torturers to inflict the suffering. Torture is used not just to hurt physically, but also to humiliate the victim, which is why prisoners are often left naked during torture sessions, and rape or pain inflicted on the genitals are among the most commonly used forms of torture.

Since the arrest in 1999 of PKK leader Abdullah Öcalan, the conflict has abated and armed clashes are rarer in Turkey's southeast. The Turkish government, determined to join the European Union, has introduced democratic reforms and improved its human rights record. Despite a government pledge to adopt a "zero tolerance" policy on torture, human rights groups say violations still occur but they are no longer systematic and appear to be on the decrease.

However, abuse of prisoners remains widespread in many countries. Moreover, there are disturbing signs that after September 11, 2001, torture, once considered abhorrent by Western public opinion and governments, is viewed by some as a necessary evil in the fight against terrorism.

Graphic photographs of detainees at Abu Ghraib prison in Iraq being humiliated, threatened with dogs and forced to pose naked in sexually explicit positions, caused a scandal in early 2004, and led to further revelations of ill treatment of prisoners elsewhere in U.S. custody. According to press reports, some detainees held by the CIA have been subjected to waterboarding, in which the victim is strapped down and water is poured over his face to induce the feeling of drowning—a practice that the United States has condemned as torture in the past when it was used by other countries.

In September 2006, the U.S. Defense Department issued a new interrogation field manual prohibiting the use of torture or cruel, inhuman or degrading treatment against any detainee held by the American armed forces. "Use of torture is not only illegal but also it is a poor technique that yields unreliable results," the manual states.

The days and nights Ferhat spent in total darkness behind a blindfold, the guards' taunts and insults, the death threats and the click of a pistol while he was waiting for an execution that never came were, according to him, even worse than the physical pain caused by the arm clamps that kept him hanging painfully for hours while electric cables were attached to his toes and genitals, and cigarettes burnt round scars in his forearms.

The Abu Ghraib prisoners piled up naked in human pyramids may not have physical scars to display but, as was the case for Ferhat, the abuse they suffered is likely to leave indelible marks on their psyche.

(See **detention and interrogation**.)

T

Total War

By Peter Rowe

Total war is sometimes used to mean the mobilization of all resources, economic and military, by a society in support of a war effort; this was the American description of its own engagement during World War II. It has also been used to mean a willingness to engage the enemy in any geographic zone, or with any available weaponry, or sometimes a willingness to fight a scorched-earth campaign, even on one's own territory. It has also been used to mean war conducted against an enemy's military and economic infrastructure, across all of its territory, in order to cripple the enemy's ability to wage war; Great Britain used the term in this sense in both World Wars. The term has also been used to mean a willingness to countenance any method or means of warfare, legal or illegal, including, for example, weapons categorically considered illegal, such as **chemical** or **biological weapons**. These extremely varied uses of the term *total war* have radically different legal implications within international humanitarian law (IHL).

The first three meanings of *total war* need not imply violations of IHL. It is possible, for example, under IHL to mobilize all of a society's resources to war ends. It is also possible to fight lawfully within IHL in any theater or with any legal weapons. It is even possible, although more difficult, to fight a war attacking military-economic infrastructure legally, provided that the attacking forces respect IHL rules regarding indiscriminate attack. Where a party to conflict runs afoul of IHL is the belief that total war permits the suspension of the laws of armed conflict.

IHL applies however intense the armed conflict. Any State that attempted to fight a total war, in the sense that it declared it would not abide by the limitations imposed on its conduct of the conflict by IHL, would be in violation of IHL and presumably would find itself the subject of UN Security Council resolutions.

In addition, it is no defense to individual or State liability for breaches of IHL that one's enemy is fighting a total war. Nor is it a defense to plead **military necessity**; military necessity only justifies actions that are themselves legal. IHL itself gives some latitude to commanders to conduct military operations, but they must act within the limitations of IHL. Nor is it a defense to argue that your breaches of IHL, as part of a total war, are in **reprisal** for the acts of your enemy. There are specific prohibitions in the Geneva Conventions of 1949 and in the 1977 Additional Protocol I of reprisals against those protected by these instruments, such as the civilian population, civilian objects, the wounded and sick, and prisoners of war. (See **legitimate military targets**; **limited war**; **military objectives**.)

Training in International Humanitarian Law

By Michael H. Hoffman

Civil and military leaders often claim that their forces always administer and obey international humanitarian law (IHL). How those leaders reply to one simple question can do much to support—or undermine—their claims. What training do your forces receive in IHL?

The 1949 Geneva Conventions contain a provision compelling States to include the "study" of IHL in "programmes of military and, if possible, civil instruction, so that the principles thereof may become known to the entire population, in particular to the armed fighting forces, the medical personnel and chaplains." By extension, insurgents are expected to provide similar instruction to their own forces. Ultimate responsibility for IHL training remains with political authorities and military leaders. The **International Committee of the Red Cross (ICRC)** and national Red Cross and Red Crescent societies also conduct IHL training for civilians in many parts of the world.

Military instruction is, generally, hands-on in nature. Effective IHL training for soldiers usually requires a practical, problem-solving approach. Some armed forces integrate IHL-linked scenarios into their training exercises, others rely more on classroom presentation. In some armed forces IHL training is by military assistance teams from other countries. There are also militaries that offer little or no training, and a few that are not aware that this body of law exists.

Two civilian institutions play an important role in IHL training. The ICRC has a Division for Relations with Armed and Security Forces that conducts IHL training using a multinational faculty composed of retired military officers. The International Institute of Humanitarian Law in San Remo, Italy, attracts military officers from around the world to its intensive IHL courses taught by IHL experts on active duty with their nations' armed forces.

Armed forces that have not yet developed a program of IHL instruction can attain it externally from the military forces of allied nations and/or internationally recognized institutions. There is no real excuse for leaders who fail to train their armed forces in IHL.

(See **command responsibility**; **soldiers, rights of**.)

T

Transfer of Civilians

By Thomas Goltz

Japarna Miruzeva, twenty-six, lives in the basement of a bombed-out Armenian house with her four children and considers herself lucky to be there. So do the one hundred or so other Azeri Kurdish refugee families who now occupy the ruins of Shariar, a once-quaint town on the lip of the disputed territory of mountainous (Nagorno) Karabakh—the majority—Armenian area that remains legally part of the former Soviet republic of Azerbaijan but that seceded in 1992 and is now a self-proclaimed independent state.

Life in Shariar is bleak at best. Well water is brackish and difficult to get; food is in short supply; there are no doctors; and the surrounding fields have been mined twice—once by the Armenians who used to till them, then by

T

the Azerbaijani Army that will have to defend the town if the Armenians come back to reclaim it.

Japarna Miruzeva and the other ethnic Kurdish families in Shariar believe they have nowhere else to go. They still hope to return to the Kelbajar, the neighboring Azerbaijani province from which they were expelled in April 1993, when Armenian and Karabakh forces effectively cleansed the territory of Azeri Turks and Kurds in order to stitch Karabakh to Armenia proper. At present, there is little hope that the day of return will occur any time soon, if ever. Although an uneasy cease-fire was established between the Armenians and Azerbaijanis in May 1994, a negotiated settlement of the war over Karabakh remains elusive due to the intransigence of both sides. Caught in the middle are people like the Miruzeva clan, who are just a few of the almost one million **internally displaced people** (IDPs) in the squalid tent cities, boxcar towns, and multifamily schoolroom domiciles that dot the Azerbaijani countryside.

In fact, from an international legal perspective, the Kurdish IDPs in

Armenian refugees flee their villages in the northern part of Nagorno Karabakh, the Armenian enclave in Azerbaijan, under Azeri assault, 1993.

T

Shariar are pawns in a war crime committed by the Azerbaijani authorities, who allowed them to move into the shattered Armenian homes in the contested town. In this instance at least, strict adherence to international law and human reality have parted company.

For a government to allow anyone to move into a zone that has been ethnically cleansed runs counter to the Fourth Geneva Convention of 1949, which protects civilians in an international armed conflict. "The Occupying power shall not deport or transfer part of its own civilian population into the territory it occupies," states Article 49. "Individual or mass forcible transfers, as well as deportations of protected persons from occupied territory" are in fact a grave breach, or war crime. Even in an internal conflict, according to Additional Protocol II of 1977, "displacement of the civilian population shall not be ordered for reasons related to the conflict."

If the security of civilians or "imperative military reasons" such as the movement of a front require it, the population may be temporarily evacuated but they must be returned to their homes when the crisis eases. Protocol II, Article 17, states: "Should such displacements have to be carried out, all possible measures shall be taken in order that the civilian population may be received under satisfactory conditions of shelter, hygiene, safety and nutrition."

Were one to ask Japarna Miruzeva or any of her fellow IDPs who come from the Azeri provinces in and around the Karabakh conflict zone who the party violating these covenants might be, the response would be very simple: Armenia and the Armenians of the mountainous Karabakh (including current Armenian President Robert Kocharian who, ironically, as a citizen of mountainous Karabakh, is legally a citizen of Azerbaijan) who flushed them from their homes and, as the occupying force, refused to let them return.

Armenia has gone farther than that. In addition to actively settling Armenian refugees from Azerbaijan into the homes of Azeri Turks and Kurds in the areas it occupies, the Armenian diaspora has constructed a multimillion-dollar paved road across the so-called Lachin Corridor, another Azeri Kurdish region that represents the shortest point between Karabakh and Armenia. It was ethnically cleansed of its citizens by Armenian forces in May 1992—and Armenia has been adamant that even if there is a future settlement that might allow the Kelbajar Kurds (including Japarna Miruzeva) to go home, Lachin will never be relinquished.

At the Nuremberg Trials, which preceded the Geneva Conventions, several Nazi government officials were indicted for the crime against humanity of deporting civilians from occupied Germany as slave labor, and transferring German nationals into occupied territory for resettlement. The final judgment against several individual defendants mentioned only deportations, not the resettlement.

The apparent gap in the law today is that in international armed conflict the law does not cover a country transferring its own nationals from refugee or IDP centers in relatively peaceful areas of the country to areas close to front lines. And the problem becomes more acute when the people in question are not being forced to move to such areas but choose to.

As one international aid worker put it, "when a family who have been dwelling in a filthy railway car in either Armenia or Azerbaijan decides that the quickest way to end the awful state of refugeehood is to take one's fate into one's own hands and starts repairing the wall of someone else's house that now finds itself on the 'friendly' side of the front lines, who is going to tell them to stop? The legal dilemma is punctured by the human need."
(See **deportation; ethnic cleansing**.)

Undefended Towns

By Adam Roberts

Towns or cities that are *undefended* or *open* (the terms are used more or less synonymously) have been the subject of regulation, and confusion, in international law and military practice since at least the late nineteenth century.

The laws of war specify that undefended places should not be attacked. The 1907 Hague Regulations on Land Warfare, still formally in force, state in Article 25: "The attack or bombardment, by whatever means, of towns, villages, dwellings or buildings which are undefended is prohibited." Similar language in the 1907 Hague Convention deals with naval bombardment.

The term *undefended* can be interpreted to encompass all places that are not fortified and do not have an active military presence. In this logic, even a town that is in the interior of a country at war and which has extensive armaments factories or military communications systems could count as undefended. However, the view that such places should be immune from attack has generally been rejected by military planners, especially by airmen, and should not be taken as indicative of prevailing law.

In practice, the words *undefended* and *open* have been defined restrictively, to mean simply places declared to be open for entry and occupation by an adverse party without resistance. In this view, the core meaning of the rule prohibiting attacks on undefended towns is simply that a town in a war zone that has declared itself ready to accept the entry of the adversary's army may not be bombed or subjected to artillery attack. This is widely agreed to be the most persuasive interpretation of the practical meaning and original intention of Article 25 of the 1907 Regulations. This restrictive view has been confirmed in the 1977 Additional Protocol I to the Geneva Conventions, Article 59, which says that a belligerent may declare as a *non-defended locality* "any inhabited place near or in a zone where armed forces are in contact which is open for occupation by an adverse Party."

There have been many cases of towns being declared "open" in this sense. When French forces abandoned Paris in June 1940, the Germans were notified that the city was open for their entry. In June 1944 the German command in Italy asked the Allies to "confirm" the status of Rome as an open city, and then made a unilateral declaration to that effect, followed by surrender of the city to the Allies. Sometimes the concept of open cities has been used differently, to refer to the idea that certain towns should be spared bombardment, even if they are not open to occupation—for example, if they are far from the front line.

Most destructive attacks in modern war have been against cities that were not undefended in the sense of open to occupation by the adversary. This has strengthened the pressure to develop other bases for protecting cities, and their inhabitants, from the ravages of modern war.

The term *open cities* has been used by the UN High Commissioner for Refugees (UNHCR) with a completely different meaning: it refers to an initiative in Bosnia-Herzegovina following the 1995 Dayton peace agreement to reward local authorities who declare their Opstina, or district, open and are committed to the return of minorities to their prewar homes.
(See **legitimate military targets**; **safety zones.**)

United Nations and the Geneva Conventions

By Roy Gutman

In November 1994, as hundreds of Bosnian and Krajina Serb troops advanced on the UN-declared "safe area" of Bihac, disaster loomed for the municipal hospital, which stood directly in the path of the offensive and for the nine hundred immobile patients inside—as well as for the town of Bihac, which lay immediately beyond the institution grounds. The Canadian commander of UN forces in Bihac was reluctant to intervene, but the UN force's civil affairs representative, an American, argued that hospitals have a "sacred" status under the 1949 Geneva Conventions, and the UN Protection Force (UNPROFOR) had to provide protection.

He sent a memo to this effect to his superior in Sarajevo, a Russian, who in turn issued a formal request. "The Geneva conventions stipulate that hospitals shall not be attacked... the support and concurrence of UNPROFOR military will also be needed. Please immediately pursue the plan with the Bihac commanding officer," it said. The UN commander thereupon instructed Bangladeshi troops to drive their armored personnel carriers onto the hospital grounds. The Serbs refrained from attacking the hospital and halted the ground invasion. Bihac, with a population of seventy thousand, was saved.

Two weeks later, the UN's Office of Legal Affairs (OLA) weighed in to ensure that the rescue of Bihac would not become a precedent. UN forces, an OLA representative said, were bound only by their Security Council mandate and were not legally obliged to uphold the conventions. "From a strictly legal point of view, obligations (such as the Geneva Conventions) are binding on States. The role of the UN is to carry out the will of the international community as expressed by it in the Security Council," OLA official Stephen Katz said.

The incident was an illustration of the UN's ambivalent relation to the Geneva Conventions at the time. Nearly every member-State is a legal party to the conventions, and each has undertaken "to respect and to ensure respect" of the provisions. But donning the blue helmets effectively provided States a way to escape their legal obligations.

When States assign troops to peacekeeping duties, the forces answer formally and solely to the Security Council, says the UN. (This is something of a fiction, because in operational terms they are officered, equipped, deployed, moved about, and directed through a national chain of command - at the insistence of the United States and many other countries.) But the United Nations as an intergovernmental institution is not a party to the conventions. Sometimes, on the eve of deployments, the Security Council would issue a statement reminding States of the applicability of the pertinent Geneva rules and the obligation to punish violations. Other times, the council would "forget" to mention the point.

When Iraq invaded Kuwait in 1990, the Security Council neglected for six weeks to mention the protections the Geneva Conventions guaranteed for civilians in Kuwait. When the council authorized the use of force to liberate

U

Kuwait, the resolution failed to remind States in the coalition of their obligations as combatants under the Geneva Conventions or humanitarian law. In fact, one of the early sanctions resolutions violated the rule that requires free passage for many sorts of humanitarian aid intended for civilians, even civilians of an adversary. Concerning its operation in Bosnia-Herzegovina, as well as that of its peacekeeping operation in Cambodia in the early 1990s, the Security Council issued no statement on the relevance of humanitarian law to the UN peacekeeping deployment.

Tension over the conventions also reflected the different institutional cultures of the UN and the International Committee of the Red Cross (ICRC). The UN's founding charter defined it as a body that would establish world peace—a lofty aim that seemingly precluded it from becoming a combatant or occupying power. The UN opted out of a role in the codification of the laws of war in 1949 with a condescending dismissal of the enterprise. "War having been outlawed, the regulation of its conduct has ceased to be rele-

Not in the mandate: A Bosnian woman from Srebrenica pleads with a UN peace-keeper, 1995.

vant," the UN International Law Commission explained. For this reason, the drafting was undertaken under ICRC auspices in Geneva.

The arms-length attitude of the UN headquarters had its counterpart in the field. In the absence of a controlling international legal regime, and with ambiguous mandates that often drifted from passive peacekeeping to active peace-enforcing, the military on the ground would take charge. Field commanders, bearing in mind the often-clearer priorities of their own governments, would answer formally to a Security Council that was incapable of managing from long distance. Often the commanders would pick and choose what they did, based on their reading of the mandate. War crimes got short shrift. In Bosnia, UN personnel in mid-1992 visited Sonja's Kon-Tiki, a restaurant-pension outside Sarajevo, on whose grounds, according to the Bosnian government, was a Serb-run concentration camp. UN forces never asked questions, investigated, or protested, explaining that neither the UN command nor their governments had provided them any lists of concentration camps. In Somalia, when Canadian soldiers killed a Somali intruder in cold blood in March 1993, the Canadian commander did not punish the crime but covered it up. (Following an official inquiry, the Airborne Regiment involved was later disbanded.) Later that year, UN forces detained hundreds of Somalis, then denied the ICRC access to them and persisted until the ICRC suspended all operations in protest.

The anomaly troubled many thoughtful UN officials. The Serb-run camp was "so blatant" a violation of international law, said Kofi Annan, who served as UN Secretary-General from 1997 to 2006. "They should have seen it and reported. And in fact if they had reported, it is the sort of thing that would have gone public much earlier than it did." As for the UN legal office's view of the conventions, "We have asked them to respect the Geneva Conventions whether we signed it or not." But he also expressed understanding for troops in the absence of explicit Security Council mandates. "Soldiers like to have a clear mandate," he said. "They will not go out of their way" to look for war crimes.

After six years of discussion between ICRC and UN experts, Annan issued a bulletin in August 1999 on the observance by UN forces of International Humanitarian Law. It stated that the rules and principles of IHL are binding on military personnel and set out many of the basic rules of the Geneva Conventions. But the statement stipulated that violations are subject to prosecution in national courts, thus thus avoiding an endorsement of the principle of universal jurisdiction. "We fought and lost that battle," commented an ICRC legal expert. Annan's statement did not result from a negotiation and is not legally binding. A number of States including some permanent members of the Security Council later voiced reservations but did not formally challenge it. Still, in the seven years after Annan promulgated the statement, it may have had a positive impact. Blatant disregard for the conventions by UN peacekeepers seems to have given way to a greater respect.

U

Unlawful Confinement

By Ed Vulliamy

The column of prisoners blinked into the sunlight as they emerged from within a dark, capacious hangar and were drilled in a straight line across a yard into a canteen under the watchful eye of a beefy machine gunner, aloft at his post.

In the minute that was permitted, the men devoured their watery bean stew. Their skin was folded over their bones like parchment. They clutched their spoons, their spindly fingers shaking. Their huge, hollow eyes fixed upon us. "I do not want to tell any lies," said one emaciated figure, "but I cannot tell the truth."

This was lunchtime at Omarska, the Serb-run camp for Muslim and Croatian prisoners. Crews from ITN television and I witnessed the scene on August 5, 1992, before we were ignominiously bundled out.

The truth—which emerged only with time—was that Omarska was a hellish **concentration camp** in our lifetime, just down the road from Venice. It was a place where killing, cruelty, and ritual humiliation had become a form of twisted recreation. The guards were often drunk and singing as they tortured, beat, mutilated, and slaughtered prisoners, and there was a particular taste for forced fellatio, forced sex with animals, and sexual mutilation. The UN Commission of Experts called Omarska a "*de facto* death camp."

One prisoner was forced to bite off the testicles of another who, as he died, had a live pigeon stuffed into his mouth to stifle his screams. An eyewitness, testifying later at the United Nations International Criminal Tribunal for the Former Yugoslavia (ICTY) at The Hague described the behavior of the guards during this barbarism as being "like a crowd at a sports match."

At the end of these orgies of violence—usually on the tarmac yard or in two outbuildings, the White House and Red House—the cadavers of the dead would be loaded onto trucks by their friends or with bulldozers. There was a macabre intimacy to this carnage: people knew their torturers; they had been neighbors. Omarska had already been emptied of most of its prisoners before we arrived and was rapidly closed the day after our visit. It was a bitter kernel at the core not just of Bosnia's war, but of our time.

Omarska also provides a textbook case of unlawful confinement, a war crime. The legacy of Omarska was dramatically recalled at the first war crimes trial since Nuremberg, at The Hague in 1996. A part-time guard at the camp, Dusko Tadic, was charged with **war crimes** and **crimes against humanity**.

The laws of war on unlawful confinement vary according to whether a conflict is internal or international; they are intricately detailed for international conflicts but impose minimal standards for internal conflicts.

In an international conflict, unlawful confinement is a grave breach of the Fourth Geneva Convention of 1949. The statute of the ICTY states that (unlawful) imprisonment directed against the civilian population is a crime against humanity. Imprisonment as a form of **persecution** on political, racial, or religious grounds is also a crime against humanity.

Based on his role in the "seizure, collection, segregation, and forced transfer of civilians to camps," the tribunal found Tadic guilty of persecution on political, racial, or religious grounds, a crime against humanity.

Not all confinement of civilians is unlawful. Article 42 of the Fourth Convention allows for a "detaining power" to intern those who pose a security threat, "only if the security of the detaining power makes it absolutely necessary." The descriptions for this are "internment" or "assigned residence." A civilian may also be lawfully interned if he or she commits certain minor offenses against an occupying power or poses a genuine threat.

The International Committee of the Red Cross (ICRC) Commentary on the Conventions calls internment a way of "getting people out of the way, and where supervision is more easily exercised." A civilian in a foreign country at war may be interned "if the security of the detaining power makes it absolutely necessary." A civilian in occupied territory may be interned if it is "necessary, for imperative reasons of security, to take safety measures concerning protected persons." There must have been some clear action threatening the security of the detaining power, such as espionage or sabotage or belonging to "organizations whose object is to cause disturbances"

Prisoner camp at Manjaca. Bosnia-Herzegovina, August 9, 1992.

or threaten (the belligerent's) security by other means. Merely being an enemy national is not enough. Civilians may be held or imprisoned as suspects or criminals, so long as they enjoy the rights relating to fair trials.

It is lawful to remove civilians for their own security in an emergency, such as an impending battle, into temporary shelters. Even so, they must be well cared for and returned home as soon as it is safe to do so. Enemy combatants, of course, may be interned as prisoners of war.

Neither the Geneva Conventions nor Additional Protocol II of 1977, which all parties to the Bosnia conflict agreed to follow, codifies the rules as to when civilians may be interned in an internal armed conflict. But the rules stipulate that if the internment is a sentence for a crime, the defendant must be allowed all the rights of a fair trial.

At a briefing inside Omarska the local police chief, Simo Drljaca (later shot dead by British troops in summer 1997 while resisting arrest), insisted that a security threat existed—the Serbs even staged a pathetic mock gun battle to try to convince us. The authorities, he said, were screening inmates in order to find Muslim insurrectionists.

This proved to be a grotesque lie; the overwhelming majority of Drljaca's captives were unarmed civilians. Even if they had been armed or hostile, the law still requires certain standards, beginning with Article 37 of the Fourth Geneva Convention, which stipulates that: "protected persons who are confined pending proceedings or subject to a sentence involving loss of liberty shall, during their confinement, be humanely treated." This stipulation includes prisoners being protected from attack, fed, clothed and otherwise cared for. Similar requirements for humane treatment apply to internal conflicts. Additional Protocol II also requires that they be properly fed, clothed, and sheltered, and "be afforded safeguards as regards health and hygiene."

If the detainees of Omarska had been prisoners of war, they would have been entitled to "not be held in close confinement except where necessary to to safeguard their health"—i.e., the stinking human chicken coop in which they were held was clearly illegal.

Detainees must have sufficient sleeping space and be allowed to hold services in their adopted religion. The detaining power is obliged to provide medical care and an "adequate infirmary"—all provisions for which Omarska was the direct antithesis.

In contrast to the watery bean stew, daily food rations must be of a proper "quantity, quality and variety" to maintain health. The "investigations" which Mr. Drljaca claimed he was carrying out "shall be conducted as rapidly as circumstances permit" and brought to a trial as rapidly as possible. It was unlawful for men to be left festering, whatever the camp conditions.

Internees in an international armed conflict must be able to "retain articles of personal use," and "articles which have above all a personal or sentimental value may not be taken away"—in contrast to the wholesale pillaging of valuables in the Serbian camps. The arbitrary and systematic or widespread imprisonment of large numbers of civilians during conflicts— internal or international—is a crime against humanity.

In a non-international armed conflict all detainees are automatically covered by Article 3 common to the four Geneva Conventions. This provision states that "persons taking no active part in the hostilities... shall in all circumstances be treated humanely, without any adverse distinction founded on race, color, religion or faith, sex, birth or wealth, or any other similar criteria."

It prohibits "violence to life... in particular murder of all kinds, mutilation, cruel treatment and torture" and "the passing of sentences and the carrying out of executions without previous judgment pronounced by a regularly constituted court."

Additional Protocol II of 1977 provides a further list of fundamental guarantees and rights for nonmilitary internees in non-international conflicts: the wounded and sick must be respected and properly treated; internees are to be provided with food and drinking water to the same extent that local civilians have them, and they are to be properly sheltered.

Under the Geneva Conventions, the detaining power is obliged to admit bodies such as the ICRC into its camps in an international armed conflict. But in Bosnia such organizations were kept out for three long, bloody months. They would have been another awkward group that knew the rules, and would recognize how thoroughly they were being torn to shreds.
(See **occupation**.)

Victims, Rights of

By Lindsey Hilsum

Hiding in her house in Kigali, hearing the cries of her neighbors as they were being slaughtered, Monica Uwimana did not know where to turn for help. Gangs of youths were moving from house to house with machetes and nail-studded clubs killing Tutsis like her. She called UN employees. They said they could not help. She called a foreign reporter and asked for advice. The journalist had none.

Many Rwandans believe that UN peacekeepers had an obligation to help them. But the UN Security Council withdrew most of the troops at the height of the Rwanda genocide in April 1994 and did not order a new force in until it was too late.

In theory, civilians can turn to a neutral country and try to make it to a foreign embassy. But even if Monica Uwimana could have gotten past the roadblocks, she might have been turned away, for most embassies take in and protect only victims who have a proven link to their country, or whose own country has formally requested that its citizens be protected.

Rwanda was the extreme example of a humanitarian crisis in which the international community and its representatives all but disappeared from the scene when they were most needed. And it encapsulates the predicament for victims of armed conflict, of crimes against humanity, or, as in this instance, of genocide. States have the obligation to pay compensation for violating international conventions and are responsible for the misdeeds of their troops. The Hague Convention of 1907 states: "A belligerent party which violates the provisions of the said Convention shall, if the case demands, be liable to pay compensation. It shall be responsible for all acts committed by persons forming part of its armed forces." Similar language is found in the first Additional Protocol of 1977. Individuals responsible for war crimes, crimes against humanity or genocide may in time face criminal charges before institutions like the war crimes tribunals for the former Yugoslavia and Rwanda, or the recently formed International Criminal Court. Ultimately in these cases there will be accountability. But at the moment of maximum violence, protection is almost nonexistent.

The **International Committee of the Red Cross (ICRC)** is one of the first places victims turn. Its mandate is based on the Geneva Conventions: to protect the most vulnerable individuals, be they prisoners of war or civilians who come under attack; to trace the missing and reunite them with their families; to supervise repatriation of prisoners; and to remind all sides in a conflict that they are obliged to uphold the conventions. During the Rwanda genocide, its expatriate and local staff expanded their mandate and sheltered as many as nine thousand Rwandans in the ICRC compound. But the ICRC was overwhelmed. Its representatives collected thousands of wounded civilians and brought them to hospital. That did not spell protection, for on one occasion, soldiers entered the hospital after the foreigners had departed and massacred the patients. On another, Tutsis were dragged out of ICRC vehicles and killed. In parts of Rwanda, local staff of the national Red Cross participated in the killing.

The UN High Commissioner for Refugees (UNHCR), by its mandate,

U

attempts to provide protection for those who flee their country because of conflict. The massive growth in the number of **internally displaced** persons (IDPs) has led UNHCR to set up operations in an increasing number of countries to handle them. And an ever-growing number of non-governmental organizations (NGOs) are attempting to help the victims of armed conflict. But few national or international NGOs operate in the midst of the conflict, unless an outside power guarantees their security. And the conflict in Bosnia shows the limits of such protection, for outside military force was deployed to protect convoys of food and medicine attempting to reach UN-declared "safe areas," but did almost nothing to safeguard the civilians or, when they came under attack, the safe areas as well.

In the post-Cold War era, aid organizations increasingly are targeted along with the civilians they are protecting. The head of the ICRC mission in Bosnia was targeted and killed in June of 1992, leading the ICRC to withdraw its entire presence from that country temporarily. It was then that Bosnian Serbs began their full-scale ethnic cleansing campaign. In Burundi, three ICRC delegates were ambushed on a main road and murdered in 1996. The same year, in Chechnya, gunmen broke into an ICRC compound and killed six delegates. And in 2003, a suicide bomber attacked the ICRC building in Baghdad, killing two officials and ten bystanders. Attacks on those who try to help victims are the most dramatic evidence of the total disregard for the laws of war that marks contemporary conflict.

Under international law, States are obliged to prevent and, that failing, punish grave breaches of the Geneva Conventions and the first Additional Protocol. For reasons of domestic politics, States often prefer to stay out of each others' conflicts; and the judicial instruments to justify intervention have at best weak enforcement mechanisms. The 1948 Genocide Convention, which requires States parties to "prevent and to punish" genocide, contains no mechanism for determining if a genocide is under way. Article 90 of Additional Protocol I of 1977 set up an **International Humanitarian Fact-Finding Commission** to investigate charges of war crimes, but it requires the consent of both parties to function and has been in general disuse. The newest attempt is the UN's recent creation of an International Criminal Court, whose prosecutor is empowered to launch investigations into war crimes and crimes against humanity while crimes are underway.

As for compensation, victims have a right under international and domestic law to sue, but after a genocide such as Rwanda's, there is rarely anyone rich enough left to pay the damages. The victims of the Nazi Holocaust received reparations from successor German governments. But "comfort women," used as sex slaves by Japanese troops during World War II, have yet to receive State compensation fifty years later, even though the government admitted in 1993 that Japan's military was responsible for the crime. On April 27, 1998, the Tokyo district court ordered compensation paid to three Korean women, but in March 2006, the Hiroshima High Court overturned this landmark decision. The UN Commission on Human Rights has advocated a set of principles to assist victims of human rights violations. The principles include a family's right to know the fate of missing people, the right to reparations, the right to criminal justice, and the principle that governments take steps to prevent recurrences. These principles are only recommendations, however.

By luck, chance, and the grace of God, Monica Uwimana survived. Her five children, who had been staying with grandparents in the countryside, were murdered. She has little faith in international law.

(See **Darfur; occupation; protected persons; refugees, rights of**.)

Wanton Destruction

By Jeremy Bowen

It seemed a little safer on the low hill on the edge of Grozny. We wanted to avoid a repeat of the day before, when we had been caught in a Russian air strike in the center of the city. I had lain in the lee of a small wall, wishing my flak jacket covered my legs as well as my back, waiting for the cluster bombs to stop exploding. About a hundred yards away the bomb fragments killed the four Chechen fighters I had been interviewing a minute or so earlier. None of us in the BBC team had been feeling very lucky before the air strike. Now we felt like marked men, like everybody else in Grozny in the first few days of 1995.

We stood on the hill, filming, at fairly long range, the fires that the Russian bombardment had started. Then, new explosions, fire and smoke started to pour out of central Grozny. Perhaps I was just knocked back by a surge of adrenaline and fear, but my memory tells me that the earth shook and the blast vibrated through my guts. In the next few seconds the line of flame and smoke moved right along the line of the city's main avenue that starts in Minutka Square and ends at the Chechen parliament building. It was a massive, coordinated attack by the heavy artillery and multiple rocket launchers I had seen on the Russian side of the lines. It was hard to believe that anybody could survive the inferno. Grozny disappeared under new clouds of flame and smoke and we got out with our tapes.

I went back into the center of Grozny most days that January. There were many more Russian attacks. Block after block of typical Soviet concrete-and-steel buildings were destroyed. In the few weeks after President Boris Yeltsin ordered his troops to end the Chechen rebellion, the Russians flattened the center of the city. Its destruction was more complete than anything I saw in the former Yugoslavia (including Mostar and Vukovar) and six other wars.

The laws of war state that an attacker must attempt to distinguish between military targets and civilians and their **property**. If he does not, he is guilty of the war crime of **indiscriminate attack**. If the attack also results in extensive, unnecessary, and willful damage then he is also guilty of wanton destruction. **Proportionality** is everything. The laws recognize that a legitimate military operation can kill noncombatants or damage their property. But any damage must not be excessive in comparison to the direct and concrete military advantage anticipated.

Despite the laws' clarity, their application is often clouded by other considerations. At the Nuremburg Trials, Hermann Goering, the German air minister, and all the major war criminals were charged with "the devastation of towns, not justified by **military necessity**, in violation of the laws of war." The charges were not pursued, perhaps because they were accused also of a wide range of other crimes and because the Allies did not want to draw attention to their own bombing campaigns in Germany and Japan.

And in Grozny, Russia could cite the fact that small groups of Chechen fighters were moving around the city almost at will, working their way up to the main confrontation line where they were killing hundreds of Russian conscripts. The shelling I witnessed followed the disastrous failure of a force of

Russian tanks to break into the city center. Moscow might argue that shelling was the best and only way to take on the highly motivated Chechens.

If Grozny itself is an ambiguous case under the laws of war, there were plenty of examples that were crystal clear. The scene was a crossroads on the road into Grozny. Refugees had been flooding out of the city in the face of the Russian attack, and enterprising traders had set up corrugated iron shacks to sell drinks and food to those who had money. You could hear the noise of shelling coming from Grozny. Sometimes Russian warplanes flew overhead on their way to bomb the city. In the middle distance the silvery shape of a Russian helicopter-gunship hovered almost motionless over one of the outlying villages. Every now and then it launched a missile into the village, where the Chechens were putting up stiff resistance.

The war was all around, but the crossroads seemed like a backwater. I never saw Chechen fighters use it. The closest bridges were three-quarters of a mile away, and the Russian Air Force had blown up one.

Grozny: A woman stands in the ruins of the Chechen capital after the Russian assault, 1996.

But one morning in January 1995, Russian warplanes had attacked the crossroads, bombing and strafing. There were wounded in the hospital and, we were told, about half a dozen dead—all civilians. There were impact craters in the road. All that was left of the food-and-drink stands were a few twisted pieces of corrugated iron. The traders were picking up where they had left off, rebuilding the stands. And the refugees were still moving out of Grozny. The devastation of the crossroads, though on a far smaller scale than the attack on Grozny, was by all available evidence, a pure example of wanton destruction.

(See **civilian immunity**; **immunity**; **legitimate military targets**; **military objectives**; **pillage**.)

W

War Crimes, Categories of

By Steven R. Ratner

The term "war crimes" evokes a litany of horrific images—concentration camps, ethnic cleansing, execution of prisoners, rape, and bombardment of cities. These images correspond in many ways to the legal definitions of the term, but international law draws lines that do not in all ways match our sense of the most awful behavior.

War crimes are those violations of the laws of war—or international humanitarian law (IHL)—that incur individual criminal responsibility. While limitations on the conduct of armed conflict date back at least to the Chinese warrior Sun Tzu (sixth century b.c.e.), the ancient Greeks were among the first to regard such prohibitions as law. The notion of war crimes *per se* appeared more fully in the Hindu code of Manu (circa 200 b.c.e.), and eventually made its way into Roman and European law. The first true trial for war crimes is generally considered to be that of Peter von Hagenbach, who was tried in 1474 in Austria and sentenced to death for wartime atrocities.

By World War I, States had accepted that certain violations of the laws of war—much of which had been codified in the Hague Conventions of 1899 and 1907—were crimes. The 1945 Charter of the International Military Tribunal at Nuremberg defined war crimes as "violations of the laws or customs of war," including murder, ill-treatment, or deportation of civilians in occupied territory; murder or ill-treatment of prisoners of war; killing of hostages; plunder of public or private property; wanton destruction of municipalities; and devastation not militarily necessary.

The 1949 Geneva Conventions, which codified IHL after World War II, also marked the first inclusion in a humanitarian law treaty of a set of war crimes—the grave breaches of the conventions. Each of the four Geneva Conventions (on wounded and sick on land, wounded and sick at sea, prisoners of war, and civilians) contains its own list of grave breaches. The list in its totality is: willful killing; torture or inhuman treatment (including medical experiments); willfully causing great suffering or serious injury to body or health; extensive destruction and appropriation of property not justified by military necessity and carried out unlawfully and wantonly; compelling a prisoner of war or civilian to serve in the forces of the hostile power; willfully depriving a prisoner of war or protected civilian of the rights of a fair and regular trial; unlawful deportation or transfer of a protected civilian; unlawful confinement of a protected civilian; and taking of hostages. Additional Protocol I of 1977 expanded the protections of the Geneva Conventions for international conflicts to include as grave breaches: certain medical experimentation; making civilians and nondefended localities the object or inevitable victims of attack; the perfidious use of the Red Cross or Red Crescent emblem; transfer of an occupying power of parts of its population to occupied territory; unjustifiable delays in repatriation of POWs; apartheid; attack on historic monuments; and depriving protected persons of a fair trial. Under the Geneva Conventions and Additional Protocol I, States must prosecute persons accused of grave breaches or hand them over to a State willing to do so.

W

The grave breaches provisions only apply in international armed conflicts; and they only apply to acts against so-called protected persons or during battlefield activities. Protected persons are, in general, wounded and sick combatants on land and sea, POWs, and civilians who find themselves in the hands of a state of which they are not nationals.

Most violations of the Geneva Conventions and Additional Protocols are not grave breaches. Of those not listed as grave breaches, many are still considered war crimes, although in those cases States do not have the same obligation to extradite or prosecute as they do for grave breaches. Other nongrave breaches are not war crimes, but simply illegal acts for which only the violating State is responsible under international law. To give one simple example, if the commander of a POW camp failed to keep a record of all disciplinary punishments (a violation of Article 96 of the Third Geneva Convention), he would likely not be committing a war crime—although some may disagree. Distinguishing among nongrave breaches to determine which are crimes is not an exact science, though it would seem that the more serious nongrave breaches do incur individual responsibility. (The U.S. military maintains that all violations of the laws of war, including those of the Geneva Conventions, are war crimes.)

Wartime atrocities not prohibited under the Geneva Conventions or Additional Protocol I may nonetheless be war crimes under the customary law rubric of "violations of the laws and customs of war" (the same phrase as in the Nuremberg Charter). For interstate conflicts, states agree that such war crimes include certain violations of the 1907 Hague Convention and Regulations, such as use of poisonous weapons, wanton destruction of cities not justified by military necessity, attacks on undefended localities, attacks on religious and cultural institutions, and plunder of public and private property. The Statute of the International Criminal Court (ICC) lists as war crimes for international conflicts not only the grave breaches of the Geneva Conventions, but some twenty-six serious violations of the laws and customs of war, most of which have been considered by States as crimes since at least World War II.

As for civil wars, unfortunately, international law today has fewer rules regulating the conduct of internal conflicts, which many States consider part of their domestic jurisdiction and, consequently, there is a shorter list of war crimes. Additional Protocol II of 1977, which contains basic rules for the conduct of internal conflicts, has no criminal liability provisions, and the reach of customary law war crimes is not as clear with respect to such wars as it is for international wars. The Statute of the International Criminal Tribunal for the Former Yugoslavia includes "serious violations of Common Article 3 of the Geneva Conventions" (the one article of the Geneva Conventions that addresses civil wars), as well as other rules to protect victims of armed conflict and basic rules on methods of warfare. The tribunal defined a serious violation as one that has grave consequences for its victims and breaks a rule protecting important values. This would presumably include violence to life or health (murder, ill-treatment, torture, mutilation, corporal punishment, rape, enforced prostitution, indecent assault), summary executions, hostage taking, collective punishment, and pillage. This list, while shorter than the list of grave breaches or other interstate war crimes, nonetheless would cover some of the most horrific acts during recent conflicts. The Statute of the International Criminal Tribunal for Rwanda includes as war crimes serious violations of Common Article 3 as well as serious violations of Additional Protocol II. The Statute of the ICC lists as war crimes for internal conflicts four serious violations of Common Article 3 (violence to life and person, outrages upon personal dignity, hostage taking, and summary executions), as well as twelve serious violations of the laws and customs of war (e.g., attacks on civilians, pillage, rape, or mutilation).

Though perhaps an obvious point, it should be noted that the laws of war only cover atrocities during armed conflict. They exclude many of the worst abuses of this century, such as Stalin's purges and destruction of the Kulaks, most of the Khmer Rouge's terror, and Mao's forced collectivizations. While these atrocities are international crimes—**crimes against humanity**, or, in some cases, **genocide**—they are not war crimes.

The definitional nexus of war crimes to armed conflict means that the atrocities against civilians committed by actors identified as terrorists do not always fit neatly within the existing categories of war crimes. As a general matter, it can be argued that the war paradigm and war crimes moniker simply should not apply to most of their actions, as they are engaged not in a war (interstate or civil), where international law accepts much belligerent activity as lawful, but rather in a criminal enterprise in which all acts are illegal. In this sense neither the Geneva Conventions nor customary law regarding war crimes captures the nature of their crimes. Insofar as terrorist activities by non-State actors are committed as part of a more paradigmatic interstate or civil war, e.g., an insurgent group working for one side blows up a civilian bus, these could well constitute grave breaches of the Geneva Conventions or other violations of the laws and customs of war, including those applying to civil conflicts. The United States government seems to hold that some terrorist acts, even those not associated with existing interstate or civil wars, are indeed "violations of the laws and customs of war." It is currently trying some suspected terrorists before military commissions at Guantanamo Bay for various offenses that it concludes are, in the words of an instruction to the commissions, "violations of the law of armed conflict or offenses that, consistent with that body of law, are triable by military commissions." The foregoing considerations make any determination whether the attacks on New York, Bali, Madrid, or elsewhere by al-Qaeda are war crimes a matter of debate. The far simpler legal characterization is to identify them as crimes against humanity, which lacks any required nexus to armed conflict.

Finally, the creation of a body of law criminalizing certain violations of the laws of war does not mean that war criminals will actually be prosecuted. This remains a matter for States and, increasingly, the United Nations and other international organizations. The Geneva Conventions require all parties to search for and either extradite or try all persons suspected of having committed grave breaches. And international law gives all States the legal right to prosecute war criminals under the theory of universal jurisdiction. While States have at times prosecuted war criminals (e.g., the U.S. trial of the My Lai offenders), the more pervasive pattern, despite the obligations of the Geneva Conventions, is either mere administrative punishment or impunity. The ad hoc tribunals for Yugoslavia and Rwanda have jurisdiction over both grave breaches of the Geneva Conventions and other crimes committed in these particular conflicts, and the ICC, as noted, has jurisdiction over most war crimes.

(See **international vs. internal armed conflict.**)

W

Water Supplies and Works, Destruction of

By Emma Daly

The old woman reached into her plastic bucket and pulled out a triangular shard of human bone, still pink and glistening, a gruesome reminder of her daily struggle to find water.

She had been waiting in line for water, at a standpipe protected, she had thought, by the ruins of an old school, when a mortar bomb crashed through

Sarajevans cross the ruined bridge across the Mitjacka River to get water, 1993.

a hole in the roof. Seven people were killed and twelve wounded, including the elderly woman herself, who had a slight graze on her forehead and a serious case of shattered nerves.

Collecting water was one of the most dangerous and dispiriting daily tasks in Sarajevo between April 1992 and December 1996. The secessionist Serb forces frequently cut off the city's water supply (and its gas and electricity as well). And even when they permitted the water to flow, they routinely fired on those queuing up for it.

As a general principle, in both internal and international armed conflict it is lawful to attack only **military objectives**. From this derives the rule stated in Article 54 of the first of the two 1977 Additional Protocols to the Geneva Conventions that "**starvation** of civilians as a method of warfare is prohibited." Denying the civilian population water is just as illegal as denying them food. Article 54 states that "it is prohibited to attack, destroy, remove or render useless objects indispensable to the survival of the civilian

W

population," and includes not only foodstuffs, livestock, and the like, but "drinking water installations and supplies and irrigation works."

But though the idea would have made little sense to the people of besieged Sarajevo, water supplies do not enjoy absolute protection under international law. If water supplies are being used exclusively by civilians, legally they are supposed to be immune. But if they are being used by both combatants and noncombatants, the picture changes.

The premise of all laws of war is that it is perfectly legal to attack **legitimate military targets.** So when water and waterworks are used exclusively to sustain military forces they can be targeted. Moreover, according to the language of Additional Protocol I, where water and waterworks are used "in direct support of military action" they can be destroyed. For example, if a water installation is being used by soldiers as a firing position or to conceal supplies then it, like other generally protected spaces such as **hospitals**, is not legally protected from attack.

Nonetheless, these exceptions are not as broad as they first appear and contain their own limitations and exceptions. The laws state that any harm to civilians must not be excessive compared to a concrete and direct military advantage. And Additional Protocol I, Article 54 states that "in no event" shall actions against targets such as waterworks be undertaken when they may be "expected to leave the civilian population with such inadequate food or water as to cause its starvation or force its movement." Military necessity alone does not give soldiers license to destroy a water installation if it is indispensable to the survival of the civilian population.

Whether what went on in Sarajevo when the Serbs cut off the water was a war crime is problematic. Often the real crime seems to have been sniping at and shelling the people lined up for water, rather than the cut-off itself. A deliberate and systematic cutting off of water to the civilian population, however, would be a war crime.

Fearing that the Sarajevo experience is the shape of things to come, and convinced that in an increasing number of conflicts the lack of clean water kills more people than bullets or bombs, the International Committee of the Red Cross (ICRC) is campaigning to have a blanket ban on attacking waterworks. It is pressing to have the immunity from attack, of the sort given to medical staff, given in practice to water engineers and other personnel seeking to keep water supplies flowing or to repair water systems. Such personnel are protected under Additional Protocol I because they fall into the category of civil defense personnel. The ICRC position asserts "the absolute imperative" of water for the survival of the civilian population.

W

Weapons

By Burrus M. Carnahan

The American Civil War saw the first use of many weapons that would revolutionize warfare—armored warships, submarines, land mines, and machine guns to list a few. One Civil War innovation would have a more dubious fate, however, becoming the first weapon specifically outlawed by international treaty. This was a rifle bullet that would explode on impact with a human body. Immediately after the war, the U.S. Army Ordnance Department concluded that exploding rifle bullets were inhumane, and should never be purchased again.

Experience during the Civil War had shown that any soldier hit by an ordinary rifle bullet was likely to be put out of action by that wound alone. In most cases, exploding bullets merely made an already disabling wound worse. The suffering caused by such bullets was therefore militarily unnecessary and inhumane.

The same conclusion had been reached at almost the same time by the Russian government, which had also developed an exploding rifle bullet. Unlike the United States, however, Russia faced a number of potentially hostile land powers, and the czar's government was reluctant to give up any new weapon unless it could be assured that potential enemies would also forgo its use. In 1868, therefore, the Russian government convened an international conference at St. Petersburg to consider this issue. (The United States did not participate—this was an era of isolationism in U.S. foreign policy.)

The resulting treaty, called the St. Petersburg Declaration, banned the use of exploding or incendiary bullets weighing less than four hundred grams. It also stated certain important general principles, as follows: "That the only legitimate object... during war is to weaken the military forces of the enemy; that for this purpose it is sufficient to disable the greatest possible number of men; that this object would be exceeded by the employment of arms which uselessly aggravate the sufferings of disabled men, or render their death inevitable; that the employment of such arms would, therefore, be contrary to the laws of humanity." These principles are now accepted as part of customary international law, binding on all nations, whether or not they are parties to the St. Petersburg Declaration.

International conferences meeting at The Hague in the Netherlands in 1899 and 1907 distilled the St. Petersburg principles into the familiar principle that it is forbidden to use weapons that cause "unnecessary suffering" or "superfluous injury." This principle, which is also part of customary international law, was reaffirmed in the first Additional Protocol of 1977.

This rule prohibits, for example, the use of explosive projectiles filled with clear glass. Glass fragments would make a soldier's wounds more difficult to treat, because a surgeon would have trouble seeing them. For similar reasons, it is forbidden to use explosive projectiles designed to injure with fragments not detectable by X-rays. The rule against the use of dumdum bullets designed to flatten on impact also reflects the principle against unnecessary suffering and superfluous injury.

In applying the principle against unnecessary suffering and superfluous injury, the military advantages of the weapon must always be weighed against the suffering it causes. After all, the very phrase "unnecessary suffering"

W

implies that there is such a thing as necessary suffering. A weapon cannot be considered forbidden simply because, in the abstract, it produces great suffering; the military side of the equation must always be considered as well.

It should be noted that a weapon may be unlawful if used for one purpose, and yet lawful if used for another purpose. For example, during World War I, the British armed the machine guns on their warplanes with incendiary bullets. The initial reaction of the German government was to threaten to try captured British airmen as war criminals for violating the St. Petersburg Declaration. Upon reflection, however, the German government backed down. Today, legal experts generally regard the use of incendiary and small caliber explosive bullets as lawful in air warfare, though their use in infantry rifles would still be forbidden.

For the same reason, the use in land warfare of shells containing white phosphorus—which burns on contact with air and can cause exceptionally severe burns—is permitted to provide a smokescreen, for marking targets or against enemy vehicles.

Customary international law also prohibits the use of indiscriminate weapons. An indiscriminate weapon is one that cannot be directed at a legitimate military objective. The V-2 rockets used by Germany in World War II were indiscriminate weapons, in that they could not be directed at any target smaller than an entire city. After the 1991 Gulf War, the U.S. Department of Defense reported to Congress that the SCUD missiles used by Iraq (which were not very much more accurate than the V-2) were indiscriminate, and that their use constituted a war crime.

One weapon that has provoked particular controversy in recent years is the cluster bomb. A "cluster bomb unit" (CBU) consists of a dispenser containing several hundred small bombs (or "submunitions"). After being dropped from a warplane, the dispenser opens at a preset altitude to disperse the submunitions over a wide area. The use of CBUs by the Israeli air force in Lebanon against the PLO in the 1970s and again against Hezbollah in 2006 was widely criticized by human rights organizations.

Cluster bombs are often denounced as "indiscriminate" weapons, but this charge is not, strictly speaking, accurate. CBUs can be directed very effectively against area targets such as tank formations, military bases, airfields, rail yards and similar legitimate targets and are not therefore indiscriminate as that term is used in international law. As with any other weapon, cluster bomb should not be used in situations where expected civilian casualties are likely to be excessive in relation to the military advantages expected from the attack.

Even when cluster bombs have been used legally, unexploded submunitions can be dangerous. Hundreds of submunitions will be dispersed in a typical cluster bomb attack (for example, each U.S. CBU-87 carries 202 submunitions). Even if 95% of the submunitions explode as designed, ten or more undetonated "dud" bomblets will be left on the field from each CBU dropped. These can create danger for civilians, peacekeeping forces and other noncombatants for decades after the conflict ends.

International law has only begun to deal with the dangers posed by the explosive remnants of war, including unexploded CBU bomblets. In November 2003, negotiations were concluded on a new treaty, Protocol V to the United Nations Convention on Certain Conventional Weapons, that would obligate countries at war to record where unexploded ordnance could exist (e.g., where CBUs have been used) and to make this information known at the end of hostilities. Another approach being pursued is to develop cluster bombs whose unexploded submunitions would self-destruct or deactivate after a given period. (See **biological weapons**; **chemical weapons**; **mines**; **poisonous weapons**.)

Willful Killing

By Peter Maass

Slobodan was being a gracious host. Whenever we entered an exposed stretch of territory, he would stop, listen like a terrier for signs of trouble, and then sprint ahead, waving me on when he felt it was safe. It was the winter of 1993, the Bosnian War was in full throttle, and Slobodan was taking me to his place of work, a ransacked apartment in a bombed-out building on the front line around Sarajevo.

Slobodan was a Bosnian Serb sniper. Because he was off duty when he showed me around, he was armed only with a pistol. Once we reached his

The body of a recently killed man by the side of a dirt track in a vineyard near the village of Xrce, Kosovo, April 1999. His identity and ethnicity are unknown.

perch, though, he cheerfully pointed it at the Sarajevans running across exposed ground a few hundred yards away. "I can shoot!" he said in excited English. "Look, look, people, pistol, pop-pop!" Then he calmed down and smiled. "No problem, no problem. No shoot people. No, no shoot."

What he actually was saying was that he didn't shoot civilians, only soldiers. This was improbable. I had been in Sarajevo long enough to know that civilians were pretty much the only targets of snipers like Slobodan. I had talked to people who were shot by snipers, I saw a youth get shot near the Holiday Inn near the front line, and I knew, as everyone did, that the cold weather and lack of food in Bosnia's besieged capital were not the worst killers. It was the snipers you worried about the most, because they were the ones firing all those bullets that found their way into so many arms and legs and heads and hearts.

There is no prohibition on sniping at combatants during wartime, but

W

427

the intentional killing of civilians is a war crime. And it was likely that Slobodan and his sniping pals were guilty of willful killing—the legal term for that crime—many, many times over.

It is well established in international humanitarian law that civilian deaths that are incidentally, even if foreseeably, caused by justifiable military operations are legal, subject to the principle of proportionality. But if the killing of a civilian, a noncombatant, is intentional or is not justified by military necessity, a war crime has been committed. For example, the execution of hostages or prisoners would be such a crime. In an international conflict, the violation could be prosecuted as willful killing under the grave breaches provisions of the four Geneva Conventions of 1949; in an internal conflict, the crime could be prosecuted as murder under domestic law or under Common Article 3 of the Geneva Conventions.

The sorts of people covered under the willful killing and murder rubrics include not just civilians in the ordinary sense of the word, but prisoners of

A couple killed on their bicycle by a sniper, Sarajevo, spring 1992.

war, sick or wounded or surrendering soldiers, and medical and religious personnel.

The crime of willful killing is an active component of international law. The International Criminal Tribunal for the former Yugoslavia has convicted defendants both of willful killing, where the crime was committed in connection with the international part of the Balkan wars, and of murder, when the crime took place during a non-international phase of the fighting. Whatever the charge, a sniper like Slobodan would likely be subject to multiple counts.

On the day he served so politely as my tour guide, I asked whether he had shot anyone. "Today, no," he replied. "Yesterday, yes. Pop, pop!" (See **civilians, illegal targeting of.**)

W

Willfulness

By A. P. V. Rogers

In trials for war crimes or grave breaches, the prosecution must generally prove not only that the accused did the act complained of but also that he intended the consequences of his act. This intent is usually referred to by lawyers as *mens rea*, criminal intent or basic intent.

If, for example, in attacking a military target, a commander causes unintended civilian casualties because of a weapons malfunction or faulty target intelligence, he would not be guilty of an offense because he lacked criminal intent, despite the consequences of his actions.

Even if treaty provisions are silent on the question of intent as in "taking of hostages," basic intent must still be proved. If a soldier is ordered to take civilians from a battlefield village under armed guard to a town well away from the fighting and there hand them over to the garrison commander and it later transpires that they were being held as hostages to protect the military headquarters in that town from attack, his defense might be lack of criminal intent as he was unaware that the civilians were hostages and assumed they were being taken to a place of safety.

Often a grave breach provision of a treaty specifies the intent as willfulness, as in *"willful* killing, torture or inhuman treatment" or *"willfully...* making the civilian population or individual civilians the object of attack." Or it may take the form of wantonness, as in "extensive destruction... of property, not justified by military necessity and carried out unlawfully and *wantonly."*

The terms *willful* and *wanton* include intentional or deliberate acts and also cases of recklessness. Criminal liability is not limited to positive acts. It can arise in the event of a failure to act when there is a duty to do so and the failure is either with intent that the consequences should follow or is due to recklessness about those consequences.

In the International Committee for the Red Cross (ICRC) Commentary on the Additional Protocols, willfulness is explained thus: the accused must have acted consciously and with intent, i.e., with his mind on the act and its consequences and willing them...: this encompasses the concepts of "wrongful intent" or "recklessness," viz., the attitude of an agent who, without being certain of a particular result, accepts the possibility of it happening; on the other hand, ordinary negligence or lack of foresight is not covered, i.e., when a man acts without having his mind on the act or its consequences. However, negligence may suffice for disciplinary action under national law.

The statute of the International Criminal Court specifies that an accused person is only to be convicted if his offense was committed "with intent and knowledge." An accused has intent if, in relation to conduct, he "means to engage in the conduct" and, in relation to a consequence, he "means to cause that consequence or is aware that it will occur in the ordinary course of events." Knowledge means "awareness that a circumstance exists or a consequence will occur in the ordinary course of events."

(See **due process; wanton destruction; war crimes; willful killing.**)

W

AFTERWORD

By Kenneth Anderson, legal editor, first edition

A Note on the Legal Standards Applied in This Book

International humanitarian law (IHL) must always balance between two poles.
On the one hand is the lawyerly desire to be legally precise, to be technically
accurate about frequently difficult concepts and distinctions of law. On the
other is the desire to codify a law to which ordinary soldiers and their officers will have allegiance because they understand it and its underlying
humanitarian rationale.

Equally important is the perception of the general public. In order to
bring this topic before the broadest possible audience, the intent behind this
book is to combine technical accuracy and readability.

As legal editor, I accept the responsibility for the legal analysis and
rules of IHL promulgated in this volume. Individual authors have retained
their independent voices as to the facts and phenomena that, frequently,
they have witnessed. Independent authorial analysis is more pronounced in
the longer country and conflict articles, such as those covering the Arab-
Israeli wars, Cambodia, and the Gulf War. The editors have generally let
authors develop their own statements of the circumstances, and social and
political causes of the conflicts. Still, insofar as is possible, I have sought to
draw my best estimation of their legal significance and status under the
terms of IHL. In our quest for accuracy and fairness we have had the benefit
of unstinting advice from many prominent legal authorities. (See **acknowl-
edgments.**) In the case of articles written by prominent legal experts in IHL,
we have given them latitude to express individual judgments on difficult or
unsettled matters, while recognizing that not all issues are settled. However,
any errors of legal analysis or judgment are mine alone.

Technical accuracy versus simplification is not the only tension that
faces a book such as this. There is always the risk that for the sake of clarity
one suggests that there are always determinate rules in IHL that yield plain
and unwavering answers to any question of application. IHL, like other bodies of law, contains important matters whose scope and interpretation are
susceptible to considerably different readings. In short, what various sources
urge as applicable law is not always uniform, and it would in fact be surprising if it were so. Of the differences that can arise, perhaps the most
important is between the aspirations of those who would like to see the rules
of armed conflict extended in one way or another and the defenders of actual
and traditional practices of States and their militaries.

In the past, it would perhaps be fair to say, Western and U.S. journalists
tended to accept the characterization of law given by their own militaries, or
worse, never questioned the legality of military actions. Today the world is
filled with international non-governmental organizations, legal scholars, and
many others seeking to influence international public opinion and happy to
offer their views on international law. Often their views are presented (and
often accepted) uncritically as objective statements of law without consideration of contrary opinions. This book does not attempt to resolve the issues
and debates between those with activist briefs and those closer to the
status quo.

Where the law or its interpretation is unsettled or contested, we seek to identify the controversy and not act as though it does not exist.

The status of Additional Protocol I of 1977 requires a special note. Protocol I has been very broadly accepted by States although the United States and other significant military powers, including, for example, Israel and Turkey, have not ratified. It is often relevant to note which countries have taken on actual treaty obligations and which have not. Additionally, ratifying States have also expressed reservations and these, too, define a country's treaty obligations. Some commentators and international activist organizations tend to be impatient with questions of which countries have bound themselves to the terms of Protocol I and which have not. Their view is that a treaty that has achieved such wide acceptance must perforce constitute customary international law, which as Professor Theodor Meron explains in his article on customary law, binds even those States that have not ratified it. Again, the intent of this book is to clarify rather than resolve the issue.

It is important to realize, however, that the United States, a State whose practices matter significantly, has accepted large portions of Protocol I as declaratory of customary international law on some of the critical substantive matters of IHL including, for example, the prohibitions on direct attack against civilians and indiscriminate attack involving civilians.

Another unsettled debate is over the weight to attach to the future of the newly established International Criminal Court (ICC). Although this book indicates how various IHL issues may be affected by the existence of the ICC, by its Statute, adopted in Rome in 1998, and by the international criminal tribunals for the former Yugoslavia and Rwanda, the fact that the United States has chosen to remain outside the ICC cannot be ignored. Whether the United States will eventually join, or whether the world will move toward some two-tier system in which most States at least nominally adhere to an international adjudication system while the world's leading military power and political guarantor of international stability stands apart, is not known at this point. In the last analysis, however, State practices still matter.

The Rome Statute of the ICC is the most important revision of IHL since the Additional Protocols of 1977. IHL is therefore on the cutting edge of movements of profoundly larger import than simply conduct upon the battlefield; those who say that the concept of sovereignty is at issue in the proper role and scope of IHL are wholly correct. This book aims to make accessible to the public, and to the journalists who write about these matters for the public, the body of law that stands at this cutting edge.

Note on the Law and Legal Terms

By Alan Dorsey

The terms *international humanitarian law,* or IHL, *laws of war, laws of armed conflict, rules of war,* etc., are, generally speaking, synonymous and interchangeable. Lawyers, human rights groups, relief organizations, the ICRC, and most States favor *international humanitarian law,* whereas militaries typically prefer the term *laws of war,* or some variation. In this book, we tend toward *international humanitarian law,* or IHL, except where an author has explicitly chosen a different usage.

International law is a complex mix of multilateral treaties, customary law, State practice, UN Security Council resolutions, judicial decisions, the work of advisory commissions and legal experts, and "general principles of law." In the simplest formulation, it might be said that the four Geneva Conventions of 1949, and the two Additional Protocols of 1977, form the heart of IHL and are the most frequently cited sources. The following list contains the major written sources of IHL but is not intended to be exhaustive.

Major International Humanitarian Law

Statements and treaties, in chronological order:
Title, place of promulgation or deposit, date, short form in italics.

Instructions for the Government of Armies of the United States in the Field. April 24, 1863. *Lieber Code*

Convention for the Amelioration of the Condition of the Wounded in Armies in the Field. Geneva, August 22, 1864. *1864 Geneva Convention*

Declaration Renouncing the Use, in Time of War, of Certain Explosive Projectiles. St. Petersburg, November 29 - December 11, 1868.
St. Petersburg Declaration of 1868

Convention II with Respect to the Laws and Customs of War on Land and its annex: Regulations concerning the Laws and Customs of War on Land.
The Hague, July 29, 1899. *1899 Hague Convention* or *1899 Hague Regulations*

Convention IV respecting the Laws and Customs of War on Land and its annex: Regulations concerning the Laws and Customs of War on Land. The Hague, October 18, 1907. *1907 Hague Conventions* or *1907 Hague Regulations*

Protocol for the Prohibition of the Use of Asphyxiating, Poisonous or Other Gases, and of Bacteriological Methods of Warfare. Geneva, June 17, 1925.
1925 Geneva Protocol

Convention for the Amelioration of the Condition of the Wounded and Sick in Armies in the Field. Geneva, July 27, 1929. *1929 Geneva Convention*

Agreement for the Prosecution and Punishment of the Major War Criminals of the European Axis, and Charter of the International Military Tribunal. London, August 8, 1945. *Nuremberg Charter*

Convention on the Prevention and Punishment of the Crime of Genocide. United Nations, December 9, 1948. *Genocide Convention*

Convention I for the Amelioration of the Condition of the Wounded and Sick in Armed Forces in the Field. Geneva. August 12, 1949.
First Geneva Convention (of 1949) or GCI

Convention II for the Amelioration of the Conditions of Wounded, Sick, and Shipwrecked Members of Armed Forces at Sea. Geneva, August 12, 1949.
Second Geneva Convention (of 1949) or GCII

Convention III Relative to the Treatment of Prisoners of War. Geneva, August 12, 1949.
Third Geneva Convention (of 1949) or GCIII

Convention IV Relative to the Protection of Civilian Persons in Time of War. Geneva, August 12, 1949. *Fourth Geneva Convention (of 1949) or GCIV*

Hague Convention on the Protection of Cultural Property in the Event of Armed Conflict. The Hague, May 14, 1954.
1954 Convention on Cultural Property

Convention on the Prohibition of the Development, Production and Stockpiling of Bacteriological (Biological) and Toxin Weapons and on their Destruction. Opened for Signature at London, Moscow, and Washington. April 10, 1972.
Biological Weapons Convention or BWC

Protocol I Additional to the Geneva Conventions of August 12, 1949, and Relating to the Protection of Victims of International Armed Conflicts. Geneva, June 8, 1977.
Additional Protocol I or API

Protocol II Additional to the Geneva Conventions of August 12, 1949, and Relating to the Protection of Victims of Non-International Armed Conflicts. Geneva, June 8. 1977.
Additional Protocol II or APII

1980 Convention on Prohibitions or Restrictions on the Use of Certain Conventional Weapons That May Be Deemed to Be Excessively Injurious or to Have Indiscriminate Effects. United Nations, October 10, 1980.
1980 Conventional Weapons Convention or CCW

Convention on the Prohibition of the Development, Production, Stockpiling and Use of Chemical Weapons and or Their Destruction. Paris, January 13, 1993.
1993 Chemical Weapons Convention

Statute of the International Tribunal for the Prosecution of Persons Responsible for Serious Violations of International Humanitarian Law Committed in the Territory of the Former Yugoslavia Since 1991. United Nations, May 25, 1993.
Yugoslavia Tribunal Statute or ICTY

Statute of the International Criminal Tribunal for the Prosecution of Persons Responsible for Genocide and Other Serious Violations of International Humanitarian Law Committed in the Territory of Rwanda and Rwandan Citizens Responsible for Genocide and Other Such Violations Committed in the Territory of Neighboring States between January 1, 1994 and December 31, 1994. United Nations, November 8, 1994.
Rwanda Tribunal Statute or ICTR

Protocol on Prohibitions or Restrictions on the Use of Mines, Booby-Traps and Other Devices. United Nations, as amended May 3, 1996.
Protocol II of the 1980 Conventional Weapons Convention

Convention on the Prohibition of the Use, Stockpiling, Production and Transfer of Anti-Personnel Mines and on Their Destruction. United Nations, September 18, 1997.
Ottawa Treaty

Rome Statute of the International Criminal Court. United Nations, July 17, 1998.
Rome Statute or ICC Statute

Second Protocol to the Hague Convention of 1954 for the Protection of Cultural
Property in the Event of Armed Conflict. The Hague, March 26, 1999.
Second Cultural Property Protocol

Optional Protocol to the Convention on the Rights of the Child on the Involvement of
Children in Armed Conflict. May 25, 2000.
Childrens Rights Protocol

Protocol on Explosive Remnants of War, November 28, 2003.
Protocol V to the 1980 Conventional Weapons Convention

Protocol additional to the Geneva Conventions of August 12, 1949, and relating to the
Adoption of an Additional Distinctive Emblem (Protocol III). Geneva, December 8, 2005.
3rd Additional Protocol

Some Titles for Further Reading

The Conduct of Hostilities under the Law of International Armed Conflict
By Yoram Dinstein, Cambridge University Press, 2004

Documents on the Laws of War
Edited by Adam Roberts and Richard Guelff, Oxford University Press, 3rd ed., 2000

Law on the Battlefield
By A.P.V. Rogers, Manchester University Press, 2nd ed., 2004

Crimes Against Humanity: The Struggle for Global Justice
By Geoffrey Robertson, The New Press, rev. ed., 2007

A Problem from Hell: America and the Age of Genocide
By Samantha Power, Basic Books, 2002

Accountability for Human Rights Atrocities in International Law
By Steven R. Ratner and Jason S. Abrams, Oxford University Press, 2nd ed., 2001

The Torture Papers: The Road to Abu Ghraib
Edited by Karen J. Greenberg and Joshua L. Dratel, Cambridge University Press, 2005

Selected Online Legal Resources

http://www.crimesofwar.org
Crimes of War Project
This site develops the themes of this book and applies them to ongoing conflicts.

http://www.icrc.org
International Committee of the Red Cross (ICRC)
Contains full texts of international humanitarian law treaties and commentaries.

http://www.un.org/law
United Nations
Contains information about international law and UN-sponsored courts and tribunals.

Contributors

Abbas is a photographer with Magnum Photos. Since 1970, he has covered wars and revolutions in Biafra, Bangladesh, Ulster, Vietnam, the Middle East, Chile, Cuba, and South Africa.

Eddie Adams was a photojournalist for AP/Wide World Photos, and won the Pulitzer Prize in 1969 for his photo of a street execution in Vietnam. He died in 2004.

Kael Alford is a freelance photojournalist who was based in south-eastern Europe from 1995-2003 and has since worked extensively in Iraq.

Ewen Allison is an attorney in Washington, D.C. and a consultant at the War Crimes Research Office at American University.

Christiane Amanpour is the chief international correspondent for CNN. She has won two Columbia DuPont Awards, eight Emmys, two Polks, two Peabodys, a Courage in Journalism Award, a Sigma Delta Chi Award, a Livingston Award, and a Breakthrough Award.

Jon Lee Anderson, a correspondent for The New Yorker, is the author of Che Guevara: A Revolutionary Life (Grove Press, 1997), The Lion's Grave: Dispatches from Afghanistan (Grove Press, 2002), Guerrillas Journeys in the Insurgent World (Penguin, 2004), and The Fall of Baghdad (Penguin, 2004).

Kenneth Anderson is a professor of law at Washington College of Law, American University, and a research fellow of the Hoover Institution, Stanford University. He was previously general counsel of the Open Society Institute and director of the Human Rights Watch Arms Division.

Thorne Anderson is a photographer who has been covering international news with Corbis/Sygma since 1999. Thorne's photographs are regularly published in magazines and newspapers including Time, Newsweek, Stern, the New York Times, the Los Angeles Times, the Times (London), the Guardian, and others.

Micha Bar-Am a photojournalist with Magnum Photos, has covered Israeli and international subjects since 1956. He was curator of photography at the Tel Aviv Museum of Art from 1977 to 1993 and was awarded the Israel Prize for Visual Arts in 2000.

Nomi Bar-Yaacov is a foreign policy adviser on Middle Eastern affairs and former head of the Middle East Conflict Management Programme at the Institute for Strategic Studies in London. Prior to that she was a Middle East diplomatic correspondent with Agence France-Presse, based in Jerusalem.

Bruno Barbey, a photographer with Magnum Photos, has journeyed across five continents and numerous world conflicts over the past four decades. He has received numerous awards for his work including the French "National Order of Merit."

M. Cherif Bassiouni is a Distinguished Research Professor of Law at DePaul University College of Law and President of the International Human Rights Law Institute. He chaired the UN Commission of Experts on the former Yugoslavia and served as the UN's Independent Expert on the Situation of Human Rights in Afghanistan.

Maud S. Beelman is Projects Editor at the Dallas Morning News. She was the founding director of the International Consortium of Investigative Journalists at the Center for Public Integrity and a veteran foreign correspondent for the Associated Press.

Dima Beliakov, a Russian photojournalist, has worked extensively on the Chechen conflicts. His photographs have been published in numerous international magazines and newspapers.

Dr. Orna Ben-Naftali heads the international law division at the Law School, the College of Management, Academic Studies, in Israel.

Marcus Bleasdale, a photojournalist, has spent several years covering the conflict in the Democratic Republic of Congo. He was named Magazine Photographer of the Year in 2005 by Pictures of the Year International and received the Olivier Rebbot Award from the Overseas Press Club of America in 2006.

Robert Block is the Homeland Security correspondent for the Wall Street Journal. He has won numerous awards for his reporting including the 1996 Amnesty International Press Award and the 2004 Elizabeth Neuffer Award for print journalism.

Jeremy Bowen is Middle East Editor for the BBC and has covered most major international stories since 1988, reporting from some 70 countries. He has won a number of awards for journalism, most recently a Sony Gold Award for coverage of the capture of Saddam Hussein. He is author of Six Days: How the 1967 War Shaped the Middle East (Simon and Schuster, 2003).

Heidi Bradner received the Leica Medal of Excellence and the Alexia Foundation Prize for her work documenting the conflict in Chechnya. Her book on the cultures of the Siberian Arctic, Land of the Second Sun, won a World Press Photo award in 2003.

Colette Braeckman is the Africa editor for Le Soir (Brussels). She is the author of L'Enjeu Congolais (Fayard, 1999) Terreur Africaine

(Fayard, 1996), and Le Dinosaure: le Zaire de Mobutu *(Fayard, 1991).*

Jess Bravin covers the U.S. Supreme Court for the Wall Street Journal. *A John Jacobs Fellow of the University of California, Berkeley, he is writing a book on the U.S. military commissions at Guantanamo Bay and the Supreme Court case that found them unconstitutional.*

Jimmie Briggs, a photojournalist, is a Goodwill Ambassador and Special Envoy for Children and Armed Conflict with the United Nations. He is author of Innocents Lost: When Child Soldiers Go to War *(Basic Books, 2005).*

David Burnett, a photojournalist based in the United States, was a co-founder of Contact Press Images. He has worked in countries around the world, and has won the Robert Capa Gold Medal, the World Press Photo Premier Award, and the Overseas Press Club's Olivier Rebbot Award.

John Burns is Baghdad bureau chief for the New York Times. *He twice won the Pulitzer Prize for international reporting, in 1993 for coverage of Bosnia, and in 1997 for reports on the Taliban regime in Afghanistan. He has also been awarded two George Polk awards and the Arthur Ross Award for Distinguished Reporting and Analysis on Foreign Affairs.*

Robert Capa was a renowned war photographer who co-founded Magnum Photos in 1947. Famous for his coverage of the Spanish Civil War and WWII, he was killed in 1954 by a landmine while covering Vietnam.

Burrus M. Carnahan is a professorial lecturer in law at George Washington University, Washington D.C. A retired USAF lieutenant colonel, he is currently employed as a foreign affairs officer in the Bureau of International Security and Nonproliferation at the U.S. Department of State.

Gilles Caron, a photojournalist, covered the Six-Day War, Vietnam, Biafra, and Northern Ireland in five short years of an exemplary career. Caron disappeared in 1970 while covering the Cambodia-Vietnam border at the age of thirty.

Anna Cataldi, one of the founding member of the Crimes of War Project, is a freelance journalist and author of Letters from Sarajevo *(Element, U.K., 1994),* Bambini di Guerra *(Valle D'Aosta, Italy), and* Fifty Years Later *(Mondadori, Italy, 1998). In 1998, the Secretary-General of the UN named her "Messenger of Peace."*

Dean Chapman is a photographer with Panos Pictures who has worked extensively in Asia. His book on Burma, Karenni: The Forgotten War of a Nation Besieged, *was awarded 1998 European Publishers Award for Photography.*

Alan Chin, photographer, has covered conflicts in Iraq, ex-Yugoslavia, Afghanistan, Central Asia, and the Middle East. He contributes regularly to the New York Times, Newsweek, *and* Time *magazine.*

Roger Cohen is the international affairs columnist of the International Herald Tribune, *and international writer at large for the* New York Times. *He is author of* Hearts Grown Brutal: Sagas of Sarajevo *(Random House, 1998) and* Soldiers and Slaves *(Random House, 2005).*

Emma Daly is the Press Director at Human Rights Watch in New York and a journalist for the New York Times. *She has covered conflicts in Europe, Central America, and Africa for the* Independent *(London) and Reuters.*

Manoocher Deghati, freelance photographer and founder of AINA Photojournalism Institute in Kabul, worked as a war photographer for Sipa and AFP, specializing in the Middle East.

Raymond Depardon is a photographer and filmmaker who co-founded the Gamma Agency and has since worked with Magnum Photos. He won the Robert Capa Gold Medal for his coverage of Chile and a Pulitzer Prize in 1977 for work in Chad.

Hamilton DeSaussure is a retired emeritus professor of law at the University of Akron, Ohio. He held the Stockton Chair in International Law at the Naval War College from 1979 to 1980.

Alan Dorsey is the former deputy project manager for the Crimes of War Project, and before that was a staff member of the ICRC Delegation to the United Nations in New York.

Corinne Dufka is a senior researcher with the Africa Division of Human Rights Watch. As a photographer with Reuters based in Nairobi, Kenya from 1989-1999, she received several awards including the Robert Capa Gold Medal, a World Press Photo Award, and the International Women's Media Foundation Courage in Journalism Award. In 2003 she received a MacArthur "genius" grant.

Nic Dunlop is a photojournalist based in South-East Asia. His book The Lost Executioner, *a real-life detective story tracking down the man responsible for some of the worst atrocities of Cambodia's killing fields, was published in 2005.*

Anthony Dworkin, co-editor of this book, is executive director of the Crimes of War Project. He is a contributing editor of Prospect, *and his writing has also appeared in the* Guardian, International Herald Tribune, TLS, New Statesman *and other publications.*

Thomas Dworzak, a photographer with Magnum, has contributed to the New Yorker, Newsweek, U.S. News, Paris Match, *the* New York Times Magazine *and* Time. *He has worked in*

Afghanistan, Chechnya, Iraq, Iran, Haiti and the United States.

H. Wayne Elliott, S.J.D., is a retired U.S. Army lieutenant colonel. He is a former chief of the international law division at the Judge Advocate General's School, U.S. Army and is an Adjunct Professor at Liberty University Law School in Lynchburg, Virginia.

Kari Eloranta is a photographer and mathematician. His images of the conditions of life of ordinary people in North-East Africa were collected in the 2002 book Time Zero Ground Zero.

Hector Emanuel is a Peruvian-born photographer based in Washington DC. His photos focus mainly on social and political issues in Latin America and the United States. He is also a founding member of Metro Collective, a documentary photographers' collective.

Douglas Farah is an investigative consultant with the Nine/Eleven Finding Answers Foundation as well as a freelance writer on terror finance and national security issues. He is a former investigative reporter for the Washington Post. He won the Sigma Delta Chi award for international reporting in 1988, and the Maria Moor Cabot award for his Latin American reporting in 1995.

Stephen Ferry is a photographer with Redux Pictures. He has worked in Eastern Europe, Latin America and North Africa, and since 2000 has focused his work on Colombia. He is the winner of two World Press Awards.

Dr. Horst Fischer is academic director of the Institute for International Law of Peace and Armed Conflict at the Ruhr-Universität in Germany, and professor of IHL at Leiden University in the Netherlands. He is also the legal advisor for international affairs for the German Red Cross and Netherlands Red Cross.

Leonard Freed, a photographer, joined Magnum in 1972 and since then has worked on assignment for numerous prominent international magazines. He has also shot four films for Japanese, Dutch and Belgian television.

Stuart Freedman is a photographer whose work has been published in Life, Geo, Time, Der Spiegel, Newsweek and Paris Match. His work on the victims of mutilation in Sierra Leone led to an invitation to speak on the subject on Capitol Hill in the United States.

Charles Garraway served for 30 years in the United Kingdom Army Legal Services and retired with the rank of Colonel in 2003. Subsequently he was a Senior Adviser on Transitional Justice to the Coalition Provisional Authority in Iraq. He is currently an Associate Fellow at Chatham House in London.

Jean Gaumy, a photographer with Magnum Photos and a filmmaker, has traveled and worked in Europe, Africa, Central America, the Middle East and Iran.

George Georgiou is a photojournalist and documentary photographer currently based in Istanbul, Turkey. He has worked extensively in the Balkans over the past six years.

Tom Gjelten is a correspondent for National Public Radio and author of Sarajevo Daily: A City and its Newspaper Under Siege (HarperCollins, 1995) and the forthcoming Bacardi and the Long Fight for Cuba. He won the George Polk Award and the Robert F. Kennedy Journalism Award for his reporting on Bosnia.

Robert Kogod Goldman is a professor of law and co-director of the Center for Human Rights and Humanitarian Law at the Washington College of Law, American University. He is the former president of the Inter-American Commission on Human Rights. From July 2004 to July 2005, Professor Goldman was the UN Human Rights Commission's independent expert on the protection of human rights and fundamental freedoms while countering terrorism.

Richard Goldstone served as the Chief Prosecutor of the United Nations Yugoslavia and Rwanda Tribunals and as a justice of the Constitutional Court of South Africa.

Kaveh Golestan was an internationally renowned photojournalist and BBC cameraman. He died on April 2, 2003, while on assignment in Kifri, Northern Iraq, when he stepped on a landmine.

Thomas Goltz has written about political and social issue in the post-Soviet Caucasus since 1991 for several American and UK publications. He is the author of Azerbaijan Diary (M.E. Sharpe, 1998), Chechnya Diary (St Martin's Press/Tom Dunne, 2003), and Georgia Diary (M.E. Sharpe, 2006). He is currently a visiting scholar in the Central and Southwest Asian Studies Program at the University of Montana/Missoula.

Patricia Gossman is director of the Afghanistan Justice Project and a consultant on human rights issues.

Joel Greenberg is a foreign correspondent for the Chicago Tribune. He was previously a reporter in the Jerusalem bureau of the New York Times, covered the first Palestinian uprising for the Jerusalem Post, and also contributed to the Christian Science Monitor.

Stanley Greene, a photographer with the VU Agency, is based in Paris. For his work in Chechnya, collected in the book Open Wound:

Chechnya 1994-2003 *(Trolley, 2003), he was awarded the W. Eugene Smith Award and a World Press Photo award.*

Christopher Greenwood, QC, *is Professor of International Law at the London School of Economics and a practicing barrister. He is the author of* Command and the Law of Armed Conflict *(H.M. Stationery Office, London, 1993).*

Philip Jones Griffiths *is a photographer with Magnum Photos. He covered the war in Vietnam and his book* Vietnam, Inc. *(Macmillan, 1971) is considered by many as the most important photographic work about the war. His later book* Agent Orange: Collateral Damage in Vietnam *was published in 2003.*

Aeyal Gross *teaches international and constitutional law at Tel-Aviv University. He is a member of the board of the Association for Civil Rights in Israel.*

Roy Gutman, *chairman of the Crimes of War Project and co-editor of this book, is foreign editor of McClatchy Newspapers. He received a Pulitzer Prize in 1993 for his writing for* Newsday *about concentration camps and other aspects of ethnic cleansing in Bosnia, and also won the Polk Award, the Hal Boyle award of the Overseas Press Club, and the Selden Ring Award for investigative reporting.*

Hale Gurland *is a photographer, sculptor and painter based in New York City.*

Ron Haeberle *was a U.S. Army photographer in Vietnam, where he documented the My Lai massacre in 1968. He later became a photographer for* Time/Life.

Françoise J. Hampson *is a professor at the University of Essex (U.K.) and co-director of its Children and Armed Conflict Unit. She is a member of the UN Sub-Commission on the Promotion and Protection of Human Rights, and has litigated many cases before the European Court of Human Rights in Strasbourg.*

Sheldon H. Harris *was a professor of American history emeritus at the California State University, Northridge. He was the author of* Factories of Death: Japanese Biological Warfare and the American Cover-Up *(Routledge, 1994, rev. ed. 2002), which won two scholarly awards. He died in 2002.*

Florence Hartmann *reported from the former Yugoslavia for* Le Monde *(France) between 1989 and 1994, and is the author of* Milosevic *(revised edition, Poche, 2002). She was the spokesperson for the Chief Prosecutor at the Yugoslavia war crimes tribunal for six years until 2006.*

Amira Hass *is an Israeli journalist for* Ha'aretz *in the West Bank and Gaza. Her awards include the UNESCO World Press Freedom Prize and the Anna Lindh Award. She is the author of* Drinking the Sea at Gaza *(Metropolitan, 1999).*

Ron Haviv, *a photographer and co-founder of the VII photo agency, has covered conflict and humanitarian crises in Latin America, Africa, the Middle East, Russia and the Balkans. He has published two collections of his photography—* Blood and Honey: A Balkan War Journal *(TV Books, 2000) and* Afghanistan: The Road to Kabul *(de.MO, 2002).*

Lindsey Hilsum *is the China bureau chief of* Channel Four News *(London), and a contributor to the* New Statesman *and* Granta. *She won 2005 Royal Television Society Journalist of the Year Award for her reporting from Iraq and Russia.*

Michael H. Hoffman *is director for international humanitarian law and policy with the American Red Cross and a retired lieutenant colonel in the U.S. Army Reserve.*

Tomas van Houtryve *is a former AP staff photographer whose work regularly appears in leading international publications including* Time *magazine, the* New York Times Magazine, Stern, *the* Independent on Sunday, Le Monde *and* Le Figaro Magazine.

Mark Huband, *former International Security correspondent for the* Financial Times *(London), won the U.K. Foreign Correspondent of the Year award in 1991. He is the author of* The Skull Beneath the Skin *(Westview, 2001) and* Brutal Truths, Fragile Myths *(Westview, 2004).*

Henri Huet, *a French combat photographer, covered Vietnam and later worked for* UPI *and the* AP. *Huet was killed when his helicopter was shot down in Laos in 1971.*

Michael Ignatieff, *a writer and historian, is deputy leader of the Liberal Party of Canada. From 2000 to 2005 he was director of the Carr Center for Human Rights Policy at Harvard University's John F. Kennedy School of Government. He is author of* The Lesser Evil: Political Ethics in an Age of Terror *(Princeton University Press, 2004) and* Empire Lite: Nation-Building in Bosnia, Kosovo and Afghanistan *(Penguin, 2003).*

Rikio Imajo *is a photographer with the Associated Press based in Tokyo.*

Stewart Innes *is a freelance photographer who has worked widely across the Middle East, and has recently covered the wars in Iraq and Lebanon.*

Christian Jennings, *a freelance journalist, covered the Rwandan genocide for Reuters and reported from Kosovo for the* Economist *and the* Daily Telegraph. *He is author of* Across the Red River: Four Years of Genocide in Rwanda and Burundi *(Victor Gollancz, 1999).*

Olivier Jobard is a photographer with Sipa Press. In 2004, he was honored with the Visa d'Or for his reportage on the Darfur conflict, and also received the Grand Prix Paris-Match for his photographs of illegal African immigrants fleeing their continent for Europe.

William E. Jones served as an aerial photographer in the Army Air Corps during WWII. During the occupation of Japan, he took low-altitude atomic bomb damage photographs of both Hiroshima and Nagasaki. These images are in the National Atomic Museum as well as in the book Picturing the Bomb (Harry N. Abrams, Inc. 1995).

Andree Kaiser, a German photographer with the Caro photo agency, has covered social and political issues in Europe and around the world for magazines such as Stern, Focus. Der Spiegel, Time and Newsweek. He covered the Balkan conflicts for Newsday and other publications.

Frits Kalshoven is professor emeritus of international humanitarian law at Leiden University and former president of the International Fact-Finding Commission. He chaired the UN Commission of Experts on the former Yugoslavia. He is the author of Constraints on the Waging of War (Martinus Nijhoff, 1987).

Ed Kashi is a photojournalist whose work has been published and exhibited worldwide. He is author of Aging in America: The Years Ahead (powerHouse Books, 2003). In 2002 he founded Talking Eyes Media, a non-profit multimedia company that explores social issues.

Yunghi Kim is a photographer with Contact Press Images. She has worked in Somalia, Rwanda, Indonesia, Kosovo Afghanistan and Iraq, among other places, and was named Photographer of the Year in 1997 by the NPPA.

Gary Knight is a photographer and co-founder of the VII Photo Agency. His book Evidence: The Case against Milosevic was published by de.MO in 2002.

Josef Koudelka, a photographer with Magnum Photos, won the Robert Capa Gold Medal in 1969 for his coverage of the Russian invasion of Czechoslovakia. Other awards include the Prix Nadar (1978) and the Grand Prix International Henri Cartier-Bresson (1991).

Antonin Kratochvil, photojournalist and co-founder of VII photo agency, has covered conflict and social and environmental issues around the world.

Danilo Krstanovic, a photographer for Reuters, has exhibited in many exhibitions in Bosnia-Herzegovina and abroad.

Daoud Kuttab is director of modern media, Al Quds University, Jerusalem, and founder of AmmanNet, the first Internet radio station in the Arab world. In 1997 he received the Committee to Protect Journalists International Press Freedom Award.

Peggy Lampl was project director for the first edition of this book and is currently a member of the Crimes of War Project's board. She has served as Deputy Assistant Secretary of State (U.S.) and as executive director of the Children's Defense Fund and the League of Women Voters.

Charles Lane covers the Supreme Court for the Washington Post. He is the former editor of the New Republic and foreign correspondent for Newsweek. He received a Citation for Excellence from the Overseas Press Club for his coverage of the former Yugoslavia.

Annie Leibovitz is a photographer with Contact Press Images. Known for her portrait photography in Rolling Stone and Vanity Fair, she went on several personal assignments to photograph Sarajevo and Rwanda in 1993 and 1994. Her most recent book is A Photographer's Life: 1990-2005 (Random House, 2006).

Roger Lemoyne, a Canadian photojournalist, has covered stories around the world and won several international awards. A selection of his work is published in the book Détails Obscurs (400 Coups, 2005).

Alex Levac is staff photographer at Ha'aretz (Tel Aviv). He received the 1993 Rita Poretzky Award for Photography from the Tel Aviv Museum of Art. He is author of An Eye to Zion (Am Oved, 1996) and Our Country (Mod, 2000).

Howard S. Levie is professor emeritus of law at the St. Louis University Law School. He drafted the Korean Armistice Agreement and served as chief of the International Affairs Division, Office of The Judge Advocate General. He is the author of Levie on the Law of War (Naval War College, 1998).

Gideon Levy, a columnist for Ha'aretz (Tel Aviv), won the Israeli Human Rights Award from the Association for Civil Rights in Israel in 1996. He served as press aide to Israeli Prime Minister Shimon Peres from 1978 to 1982.

Pedro Linger Gasiglia, photographer, documented the work of the Argentine Forensic Anthropology Team in conjunction with local human rights organizations in El Salvador. Born in Argentina, he is now based in New York.

Paul Lowe is a freelance photographer and teacher living and working between Sarajevo and London. He has covered international events in Europe, Asia, Africa and the Middle East. Since 2004, he has been course director of the masters program in photojournalism and documentary photography at the London College of Communication

Peter Maass, a contributing writer at the New York Times Magazine, reported on the invasion of Iraq and its aftermath. He also reported from the former Yugoslavia for the Washington Post in the 1990s and is the author of Love Thy Neighbor: A Story of War (Knopf, 1996), which won the 1996 Los Angeles Times Book Prize and the 1996 Overseas Press Club Book Prize.

Sean Maguire is the editor of Reuters' political and general news coverage across Europe. He is the former chief correspondent in Warsaw for Reuters News Agency, and covered Kosovo and other eastern European issues. He has reported on both the Gulf War and the Iraq War.

Stephanie Maupas is a journalist in the Hague reporting on the Yugoslav war crimes tribunal and the International Criminal Court for Le Monde.

Don McCullin is a photographer with Contact Press Images. A collection of his work, Don McCullin, was published by Jonathan Cape in 2001. He was awarded the CBE in 1993.

Steve McCurry, a photographer with Magnum Photos, has covered conflicts around the world. His most recent book is Looking East (Phaidon, 2006).

Susan Meiselas is a photographer with Magnum Photos, who is known for her coverage of Latin America. She received the Robert Capa Gold Medal in 1979 for her work in Nicaragua and more recently published the book Kurdistan: In the Shadow of History (Random House, 1997).

Eric Mencher, staff photographer at the Philadelphia Inquirer since 1987, has covered regional, national and international assignments. He received the 1999 Overseas Press Club/John Faber Award for his work in Rwanda.

Sheryl A. Mendez is a widely published photojournalist whose work has appeared in the London Sunday Times Magazine, the Independent, the Washington Post, the Christian Science Monitor, Nouvel Observateur, and on National Public Radio. She covered the war in Iraq and its aftermath from 2003 to 2005 and the Lebanon War of 2006. She is on the Board of November Eleven—a non-profit organization supporting independent media and humanitarian aid efforts worldwide.

Theodor Meron is Charles L. Denison Professor Emeritus at New York University Law School, and a judge on the Appeals Chamber of the war crimes tribunals for Rwanda and the former Yugoslavia. He was president of the Yugoslavia tribunal from 2003-5. He is the author of War Crimes Law Comes of Age (Oxford University Press, 2006) and Bloody Constraint: War and Chivalry in Shakespeare (Oxford University Press, 1998).

Frits Meyst, a Dutch photographer, has covered conflicts in Europe and the Middle East for many newspapers and magazines. He won the Silver Camera Award for best press photo of the year in 1991.

Ed Miles was the associate director of the Vietnam Veterans of America Foundation (VVAF), and worked on the International Campaign to Ban Landmines for which VVAF shared the 1997 Nobel Peace Prize. He died in January of 2004.

Etienne Montes is a photographer who has covered conflicts in Spain, El Salvador, Nicaragua, Guatemala, Honduras, Cuba, Chile, Peru, South Africa, Lebanon, and Ireland.

Benny Morris is a professor of history at Ben-Gurion University, Beersheba, Israel. He is author of Israel's Border Wars, 1949-1956: Arab Infiltration, Israeli Retaliation, and the Countdown to the Suez War (Oxford University Press, 1997), Righteous Victims: A History of the Arab-Zionist Conflict (Knopf, 1999), and The Birth of the Palestinian Refugee Problem Revisited (Cambridge University Press, 2004).

Seamus Murphy is a photographer for AWP/World Picture News.

Karma Nabulsi is a university lecturer in international relations at Oxford University, and fellow in politics at St. Edmund Hall. She is the author of Traditions of War: Occupation, Resistance and the Law (Oxford University Press, 1999).

James Nachtwey, photojournalist, has been a contract photographer with Time magazine since 1984. In 2001, he became one of the founding members of the photo agency, VII. He has won the Robert Capa Gold Medal five times, and the World Press Photo Award twice, among many other prizes.

Hrant Nakashian photographed conditions in Palestinian refugee camps in Gaza and the West Bank for the United Nations Relief and Works Agency after it was established in 1949.

Zed Nelson is a photographer based in London. He has covered wars in Africa and Afghanistan, and won several prizes for his work on the gun culture in the United States, Gun Nation.

Elizabeth Neuffer was a foreign correspondent for the Boston Globe and author of The Key to My Neighbour's House: Seeking Justice in Bosnia and Rwanda (Picador, 2001). She was awarded the 1998 Courage in Journalism Award. She was killed in an automobile accident while on assignment in Iraq on May 9, 2003.

Don Oberdorfer is a distinguished journalist in residence and adjunct professor at the Johns Hopkins University's Nitze School of Advanced International Studies. He is the author of The

Two Koreas (Basic Books, 2001), Tet: A History of the 1968 Tet Offensive in Vietnam (Johns Hopkins University, 2001), and Senator Mansfield (Smithsonian Books, 2003).

Diane F. Orentlicher is a professor of international law at American University's Washington College of Law and co-director of the Center for Human Rights and Humanitarian Law. In 2004 she was appointed by the UN Secretary General to update the United Nations' principles on combating impunity.

William A. Orme, Jr. is chief of external communications at the United Nations Development Programme. He was a reporter for the New York Times in Jerusalem and served as executive director of the Committee to Protect Journalists from 1993 to 1998.

Ramazan Ozturk works as a freelance photographer for Time magazine and for the daily Sabah (Turkey). He has covered the Iran-Iraq war, the Halabja gas attack, the wars in Bosnia, and many important events in Turkey since 1974.

George Packer is a staff writer for the New Yorker. He was awarded two Overseas Press Club awards for his work in 2003, one for his Iraq coverage and the other for his reporting on the civil war in Sierra Leone. He is author of The Assassins' Gate: America in Iraq (Farrar, Straus and Giroux, 2005).

Paolo Pellegrin is a photographer with Magnum Photos and a Newsweek contract photographer. He has produced award-winning reports covering Albania, Kosovo, Aids in Uganda, and children in war zones.

Gilles Peress is a photographer for Magnum Photos who has covered conflicts in Northern Ireland, Iran, Bosnia, Rwanda, Kosovo, and the Middle East. He was twice president of Magnum and has received numerous awards for his work. His books include Telex: Iran (Scalo, 1994) and A Village Destroyed, May 14, 1999: War Crimes in Kosovo (University of California Press, 2002).

Mark Perry is a military, intelligence and foreign affairs analyst and co-director of Conflicts Forum. He was formerly a senior foreign policy analyst for the Vietnam Veterans of America Foundation, which shared the 1997 Nobel Peace Prize for its role in the campaign to ban land mines. He is the author of A Fire in Zion (William Morrow, 1994), and Conceived in Liberty (Viking, 1997).

Nicole Pope is a journalist and writer based in Istanbul, who was Turkey correspondent for Le Monde (France) for 15 years and formerly worked for the ICRC. She is the co-author of Turkey Unveiled: a History of Modern Turkey (Overlook Press, 1998).

John Prendergast is the Senior Adviser to the President of International Crisis Group and former Director of African Affairs at the National Security Council.

Dana Priest reports on U.S. intelligence and military special operations for the Washington Post. She was awarded a Pulitzer Prize in 2006 for her coverage of the CIA's counterterrorism operations. She is author of The Mission: Waging War and Keeping Peace With America's Military (Norton, 2003).

Peter Pringle is a freelance journalist and author. He was bureau chief in Washington, New York and Moscow for the Independent (UK). He has written several non-fiction books, including most recently Food Inc.: Mendel to Monsanto—The Promise and Perils of the Biotech Harvest (Simon & Schuster, 2003).

Gerard Prunier is a research professor at the University of Paris and director of the French Center for Ethiopian Studies in Addis Ababa. He is author of Darfur: The Ambiguous Genocide (Cornell University Press, 2005) and a forthcoming book on the war in the Democratic Republic of Congo.

Noel Quidu, a photojournalist with the Gamma Presse agency since 1988, has covered numerous conflicts, notably in Afghanistan, Lebanon, the Persian Gulf, former Yugoslavia, Rwanda and Chechnya. He has received three World Press Photo awards.

Gaby Rado was the foreign affairs correspondent for ITN's Channel Four News in the U.K. He died after falling from the roof of a hotel while on assignment in Sulaimaniya, Iraq, on March 30, 2003.

Jonathan C. Randal is a former foreign correspondent for the Washington Post from 1969 to 1998. He is the author of After Such Knowledge, What Forgiveness? My Encounters in Kurdistan (Farrar, Straus & Giroux 1997) and Osama: The Making of a Terrorist (Vintage Books, 2005).

Erich Rathfelder is a German journalist for Die Tageszeitung (Berlin) who has reported extensively on the former Yugoslavia. He is the author of Schnittpunkt Sarajevo (Schiler, 2006, and Sarajevo und Danach (Beck-Verlag, 1998).

Steven R. Ratner is a professor of law at the University of Michigan. He was a member of the UN's expert group investigating potential prosecution of Khmer Rouge officials for their atrocities in Cambodia. He is co-author of Accountability for Human Rights Atrocities in International Law: Beyond the Nuremberg Legacy (Oxford University Press, 2nd ed. 2001).

Barry Renfrew is vice president of global business for Europe, Africa and the Middle East for the Associated Press. He covered the Soviet intervention in Afghanistan and was bureau chief in Islamabad, Seoul, Johannesburg, Moscow, Sydney and London.

David Rieff, co-editor of this book, is a contributing writer for the New York Times Magazine. He has also written for Foreign Affairs, Harper's, the New Republic, the Nation, Prospect, the New Yorker and other publications. His books include Slaughterhouse (Simon & Schuster, 1995), A Bed for the Night (Simon & Schuster, 2002) and At the Point of a Gun (Simon & Schuster, 2005).

Patrick Robert is a freelance photographer with Corbis. He has covered almost every war in Africa and the Middle East in the last twenty years. He was seriously injured by small arms fire in Liberia in 2003.

Sir Adam Roberts is the Montague Burton Professor of International Relations at Oxford University. He is co-author of United Nations, Divided World: The UN's Roles in International Relations (2nd ed., Oxford University Press, 1993) and is the co-editor of Documents on the Laws of War (3rd ed., Oxford University Press, 2000).

Gwynne Roberts, an independent filmmaker, has produced documentaries for broadcasters around the world including PBS (USA), BBC and Channel Four (UK), and ZDF, ARD (Germany). His films have highlighted major human rights violations in Iraq—in particular the gassing of the Iraqi Kurds and the regime's mass killing of Kurdish civilians. In 1992 he received an Overseas Press Club Award for Wings of Death, a landmark documentary establishing the gassing of the Iraqi Kurds.

George Rodrigue is vice president and managing editor of the Dallas Morning News. A former Washington correspondent and European bureau chief for the Dallas Morning News, he shared the 1986 Pulitzer Prize for national reporting and the 1994 Pulitzer for international reporting.

A. P. V. Rogers, OBE, is a retired major general in the British Army and a recognized expert on the laws of war. He is a fellow of the Lauterpacht Research Center for International Law at Cambridge University. He received the 1997 Paul Reuter prize for Law on the Battlefield (Manchester University Press, 1996, 2nd ed. 2004).

David Rohde is a reporter for the New York Times and author of Endgame: The Betrayal and Fall of Srebrenica (Farrar, Straus, Giroux, 1997). His investigation of mass graves at Srebrenica for the Christian Science Monitor won the 1996 Pulitzer Prize for international reporting as well as the George Polk, Sigma Delta Chi and Overseas Press Club Awards.

Daniel Gyula Rosenthal is a staff photographer for the Dutch national daily De Volkskrant covering news and personal projects worldwide.

Richard Ross, photographer and professor of art at UCSB, has photographed for many American and international publications. He is the principal photographer for the Getty Conservation Institute documenting the research work of the GCI in El Salvador, Honduras, Tunisia, and China.

Peter Rowe is a professor in the Department of Law, the University of Lancaster in England. He is the author of The Impact of Human Rights Law on Armed Forces (Cambridge University Press, 2006).

Elizabeth Rubin is a contributing writer for the New York Times Magazine. She covered the U.S. wars in Afghanistan and Iraq for the New Republic, and has also written for the New Yorker and Harper's. She received an Overseas Press Club citation for her reporting on mercenaries for Harper's.

John Ryle is Legrand Ramsey Professor of Anthropology at Bard College, NY, and Chair of the Rift Valley Institute.

Q. Sakamaki is a photographer with Redux Pictures who has coverd wars in Afghanistan, Israel/Palestine, Algeria, Bosnia, Kosovo, Iraq, Liberia and Sri Lanka. He won a World Press Photo award and two Pictures of The Year International prizes in 2007.

Sebastião Salgado is a photographer with Contact Press Images. Twice named Photographer of the Year by the International Center of Photography, he has received numerous awards and honorary degrees. His books include Workers (Aperture, 1993), Migrations: Humanity in Transition (Aperture, 2000) and The End of Polio (Bulfinch, 2003).

Kyoichi Sawada was a photojournalist best known for his photos of Southeast Asia. He won a Pulitzer Prize in 1966, a World Press Photo contest Grand Prize, and the Overseas Press Club Award. After his death in Cambodia in 1970, he was awarded the Robert Capa Gold Medal.

Sydney H. Schanberg currently writes for the Village Voice. He won the 1976 Pulitzer Prize for his New York Times reporting on the fall of Cambodia. He also won two Overseas Press Club Awards, two George Polk Memorial Awards, two Newspaper Guild Front Page Awards, and the Sigma Delta Chi Award for distinguished journalism.

Michael N. Schmitt, legal editor for the second edition of this book, was formerly professor of international law at the George C. Marshall European Center for Security Studies in Germany, and in 2007 will take up a two-year appointment as Charles H. Stockton Visiting Professor of International Law at the U.S. Naval War College.

Kurt Schork was a war correspondent for Reuters News Agency, and covered numerous conflicts including those in Afghanistan, the Balkans, Cambodia, Chechnya, East Timor. Iraq, Kashmir, South Africa, Sri Lanka, and Turkey. He was killed in an ambush in Sierra Leone on May 24, 2000.

Heidi Schumann is an independent photojournalist and documentary photographer. She photographs for the New York Times, and has also worked with several other magazines and newspapers.

Thom Shanker covers national security and foreign policy issues for the New York Times in Washington. At the Chicago Tribune, he was foreign editor, Moscow bureau chief. and, while Senior European correspondent. covered the war in Bosnia from 1992 to 1994.

William Shawcross is a freelance journalist who has written about Eastern Europe. Southeast Asia and the United States. He is author of Sideshow: Kissinger, Nixon, and the Destruction of Cambodia (Simon & Schuster, 1979), The Quality of Mercy: Cambodia, The Holocaust, and Modern Conscience (Simon & Schuster, 1984), and Allies: The United States, Britain, Europe and the War in Iraq (Atlantic Books, 2003).

Jean-Marie Simon trained as a lawyer and worked as a journalist and photojournalist in Guatemala for several years. She was a consultant to a number of human rights organizations and is the author of Guatemala: Eternal Spring, Eternal Tyranny (W.W. Norton, 1988).

Lewis M. Simons is a freelance writer for National Geographic and other publications. He shared the 1986 Pulitzer Prize for international reporting, and has won a George Polk Award, three Overseas Press Club Awards, and an Edward R. Murrow Award.

P.W. Singer is Senior Fellow and Director of the 21st Century Defense Initiative at the Brookings Institution. He is the author of Corporate Warriors: The Rise of the Privatized Military Industry (Cornell University Press, 2003) and Children at War (Pantheon, 2005).

E. Benjamin Skinner is the author of the forthcoming book "A Crime So Monstrous": A Living History of Contemporary Slavery, which chronicles modern-day bondage on five continents as well as American abolitionist efforts. His work has appeared in Newsweek, Travel + Leisure, the Los Angeles Times, Foreign Affairs, the Foreign Service Journal and others.

Patrick J. Sloyan is a freelance writer and former senior Washington bureau correspondent for

Newsday. He received the 1992 Pulitzer Prize for international reporting, and has won the American Society of Newspaper Editors', George Polk, and Raymond Clapper Awards for outstanding journalism.

Frank Smyth is a freelance journalist and Washington Representative of the Committee to Protect Journalists. He has served as an investigative consultant to Human Rights Watch and Amnesty International.

Sgt. Graham Spark is a photographer with the British Royal Air Force. He was stationed in Sarajevo in 1997 to document the work of multinational soldiers traveling through Bosnia. He was awarded the MBE in 2000.

Dr. Heike Spieker is Head of the International Law and International Institutions Department of the German Red Cross and visiting professor at the Institute for International Law of Peace and Armed Conflict in Bochum, Germany, and at the University College Dublin, Ireland.

Amy Stevens is a designer and entrepreneur based in New York.

Bruno Stevens became a photojournalist in 1998 after 20 years in the music business. His work has been published in Stern, Libération, the Sunday Times Magazine, Time, Newsweek, Paris-Match and other publications.

Alexandra Stiglmayer covered the wars in the former Yugoslavia for Time magazine and is the author of Mass Rape: The War Against Women in Bosnia-Herzegovina (University of Nebraska Press, 1994). She is currently a speechwriter at the European Commission in Brussels.

Tom Stoddart, a photographer with Getty Images, has covered international stories for publications including the Sunday Times and Time. Recently he has worked on the impact of AIDS in Africa. He is the author of iWitness (Trolley Books, 2004).

Eric Stover is Director of the Human Rights Center and Adjunct Professor of Public Health at the University of California at Berkeley. He is author of The Witnesses: War Crimes and the Promise of Justice in The Hague (University of Pennsylvania Press, 2005) and co-editor of My Neighbour, My Enemy (Cambridge University Press, 2005).

Jeff Streeper is Director of Modern IDENTITY in New York. In partnership with Gilles Peress, he designed and produced both editions of this book and helped establish the Crimes of War Project. He was co-designer/author of A Village Destroyed, May 14, 1999: War Crimes in Kosovo (University of California Press, 2002).

Sean Sutton worked for nine years as a photo-journalist for the international press and aid agencies. In 1997 he became Information Manager for the Mines Advisory Group (MAG), an NGO which works to clear landmines and other remnants of conflict.

Terence Taylor is director of the International Council for the Life Sciences and was previously the president and executive director of the International Institute for Strategic Studies-U.S. In October 2006, he was appointed to the five-member special advisory group for the UN Secretary-General's initiative on biotechnology.

Andrew Testa is a photographer who has worked extensively in the Balkans. He has won many awards and received a Getty grant in 2006 to continue his work in Kosovo.

Colin Thomas-Jensen is based in the International Crisis Group's office in Washington DC, where he has a range of responsibilities across the Africa program. He worked for the U.S. Agency for International Development (USAID), where he was an information officer on the humanitarian response team for Darfur.

Guy Tillim is a photographer who has worked extensively in central and southern Africa. In 2005 he won the Leica Oskar Barnack Award for his Jo'burg series, and in 2006 he was awarded the Robert Gardner Fellowship at Harvard.

Sven Torfinn is a photographer who has been based in Nairobi since 2000. In 2005 he won a World Press Photo Award for his coverage of the Democratic Republic of Congo.

Larry Towell, a photographer with Magnum Photos, is best known for his works on Palestine and Central America. He has received several World Press and Pictures of the Year awards, as well as the Henri Cartier-Bresson, Eugene Smith, and Oskar Barnack awards.

David Turns is a Lecturer in Law at the University of Liverpool in England and a Visiting Lecturer for the International Institute of Humanitarian Law in San Remo, Italy. He is the editor of International Law and Espionage (Martinus Nijhoff, 1995, begun by the late Dr. J. Kish) and has written widely on international law.

Geert Van Kesteren is a photojournalist who has worked in Africa and Iraq. His images from Iraq were published in the book Why Mister, Why? (Artimo, 2004).

Dejan Vekic, a photographer and videographer based in Sarajevo, documented the destruction of the city for the Commission on War Crimes during the Bosnian war.

Marita Vihervuori is a Finnish journalist who covered the wars in the former Yugoslavia for the Austrian Press Agency. She has written books on Iran, Libya, and the Balkans, and was named as Finland's Journalist of the Year in 2003.

Teun Voeten is an award-winning war photojournalist and author. His work from Colombia, Afghanistan, Iraq, Liberia, Sierra Leone, and Bosnia has been published in leading publications worldwide. He lives in New York and Brussels.

Ed Vulliamy is a journalist with The Guardian and the author of Seasons in Hell: Understanding Bosnia's War (Simon & Schuster, 1994). His prizes include: British Press Awards, International Reporter of the Year (1992 and 1996); Amnesty International Award for newspaper journalism (1992); James Cameron Memorial Award (1994), and "What the Papers Say" Foreign Correspondent of the Year (1992).

Lawrence Weschler is director of the New York Institute for the Humanities at New York University. A retired staff writer for the New Yorker, he is a two-time winner of the George Polk Award and 1998 winner of the Lannan Literary Award. He is the author of A Miracle, A Universe: Settling Accounts with Torturers (University of Chicago Press, 1998), Vermeer in Bosnia (Vintage, 2005) and Everything That Rises: A Book of Convergences (McSweeneys Books, 2006).

Alvaro Ybarra Zavala is a photographer with the VU agency. His project Children of Sorrow documented the condition of children affected by violence around the world. He has also worked extensively in Fallujah, Iraq.

Acknowledgments

This book is that rarest of works, breathed into being by an enormous number of people who agreed it was urgently needed. For our editors, legal advisers, expert readers, and, most of all, our writers, who worked for a pittance and suffered through double editing and repeated requests for rewrites, it was clearly a labor of love, and there is no way to thank them adequately. At the same time, we are deeply grateful to the individuals and institutions who provided the funding and facilities to do the job.

Herbert and Marion Sandler and The Sandler Family Supporting Foundation quickly saw the potential and stepped forward with the funds that enabled us to launch the project. The Ford Foundation, through the efforts of Larry Cox, our program officer, provided the rest of the budget, permitting completion in the shortest possible time.

Sanford J. Ungar, dean of the American University School of Communication, graciously provided an office and every possible form of administrative support with the help of assistant dean, Patrick Martin. Claudio Grossman, dean of AU's Washington College of Law, enthusiastically supported the involvement by WCL's unique faculty. Professor Diane Orentlicher threw herself behind the project and, aided by the WCL War Crimes Research Office and a grant from the Open Society Institute, organized a conference in October 1996 that helped determine our agenda; she suggested authors, critiqued plans, and closely supervised a large portion of the articles. WCL Professor Kenneth Anderson took on the enormous task of legal editing, and Professor Robert Kogod Goldman was a source of solid advice throughout. The War Crimes office with OSI funding sponsored the legal research by Ewen Allison, an indefatigable WCL graduate who put himself on call around the clock and had the assistance of Deans' Fellows, Mair McCafferty and C. Jeffrey Tibbels.

Eric Stover, former executive director of Physicians for Human Rights, organized a critical second conference in April 1997 at the Human Rights Center he heads at Berkeley. He brought clarity of purpose to every strategic moment and played a central role in obtaining funding. Aryeh Neier, President of the Open Society Institute gave wise counsel at both conferences, offered moral support when it was most needed, and also critiqued a number of articles. Anna Cataldi, the Italian writer, assembled the journalists, photographers, and legal scholars for our first brainstorming session and prodded and promoted our efforts from beginning to end.

It was essential in a book combining law and journalism that we strive to meet the standards of both professions. Maj. Gen. (ret.) A. P. V. Rogers of the British Army, our consultant on military law, undertook a detailed legal review. Louise Doswald-Beck, Urs Boegli, and Jean-Francois Berger of the International Committee of the Red Cross read the text and made useful suggestions. Lt. Col. Scott Morris of the U.S. Judge Advocate-General corps and Lt. Col. (ret.) H.

Wayne Elliott, a former chief of the JAG international law division, gave us valuable criticism and encouragement. Jim Toedtman, *Newsday's* Washington bureau chief, made numerous helpful suggestions. Thom Shanker of the *New York Times* edited the three articles on sexual violence and read the f text. Views expressed in the articles are those of the authors and do not represent the position of any government, institution, or organization, nor our expert readers. Editorial judgments are the responsibility of the writers and editors.

Tremendous energy and time went into photo-editing and design. Sheryl Mendez broke off work on two projects in the Middle East to join the project as photo editor and researcher, a task to which she brought visual and political astuteness, moral commitment, and astonishing drive. Brooke Hellewell, our unflappable deputy design editor, was a key player, whose formidable design and organizational skills were matched by her stamina.

Peggy Lampl, our long-suffering project manager, defused every crisis, and played a key role in editing. One of our luckiest breaks was the appearance of Alan Dorsey, former librarian for the ICRC in New York, who had begun graduate studies at AU. Serving as deputy project manager, he brought invaluable experience and knowledge of IHL, and imposed order on the project and our office.

Ron Goldfarb, our devoted literary agent, stayed on as general counsel in future project activities. Tabitha Griffin, our editor at W. W. Norton gave us constructive criticism and enthusiastic support. Carole Kismaric advised us at crucial early moments on budget and organization. Professor Brad Blitz of Lewis & Clark College, Pat Watson, Evelyn Leopold of Reuters, Ian Williams of the *Nation*, Chuck Lane of the *New Republic*, Tom Gjelten of National Public Radio, and Michael Muskal and Jim Dooley of *Newsday*, provided wise guidance. W. Hays Parks, Special Assistant to the Judge Advocate General, and Professor Steve Ratner, of the University of Texas at Austin, gave us welcome moral support and timely legal guidance.

Newsday editor Anthony Marro, A.M.E. Les Payne, foreign editor Tim Phelps, and Washington news editor Anne Hoy enthusiastically backed the book and tolerated my absences. And on a personal note, truly special thanks go to my patient wife, Betsy, and daughter, Caroline, who let me give up practically every evening, weekend, and vacation day for eighteen months.

Every participant and every outside supporter made a difference. I hope each will look on the finished product with pride, bearing in mind that the educational effort to be built around the book is still a work in progress.

—*Roy Gutman*

Acknowledgments for the Second Edition

Given how much has changed in the field of law and armed conflict since 1999, revising and updating this book proved to be a big undertaking. It would not have been possible without the generous support of the JEHT Foundation, which gave us a grant to produce this new edition, and the Carnegie Corporation, Ford Foundation, Knight Foundation, and the Hamburg Institute for Social Research, which provided general funding during the period when we were working on it. We are also grateful to the Open Society Institute for supporting the foreign language editions of this book over the last several years.

Since the first edition was published, the Crimes of War Project has become an established organization and its staff members all played an important part in the revision of our flagship book. Elisa Munoz, executive director during the early part of the editorial process, helped get it underway. Lauren McCollough, program manager, was involved in administering all aspects of our work and in addition did much valuable research and proofreading. Marika Theros, program and development officer, ably organized our finances. As with the first edition, the book benefited greatly from the involvement of Anna Cataldi, Peggy Lampl, Gilles Peress, and Eric Stover, all now members of our board of directors, as well as John Owen and Gary Knight who joined the board later.

Professor Michael N. Schmitt generously agreed to serve as legal editor for the second edition and has been an invaluable source of guidance on legal and indeed editorial questions. Caroline Cross provided superb research help that has underpinned many of the revisions and Kimberly Grant also helped with research. Thanks to Jasmine Moussa for her proofreading assistance. I am very grateful to the following people who provided advice on particular areas or reviewed drafts of the articles: Kelly Askin, Jennifer Dworkin, Françoise Hampson, David Kretzmer, Joanne Mariner, Antonella Notari, Rodney Pinder, Ian Piper, and John Ryle.

As with the first edition, Sheryl Mendez did a superb job of selecting the photographs, and her contribution is central to this new edition. We were very lucky also to retain Jeff Streeper as the book's designer, and he played a vital role in shaping the finished book. Amy Stevens gave valuable assistance on design and layout. Thanks also to Jim Mairs, our editor at W.W. Norton, for his enthusiastic support of this new edition and his judgment.

Finally, thanks to all the contributors and to all those others who have given their time and effort to assist the work of the Crimes of War Project during the ten years since it was first launched.
    —Anthony Dworkin